External Mission

D1609840

External Mission

The ANC in Exile, 1960–1990

Stephen Ellis

HURST & COMPANY, LONDON

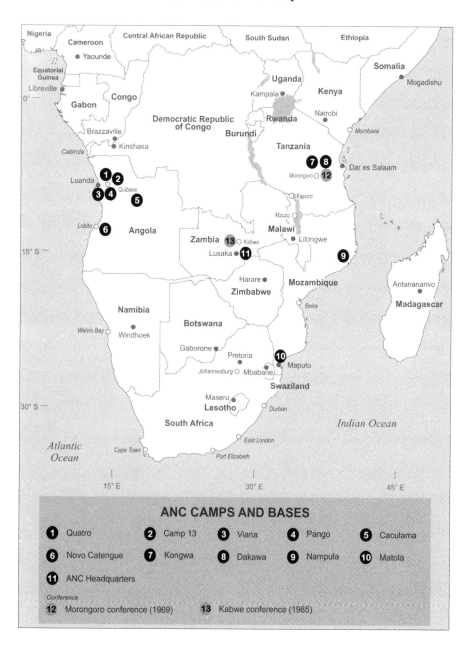

ANC CAMPS AND BASES

1 Quatro   **2** Camp 13   **3** Viana   **4** Pango   **5** Caculama

6 Novo Catengue   **7** Kongwa   **8** Dakawa   **9** Nampula   **10** Matola

11 ANC Headquarters

Conference

12 Morongoro conference (1969)   **13** Kabwe conference (1985)

One thing the 'old' and the 'new' South Africa have in common is a passion for inventing history. History is not seen as a dispassionate inquiry into what happened, but rather as a part of political mobilisation promoting some form of collective self-interest.

– Frederik van Zyl Slabbert

Hardback edition first published in the United Kingdom in 2012
by C. Hurst & Co. (Publishers) Ltd.,
41 Great Russell Street, London, WC1B 3PL

This paperback edition, 2014

Printed in India

The right of Stephen Ellis to be identified as the author of this
publication is asserted by him in accordance with the Copyright,
Designs and Patents Act, 1988.

A Cataloguing-in-Publication data record for this book
is available from the British Library.

ISBN: 978-1-84904-506-3 *paperback*

This book is printed using paper from registered sustainable
and managed sources.

www.hurstpublishers.com

Praise for 'External Mission'

'[*External Mission*] will probably cast Ellis as a troublemaker in the ANC's South Africa, but there can be little doubt that his research is sound and his interpretations credible ... He provides exhaustive evidence for what are now recognised to have been the most significant weaknesses of the ANC in exile [and] adds much data on the extent of corruption within the party ... Ellis's book will undoubtedly stand as the definitive account of the ANC in exile.'
— Patrick Chabal, *International Affairs*

'*External Mission* clarifies what has long been a rather murky area: the precise origins of the armed struggle. [...] Ellis marshalls this information convincingly. Best of all, he weaves it all into a densely patterned history that combines local detail and broader context — and still comes out as a very readable narrative. [...] If you read only one work of history in the coming year, this should be it.'
— Shaun De Waal, *Weekly Mail & Guardian* (South Africa)

'This thoroughly researched book explains much about why SA is in the condition it is today. It makes it depressingly obvious that our "rainbow nation" is no longer the legacy of Nelson Mandela, or even Thabo Mbeki, but rather of Joe Modise. [...] a remarkable new study of the ANC in exile.' — *Financial Mail* (South Africa)

'Ellis has produced an excellent, even brilliant, book that greatly adds to our knowledge of the ANC.' — Professor David Welsh, author of *The Rise and Fall of Apartheid*

'It is time that the ANC's mythology about its years in exile gives way to critical history. Stephen Ellis's new book is to be welcomed as a step along the journey from myth to history.' — Jonny Steinberg, author of *The Three-Letter Plague*

'An explosive exposé that is timeous and relevant as much as it may be discomforting to some.' — Barney Pityana, theologian and human rights lawyer

'Stephen Ellis lays bare a history that the ANC would prefer to forget. Basing his account on ANC and other historical archives, including those of the Stasi — the former East German secret police — complemented by confidential information from former comrades, he shows that the history of the ANC is less noble than usually presented. This book is full of shocking surprises. Not only does Ellis shows the crucial role of the South African Communist Party in the ANC's decision to launch the armed struggle, but he also reveals Nelson Mandela's role as a secret Party member.' — Rian Malan, *Media24* (South Africa)

'This is a book ANC-ologists will pore over (or maybe pour things over), dissect, discover what's new, what's already out in the open but newly contextualised, by a tireless student of the liberation movement and South Africa's Communist party. ... At the conclusion of this densely-researched roller-coaster of a book, Ellis writes that the ANC's "sanitised" version of its immediate past, propagated by means of official documents, speeches, monuments and commemorations, is that the liberation movement initiated an armed struggle that, after much sacrifice, was the main factor forcing the apartheid government to negotiate in circumstances that handed effective victory to the majority of the population.'
— Denis Herbstein, *African Arguments*

'Stephen Ellis' book provides a readable, detailed and well-researched account of these events ... If you read nothing else, I would strongly recommend his brilliant final chapter entitled "Perspectives".' — Nigel Watt, *Chartist*

'The depth of evidence makes this an important work, especially given how the micro-history of ANC archives raises questions about what may never be known. ... Ellis open[s] new pathways for the study of the uncomfortable realities of exile.' — *Journal of African History*

Contents

Appendix: A Note on Method 305

Acronyms and Abbreviations

AAM   Anti-Apartheid Movement
ANC   African National Congress
APLA   Azanian People's Liberation Army
ARM   African Resistance Movement
AZAPO   Azanian People's Organisation
BCM   Black Consciousness Movement
BOSS   Bureau for State Security
BPC   Black People's Convention
CIA   Central Intelligence Agency
CP   Conservative Party
COSATU   Congress of South African Trade Unions
CPSA   Communist Party of South Africa
CPSU   Communist Party of the Soviet Union
FNLA   Frente Nacional de Libertação de Angola
FRELIMO   Frente de Libertação de Moçambique
HNP   Herenigde Nasionale Party
IRA   Irish Republican Army
KGB   The security agency of the Soviet Union from
          1954 to 1991

TRC	Truth and Reconciliation Commission
UDF	United Democratic Front
UFH	University of Fort Hare
UFS	University of the Free State
UN	United Nations
UNITA	União Nacional para a Independência Total de Angola
USA	United States of America
USSR	Union of Soviet Socialist Republics
ZANU	Zimbabwe African National Union
ZAPU	Zimbabwe African People's Union
ZIPRA	Zimbabwe People's Revolutionary Army

MfS	Ministerium für Staatssicherheit (Stasi)
MI6	The foreign intelligence service of the United Kingdom
MK	Umkhonto we Sizwe
MNR	Mozambican National Resistance
MPLA	Movimento Popular de Libertação de Angola
NAT	National Department of Intelligence and Security
NCL	National Committee for Liberation
NEC	National Executive Committee
NIA	National Intelligence Agency
NIS	National Intelligence Service
NLM	National Liberation Movement
NP	National Party
NSMS	National Security Management System
OAU	Organisation of African Unity
OPEC	Organisation of Petroleum Exporting Countries
PAC	Pan-Africanist Congress of Azania
PMC	Politico-Military Council
RC	Revolutionary Council
RENAMO	Resistência Nacional Moçambicana
SACP	South African Communist Party
SACTU	South African Congress of Trade Unions
SADET	South African Democracy Education Trust
SADF	South African Defence Force
SAP	South African Police
SAHA	South African Historical Archive
SAIRR	South African Institute of Race Relations
SANDF	South African National Defence Force
SAS	Special Air Service
SIDA	Swedish International Development Cooperation Agency
SSC	State Security Council
SWAPO	South West African People's Organisation

CHAPTER ONE

Call to Arms

One day in May 1948, a 30-year-old man, well groomed and well dressed in the fashion of the time, had an experience that marked him for life. He was a university graduate, a science teacher by profession, who just that month had been accepted for retraining as a solicitor, although a passerby observing the ritual scars on his cheeks could deduce that he had been born in a rural area into a traditional African family.

While he was walking down a street in Johannesburg, a white man accosted him and spat in his face.

The victim of this assault was Oliver Tambo, an activist in the African National Congress Youth League. Tambo recalled the event almost 40 years later while he was talking to a group of South African businessmen in one of a series of meetings with key sectors of the white establishment at a time when the African National Congress (ANC) was still illegal in South Africa. Tambo told them he still had the silk handkerchief with which he had wiped away the spit,[1] a detail that suggests how deeply the incident disturbed him.

Oliver Tambo played a vital role during the 30 years of the ANC's exile. Holding the rank of deputy president, he was sent abroad by the ANC's governing body in March 1960, the month in which police shot dead 69 demonstrators at Sharpeville, an event that opened a new chapter of South Africa's history. His instructions were to set up an external mission of the ANC in the likely event that the organisation was banned. When the National Party government led by Hendrik Verwoerd, panicked by the Sharpeville incident, outlawed the ANC and some other anti-apartheid formations the following month as predicted, Tambo was the ANC's top-ranking official outside the country. He worked to generate international support, not least from Africa's newly emerging independent states, of which no fewer than 18 hoisted their flags in that same year.

Unknown to Tambo, a closely allied organisation, the South African Communist Party (SACP), was securing international backing for an armed struggle at the very same time that he was establishing the ANC's external mission. Leaders of the SACP met the Chinese ruler, Mao Zedong, on 3 November 1960 to discuss taking up arms. A few weeks later, the SACP formally voted to prepare a campaign of violence.[2]

These crucial events remained unknown to South Africans, outside a tiny circle, for years. Even now, few people are aware how the war that made South Africa what it is today actually began.

Those in the ANC who advocated the use of violence against a ruthless and uncompromising regime, led by Tambo's friend and former law partner Nelson Mandela, never imagined that their campaign would last for three decades. By the time Tambo came home in 1990, he had suffered a stroke, his health ruined by years of overwork and unrelenting travel.

The ANC was transformed by the experience of exile and war. This book is an account of that process.

Resisting apartheid

Oliver Tambo had no doubt that the spitting incident in 1948 was related to the fact that the National Party had just won parliamentary
elections held on 26 May. This grossest of insults was not directed at
Tambo personally, but at the black population in general.

At that time, only white South Africans enjoyed voting rights,
with the exception of some coloured[3] people in the Cape Province.
For many voters, the key issues in the campaign leading up to the
1948 election concerned the relationships between South Africa and
the old colonial power, Great Britain, and between English- and
Afrikaans-speaking whites. Standing for a radical Afrikaner nationalism, the National Party claimed to speak for whites who were in
favour of full independence from Britain in every field, not only
political but also economic and cultural.[4] During the world war
that had ended just three years earlier, the Nats had opposed the
pro-British policy of Jan Smuts's United Party government. They
advocated only legal methods of protest, while radicals in the rival
Ossewabrandwag made use of sabotage. Both hoped to see a South
African republic arise from a German victory and were disappoint-
ed by the war's outcome. National Party candidates campaigning
for election in 1948 generally appear to have said relatively little
about policy towards black South Africans or, more explicitly, about
apartheid, the policy for which the National Party was to become
notorious.[5]

During the 1948 election campaign, a National Party functionary
called Pieter W Botha – later to become state president – wrote a
pamphlet attacking the ruling United Party for being soft on communism.[6] The Communist Party of South Africa (CPSA) had flourished since 1941. Until then, in line with the 1939 non-aggression
pact between the USSR and Germany, the CPSA had condemned the
war as an imperialist venture, but its unwavering allegiance to the
Soviet Union caused the Party to change course as soon as Germany

attacked the USSR, the homeland of international communism. The CPSA's declaration of support for the Allied cause put it on the same side as the South African government for the first time in its history. Accordingly, it enjoyed an unusual measure of official tolerance for as long as the war lasted. Having almost destroyed itself with factional quarrels in the 1930s, the Party now succeeded in recruiting fair numbers of white servicemen politicised by their experience of war, as well as black workers in the factories that had burgeoned with the war economy.[7] Its membership, previously tiny, rose into the thousands.

The CPSA's leaders had no illusions about the depth of the National Party's anti-communism, and they braced themselves for harsh new measures. The CPSA general secretary, Moses Kotane, who had been trained in Moscow, was already a member of the national executive of the ANC, in those days a genteel lobbying group with no ideology beyond a commitment to speak for black Africans of all political persuasions. It was more a movement than a party. Kotane encouraged communists to join the ANC. He and other CPSA leaders saw entry into the ANC not only as a way for some of its members to take cover against the anti-communist measures they grimly anticipated, but also as a way of countering the influence of Trotskyist rivals already situated within the ANC.[8]

The election of a National Party government in 1948 was a decisive moment in South Africa's long drift towards the formal state of hostilities known as the armed struggle.[9] Raymond Mhlaba, later to become the second commander of the guerrilla army Umkhonto we Sizwe (MK), recalled in his memoirs how even in those days some South Africans talked about taking up arms. Mhlaba was one of the black workers who joined the CPSA during the war years. He found the Party's meetings in Port Elizabeth refreshing for the opportunity to meet activists of other racial groups, and he was not the only person to think this way. Only in 1944, when he was already a member of the Party, did Mhlaba join the ANC, which he thought to be 'moribund' at the national level at that time.[10] He attended the ANC's momentous annual conference of 1949, when radicals from the Youth League, founded just five years earlier, argued for communists to be expelled from the ANC[11] on the grounds that association with a party top-heavy with whites would dilute the ANC's nature as the political vehicle of black people. The anti-communist resolution presented at the 1949 conference didn't muster a majority of votes and failed to pass, but one measure the Youth Leaguers did succeed in getting the ANC to adopt was their plan of action against the National Party government. Moreover, a Youth League member, Walter Sisulu, was elected to serve as the ANC's secretary-general. Many ANC leaders of the late 20th century entered politics in the 1940s through the Youth League – not only Mandela, Tambo, Sisulu and others, but also future opponents like Robert Sobukwe, who was to lead a breakaway faction that established the Pan-Africanist Congress (PAC) in 1959. Many of the Youth Leaguers were graduates of Fort Hare university college, the premier seat of higher education for black people.

By early 1950 it was clear that the government intended to declare the Communist Party illegal. Knowing that the police held a complete list of its members and that going underground would simply get them all arrested, the CPSA chose to dissolve itself, probably the first time that a communist party anywhere in the world had disbanded itself.

The ANC proceeded to implement the Youth Leaguers' Plan of Action with a series of protests and strikes implemented from 1952. Known as the Defiance Campaign, for the first time this brought large numbers of ANC members into regular cooperation with militants from other racial groups, united by their opposition to the apartheid system. Anticipating the difficulties ahead, Nelson Mandela, the president of the ANC's Transvaal section, conceived a plan to reorganise in small neighbourhood units in the event of the movement being banned. It was dubbed the M-Plan after him.

At that time, domination of South Africa by whites had not yet erased memories of wars of resistance a couple of generations earlier. Another future state president, Jacob Zuma, born in 1942 in rural KwaZulu, remembers as a child having met a veteran of the last Zulu resistance to colonisation, the 1906 Bambata war. As a teenager, Zuma, like many others his age, was impressed by what he heard about Kenya's Mau Mau and Ghana's independence and he was outraged by the 1961 murder of Congolese prime minister Patrice Lumumba.[12] As the Defiance Campaign rolled on, more people within the ANC began to wonder about armed resistance in a form adapted to the current age. In 1952 Mandela discussed this with his close friend ANC secretary-general Walter Sisulu.[13] Both men had shifted from their earlier 'Africanist' position of opposing collaboration with communists. They had come to trust the white and Indian communists they met in the course of their political work and had developed real friendships across the racial boundaries that apartheid aimed to carve in stone.

The Communist Party was, as one of its members, Lionel 'Rusty' Bernstein, put it, 'a sect'.[14] After its banning, its members adopted the practice of joining other organisations through which they could exercise their self-appointed role in the vanguard of revolutionary change. Black communists more than ever threw themselves into work with the ANC. Their Indian colleagues joined the existing Indian congresses. White communists worked with ex-servicemen especially to form the Congress of Democrats, which effectively became their front organisation. The idea of a broad anti-government coalition between all of these gained ground. Leninist techniques of political organisation were perfectly adapted to circumstances like these. The Communist Party activist Ben Turok – today a parliamentarian – was later to recall 'how easy it was for a small group like ours to exert much influence in the mass movement without giving away our existence'.[15] Senior communists secretly re-established their party in 1953. It was now called the South African Communist

Party, but was generally known to insiders as 'the Party' or, in coded language, 'the family'.

In that same year, white comrades working under cover in the Congress of Democrats invited Walter Sisulu, earmarked as a possible recruit to the Party, to go with a couple of other ANC members on an extended overseas tour funded by the World Federation of Democratic Youth, a Soviet front organisation. Sisulu accepted. The experience made a tremendous impact on him. 'He said it was the first time he'd ever been treated like a human being', one associate recalled.[16] The tour took in Romania, Poland, the USSR, China and elsewhere. It was while Sisulu was preparing for this trip that Mandela again raised the question of taking up arms, asking his friend 'to discuss the possibility of armed struggle with the Chinese'.[17] Sisulu duly raised the issue with members of the Central Committee of the Chinese Communist Party whom he met during his stay in Beijing. His Chinese hosts are said to have responded cautiously, commenting only that 'you have to do it when the conditions are right'.[18]

Others too were speculating about the eventual necessity for armed struggle. Oliver Tambo, who succeeded Sisulu as ANC secretary-general in 1955, later recalled that 'the question of violence was raised but deferred because of [the] situation' at that time.[19] In short, by the mid-1950s several of the younger generation of ANC leaders, especially former Youth League members, were anticipating the adoption of a policy of armed struggle at some future point. Sisulu and Mandela regarded it as inevitable.[20] Many of the first generation of Youth Leaguers had abandoned their insistence on blacks organising alone and were now open to working with whites, coloureds and Indians. In some urban areas they were successful in recruiting 'home-boy' groups of people with roots in one or other rural area. Generally known as residents' associations, these provided solid building blocks of support. In the Johannesburg townships especially, the Youth Leaguers came face to face with local gangsters, or *tsotsis*. For all their hatred of the police, these hard men generally had no understanding of the type of politics being advocated by the Fort Hare graduates who were radicalising the ANC in the early 1950s.[21] Nevertheless, 'quite a lot' of *tsotsis* from Sophiatown joined the ANC, particularly the Youth League. 'Those who were known as street fighters and things like that. They joined the movement,' recalled Tennyson Makiwane,[22] who had been expelled from Fort Hare for political activity before moving to Johannesburg. The *tsotsis* were useful as strong-arm men who could police meetings and repel attempts at disruption.

Some members of the secretly reconstituted Communist Party were in occasional contact with Moscow and Beijing. In 1954, shortly after Walter Sisulu had raised the question of armed struggle for the first time with officials in China, Party member Molly Fischer attended the fifth anniversary celebration of the revolution in Beijing, having received a visa through the good offices of fellow Party member Vella Pillay.[23] Having joined the CPSA as a student in South Africa, Pillay settled in London in 1949 after new apartheid legislation had made it impossible to live in South Africa legally with his white wife, Patsy. He found a job at the Bank of China office in the City. Eventually rising to a senior position in an institution that was at the heart of China's foreign-exchange dealings, he maintained a close link with Beijing for the next three decades.[24] His connections there and in Moscow were to prove crucial in the development of the armed struggle.

During these years, the National Party government was implementing its vision of a South Africa rigorously separated into distinct ethnic and racial zones. Determined to break the broad alliance of forces that had emerged during the 1952 Defiance Campaign and in the preparation of the Freedom Charter – a socialist-flavoured manifesto published in 1955, largely authored by the SACP's Rusty Bernstein – in 1956 the authorities indicted 156 people associated with the ANC and allied organisations on charges of treason. This was a huge tactical mistake by the government. By taking people from all parts of the country, and from a variety of backgrounds, and placing them in the same courtroom for months on end, seated in alphabetical order regardless of race, the Treason Trial served only to consolidate the opposition to apartheid. It was all to no purpose, as the trial eventually collapsed without a verdict. Bernstein described the Treason Trial as 'the great underestimated factor in the history of the South African movement'.[25] However, he and other Communist Party theoreticians missed an important point, failing to consider the implications of the fact that a conservative bench of judges felt obliged to acquit in the face of insufficient evidence. The collapse of the Treason Trial indicated that, even under apartheid, South Africa retained some of the civil freedoms associated with a liberal dispensation. The existence of this political space was to become a crucial factor in decades to come.

Meanwhile, popular disturbances in the rural areas of Zeerust and Sekhukhuneland were engaging the attention of militant ANC and SACP members, who were able to connect with local activists through migrant labour networks.[26] The most serious of a series of rural uprisings caused by the implementation of apartheid was an armed revolt by peasants in Pondoland, which 'profoundly influenced the whole orientation of the ANC leadership', in Bernstein's words, 'because there was the beginnings of an armed resistance movement'.[27] Some SACP and ANC members were in communication with the Pondo insurgents.[28] A Communist Party activist, Rowley Arenstein, provided legal defence for some of those charged in connection with these events.

The international environment was changing rapidly. The emancipation of what was becoming known as the Third World, including European colonies in Africa, was perhaps the most important emerging theme of world affairs within the overall context of the Cold War. When Ghana became the first colonial territory in tropical Africa to receive independence, in 1957, its prime minister and later president, Kwame Nkrumah, proclaimed himself the leader of a pan-African

movement to overthrow colonial rule. Becoming steadily more militant – as well as more pompous and deluded – during the course
of his presidency, Nkrumah developed an alliance with the Soviet
Union and China, which in time provided him with instructors for
a training centre for guerrilla warfare where radicals from all over
Africa could receive instruction.[29] Further north, Algerian nationalists were fighting a bloody war against France. Moses Kotane, the
SACP's general secretary, attended the famous Bandung Conference
in Indonesia in 1955. There he met heroes of the anticolonial left,
including Indian prime minister Jawaharlal Nehru, Egypt's Gamal
Abdel Nasser and Chinese foreign minister Zhou Enlai, before going
on to visit India and China.[30] An inspiration to the left worldwide
was the 1959 overthrow of the Batista government in Cuba by a
guerrilla force under Fidel Castro.

In this changing climate, Raymond Mhlaba found that his persistent advocacy of armed struggle was now gaining a respectful
hearing 'It was only later, towards the end of the 1950s, that Rusty
Bernstein asked why my question was not taken seriously within
the new Communist Party,' Mhlaba recalled. 'From then on we discussed the issue of orchestrating an armed struggle. We discussed the
recruitment and training of soldiers, how to obtain assistance from
abroad and how to acquire weapons and explosives.'[31] Within the
ANC, many of the most radical members were in the eastern Cape
Province, Mhlaba's home, and the Transkei. The university college of
Fort Hare, formally incorporated into the apartheid system in 1959,
became a breeding ground of radicalism that exercised an influence
way out of proportion to its 500-strong student body.[32] 'I remember
that a group of us at Fort Hare actually formed a group to prepare for
the eventuality of an armed struggle,' recalled Andrew Masondo, in
those days a young Mathematics lecturer.[33] This outfit soon expired,
however, 'because we were not a homogenous group ideologically'.[34]
ANC radicals became impatient with their organisation's policy of
nonviolence, particularly after a split in 1958–59, when an Africanist

wing broke away to form the rival PAC and threatened to outbid the ANC in militancy. There had long been semi-secret networks inside the ANC that were hard to distinguish from the 'Freedom Volunteers' recruited to help in ANC campaigns. Some of these militants seem to have been responsible for a spate of arson attacks in the mid-1950s.[35] A couple of years later, ANC Volunteers in the eastern Cape were able to acquire explosives through contacts with workers in the mines.[36] In 1959, tracts appeared, issued by something called the Underground Army for the Liberation of Africa. The ANC claimed that these were government disinformation, intended to smear it and to divide popular opposition.[37]

An armed struggle was emerging in bits and pieces. Yet few militant opponents of the government had military experience. Among the exceptions, many were white members of the underground Communist Party, the SACP. Arthur Goldreich, for example, had been part of a Zionist urban guerrilla group in Israel in the late 1940s. Others had fought in the Second World War. The most militant of all the communist combat veterans was Percy 'Jack' Hodgson, whose wartime service had included a spell with a crack army unit in North Africa. He also had an expert knowledge of explosives from his time as a miner. After the Sharpeville killings Hodgson began experimenting with bomb-making equipment at home. He even suggested, his widow recalled, that 'we should be robbing banks to raise money for our revolution'.[38]

When the government imposed a state of emergency from March to August 1960, in reaction to the Sharpeville protests, detaining thousands of people, some of those behind bars discussed how they would organise an armed struggle as soon as they were released.[39]

Securing a mandate

Whether they supported the PAC, the ANC or another organisation, those in favour of taking up arms faced enormous problems. They had no modern weapons and no international allies. In the case of ANC members, the leaders of their own movement remained formally committed to nonviolence even after Sharpeville. Chief Albert Luthuli, the ANC president, was a strong Christian. Having studied the methods of Gandhi and Martin Luther King, Jr, he did not think that violence was the most effective way to confront the apartheid state. But Luthuli was forbidden by government order to leave his home town north of Durban and so was unable to take part in the heated debates on switching to the use of violence that were taking place among ANC leaders especially in the Johannesburg region and in the eastern Cape.

The people who made the most progress towards organising an armed force were the small band of communists, no more than 450 to 500 in number countrywide.[40] Operating underground, they were able to meet only in small groups. In the course of 1960 some of the Party's leading figures began to talk seriously about taking up arms. In July 1960, for the first time since the SACP's foundation seven years earlier, a delegation of South African communists travelled to Moscow for official meetings. A member of the Central Committee, Yusuf Dadoo, who had moved to London earlier that year on instructions from the Party, and Vella Pillay, living in England for 11 years already, had a first round of meetings in Moscow on their own.[41] They were joined from South Africa[42] by two other Central Committee members, Michael Harmel and Joe Matthews, invited to attend a congress of communist and workers' parties scheduled for November 1960.

Before the start of this important conference, Dadoo and Pillay[43] took the opportunity to visit Beijing, inferior to the Soviet Union in prestige in the communist world, but increasingly asserting its political and ideological independence. The Chinese government at this time was in revolutionary mode. Faced with a massive famine brought about by the Great Leap Forward, a disastrous policy he had initiated in the face of opposition from some of his own colleagues, Chairman Mao had reacted by becoming more radical still, in a logic that was to end with the Cultural Revolution and a decisive break with the more cautious and experienced Soviet communist party.

It was in this context that the two South Africans, Dadoo and Pillay, presented a request for military training to leading party official Deng Xiaoping.[44] On 20 October 1960, they met Zhu De, China's military chief.[45] On 3 November, they were received by Mao Zedong, the country's leader and Chairman of the Chinese Communist Party.[46] During their conversation Dadoo is said to have provided Chairman Mao with his views on armed struggle.[47] Subsequent events suggest[48] that Mao's response was far more positive than when Walter Sisulu had raised the matter for the first time in Beijing seven years earlier. After this meeting, Dadoo and Pillay returned to Moscow to take part in the November congress of communist and workers' parties.

Matthews and Harmel seem to have remained in Moscow throughout this period, during which Matthews recalled 'putting forward the policy of armed struggle'.[49] He later recalled that he and Harmel had extensive talks with Soviet officials and military officers at Stalin's former dacha outside Moscow, used by the Soviets to receive representatives of 'fraternal parties', particularly clandestine ones.[50] However, Vladimir Shubin, the author of the most detailed study of relations between the South African and Soviet communist parties, and himself formerly a senior Soviet official, makes no mention of this. He refers to several matters discussed by the South African delegation with their Soviet counterparts, including notably an agreement by the Communist Party of the Soviet Union to give financial aid to its South African counterpart that amounted to $30 000 before the end of 1960, but writes that the SACP raised the question of armed struggle with its Soviet counterpart 'for the first time only a year later, on 21 October 1961.[51]

Soviet perspectives on issues of national liberation were changing fast. Having taken little previous interest in African affairs, Soviet thinkers had come to believe that the decolonisation movement in Asia and Africa was a precursor to the collapse of the capitalist system worldwide.[52] The Communist Party of the Soviet Union (CPSU) began to give enthusiastic backing to radical and revolutionary movements in Africa. Its Central Committee appointed a group of advisers to work on theoretical issues concerning national liberation,[53] and in late 1960 an Africa section was formed within the Central Committee's international department.[54]

In developing a new perspective on African nationalist movements with a view to determining their suitability as allies, Marxist-Leninist theoreticians were able to draw on views expressed by Lenin himself and on ideas about a two-stage revolution that went back to the early days of the Russian Social Democratic Party, the forerunner of the Communist Party. In a series of speeches and articles starting with an address to the second congress of the Communist International, or Comintern, in 1920, Lenin had argued that national liberation movements were potential allies of the CPSU.[55] He maintained that a nationalist revolution could be the precursor to a socialist one, and it therefore made sense for communists in a colonial territory to work for a nationalist revolution in the first instance. In 1928, this line of argument was adopted by the CPSA after the sixth congress of the Comintern had instructed CPSA delegates present in Moscow to campaign for the establishment of an 'independent native republic' in conformity with current Soviet thinking. The decision caused consternation among many CPSA members, who regarded South Africa's white proletariat rather than its black population as the focus of their action. In 1935, the seventh Comintern congress made an about-turn, withdrawing the independent native republic slogan 'as abruptly and as harshly as it had introduced it'.[56] Obedient to direction from Moscow, the CPSA turned its attention away from black political emancipation to the struggle for workers' immediate interests, concentrating on trade unions. After the Soviet Union's entry into the Second World War in 1941, the CPSA had no strategic interest in encouraging nationalist activity among the black population. Accordingly, the CPSA's official programme published in 1944, and supplemented in 1947 and 1949, made no mention of a national liberation struggle. It proclaimed the Party's goal to be 'the establishment of a Socialist Republic, based on common ownership of the means of production and the rule of the working class and providing equal rights and opportunities for all racial and national groups'. It made no substantial mention of race at all.[57]

It was the election of a National Party government in 1948 that caused the CPSA to revert to exploring an alliance with black nationalists. At the CPSA's January 1950 conference, its last before its dissolution, a discussion on a possible alliance between communists and bourgeois proponents of a national-democratic revolution was greeted 'with great acclamation'.[58] Subsequently, the CPSA's successor, the SACP, worked consistently with the ANC and other anti-apartheid organisations to form a grand congress alliance, yet without placing this in any clear ideological or theoretical framework. A useful idea in this regard was contained in the report of the CPSA Central Committee to the 1950 Party conference, which asserted that South Africa was itself a colonial power of sorts.[59] The most articulate exponent of this concept was not a communist at all, but a member of the Liberal Party, Leo Marquard, president of the South African Institute of Race Relations (SAIRR). He argued that South Africa was by nature a colonial power and that the country's African reserves were its colonies.[60] Despite their political differences, Marquard was a friend of the communists Jack Simons and Bram Fischer.

Given the direction already taken by their own party, the South African communists who visited Moscow in 1960 were delighted to find an atmosphere in which national liberation was so much in vogue. The new theories on nationalism emanating from advisers of the CPSU Central Committee offered the South Africans a way of resolving the contradiction between their long-term aim of a socialist revolution and their efforts to resist the white minority government in partnership with others who were not committed to the same ultimate goal. It meant that South African revolutionaries, acutely aware of events in Algeria and the Congo, could concentrate in the first instance on the task of liberating the majority population, as in colonies elsewhere in Africa, and leave a socialist revolution to a later date.

Back in South Africa, there was keen discussion on the implications of this analysis in a context where both the SACP and the ANC were illegal. Some people argued for creating a new, legal, African nationalist body to replace the ANC, while others wanted the ANC to continue underground. Still others argued that, on the contrary, it was the Party that should dissolve itself so as not to provoke the hostility of nationalists within the ANC.[61] They were acutely aware of the challenge offered by the PAC, which had the support of large numbers of black people and was threatening the ANC's status as the prime vehicle for black political expression.

Thanks to the new insights gleaned in Moscow, debates about the degree to which the South African struggle was nationalist or class-based could now find a formal place in Marxist-Leninist ideology. SACP theoreticians duly determined that South Africa was the site of a 'colonialism of a special type', unusual in that coloniser and colonised lived in the same national territory. This was to become the key analytical concept in the programme adopted by the SACP at its fifth congress in 1962, entitled 'The Road to South African Freedom'.[62] Some passages in this manifesto were lifted from the documents of the 1960 meeting of communist and workers' parties attended by Harmel and others.[63] The SACP is said actually to have sent the draft of its 1962 programme to the Central Committee of the CPSU for perusal before it was passed.[64] Colonialism of a special type was adopted as a dogma in spite of the fact that, as Jack Simons pointed out, 'it was no more than an analogy – a partial, superficial similarity'.[65]

Having received promises of support in both Moscow and Beijing, the SACP moved to adopt a new policy in conformity with the finding that it was correct for the Party to give its full support to a nationalist revolutionary movement.[66] In December 1960 the Party convened a national conference in the Johannesburg suburb of Emmarentia, held at a house rented for the purpose. The meeting was of course secret. Among the 25 people who attended were Mandela, Sisulu, Govan Mbeki, Mhlaba, Kotane and at least three others who were members of the ANC as well as the Party. According to one of those present,[67] the aim of the conference was to sum up the lessons of the emergency period and reassess the Party's strategy and tactics in light of the new situation. The agenda was in three main parts: first, a report on the political situation presented by Rusty Bernstein; second, a report on Party organisation by Joe Slovo; third, a report on the national liberation and trade union organisations delivered by Walter Sisulu. In addition, there were elections to the Central Committee.

It was the unanimous view of the conference that the imposition of a state of emergency and the banning of the ANC indicated the arrival of a new phase characterised by a shift from legality to illegality as the context in which political activity took place. Armed resistance would have to replace nonviolence as an instrument of the struggle to overthrow the regime. Rusty Bernstein read out the draft of a resolution instructing the Central Committee to take all steps necessary to establish military units.[68] The debate on Bernstein's resolution was short, with only a minority wondering whether the Party was ready for military action, even of a sort falling short of guerrilla warfare. No one voted against the motion. There does not appear to have been any discussion about who would control the proposed military unit; it was taken for granted that this new body would be directly controlled by the Party. After the resolution had been duly approved, Bernstein dramatically burned the paper on which it was written and scattered the ashes.[69] The resulting decision was officially described as a 'secret' one, meaning that it was not recorded and not reported to members of the Party. It was the real starting point of Umkhonto we Sizwe.

'This is one part of our history that is not known,' Eric Mtshali, SACP and ANC member and founder-member of Umkhonto we Sizwe told an interviewer many years later. 'That is that the South African Communist Party arrived at the decision [to commence an armed struggle] ahead of the ANC.'[70]

The formation of Umkhonto we Sizwe

'Congress activists everywhere were questioning the policy of non-violence' after the Sharpeville killings, Rusty Bernstein recalled.[71] So were many other people, too. On 9 April 1960, a white farmer, said to have been deranged, tried to murder Prime Minister Hendrik Verwoerd, firing two shots into his face. Verwoerd was fortunate to recover.

Nelson Mandela, as a leading ANC militant, was keenly aware of the wave of radical feeling. According to police sources, in May 1960 he persuaded some people who had been preparing to launch acts of sabotage to postpone their plans in favour of a coordinated approach.[72] This is perhaps a reference to the ANC Volunteers in the eastern Cape, the militant group that had been 'able to go underground with the whole force still intact'[73] after the ANC's banning. The Volunteers included Robert Resha, an eastern Cape man who had moved to Johannesburg to work on the mines and who was later to become one of the ANC's top people.

There was a notable increase in radical activity after the lifting of the state of emergency in August 1960 had let thousands of militants back onto the streets. Some ANC members were making common cause with other networks to form ad hoc sabotage groups, sometimes sporting fancy titles. Others were taking their own initiatives, like the former ANC Youth League activist Joe Modise, part of a small group that tried to blow up the railway line between Soweto and Johannesburg in May 1961.[74] There were groups outside the ANC and the SACP intent on demonstrating their opposition to the apartheid state by means of violence. The Trotskyist Baruch Hirson wrote in his memoirs that 'we could see the possibility of one of these movements outstripping everyone else, leaving people like us behind'. He went on to recollect how 'the only way to prevent our eclipse was to seize the moment'.[75] Monty Berman, a former Communist Party member, formed a partnership with John Lang of the Liberal Party to set up the National Committee for Liberation (NCL). The NCL soon merged with yet another group to become the African Resistance Movement (ARM).[76] Although the ARM was established only in 1964, its direct antecedents went back at least three years earlier.[77] According to the Fort Hare lecturer Andrew Masondo, the radicalism of the nascent ARM was attractive to ANC militants frustrated by their own organisation's official policy of nonviolence.[78] The most threatening group of all was the PAC, which as yet had no armed wing, but which had the potential to mobilise a large constituency for a race war.

Many of the bewildering number of subversive groups founded in the early 1960s had a rather weak institutional identity. Many were probably better described as networks than organisations, arising from within a fairly limited pool of activists. What could not be doubted was the diversity of the people who concluded that force was needed in opposition to the state.

The government, meanwhile, faced the post-Sharpeville crisis with a show of unshakeable resolve. Prime Minister Verwoerd, stung by a public warning from his British counterpart Harold Macmillan about the wind of change sweeping through Africa, rather than offer any concession that might be construed as weakness prepared to withdraw South Africa from the Commonwealth and to declare it a republic. He did not deign to consult any organs of opinion outside the white community. Having banned the ANC and the PAC, he had in any case cut off any possibility of talking to the leading representatives of black political opinion.

It seems that neither the South African government nor any of the disparate groups and networks plotting acts of violence had any idea that before the end of 1960 the SACP had already discussed with senior officials of two major powers the opening of a campaign of violence against the apartheid state. The SACP had at its disposal a unique international network by virtue of being a trusted member of the family of communist parties. Nor was this the SACP's only asset, despite its small size. The Party had a discipline that no rival organisation could match. Its members were highly dedicated, with a ready guide to conspiratorial work in the form of texts by Lenin and other theoreticians of struggle. Some could recite passages of the Marxist classics from memory. There were SACP members with combat experience, and others who were professional engineers or had other skills that could be used for bomb-making. The Party had long experience with journalism, too. *armed struggle. UK*

In order to prepare its campaign, it was clear that the Party would need to address public opinion and, more specifically, that it would require some sort of arrangement with the ANC. This had to be achieved at a time when both organisations were outlawed, many individuals were subject to legal restrictions, and the ANC's president, Albert Luthuli, remained committed to a strategy of nonviolence. Luthuli and most of his colleagues were unaware of the talks on armed struggle between the SACP and its opposite numbers in the USSR and China. The only ANC members who definitely knew of the progress being made by the SACP towards organising armed resistance were those who were also senior members of the Party. Since ANC membership was formally open only to black South Africans, a crucial position was occupied by the handful of senior black communists who were also ANC members, most of whom lived in the Johannesburg region. Of the 15 people elected to the SACP Central Committee in 1958,[79] five were also members of the ANC. These five included most notably Moses Kotane, the chief functionary of the SACP as well as an influential member of the ANC's National

Executive Committee. Others were Walter Sisulu and Raymond Mhlaba, long-term advocates of armed struggle. It is notable that one of four people coopted to the SACP Central Committee in mid-1960 was ANC member Joe Matthews,[80] who participated in the meetings in Moscow later that year that were so crucial to the decision to launch an armed struggle. The promotion of blacks who were also members of the ANC reflected a move by the Party to bring in new blood[81] and, not least, to incorporate some of the nationalists who were pushing the ANC to adopt a more militant position.

According to Matthews, among the ANC militants coopted by the Party's Central Committee at this time was Nelson Mandela. Near the end of his life Matthews stated that Mandela had sat on the Party's Central Committee at the same time as himself.[82]

The police often suspected Mandela of being a SACP member. At his trial in 1964, the prosecution produced as an exhibit a 62-page manuscript entitled 'How to be a Good Communist' written in Mandela's own hand, one of the hundreds of documents found by police in a raid on Umkhonto we Sizwe and SACP headquarters in July 1963. This text, which Mandela had apparently acquired from Joe Matthews[83] or Rusty Bernstein[84] appears to have been a translation of an original by Liu Shaoqi,[85] the Chinese head of state from 1959 to 1968 who later opposed Mao and died in prison. When asked to explain this document, Mandela claimed that he had been requested to edit 'How to be a Good Communist' to improve its readability.[86] When he was asked whether he was ever a communist, Mandela was evasive: 'Well I don't know if I did become a Communist,' he replied to a question from his own attorney towards the end of the marathon Treason Trial in 1960. 'If by Communist you mean a member of the Communist party and a person who believes in the theory of Marx, Engels, Lenin and Stalin, and who adheres strictly to the discipline of the party, I did not become a Communist.'[87] In 1966 he wrote to the Department of Justice to 'emphatically deny that I was a member of the CPSA'[88] – a telling formulation, since he well knew that the CPSA had been extinct since 1950. Nevertheless, the police concluded that Mandela joined the Party in 1960[89] and was appointed to the Central Committee[90] at more or less the same time, as Joe Matthews's testimony seems to confirm.

Evidence of Mandela's SACP membership includes his participation in the Party's December 1960 conference, where the decision was made to launch the organisation later known as Umkhonto we Sizwe. Furthermore, at least seven prominent members of the SACP, in addition to Joe Matthews, have testified to Mandela's Party membership, and others have hinted at it. In 1982, former Central Committee member John Pule Motshabi recalled during the course of a Party meeting that Mandela had been recruited at the time JB Marks was campaigning for chairmanship of the Party.[91] Former Central Committee member Hilda Bernstein told an interviewer in 2004: 'Mandela denies that he was ever a member of the Party but I can tell you that he was a member of the Party for a period,'[92] and the same interviewer received confirmation from Brian Bunting,[93] son of one of the CPSA's founders and himself a senior communist for many decades.

Mandela's cooptation by the SACP Central Committee suited both sides. By embracing the ANC's leading militant, the Party was able to take strategic control of an armed movement that was gaining momentum among ANC members, especially in Johannesburg and the eastern Cape. As for Mandela himself, 'through joining the SACP,' writes Paul Trewhela, himself a Party member in the early 1960s, 'Mandela trumped both the National Party and the PAC. Of course he went straight to the Central Committee. Joining made no sense otherwise. In this way, MK was conceived and born.'[94]

The fact that Mandela's name does not figure in the Central Committee membership list quoted by Vladimir Shubin from his research in Soviet and South African archives[95] is by no means strong counter-evidence since, as the SACP activist Ben Turok writes, 'few, if anyone, knew the entire membership'[96] of a Party that had organised itself in a series of cells to avoid detection and that operated on a need-to-know basis.

The revelation of Mandela's Party membership throws light on the sequence of events as the Party moved to implement its December 1960 decision to begin an armed struggle. In early 1961, Mandela took the lead in a public campaign urging the government to convene a national convention that would be a last chance for it to talk to the extra-parliamentary opposition. A close analysis of the campaign for a national convention concludes that this initiative was actually intended to provide proponents of armed struggle with a paper trail that would justify their change of policy.[97] In other words, knowing that the government remained closed to dialogue, the Party was concerned to create the best possible climate for its forthcoming declaration of war to be received by the national and international public. 'By June 1961,' Joe Slovo wrote, 'the Central Committee of our Party and the Johannesburg Working Group of the ANC had reached a consensus on the need for a military wing and to prepare for its initial phase of armed action'.[98] The ANC's Johannesburg working group included Kotane, Marks, Mandela, Sisulu and Duma Nokwe, all senior members of the Communist Party.

It was in order to deal with the position of the ANC and other members of the Congress Alliance that, in mid-1961, the main advocates of armed struggle within the ANC, led by Nelson Mandela, set up a series of meetings within the decision-making organs of the ANC and its partners. After consulting Sisulu, Mandela convened a meeting of the ANC working committee in June 1961, where he presented the proposal for the formation of a military organisation[99] along lines the Party had resolved six months previously. This meeting was secret, like all meetings of the banned ANC at that time.

It is most striking that one of the senior ANC members present who argued most strongly against the proposal to adopt a policy of armed struggle was Moses Kotane, who spoke in favour of continuing with nonviolent protest. Kotane's reasoning was simply that the advocates of armed struggle were unprepared for the reaction it would provoke. He had already warned about this the previous year when members of his Party wanted to step up their activities. 'The backlash will be fantastic,' he had said then. 'The police will go mad.'[100]

Kotane's opposition to the use of violence is surprising because he was the general secretary of the SACP as well as being a member of the ANC's governing body. How could he argue against a policy of armed struggle within the councils of the ANC when the Communist Party had already decided in favour, and especially when the practice of democratic centralism required that, once the Party's senior organ had decided on a policy, all members must concur? The most likely answer to this question is that Kotane managed the problem posed by dual membership by reasoning that he spoke within ANC fora as an ANC member, and was therefore entitled to articulate his personal view rather than that of his Party.[101] If so, it is a measure both of the depth of Kotane's conviction concerning the folly of armed struggle and of his standing within the SACP, as his action carried the risk of him being stripped of his office. But despite his personal opposition to armed struggle, Kotane told Mandela that he could agree to the issue being raised with the ANC's highest authority, the national executive.[102] This led to a subsequent meeting, also in Durban, the next week.

Today, the June 1961 meeting of the ANC's National Executive Committee is presented in popular histories as the most dramatic of all the occasions on which the issue of armed struggle was debated, not least because Luthuli was present. It is generally presented as the real start of the new armed unit,[103] occluding the decision already taken by the SACP. The session was held at night, again in secret. Luthuli, recognising that there was a substantial current of opinion inside the movement in favour of taking up arms, accepted that a military organisation could be formed provided it was separate from, and independent of, the ANC. The National Executive Committee agreed to this formula.[104] This meant that as from June 1961, the ANC remained formally committed to nonviolence even though some of its leading members were engaged in preparing violent activities on behalf of another organisation, later to be dubbed Umkhonto we Sizwe, Zulu and Xhosa for 'the spear of the nation'. This became contracted to MK, initials originally applied to the Amadelakufe ('Those who do not fear death'), the name given to resisters of an earlier period.[105]

The decision of the ANC's national executive to turn a blind eye to the formation of a new militant organisation paved the way for a discussion to be held by the joint executive of the entire Congress Alliance, which met just a day later, also in Durban. This included representatives not only of the ANC but also the Indian Congress, the Coloured People's Congress, the South African Congress of Trade Unions and the Congress of Democrats, all of which included members of the SACP in their ranks. This meeting, too, gave Mandela a mandate to proceed with forming an armed group.[106] The way was now open for militants to assemble the people and the resources to initiate a campaign of sabotage, secure in the knowledge that they had substantial backing within organisations with a popular base far wider than that of the tiny SACP.

In a speech in 2010, President Jacob Zuma claimed not only that Luthuli supported the foundation of Umkhonto we Sizwe, but that it was in fact he who gave it its name.[107] Yet a study of Luthuli's writings concludes that he never renounced his personal commitment to nonviolent methods,[108] on account of which he was awarded a Nobel Peace Prize in 1961, and that he never underwent a conversion to the cause of armed struggle. It is possible that both accounts contain some truth, in the sense that Luthuli remained a partisan of nonviolence while wishing to remain informed of events affecting the movement of which he remained the nominal president until his death in 1967. He continued to attend meetings that tracked the progress of the ANC abroad, without questioning the existence of

Umkhonto we Sizwe.[109] What is most clear, however, is that once leading members of his organisation had committed themselves to a policy of violence, albeit under the flag of the nominally autonomous organisation called Umkhonto we Sizwe, the authority of Luthuli, banned by the government and presiding over a movement that was proceeding on a new path, drained away. Luthuli played little further role in ANC decision-making, which passed swiftly into the hands of members who went into exile.[110]

The Durban communist Rowley Arenstein, who was not present at the December 1960 conference in Emmarentia, and who believed that the time was not ripe for armed struggle, saw the adoption of this position by the ANC simply as 'the act of the Johannesburg SACP clique – a hijacking!'[111] He told an interviewer that 'Luthuli was simply brushed aside. He was told that MK was separate from the ANC, that the ANC should stay committed to non-violence but that he shouldn't expel individual ANC members who participated in MK.'[112] Lying in an archive in Ghana is a document suggesting that Mandela and others indeed intended the description of Umkhonto we Sizwe as a nominally autonomous organisation only as a tactical ploy. This is a memorandum written in May 1962 by Mandela and two leaders based outside the country, Oliver Tambo and Robert Resha. The memorandum, addressed to the government of Ghana, describes Umkhonto we Sizwe as 'an armed organisation formed by the ANC to carry out planned attacks'.[113]

In late 1962, Resha stated publicly in London that Umkhonto we Sizwe was the ANC's armed wing.[114] After this revelation, the ANC dropped the line that it was not committed to violence. Soon, few people remembered the legalistic contortion that the ANC remained committed to nonviolence in spite of the fact that some of its leading members were also the commanders of a guerrilla force. Umkhonto we Sizwe became regarded simply as the ANC's army. A hazy perception was created that somehow the ANC as a body had decided on an armed struggle and created its own armed wing. The bulk of ANC members, then and now, have never known how their organisation was bounced into adopting the armed struggle.

Preparing for war

'To constitute the [Umkhonto we Sizwe] High Command the ANC appointed Mandela and the Party appointed me,'[115] Joe Slovo, one of the architects of the armed struggle, later wrote. The SACP and the ANC each began setting up sabotage units, although these soon merged to form the first units of Umkhonto we Sizwe.[116] Since in fact Mandela was also a member of the Party's Central Committee, this joint division of labour with the ANC was a device that disguised the degree of the Party's influence, and that also served to keep these two ambitious men on the same track. Slovo later wrote of 'the important role which the Party played in the creation and building of MK', acknowledging that this 'was not generally known'.[117] He maintained that 'there was perhaps no other period in our history when the Party played such a seminal role in the unfolding of the struggle as in the years between 1960 and 1963'.[118] In the many cases where Party members were also members of another organisation, such as the ANC or the Congress of Democrats, internal Party discipline required that 'at all times, the first loyalty of Party members is to their Party',[119] the very rule that Kotane flouted when he argued in ANC meetings against adopting a policy of armed struggle.

Mandela and Slovo set to work recruiting people for the new organisation, and by December 1961 Umkhonto we Sizwe could count some 250 operatives.[120] Party member Mac Maharaj, then studying in England and in close contact with Vella Pillay, 'was approached ... to go for training' in East Germany as early as March 1961, originally as a printer, but subsequently in sabotage.[121] Almost all the people recruited to MK were from the Communist Party. Joe Modise, an organiser for the ANC Youth League in Sophiatown with good contacts in the underworld of the *tsotsis*, was one of the very few non-Party members enlisted.

The SACP Central Committee now implemented the plans for foreign training that it had been preparing since the visits to Moscow and Beijing by leading members the previous year. In October 1961, the Central Committee sent a coded message to Raymond Mhlaba instructing him to leave for military training abroad. He slipped out of the country in company with Andrew Mlangeni.[122] Travelling via Tanzania, Ghana and the USSR, on arrival at his final destination in China, Mhlaba met others who were also going to China for training. They were Joe Gqabi, Wilton Mkwayi, Patrick Abel Mthembu and Steve (later known as Nandhagopal) Naidoo, the latter coming from London, where he had been living for some years and had been recruited for military work by Vella Pillay.

After arriving in China, the trainees were divided into two groups, one sent to Shen-Yon military academy, the other stationed in Nanjing.[123] They were received in Beijing by Chairman Mao in person. 'Mao [Zedong] met and welcomed us in China,' Mhlaba recalled, and asked the trainees about their opinions on China and the USSR.[124] Others reported that Mao asked about the nature of the terrain and the general situation in South Africa and gave advice on military strategy.[125] He 'urged his listeners not to follow blindly the experience of the Chinese Red Army. He suggested to them that the experience of the FLN [Front de Libération Nationale] in opposition to French colonial rule in Algeria might be more relevant,' according to Paul Trewhela,[126] who received the information from his brother-in-law, Nandhagopal Naidoo, in confidential discussions in 1970.

So secret was the military training given by China that even senior ANC officer-holders remained uninformed for some time. On his way back from Nanjing to rejoin the underground in South Africa, Raymond Mhlaba passed through Tanzania, where he met Oliver Tambo, the official leader of the ANC's external mission and soon to take over the effective leadership of the ANC as its internal structures crumbled in the face of government repression. Tambo 'did not know about our military training in China', Mhlaba noted.[127] Another China trainee recalled: 'OR said to me that he was unhappy about the fact that he had not been informed about the trip to China by the movement.'[128] Nevertheless, by 1965 at the latest, the security police had learned about the China trip.

Most early military trainees were sent not to China but to other African countries. In June 1962, some 32 recruits left South Africa for this purpose,[129] and a further 135 fighters from camps in Tanzania were sent to various countries throughout the continent in the half-year from September 1962,[130] with larger groups to follow. The preferred exit route from South Africa was generally via the border with Botswana (in those days still the British protectorate of Bechuanaland). Within months, Joe Modise, a Tswana-speaker whose own mother was from Bechuanaland,[131] together with Fish Keitsing had created an excellent network of contacts from Johannesburg across the border.[132]

Umkhonto we Sizwe planned to launch its sabotage campaign on 16 December 1961, a highly symbolic date known to Afrikaners as Dingane's Day or, later, the Day of the Covenant, the anniversary of the 1838 Battle of Blood River, at which a party of Voortrekkers had defeated a Zulu army. Yet there were sporadic sabotage attacks by various groups and networks protesting against the government throughout the preceding months, such as an arson attack in September 1961 by Monty Berman's network.[133] Another armed movement, Poqo, was in the process of formation within the Pan-Africanist Congress, the ANC's rival. The SACP did everything it could to control or contain attacks by these other parties. It infiltrated some of its own people into the anti-communist ARM,[134] many of whose members also suspected that a dashing British war veteran who trained them in sabotage techniques, Robert Watson, was an agent for his country's own foreign intelligence service, MI6. The SACP regarded all of these rival groups as potential spoilers.

In their memorandum to the Ghanaian government, Mandela, Tambo and Resha went as far as claiming that Umkhonto we Sizwe's first act of sabotage was an attack on Johannesburg's phone system in October 1961,[135] although this was almost certainly the work of another group; the networks that formed the ARM had more expertise in sabotage than Umkhonto we Sizwe, which claimed several of its rivals' attacks as its own. Even the first official attacks by Umkhonto we Sizwe, on 16 December 1961 (with one premature effort on the previous day), took place at the same time as attacks by other networks.[136] According to a later chief of security police intelligence, there were in total some 400 acts of sabotage by various groups in the years 1961–63,[137] of which the first MK high command was responsible for 193, or just under half.[138]

The formation of Umkhonto we Sizwe reflected the ANC's adaptation to life underground, with local units still based on the neighbourhood residents' associations that were its bedrock. These now responded to a centralised command structure for the first time in the ANC's history,[139] namely, the Umkhonto we Sizwe high command, chaired by Mandela. Writing from prison six years later to an official in the Department of Justice, Mandela stated that the SACP had only a minority of representatives on the high command 'and did not in any way direct its policy'.[140] Still later, however, he told the ghostwriter of his autobiography that 'the Communist Party and the ANC met from time to time, to give us, the High Command … instructions'.[141] Evidence produced at the so-called Little Rivonia trial in 1964 left little doubt that, certainly after Mandela's arrest, the Umkhonto we Sizwe high command was under the direction of the SACP Central Committee.

The initial plan of the Umkhonto we Sizwe high command was to attack economic and symbolic targets without risk to human life.

However, in the eastern Cape, where a group of ANC Volunteers had been preparing for war even before 1960, some militants were intent on going beyond sabotage attacks to root out enemies in their midst.[142] On 15 December 1962, the MK regional commander, Washington Bongco, firebombed the house of one Inkie Hoyi in Duncan Village. Hoyi was well known in the neighbourhood as a counsellor of the Xhosa royal house of Phalo. His fault, in the eyes of the local MK unit, was to have supported Kaiser Matanzima's campaign for a self-governing Transkei homeland, in conformity with apartheid policy. The arson attack, one of several petrol-bombings on the first anniversary of the unveiling of Umkhonto we Sizwe, resulted in the death from burns of Hoyi's 14-year-old niece.[143] When Bongco was duly convicted and hanged in December 1964, the ANC issued no statement, suggesting that the high command did not endorse actions of this nature. In May 1963, Vuyisile Mini, MK commissar in the eastern Cape,[144] was arrested and subsequently convicted with two others for the shooting to death of an alleged police informer, although none of the three had actually pulled the trigger of the murder weapon.[145]

By March 1966, according to official statistics,[146] the insurrection throughout South Africa had resulted in 15 deaths. This figure includes killings by other organisations, notably Poqo, as well as MK. The bitterness caused by ideologically motivated murders among people living in the same neighbourhoods in East London was a foreshadowing of what was to happen a couple of decades later, when some communities became split into armed factions subsumed in the ANC's people's war and the government's counterinsurgency campaign.

Amid the practical problems caused by illegality, the Umkhonto we Sizwe high command strove to create some coherence. Arthur Goldreich, acting on behalf of the SACP Central Committee, bought a property where the Party and the MK high command could hold meetings and store documents. This was the famous Liliesleaf Farm in Rivonia, now a national museum in what has become a suburb of Johannesburg, but in those days a farm in the grassland between Johannesburg and Pretoria. Nelson Mandela spent much of his time there in late 1961, receiving visits from his wife and children. It was at Liliesleaf that he copied by hand the text of 'How to be a Good Communist' while he read voraciously on guerrilla warfare in Algeria, Cuba, Israel and elsewhere. It was also at the farm that the MK high command, including Mandela, Sisulu, Govan Mbeki, Mlangeni and Mhlaba, Party members all, worked on a strategic plan of campaign known as Operation Mayibuye, a six-page document drafted by Slovo and Goldreich. It envisaged broadening the sabotage campaign into a guerrilla war, using MK members trained abroad.

Security at Liliesleaf Farm was astonishingly poor. Arthur Goldreich, the legal owner of the property, used to leave every morning to go about his business. This was odd behaviour for someone who purported to be a farmer, and it made the neighbours curious. Wilton Mkwayi recalled: 'One of [them] – a white farm owner – said to us (he thought that we were farm workers): "We always invite your boss to all our social events and he does not invite us to his events. Why? There are always cars parked outside his yard, seven or so, even though he is supposed to be at work together with his wife?"'[147] Mkwayi was also alarmed by the number of people from a nearby township who would visit the farm. 'I ask myself why this place seems to be known by so many people,' he mused.[148]

In January 1962, Mandela left the country to solicit international support for Umkhonto we Sizwe. His trip took him to Egypt, Morocco, Algeria at the moment of its independence, Guinea, Liberia, Ghana (the 'black star' of Africa), Tanganyika, imperial Ethiopia and other countries, including Britain. He underwent basic military training in several places, and many of the countries he visited were subsequently to provide military training to MK recruits. At this early stage, the MK high command's strategic thinking was based largely on the experience of Cuba, where a small body of guerrillas had been able to establish itself in the countryside before spreading from its rural bases to raise the population in support. Inspired by this example, the aim of Umkhonto we Sizwe's commanders was to send trained guerrillas into South Africa with a view to setting up bases in rural Transkei and elsewhere, from where they could launch attacks and train a new cohort of fighters. 'When we left South Africa in 1962,' wrote one early recruit, 'the expectation within ANC circles was that an insurrection toppling the oppressive regime would occur within a matter of months'.[149]

As he toured Africa, Mandela sensed that the ANC's connection with the SACP was not universally popular. Many African governments had a preference for the rival PAC, with its simple brand of African nationalism, and were suspicious of the ANC's links with white communists.[150] In Cairo, Mandela was received coldly by officials who had read a hostile commentary on Colonel Nasser in *New Age*, a Cape Town weekly edited by Party members.[151] Passing through London in June 1962, he had a difficult meeting with Pillay and Dadoo, who were not impressed by his argument that the ANC and MK should cultivate a more 'African' profile.[152] Arriving back in South Africa on 24 July and heading straight to Liliesleaf Farm, Mandela briefed the ANC's National Working Committee on his tour, articulating the views he had formulated over the previous six months. From there he went to Natal to see Chief Luthuli, still the president of the ANC. 'I remember when Mandela came back from his tour of Africa in 1962 and wanted to report to Luthuli as the ANC leader,' Rowley Arenstein reminisced. 'Joe Slovo and Ruth First were very contemptuous of this – they saw Luthuli as sidelined and rather irrelevant. Mind you, Slovo was upset about Mandela's trip in general: "We sent Nelson off to Africa a Communist and he came back an African nationalist," he used to complain.'[153]

Despite Slovo's disappointment at the cooling of Mandela's communist sympathies, it is evident that Mandela's brief membership of the Party was motivated by pragmatism rather than ideological commitment, that his opinions on communism had a strongly Christian tint, and that his primary allegiance was to Africa.

It was after briefing Luthuli that Nelson Mandela was arrested at a police roadblock in Natal in August 1962. It was clear that the police had been tipped off that he would be travelling along that particular road. Ever since that moment, there have been rumours that information on his movements was given to the police by the US Central Intelligence Agency (CIA). Gerard Ludi, a government agent who succeeded in penetrating the SACP, later wrote: 'I know for a fact that the CIA gave [Mandela] away.'[154] Ludi was well placed to know the truth of the matter, as he and Millard Shirley, the chief CIA operative in the country, became so close that they eventually went into business together. One of Mandela's colleagues in Umkhonto we Sizwe later stated that it was 'known that Nelson Mandela was betrayed by the United States CIA'.[155] According to a newspaper investigation carried out after Mandela's eventual release, CIA officers initially considered Mandela's arrest one of their 'greatest coups'.[156] The US government has denied the allegation of CIA involvement. Nevertheless, three decades after Mandela's arrest, the story of a CIA tip-off was regarded as accurate by former staff who had served at the US embassy during that period,[157] as well as by old hands in the apartheid intelligence service.[158]

The US intelligence agency and the South African government of the early 1960s shared a strong anti-communism. In those days, the National Party government was still in the process of establishing an intelligence service suited to its requirements. Following its rise to power in 1948, the National Party had cleared out United Party supporters from the police Special Branch and replaced them with its own people. At the same time, some of the Ossewabrandwag radicals who had advocated paramilitary action during the Second World War years joined the National Party and became prominent on its right wing. The events of 1960–61 strengthened their position, to the extent that in 1961 Prime Minister Verwoerd appointed to the Justice ministry a former Ossewabrandwag general, John Vorster. Vorster's friend HJ van den Bergh, the former head of Ossewabrandwag counterintelligence, and with whom he had been interned during the war, was parachuted into a senior position in the security police, the successor to the Special Branch, and soon acquired the rank of general. In secret, he worked at the same time to establish a new agency within the security police known as the Republican Intelligence Service. Van den Bergh struck up a close relationship with the CIA.[159]

Various trial records indicate that, by 1965, the police were well informed about the extent of Umkhonto we Sizwe's relationship with China in particular. At first, the USSR and China both gave support to the SACP and its ANC ally, but in later years, after their split with Moscow, the Chinese developed a relationship with the PAC. The CIA, meanwhile, was playing an altogether more complex game. Piet Swanepoel, an analyst employed by Van den Bergh's new intelligence outfit, discovered that the CIA was, from about mid-1960, providing funds to John Lang and others to finance a movement dedicated to calling a national convention.[160] Some of this money may have found its way to the ARM,[161] whose John Harris planted a bomb at Johannesburg station in 1964, killing a bystander. As a result, Harris became the first white to be hanged in South Africa for a politically motivated crime. This meant that the CIA was cooperating with the state security services even while it was also channelling funds to anti-apartheid networks that were dabbling in sabotage. Furthermore, it enjoyed a close relationship with the PAC, and in particular with its future leader Potlako Leballo, whose South African security police file indicated that he was on the CIA payroll.[162] The common denominator in all the CIA's connections was opposition to Soviet communism.

After Mandela's arrest, the MK high command continued to operate from its headquarters at Liliesleaf Farm, now reinforced by the return of the first batch of China trainees. In October 1962, some

ANC cadres from inside the country were able to meet staff of the external delegation, old friends and comrades including Oliver Tambo, at an ANC conference held at Lobatse in Bechuanaland. Some 50 delegates attended this meeting,[163] the last to be organised by the ANC from home until 1991. Its main purpose was to review the armed struggle.

Rivonia

On the afternoon of 2 July 1963, Lieutenant Willem van Wyk was sitting in his office on the sixth floor of The Grays, the security police headquarters in Johannesburg, when his phone rang. The call was from a colleague who said that he had with him someone claiming to know the whereabouts of Walter Sisulu, a member of the MK high command who had made a provocative radio broadcast from a secret transmitter somewhere in the Johannesburg area. It has never been established who the police's informant was, but he seems to have been someone that MK had earlier taken through Bechuanaland for military training.[164] After he had eventually led police to Liliesleaf Farm, the informant was paid a reward of R6 000, at that time a massive sum.[165] When the police launched a raid on the farm on 11 July, they found not only most of the MK high command, but also some 800 documents, including the strategic plan known as Operation Mayibuye, as well as Goldreich's notes on meetings with Chinese officials.[166]

Even before this spectacular bust the police had been making inroads into MK. Joe Slovo left the country in May 1963 to seek outside help. His mission was undertaken on orders from the Central Committee, although the man who took Slovo's place in MK on behalf of the SACP, David Kitson, later claimed that Slovo left after one of his protégés had been arrested and had broken under torture, causing Slovo to fear for his own position.[167] Kitson was to pay for his own steadfastness with 20 years' imprisonment.

More important even than their amateurism as saboteurs, (the SACP's intellectuals had badly misjudged the situation in South Africa) The official line peddled by the MK leadership was that the organisation in its first phase, 'through acts of largely small scale sabotage, would convince the state of the need to back down and start acting properly'.[168] Nevertheless, as an early recruit wrote, 'few of us really believed this fully. We recognised that from our small beginnings, MK would have to expand its operations.'[169] The Mayibuye plan indeed foresaw rapid progress towards a semi-conventional war. Party strategists were convinced that the apartheid state would not last long. Sharing the analysis current in Moscow that the decolonisation of Africa was a forerunner of the collapse of capitalism, and inspired by the unlikely success of Fidel Castro's 1959 seizure of power in Cuba, they believed that the sabotage campaign formally unveiled in December 1961 would serve as a detonator, provoking a more general rising against a state that they believed to be brittle. One SACP document of the time referred to 'the African Revolution', maintaining that it 'spells the certain doom of apartheid in the near future'.[170] Another explained that 'Umkhonto provides the basis for the rapid establishment of a people's liberation army, should such a stage become necessary in the future'.[171] Many of the liberal activists who embraced violence as a tactic, like John Harris of the ARM, also believed that a few acts of exemplary violence would spark a general rising. The possibility that the state might reorganise itself and develop a particularly ruthless and effective security apparatus does not seem to have crossed many minds. Joe Slovo, for one, later admitted frankly how massively he had underestimated the National Party government's capacity to counterattack.[172] Further afield, the CPSU and the Soviet government were themselves very ignorant of Africa at this stage. In 1964, during a meeting with counterparts from the East German security service, better known as the Stasi, the chairman of the KGB, Vladimir Semichastny, noted just how little either organisation knew about the continent. 'We are only at the beginning,' he observed, listing liberation movements in Angola and Mozambique among the most promising allies in the continent.[173]

The most prudent of the SACP leaders, oddly enough, was the Party's general secretary, Moses Kotane. Less steeped in theory than many of his colleagues, and with a canny instinct for survival, Kotane warned consistently of the backlash to be expected if the Party over-played its hand. Bram Fischer, sometime chairman of the Communist Party, often recalled during his years in prison Kotane's warning that 'if you throw a stone into the window of a man's house, you must be prepared for him to come out and chase you'.[174]

It could be argued that an armed struggle actually started with the peasant risings that occurred in some parts of South Africa in the late 1950s, and that it spread to urban areas after the Sharpeville killings, when various political groups became intent on perpetrating violence against the state. From this point of view, the SACP had the distinction of being the first organised group to adopt a policy of armed struggle formally. Of all the militant groups existing at the time, it had by far the best international contacts. For strategic reasons, however, it chose to conceal its own declaration of war, preferring to represent Umkhonto we Sizwe as an autonomous organisation that was later adopted by the ANC.

A still wider perspective might suggest that the historical origins of violent resistance went back to a time before apartheid, since racial segregation and massive inequality were features of South African life long before the National Party took power. However, there is no historical law dictating that certain fundamental forces produce inevitable outcomes – the error labelled 'historicism' by philosophers writing in the mid-twentieth century.[175] Historicism was precisely the great weakness of the SACP's analysis of events, the result of Marxist-Leninists thinking of history as a matter that could be dissected with precision by people skilled in the science of revolution to reveal forces as predictable as gravity. In reality, history does not unfold in conformity with principles that can be calibrated exactly by scientific methods. Perceptive analysts and politicians do well to study and identify the fundamental forces that are driving change in their own lifetimes, but they must always be prepared to be surprised by events.

CHAPTER TWO

The External Mission

A fter Oliver Tambo left South Africa in March 1960 with instructions from the ANC's governing body to set up an office
abroad, it was three years before he found a house for his
family in London, in the middle-class neighbourhood of Muswell
Hill.[1] To be more precise, it was home mostly for Adelaide Tambo
and their children, as Oliver was travelling constantly. Living close by
were Vella and Patsy Pillay. Vella Pillay, although rarely mentioned in
ANC histories, was one of the main intermediaries between the SACP
and Moscow until he eventually sided with Beijing in the dispute
that split the communist world. He was also a founder of Britain's
Anti-Apartheid Movement, being appointed treasurer when it was
inaugurated in April 1960.[2] Another Muswell Hill resident was Yusuf
Dadoo, sent abroad by the SACP to organise support for the struggle
in South Africa.[3] In London, Tambo found yet other South Africans
who were to play an important role in the years to come. They included the former Treason trialist Tennyson Makiwane and the latter's cousin Mzwai Piliso, who had been working in England as a
pharmacist for some years without being politically active.

In Africa itself, many of the governments newly minted in the late 1950s and early 1960s as Britain and France divested themselves of their colonies preferred the PAC to the ANC, and they put pressure on the two organisations to reunite, or at least to form an alliance. Tambo sat with exiled representatives of the PAC at meetings of the South African United Front launched in London in May 1960[4] until its collapse a year later.

Meanwhile, the bulk of the ANC and MK cadres who had left home in the early 1960s were parked in Tanzania or scattered around the other countries where they were sent for training. Some married local women, and a handful settled permanently in Tanzania.

Taking stock

After the Rivonia disaster, the first task of the external mission was to assess the damage. One of the high command who had been staying at Liliesleaf Farm, Wilton 'Bri Bri' Mkwayi, managed to escape and became the new commander of Umkhonto we Sizwe, its third in two years. He reconstituted the high command in November 1963. According to official statistics, MK under his leadership was responsible for 58 attacks.[5]

The police launched a new wave of arrests in mid-1964. David Kitson, Mac Maharaj and other members of the new leadership were arrested, and Mkwayi followed them into custody before the end of the year. After Robert Resha had given a speech in London in 1962 describing Umkhonto we Sizwe as the ANC's armed wing – probably a deliberate attempt to show the world that the ANC was no less militant than its PAC rival – the police had an excuse to detain and interrogate all known ANC members, even those who had been inactive for years.[6] 'We are completely stripped of our best and capable workers,' one activist lamented.[7] Joe Slovo acknowledged that 'for all practical purposes the internal movement as an organised structure had been destroyed'.[8] The police pressed home their advantage by 'using [the] M-Plan in reverse', as another ANC member put it,[9] by cultivating informers in every neighbourhood.

Just as Moses Kotane had feared, the premature declaration of an armed struggle had deprived the ANC, the Party and the communist-led South African Congress of Trade Unions (SACTU) of many of their best people. ANC units still existing inside South Africa found it difficult to communicate with one another. In Natal, at the time of the Rivonia arrests, the ANC had four provincial sub-units in operation, despite the organisation's illegal status, and no fewer than 20 branches in Durban alone. In rural Pondoland, the scene of the peasant rising three years earlier, ANC branches had stubbornly refused to adopt the M-Plan cell structure as ordered by the ANC national executive after it had received its banning order in 1960.[10] By 1965, there were still five underground ANC organisers in Port Elizabeth and the Border, four in Natal and two in the southern and western areas of the country. There were still functioning branches in 22 townships.[11]

Even more than for the ANC, Rivonia was a disaster for the South African Communist Party. The Central Committee was able to struggle on under the leadership of Bram Fischer for a few months, but even before his second arrest, in November 1965, no more organised Party formations existed inside South Africa.[12] The SACP's first major meeting after the Rivonia raid, held in Prague in May 1965, formally decided to establish the Party secretariat in London.[13] Here the SACP had its financial administration, dependent on a subsidy from the Soviet government and run by Yusuf Dadoo and Julius First, father of Ruth First, whose husband, Joe Slovo, was already established as one of the SACP's most ambitious leaders. The main concern of the Party's London-based leadership was to stay in touch with what was going on in Africa. Using codewords for security, an instruction was sent out as follows: 'To enable the CC [Central Committee] to provide adequate political leadership and guidance, the comrades from Hull [Dar es Salaam] will keep the CEC [Central Executive Committee, in London] informed on the main outline of what Jane [the ANC] is doing both inside and outside the country.'[14] The information that came back from Africa was not encouraging. The police had concluded, from a study of the vast archive confiscated at Rivonia, that the Party's Central Committee was the real power behind the new guerrilla army, Umkhonto we Sizwe. Party leaders were alarmed to learn that many senior members arrested in South Africa had broken under torture by the police. 'This has resulted in the disclosure of the workings of the Party and the identity of nearly all our members, even many now in exile,' one document noted.[15]

One of the few leading communists to remain at liberty after the Rivonia disaster was the nominal owner of Liliesleaf Farm, Arthur Goldreich. He was actually arrested with the other MK and SACP leaders, but managed to escape from police custody by bribing a guard. He settled in Israel, where he had lived previously and was well connected. After his arrival there in January 1964, he lobbied continuously on behalf of the ANC and its armed wing. In response to his urging, two senior Israeli government officials offered to conduct secret military training for MK cadres. Goldreich passed this proposal on to Tambo, as head of the external mission,[16] but nothing seems ever to have come of it.

Slovo's later admission that 'our misassessment of the situation' had been 'an important factor'[17] leading to this state of affairs was an understatement. With the notable exception of Moses Kotane – who had seen at first hand what a secret police could do, in the USSR in the 1930s – Party leaders simply had not envisaged that the state would reinforce its repressive apparatus as effectively as it did, through measures such as the 90-day detention law introduced by the Minister of Justice, John Vorster, and through the ruthlessness of the security police. Several detainees reported being interrogated by a special unit led by Captain Theunis 'Rooi Rus' Swanepoel that made systematic use of torture when dealing with suspected saboteurs, and torture became routine. Decades later, South Africa's Truth and Reconciliation Commission (TRC) reported that Swanepoel's team had been trained in France,[18] although this remains unconfirmed. Donald Card, the eccentric, Xhosa-speaking East London detective who did so much to break open the MK structure in the eastern Cape through his knowledge of local society, was transferred from the detective branch to the security police in 1965, becoming one of the very few English-speakers in an Afrikaans enclave. His new bosses provided training in sabotage techniques, telling him that this might prove useful if the government were overthrown. He received secret premiums on top of his normal salary.[19] Training in military skills unsuited to a conventional police force, and hints of corruption, thus became features of the police as it was redesigned to take on saboteurs. These were traits that were to recur in later years.

Afflicted by the Rivonia arrests, the ANC and the SACP depended on their Soviet ally more than ever before. The first batch of MK trainees was received in the USSR in 1963, and in time a special base was set up at Perevalnoye in the Crimea for training guerrillas from all over southern Africa.[20] In total, more than 2 000 ANC people were to train in Soviet military institutions in the following 28 years.[21] The Soviet alliance brought with it the support of socialist organisations in many parts of the world, not to mention in the United Nations, where, from 1963 to 1989, the USSR every year proposed a resolution demanding sanctions against South Africa, sustaining an atmosphere of hostility against the apartheid government.[22]

The USSR was not only a leading trainer of manpower, but also a leading funder. At first, Soviet subsidies to the ANC came via the SACP, but after a visit by Tambo to Moscow in 1963, the Soviet government supplied the ANC directly with $300 000 per year, with a separate subsidy of $56 000 for the SACP.[23] Soviet financing, although eventually surpassed by the sums donated by Sweden, had the great advantage of being free of conditions – a sign of the trust the USSR placed in the ANC. Joe Matthews played an important intermediary role, passing some of these funds to ANC members inside South

Africa, including for the purpose of paying the lawyers representing the Rivonia trialists.[24] Despite its Soviet subsidy, the ANC at this stage was teetering 'on the verge of bankruptcy', according to its treasurer, Moses Kotane. In May 1965, Kotane, keeping his accounts in sterling rather than dollars, estimated the organisation's annual budget at £210 000, of which £150 000 was for MK, £40 000 for running the camps where most of the cadres lived, and £20 000 for pay and expenses for officials. The organisation had some £17 000 in cash but this was less than its outstanding debts.[25]

Not only was the ANC almost penniless, but it was struggling to set up an effective administration abroad. Formally speaking, the president of the ANC remained Luthuli, but he was under permanent restriction at his Natal home. Oliver Tambo, as deputy president, ranked as number two and derived status from the fact that he had been mandated by the national executive to set up an external mission, but his authority was by no means uncontested. ANC heavyweights Tennyson Makiwane and Robert Resha 'proclaimed that Africa is their place. They said that OR Tambo must operate in Europe,' Wilton Mkwayi recalled.[26] 'Tennyson used to stress the point that: "Africa is ours. Others must stay in Britain."'[27] The fact that the ANC secretariat was located in Tanzania reinforced the influence of officials based in Africa. Nevertheless, Tambo was able to convene meetings of the national executive in London. In 1964, this body set up a planning council to replace the MK high command,[28] which had collapsed entirely after its second generation of internal leaders had been detained. Besides being based in exile rather than in South Africa, the planning council was notable for being a subcommittee of the ANC's national executive, its governing body. Formally placing MK under the authority of an ANC body was a significant change from the days when it had been under a high command that was technically autonomous but in fact under the control of the SACP Central Committee.

Noting that the massively influential position it had built up during the first phase of the armed struggle was now diminished, the SACP leadership believed that it was vital for it to restore its influence in the new context. Considering itself 'indispensable',[29] it voted repeatedly in favour of reinstating its privileged position with regard to the ANC. In the words of one Party document, the SACP believed that it 'should work towards a position where [it] has direct representation on the leading organs which implement military aims and revolutionary strategy'.[30] As a result of pressure from the Party, white, Indian and coloured Communist Party members who were not technically part of the ANC were occasionally included in ANC delegations to international meetings. Some ANC members in London became irritated by the role played in ANC affairs by people from minority groups who were not officially permitted to join the ANC at all.[31]

The formal arrangements that had worked well enough in the past were obsolete in the circumstances of exile. Before 1960, back in South Africa, the grand Congress Alliance had provided a space big enough to house the ANC and a number of allied organisations, with a committee to coordinate relations between them. The Communist Party, being banned by law, had never formally been a member of the Congress Alliance. Instead, individual Communist Party members joined the component units of the alliance: blacks in the ANC, whites in the Congress of Democrats, Indians in the Indian congresses, and so on. This made no sense once the leadership was outside the country. The SACP was not illegal in London, and could run its affairs openly from its tiny office in Goodge Street. By the same token, the Indian congresses were not illegal in South Africa, and therefore associating them with the ANC, which by this time formally included an armed wing that had declared war on the Republic of South Africa, would only get people arrested back home. Clearly, some new arrangement was needed.

The Party saw itself as a vanguard, in the forefront of diverse groups that constituted a common front against apartheid. In pursuit of their strategic goals, influential SACP leaders believed that the ANC would sooner or later have to shed its character as a forum for black South Africans of all shades of opinion. If the ANC were to become a vehicle for the emancipation of the whole population, as the SACP believed it should, it would need to find a way of accommodating people of all population groups, and not reserve membership for Africans only (as black South Africans were generally called at that time). It would also have to become more focused ideologically in order to respond to the needs of an armed struggle led from exile.

Reasoning on these lines, Party strategists saw that one option was to create a formal alliance between the Party and the ANC, each retaining its own set of rules, and both responding to a decision-making structure on which each was represented. One of the disadvantages of such an arrangement, from a communist point of view, was that it risked turning the Party into a junior partner of the ANC, since the SACP could not claim the same number of members. Moreover, it would supply ammunition to anti-communists by making public the nature of the association between the two organisations.

Another option was simply to open the ANC to people of every ethnic origin. The problem here was that the people pressing the ANC hardest for the negotiation of a new arrangement governing relations between the organisations in exile were Party activists from minority groups – whites, Indians and coloureds. Any change in their formal relationship to the ANC risked reviving old sensitivities about collaboration between the ANC and the whites and Indians who were so prominent in the Communist Party. This was a point that had been a central plank of the Youth League programme in the 1940s and which had led to the breakaway of an Africanist bloc in 1958 and the establishment of the PAC the following year.

In 1965, Slovo convened a meeting to discuss the matter at the London home he shared with his wife, Ruth First, and their daughters. Gathered in the Slovo family living room were nine people from the SACP and four from the ANC. The latter group was led by

Tambo, although some of the other ANC delegates were also Party members. As the discussion went on, two of the ANC people present, Robert Resha and Alfred Kgokong (a Communist Party member also known as Temba Mqota), said they were opposed to opening up membership of the ANC to people from minority groups.[32]

While the Party had far fewer members than the ANC, it had greater cohesiveness. One of the SACP's outstanding features was its distinctive style of legalism, as members were required strictly to abide by the rules the Party had made for itself. Party committees could thrash out the SACP line on leading issues before they were aired within the councils of the ANC. The fact that the Party had a separate (and secret) structure enabled members sitting in ANC meetings to state their case with particular effectiveness, since it had often been rehearsed. Tambo drew the line at allowing the Party to form its own cells inside Umkhonto we Sizwe, as some Party leaders were suggesting,[33] and Moses Kotane supported him on this. The Party's closeness to the USSR was also a crucial factor giving the Party leverage in its relationship with the ANC. Thanks to its Soviet connection, the SACP had at its disposal the grant of privileges such as bursaries for political training in Moscow at the prestigious Institute of Social Science, known in the ANC as the Lenin school or the Party school.[34] The first cohort of students from the ANC to be sent to this institution included Flag Boshielo, a veteran of the 1950s Sekhukhuneland rising, Ruth Mompati, former secretary at the law practice run by Tambo and Mandela in Johannesburg, and Alfred Kgokong, an important figure in the external mission – the very person who argued at the Slovos' home in favour of keeping ANC membership restricted to black people.

Tambo was in favour of strengthening the relationship between the ANC and allied organisations, and kept an open mind as to how this should be done. In September 1965, he asked Party heavyweights Dadoo, Slovo and Matthews to form a committee to examine the issue. This trio duly recommended the creation of a new strategic body, described as 'a sort of *Council of National Liberation* enjoying the support of all constituents of the Congress Alliance'.[35] Creating a war council of this sort would effectively have restored the situation pre-Rivonia, with Umkhonto we Sizwe being responsible not to the ANC but to a superior organ that would include white, Indian and coloured communists who were not, formally speaking, members of the ANC. The Party's Central Committee also appears to have established its own body to examine the role of minority groups in relation to the ANC.[36] For many ANC members, the suggestion of a Council of National Liberation was a step too far, as it would make the ANC subordinate to another body. The ANC's national executive set up a subcommittee to study the matter further. Although this subcommittee was composed entirely of people who were also prominent SACP members, it produced a different formula, proposing that the ANC, led from abroad, should function as 'the leading organ of the liberation movement'.[37] Twice, in 1965 and 1966, the ANC held what it called 'consultation conferences' in Tanzania to wrestle with the question of the proper relationship between itself and its allies.[38]

The National Executive Committee rejected the suggestion of setting up a council of war, on the grounds that it was an attempt to revive the defunct Congress Alliance, in which a rough parity had operated. Such an arrangement might imply giving the same weight to the ANC, the vehicle for black African aspirations, as to far smaller organisations representing coloureds, whites and Indians, respectively. What the position adopted by the ANC's National Executive Committee boiled down to was that whites, coloureds and Indians were welcome to join Umkhonto we Sizwe, the army of the ANC, as individuals, but not as representatives of other organisations, and they could not aspire to positions of command. People from these minority groups could not seek formal membership of the ANC. However, the consultation conference convened at Morogoro in November 1966 voted to set up a sub-subcommittee, to include representatives of the racial minorities, that could work with the ANC's planning

49

council.[39] Setting up committees was fast becoming a hallmark of the ANC in exile. While it is a conventional way for organisations to sound out opinion and reach consensus, it can easily become a technique for postponing difficult decisions.

At this point, a complicated position could be summarised as follows. The ANC's governing body was its National Executive Committee. This had two subcommittees. The first of these two entities was a planning council that consisted of ANC members – in other words, black Africans only – but which took advice from a sub-subcommittee on which other groups were represented. The second entity was the cooperation and coordination committee, in which members of allied organisations were represented, and which therefore included people from minority groups.[40] Therefore, representatives of minority groups did have some representation in the councils of the ANC, but only on advisory bodies and not as full members of the most senior organ. Above all, Umkhonto we Sizwe remained under the authority of an ANC committee that did not contain people from any of the minority groups and on which no other organisation was formally represented. This was a significant change from the early days of Umkhonto we Sizwe, when it had been a Party fief. The situation was made more delicate, though, by the fact that several of the ANC heavyweights who sat on these key committees were also Party members.

There was one obvious way of cutting through all this complexity. That was simply to declare the ANC open to all South Africans, irrespective of race. But Moses Kotane, general secretary of the SACP and influential member of the ANC's national executive, was opposed. Ever cautious, he argued in favour of the status quo. He is said to have stated that every true revolutionary should 'subordinate himself to the will of the African people without demanding membership'.[41]

Kongwa

While ANC leaders in Dar es Salaam and London formed committees and subcommittees, wrote letters and scraped together money for plane tickets, the bulk of the troops led a poor existence in camps in rural Tanzania. Hundreds of people, overwhelmingly men, had left South Africa in the early 1960s, believing that they would be back home, gun in hand, after a few weeks' training. From 1963, many of these recruits went on training courses in Algeria, Egypt, Ethiopia, the USSR and elsewhere. After these interludes, they were generally sent back to Tanzania. There, they remained stuck.

The biggest of four ANC camps in Tanzania was at a railway junction at Kongwa, near Dodoma, some 400 kilometres from Dar es Salaam. It was situated in a hot, dry basin between hills. The first occupants built the camp themselves, making their own bricks. Once this was done they kept busy with drills and shooting practice. The first commander of the camp was Archie Sibeko (also known as Zola Zembe), whom some inmates recalled as a blatant tribalist, 'Xhosa first and ANC second'.[42] By early 1965, he had been replaced by Ambrose Makiwane, cousin of the influential Tennyson Makiwane. He was followed in turn by his deputy, Joseph Jack. The camp commissar was a young man whom Ambrose Makiwane had recruited into the ANC when both were students at Fort Hare. His name was Chris Hani.[43]

Even after Sibeko's replacement, Kongwa remained a nest of ethnic and factional rivalries. It was generally agreed that these were aggravated by conflict between two people who were vying for ultimate control of Umkhonto we Sizwe. One of the two was Ambrose Makiwane, a Party member. As someone from the eastern Cape and a Fort Hare graduate, he was central to many of the networks of family and schooling that linked so many people in the ANC's external mission. The other contender was Joe Modise, a Tswana from the Johannesburg townships, one of the very few non-communist founder-members of the original Umkhonto we Sizwe, who had set up the main network for taking recruits out of South Africa via Bechuanaland that was used by cadres heading into exile. Modise's roots were in the gangster milieu of Sophiatown, where, in the old days, few of the Fort Hare graduates had had much of a following and the most admired ANC leader was Robert Resha, a renowned street fighter and former gold miner[44] with family roots in the eastern Cape. It was well known that what Wilton Mkwayi once called 'that element of *tsotsis*' existed particularly among the Transvalers in Umkhonto we Sizwe.[45]

So intense was the rivalry between Modise and Makiwane that Tambo, Kotane and SACP chairman JB Marks had to impose a compromise, confirming Makiwane as camp commander at Kongwa and Modise as commander of the army as a whole.[46] 'There is a need to go into details about what goes on there in [Kongwa],' one source reported. 'It is an old story, of the struggle for power … There has long been struggle between the present Camp Commander and some old J. dating back from the days of Odessa. The rift between the two has never been healed.'[47] This suggests that the feud between Ambrose Makiwane and Modise had started during their training in the USSR.

Bitter rivalries, plus frustration and poor living conditions, made a noxious brew. Ambrose Makiwane reported to the national executive that one cadre, a certain Vincent Khoza, had stabbed another in the belief that his victim was an informer for Joe Modise, whom he said he wanted to kill.[48] Khoza held a grudge against Modise because, he believed, the latter was out to destroy him and was highly partisan in the way he dealt with the troops. Interestingly, there exists a second version of this story, as relayed by 'Radio Potato', the name given to the ANC rumour mill. It was written down only many years later.[49] In this version, the stabbing incident occurred in the USSR, not Tanzania, and Vincent Khoza attempted to stab Modise himself because he believed him to be a government spy. The second version of the incident is clearly garbled, but it nevertheless indicates the degree to which Modise was a controversial figure, as well as the existence of rumours about his loyalty.

As camp commander, Ambrose Makiwane liked to take regular evening trips to the local town, where 'he drank until late with the local traders'.[50] He would sometimes come home roaring drunk and force the cadres to do military exercises in the middle of the night, lashing out at them with a sjambok.[51] He was generally suspected of doing corrupt business deals for the procurement of supplies. Many camp inmates wore rags because their leaders were selling the second-hand clothes sent by sympathisers for their use.[52] Nevertheless, many members of the Luthuli detachment, the name given to the first generation of Umkhonto we Sizwe exiles, were later to recall Makiwane with a certain affection, laughing at the memory of his famous riposte to an ideological challenge: '*Ndibomvu, ndibomvu, nomnqundu lo*' (I'm red, red, even my arse is red).

Kongwa was notorious for 'discrimination against recruits, failure to look after their wellbeing or correct bad treatment by seniors, including P[arty] members'.[53] Homosexuality was rife, prison-style.[54] Everyone with experience of Kongwa agreed on the existence of tribalism in the camp: 'There was less pressure and more hesitation in taking disciplinary action when Xhosa-speaking people are involved than is the case with Zulu-speaking people,' a disillusioned cadre, himself a Zulu, wrote.[55] Another provocative statement was to the effect that it would be 'better to take a gun and shoot Zulus because they are not wanted'.[56] In regard to the feud between Makiwane and Modise, it was said that 'there are great possibilities that either of them have told the Officers such & such a tribe is not prepared to go home and fight'.[57] John Pule Motshabi, a Sotho and a confidant of Tambo who was familiar with conditions at Kongwa, agreed that there was what he called 'one-sided development (Xhosa) political domination'.[58] Conflicts sometimes had an ideological edge, as some cadres took Beijing's side in the Chinese Communist Party's dispute with its Soviet opposite number. In October 1965, a group of some 29 Zulus hijacked a truck and headed for the town of Morogoro, where the ANC had an office, with the aim of confronting the leadership with a demand to be sent home to fight. Makiwane called in Tanzanian government troops to arrest them. The group was put on trial but treated leniently, as most Kongwa residents supported the protestors. Three weeks later, the infliction of a punishment beating led to a firefight between Xhosas and Zulus. Those implicated were detained, but so too were others who were not involved but whom the camp administration regarded as troublesome, including Patrick Molaoa. Reputed to be a former *tsotsi*, Molaoa had the distinction of being the last president of the ANC Youth League elected before its banning by the government in 1960. He had trained in China and was sent for retraining in the USSR after the Sino-Soviet split, in an effort to rid him of Maoist ideas, now regarded by the SACP as heretical.[59] Some of the 27 people who were detained for over a year were accused of having tried to contact the Chinese embassy.[60]

The overall conclusion drawn by two former residents was that 'it is difficult to measure the level of demoralisation that saturated MK's ranks at Kongwa'.[61] Not the least of the frustrations endured by ANC cadres stemmed from the fact that there were other camps close by occupied by guerrillas from the Mozambican liberation organisation FRELIMO, the Angolan MPLA, the South West African People's Organisation (SWAPO) and the Zimbabwean ZAPU, all four allies of the ANC. The disheartened Umkhonto we Sizwe troops at Kongwa knew that the Mozambican and Angolan organisations were sending their people to fight in the front line back home.[62] Among the ranks of MK, 'eventually the suspicion grew that the external leaders had no intention of returning to South Africa to fight and free the people. The belief was they were living in luxury in the city while the soldiers were stuck out in bush camps with virtually no facilities.'[63]

Beyond personal animosities, the conflict between Makiwane and Modise was really about patronage. Kongwa camp with its 400 to

500 residents was the main concentration of ANC personnel in exile, and mastery of the camp therefore provided a platform for influence within the organisation as a whole. A camp commander could control the provision of food and resources, and issue invitations to train elsewhere, in effect giving rewards to favourites so as to build a personal clientele. For those other ANC chieftains who did not have control of large numbers of people, the stuff of patronage was more likely to be invitations to international conferences with the chance of getting cash allowances and other perks. These rivalries took on ideological overtones, not only in regard to the Sino-Soviet dispute but also on other issues. Leaders based in London, where the influence of white SACP members was greatest, tended to be distinctly less attentive to racial issues than those based in Africa, who were generally more Africanist because of their exposure to the views of Tanzanian officials. As Mandela had detected during his 1962 African tour, many African governments were frankly suspicious of the ANC's links with a communist party run largely by whites.

Conflicts of any description could quite easily be interpreted as security threats, real or imagined. Thus, John Pule Motshabi found himself under surveillance when he returned to Tanzania after 11 months in the USSR. When he appealed for help to Party chairman JB Marks and ANC secretary-general Duma Nokwe, they told him he was under suspicion because 'I had something to do with the Boers and there was [an] allegation that I am an enemy agent'.[64] Similar difficulties were experienced by Flag Boshielo when he returned from the USSR after his stint at the Lenin school. Even his mentors Marks, Kotane, Harmel, Slovo and Dadoo could not protect him from the unwelcome attentions of the security people.[65] Control of a security network was of great value in the ANC's factional politics as it enabled the leader of one faction to attack the clientele of a rival.

It is not entirely clear what the status of the security services was in those days. According to the ANC's own submission to the later Truth and Reconciliation Commission, the organisation established

a military intelligence unit in the 1960s with responsibility for un-
dertaking reconnaissance missions to find routes for the infiltration
of trained MK cadres, the establishment of reception areas inside the
country for these cadres, and the selection of targets for armed propaganda attacks.[66] This military intelligence unit is said to have had no
counterintelligence capacity and there was no structure specifically
tasked with the screening of new recruits. A variety of informal security networks seems to have sprung up within the ANC and MK in the
mid-1960s. What one senior official called the 'James Bond-type-of
spies' were active 'against their colleagues in all camps'.[67] A unit pop-
ularly known as the James Bond section was headed by Eric Manzi
(whose real name was Bonnie Njamela). Born in Queenstown in
1937, Manzi had attended Fort Hare, where he came under the influence of Ambrose Makiwane when the latter was president of the
students' representative council. Manzi joined the ANC Youth League,
and, while he was still at Fort Hare, in May 1961, he organised a
strike with his fellow student, Chris Hani. Manzi was talent-spotted
by Govan Mbeki, who recruited him to the Party. As was standard
practice, Manzi was made to read some of the Marxist-Leninist classics as an initiation into the Party's intellectual life, beginning with
A Leontiev's *Political Economy*, a stodgy textbook first published in
Russian in 1935. It was Manzi's proud boast that he set up the first
SACP cell at Fort Hare.[68] Manzi arrived in Tanzania in January 1963.
Described as a 'blue-eyed boy of senior leaders',[69] he seems to have
remained a protégé of Ambrose Makiwane, who used him to run a
security service at Kongwa. By 1967, Manzi was described as MK's
'regional head of intelligence'.[70] He was said to have 'destroyed some
senior leaders' by placing them under investigation.[71]

Disillusionment with the pettiness of the intrigues within the ANC
in Tanzania caused some cadres to seek asylum elsewhere. Some 80
escapees from the Tanzanian camps are said to have taken refuge in
Nairobi.[72] One promising youngster who abandoned ANC work in
disgust was Walter Sisulu's nephew, Gerald Sisulu, who for a while

had played a significant role in liaising between the internal and external movements.[73] Eventually, Manzi himself baled out of the ANC, probably because he saw the star of his patron Ambrose Makiwane waning. Manzi was last heard of living a quiet life in Sweden. By the time he left Africa, the ANC had acquired an official security organisation headed by the secretary-general, Duma Nokwe, which seems to have assimilated Manzi's network. The official security service run by Nokwe was powerful enough to have people detained, tried and even executed.[74]

Security networks

Meanwhile the SACP ran its own security system in its stronghold in London. To judge from surviving reports,[75] this was formal in nature and must therefore have been approved by the Party's Central Executive Committee. It kept files on security suspects in the United Kingdom at least from 1967. It also had at least one source inside South Africa's security police.[76] The Party security unit made notes on possible recruits, commenting on the young Thabo Mbeki while he was a student at the University of Sussex, 'if he is not already in our outfit he should be brought in at once'.[77] After the diplomatic and ideological split between China and the Soviet Union in the mid-1960s, one of the main concerns of SACP chieftains was to keep the Party loyal to Moscow, causing a security operative to send to Yusuf Dadoo a report on Maoist influence in SACP circles in Britain.[78] Although Dadoo was not formally the Party chairman at this time, 'in reality he headed everyday activities of the Party'[79] from his London office. Even though the Party's security apparatus was small, it was of considerable importance because of the Party's influence on the various networks based in London. In particular the Anti-Apartheid Movement (AAM), originally founded as a boycott movement in 1959, had grown into a formidable lobby in the aftermath of the Sharpeville killings,[80] developing excellent contacts among journalists and other opinion-formers and in Britain's governing Labour Party. SACP members in exile such as Vella Pillay and Alan Brooks played a much-underestimated role in turning the AAM into one of the most formidable public pressure groups seen in Britain for decades.

The importance of London as a node of influence did not escape the attention of ANC chieftains elsewhere, such as Maindy[81] Msimang, a former clerk at the famous Mandela and Tambo law firm, who by the mid-1960s was in charge of youth affairs in East Africa. Although based at ANC headquarters in Dar es Salaam, Msimang ran his own intelligence-gathering apparatus in London from an early date. 'The individuals contacted were given specific instructions as to the nature of the intelligence they were to garner and directed to forward it to him personally', the SACP security unit reported concerning this rival network. 'They were further directed to keep the whole matter secret', although Msimang shared his information with close associates.[82] When some of Msimang's colleagues discovered the existence of his network and confronted him in early 1967, he refused to give any explanation.[83]

The existence of personalised security networks like those run by Manzi and Msimang, as well as the Party's own outfit, lends credence to the assertion by an authoritative source that a formal ANC security organ 'came into being over a period of time. It came into being through evolution ... It was not planned nor was its birth a subject of discussion.'[84] A later head of the ANC intelligence and security organ commonly known as NAT was Sizakele Sigxashe, yet another graduate of Fort Hare. He had studied with Hani, Manzi and others who were to make their mark in the ANC, most of them associated with Govan Mbeki.[85] Seeking to compile a history of ANC security, he wrote that 'a secret embryo' of an intelligence and security structure was formed 'as from the 1960s', consisting of 'a few specially selected cadres'.[86] More specifically, he described the 'formation of

NAT embryos' as having taken place in the period 1962–68.[87] A formal security organisation headed by Duma Nokwe certainly existed by early 1969, as this was referred to explicitly in a document written by Chris Hani and others in the first quarter of that year.[88] We may perhaps deduce from this that the ANC's official apparatus was actually founded in 1968 and placed under the authority of Duma Nokwe, and that it existed for a while alongside a number of less formal structures associated with factions inside the movement, which it soon absorbed. The ANC itself has reported that 'during this period, the embryonic Department had no formal structure, and all members of the Department were also members of MK'.[89] One might add that it already seems to have been an SACP fief.

No one seems to have doubted that a security problem indeed existed insofar as the ANC's ranks included people who were passing information to the police or intelligence agencies of the South African state. As early as 1962, before large numbers of cadres had gone abroad for training, the police were reported to have informers in the ranks of the ANC's external mission 'fairly high up in the ANC's East Africa hierarchy'.[90] The security police circulated forged pamphlets and used various other methods intended to disrupt and discredit the ANC abroad. A couple of years later, Robert Resha told a dinner companion that the ANC knew it had informers in its midst and that most of them were motivated by money.[91] In 1963, the security police acquired a farm where they trained potential infiltrators into the ANC and the PAC.[92] The East London detective-turned-security cop Donald Card claimed to have informants in MK camps.[93]

This offensive capacity on the part of the state security police reflects its development as a result of legislation introduced by John Vorster at the Ministry of Justice and the work of his close friend Hendrik van den Bergh, after his appointment to the Security Branch in January 1963. A 90-day detention law in effect licensed the use of torture. The police, protected by legislation placing them to all practical purposes beyond the reach of the law, made extensive use of torture to break open their enemies' underground networks. One of the first of many cases of a political suspect dying in detention occurred on 5 September 1963 when Looksmart Ngudle, a leader of MK in the Cape, was found hanged in his cell. It was generally supposed that he had been murdered by the police. In addition to the police there now existed the Republican Intelligence Service, which Van den Bergh had set up to function as South Africa's first home-grown secret service. As its name suggested, it was intended to take over responsibility for the international contacts that had previously been supplied by the former colonial power, Great Britain.[94]

After the conviction of SACP chairman Bram Fischer in 1966, the police were confident of having neutralised both the ANC and the SACP within the country. Yet there still existed inside South Africa not only individual ANC sympathisers and former members, but even small groups.[95] A memorandum written by a security police officer in 1968 claimed that his service was aware of the existence of what it called the ANC national secretariat in Johannesburg, chaired by John Mavuso and including John Nkadimeng. It also knew of a second group – 'if it could be called a group', noted the report – associated with Cleophas Sibande in Benoni.[96] The author of this document claimed that it was unnecessary to arrest those concerned as the ANC had already been effectively incapacitated. The police could afford, it seems, to allow a few known ANC members to stay at liberty.

The Rhodesian campaign

It was the commander at Kongwa, Ambrose Makiwane, knowing the cadres' frustration, who first began systematically soliciting their opinions about launching a campaign at home. The camp residents tended to form groups according to where they had trained, and this was reflected in their answers to his question. Those who had trained at Odessa in the USSR favoured a return en masse, weapons in hand.

Others advocated piecemeal infiltration into South Africa without weapons.[97]

These debates about returning to South Africa acquired a momentum that continued throughout 1966. A small team entered Botswana in September-October 1966, at the moment of the country's independence, to explore the possibility of reaching South Africa by this route. The infiltrators were detained and interrogated by a British officer working for Botswana's police Special Branch and eventually deported to Zambia.[98] Another way home via Mozambique was investigated in May 1967, when two small groups of MK guerrillas went in alongside FRELIMO with a view to reconnoitring a corridor into South Africa.[99] The distances involved turned out to be too great for this route to be viable.

After Makiwane's removal from command at Kongwa, army commander Joe Modise cancelled his rival's plans for sending small unarmed groups back home. Himself favouring the use of large units,[100] Modise reverted to the Odessa trainees' idea of a mass infiltration. According to Oliver Tambo, a proposal along these lines was debated 'not only by the PC [Planning Committee] or HQ but by the army commanders and commissars after lengthy deliberations'.[101] Under pressure from the rank and file, the top brass agreed to a plan 'of going home via Rhodesia' that 'came from the soldiers themselves'.[102] Members of the national executive feared that a failure to act could result in 'a mass defection among our ranks' as the soldiers simply went home under their own steam.[103] Specifically, it was decided that a contingent from MK would enter Rhodesia in company with cadres from its sister-organisation, the Zimbabwe People's Revolutionary Army (ZIPRA), the armed wing of ZAPU, with a view to establishing a route for infiltrating fighters from the camps in Tanzania via Rhodesia into South Africa. It was never the intention for this group to launch an attack on Rhodesian or South African forces, but only to set up a logistical network in order to facilitate future infiltration. Insofar as there was any strategic thought behind the initiative, dictated primarily by the need to provide some action for the troops, it was based on the Cuban model that had attracted MK chiefs from the start. Those who eventually made their way to South Africa were supposed to establish themselves in rural areas where they could reach out to the local population, thought to be ripe for insurrection, as the Pondoland rising of 1960 had suggested. Modise informed the troops 'that large groups would enter Zululand, Sekhukhuneland and the Transkei ... Only a route in [South Africa] remained to be found.'[104]

Cadres from Kongwa summoned for active service – *mchina* was their name for call-up, so called after a gambling game popular in the townships – were transferred to Zambia. Most of the fighters were lodged at a farm outside Lusaka, but a few received hospitality in private households. The academic Bernard Magubane, who was working at the university in Lusaka in mid-1967, recalls meeting the young coloured intellectual Basil February, a poet and author of political texts, who was one of those chosen to take part in the expedition. Another person staying in Lusaka at this time was Chris Hani,[105] a Party member already regarded as one of the leaders of his generation. Hani was appointed chief political commissar of a joint force that was to enter Rhodesia. It would be composed of troops from MK and ZIPRA. The ANC's military headquarters moved from Morogoro to Lusaka to organise the operation, and Lusaka was to remain important thereafter, even though the ANC remained formally headquartered in Tanzania.

The Wankie campaign, as it was to become known, was notable for its lack of planning. The troops were not even provided with proper maps. Although Joe Modise claimed to have ventured into Rhodesia beforehand to reconnoitre the terrain, getting his boots muddy, he was not widely believed and acquired the derisive nickname 'Nyawo Zinodaka' (dirty feet).[106] Tambo accounted for the lack of preparation by explaining that he and his colleagues had been relying on their ZAPU allies. 'In entering Zimbabwe,' he wrote, 'we were taking advantage of the fact that ZAPU was sending in its men anyway, and we were told they knew the terrain, although there were no maps and no proper reconnaissance of the route'.[107] The timing of the campaign was dictated by the desire of the troops to see action: 'one does not know how impatient our men were', Tambo wrote.[108] Another official recalled that 'the patience of the cadres in the camps was running out and they were pressing for action, such that in fact more of our people went into Zimbabwe than had in fact been agreed to by the leadership of the ANC'.[109]

The first group of some 80 ZAPU and MK entered Rhodesian territory at the end of July 1967. Unable to navigate effectively, travelling through largely unpopulated and waterless terrain, they bore hardships stoically. When, inevitably, they were detected and attacked by Rhodesian troops, they fought bravely in a series of skirmishes, going on until most of the ZAPU and MK fighters had been killed or captured. The Rhodesians were impressed by the morale and standard of training of their adversaries, who, according to the intelligence chief in Salisbury, were 'defeated only by the Security Forces' air power, mobility and much greater effectiveness in communications and medical services'.[110] A couple of dozen fighters in two groups – Chris Hani among them – managed to reach the relative safety of Botswana. There they were arrested and sentenced to between three and six years in prison,[111] although Hani and some others were released after just over a year as a result of heavy lobbying by African governments.[112] There were further infiltrations of a similar type in Sipolilo before the end of the year and in early 1968.

According to the South African police, a total of 81 Umkhonto we Sizwe members took part in the Wankie campaign alone.[113] The ANC later published a figure of 48 Umkhonto we Sizwe soldiers killed in the Wankie and Sipolilo campaigns combined in 1967–68,[114] a very high level of casualties for a small army. The expeditions failed in their aim of establishing a route to South Africa. Yet they were hailed by the ANC as a success. As a former editor of the ANC's main publication recalled, 'the ANC, and myself in *Sechaba*, continued to trumpet our great achievements, even when conditions were dire'.[115] This reaction resulted from more than a simple wish to put a positive spin on events. Not only was the leadership under intolerable pressure from the MK rank and file to take an initiative, but it also had to be seen to be doing something to satisfy its main international backers, the Soviet Union and the Organisation of African Unity, that it really was a fighting organisation and not just a talking shop. In 1967, the USSR recognised the ANC as one of southern Africa's 'authentic' liberation movements,[116] a status that had to be worked for.

For all their tactical failure, the Wankie and Sipolilo campaigns did have at least one positive outcome. They became an inspiration to later generations of MK fighters, producing living heroes like Hani and martyrs like Basil February, better known by his nom de guerre of Paul Peterson. Breaking off from the main group, February hijacked a car and headed for South Africa before eventually being cornered near Plumtree and killed in a shootout.[117] Patrick Molaoa was another noted casualty. He was a close friend of Vincent Khoza, the man who had wanted to kill Joe Modise at Kongwa, and was regarded by the army's top brass as a troublemaker. Some cadres believed that he was 'launched' by Modise into the Rhodesian campaign – 'an MK expression for being sent on a mission of no return'.[118] In later years Molaoa was regarded as a hero in the ANC pantheon, not least because cadres assumed that, as an ex-president of the Youth League, he could have avoided active service if he wished. MK, like many other armies, most admired leaders who put themselves in the front line.

In addition to Hani and his companions, many participants in the Wankie and Sipolilo campaigns were arrested by the Rhodesian police. Many were convicted and served prison sentences. A list of ANC prisoners held in Rhodesian gaols 12 years later recorded 32 names, probably all veterans of the 1967–68 campaigns.[119] Others had died in prison in the interim, including some held in punishment cells after trying to escape.[120] Some of those arrested in Rhodesia were subsequently handed over to South Africa, including one Charles Makaya, who later went on to become a security policeman.[121] Two are said to have made it to South Africa before being arrested.[122] Only one guerrilla, Leonard Nkosi, actually reached South Africa undetected. Returning to his home in Natal, he was betrayed to the police and arrested. Like Makaya, he was 'turned', acting as a prosecution witness in several trials and eventually becoming an officer in the KwaZulu police. Shortly after the Rhodesian campaigns, a few individual MK guerrillas succeeded in slipping into South Africa by land or sea, but were arrested and tried in Pietermaritzburg in 1969.[123]

Some ANC members, disillusioned and claiming that the Wankie expedition was a suicide mission, sought asylum in Kenya. A few of these defectors tried to launch a new movement known as the National Liberation Front of Southern Africa.[124] At least one frustrated cadre, Nimrod Sejake, left the ANC in favour of the rival PAC. Flag Boshielo was one of several others who seriously thought of resigning, but one of his friends talked him out of it by convincing him that 'resignation was tantamount to committing suicide'.[125] The most prominent ANC member actually to leave the organisation was James Hadebe, the official representative in East Africa, who resigned in December 1967 after making a series of complaints about conditions in the movement. Among other things, he accused leading members of alcoholism and tribalism. 'I am only a Zulu *nkwenkwe*, after all, and not of the circumcised better tribe,' he wrote sarcastically.[126] He alleged that certain colleagues, whom he named, had sexually harassed his daughter. The ANC, Hadebe claimed, was intent on creating a romantic image for itself, but actually ignored the rank and file. His resignation caused no lasting damage, and nor did his attempt to set up a new organisation that would renounce violence, called Umbuto we Sizwe.[127] Both Hadebe and his new outfit were soon forgotten.

The Rhodesian intelligence chief, Ken Flower, wrote that 'within hours' of Rhodesian security forces detecting the MK/ZIPRA infiltration into Wankie, he received a phone call from Hendrik van den Bergh, the chief of South Africa's security and intelligence services. Van den Bergh 'telephoned me from Pretoria to say that he had arranged through the South African Prime Minister for a detachment of South African "Riot Police" and helicopters to be sent to share in our defence of the Zambian border', Flower wrote.[128] After this, South African police 'used Rhodesia as a training ground' in counterinsurgency.[129] Hundreds or even thousands of South African policemen were to serve in Rhodesia over the next 13 years, including Eugene de Kock, later to be notorious as head of a police death squad, and Hans Dreyer, founder of Koevoet, the counterinsurgency unit deployed by the police in Namibia. Officers of the South African Defence Force (SADF) were furious that their own service, trained to operate outside the country's borders, had been ignored in favour of the police, the institutional base of their rival, Van den Bergh. Sharing their sense of outrage was the SADF's political chief, Defence Minister PW Botha, who suffered the added indignity of learning that Van den Bergh had opened a file on him.[130] Only later were a few soldiers from South Africa's fledgling special forces sent to work with the Rhodesian SAS, which itself remained inscribed on the British army's order of battle as C Squadron of the mother regiment.[131]

At more or less the same time as South Africa was becoming militarily involved in Rhodesian affairs, albeit by means of its police more often than its armed forces, a shift in the country's military disposition was taking place that strengthened the grip of the Broederbond, the powerful Afrikaner nationalist secret society, over an institution that many *Broers* found rather too Anglophile for their taste. Having been largely inactive since the Second World War, the SADF still contained senior officers who had started their career in the days before the National Party had come to power and who lacked a strong political connection to the ruling party. Military intelligence officers continued to be trained by Britain, and a number of officers who had previously worked for the British colonial administration were given jobs in South African military intelligence after the break-up of the Central African Federation in 1963. There was rivalry between military intelligence and the police intelligence agencies controlled by Hendrik van den Bergh.[132] In 1965, General Rudolph Hiemstra, who had refused to fight in the Second World War on political grounds, was appointed head of the defence force. In 1966, the same year that PW Botha took over the Defence portfolio, Brigadier General Fritz Loots became head of military intelligence. Hiemstra, Botha and Loots were all *Broers*.[133] Loots immediately identified six military intelligence officers as foreign spies – on behalf of Britain, presumably – and had them fired.[134] Over the next few years, Botha, a formidable political infighter, was to mould the officer corps of the SADF, weeding pro-British officers out of military intelligence. One young officer whose career blossomed was Magnus Malan, who rose to become the head of the SADF and eventually to succeed Botha at the defence ministry. He was the son of one of Botha's patrons, Professor Avril Malan, an influential figure in the National Party in the Cape, a parliamentarian and chairman of Volkskas bank. Needless to say, he was also a senior member of the Broederbond.

It is interesting to note that, just as there was a secret organisation at the core of the ANC in the form of the Communist Party, so was there one within the ranks of its arch-enemy, the National Party. Nevertheless, the Broederbond, for all its influence, never controlled the National Party or the apartheid state to anything approaching the degree that the SACP dominated the ANC on the other side of the fence.[135]

The Hani memorandum

After months behind bars, Chris Hani and some others were released early from the prison in Botswana where they had been held since their retreat from Rhodesia. Hani himself returned to Zambia on 16 September 1968.[136]

Hani and his comrades were angry men.[137] Thrown into a campaign that had not been properly planned, they returned to Lusaka to find no senior official prepared even to reflect on what had happened. Among junior MK members they found seething discontent. Three cadres, one of them a Wankie survivor, made an appointment to discuss their grievances with the ANC secretary-general, Duma Nokwe. When they finally managed to see him, Nokwe was at first nonchalant, but grew angry when the three pointed out that his wife was working for a company that they claimed was a front for Israeli intelligence. The complainants insisted on meeting the full national executive, whereupon they were asked to put their points in writing. This resulted in the production of a lengthy memorandum that seems to have been drafted by Chris Hani. It was signed by him and six others, two of them fellow veterans of Wankie who had been imprisoned with him in Botswana.

Having written their document at the invitation of their leaders, the signatories were alarmed to find that their memorandum was being treated as a disciplinary affair. They were detained on suspicion of treason. It seems that there was a faction within the ANC leadership that intended to have the signatories of the memorandum shot, and that there was also a specific plot to murder Hani, a fate he was lucky to avoid.[138] Oliver Tambo intervened to secure the release of the seven, although they were suspended from membership of Umkhonto we Sizwe and prevented from attending meetings.

It is unclear just how much support the seven had among the rank and file, but the affair was serious enough for Tambo to address a general meeting of the ANC held at a ZAPU camp near Lusaka in February 1969. He tried to calm things down by announcing that there would be a national consultative conference, to be held at Morogoro in Tanzania. The seven plaintiffs were then brought before a five-person tribunal, which expelled them from the ANC on 25 March 1969.

The memorandum written by the seven, and generally known as the Hani memorandum, was explosive. It described the ANC in exile as being in 'a deep crisis', attributing much of the reason to a leadership that had 'created a machinery which has become an end in itself'. It mentioned two people by name, army commander Joe Modise and secretary-general Duma Nokwe.[139] It claimed that leaders were satisfied with their life in exile, making no attempt to give an account of themselves to the rank and file or to stay in touch with events inside South Africa. It accused them of 'careerism', of being 'professional politicians rather than professional revolutionaries', who travelled the world from one conference to the next. It pointed out that leaders were exempt from taking the oath of allegiance that the rank and file were required to swear. It also alleged the existence of corruption in the form of businesses in Zambia that engaged the attention particularly of Modise, and that were run from day to day by 'dubious characters with shady political backgrounds'. Modise, the critics alleged, was running the army as a personal fief without political direction and without effective input from the political leadership of the ANC as a whole. Not only did the army apply vicious punishments, but the ANC was also running a security department – set up apparently the previous year – that was directed more at stifling internal dissent than at acquiring intelligence about South Africa. 'Those who serve in it have the central task of suppressing and persecuting dedicated cadres of MK,' the seven alleged, adding that there were 'secret trials and secret executions'. Finally they suggested that relatives of senior officials were colluding with the Peace Corps, assumed to be connected to US intelligence.

There is some indication that Hani was not the only Wankie veteran who issued a formal protest against the conduct of Joe Modise at this time. On 16 July 1968, half a year before the Hani memorandum, Modise – using his nom de guerre of Thabo More – wrote to Moses Kotane, referring to statements critical of himself that amounted to an act of indiscipline. Modise proposed to deal with the problem by setting up a tribunal composed of members of the NEC's planning council and of staff from his own military headquarters. He wished to recuse himself, however, noting: 'I find it difficult to sit in judgement over this case, in that most of the accusations are directed against me.'[140] It is unclear exactly what this refers to, as Hani and his comrades were still in prison at the time of this incident, which seems to concern another person or persons who had made a personal criticism of Modise. It is known that some veterans of the Rhodesian campaigns – other than Hani's group – were hounded out of the organisation 'for daring to raise their voice and to challenge the opulent lifestyle of their leaders in exile'. They were rehabilitated only years later.[141]

The Wankie campaign, itself born of frustration, was such a resounding military failure and had aroused such strong feelings that blame had to be pinned somewhere. The appearance in Zambia of Chris Hani and his friends, fresh from prison in Botswana and furious at the incompetence of the military leadership, therefore gave fuel to factional battles of exceptional ferocity. The truth behind specific allegations is often difficult to identify as different sides tried to 'spin' or deflect the criticism by Hani and his six companions, and many accusations were made that cannot be substantiated. What is clear is that the signatories were used 'as brooms by which the leadership swept its dirt', as Tambo put it.[142]

The public accusations made as a result of the Hani memorandum reverberated widely. Tennyson Makiwane and Alfred Kgokong (alias Temba Mqota), the ANC director of publicity, were suspended from the ANC's national executive in early 1969 on suspicion of being implicated in the drafting of the document.[143] Makiwane's enemies claimed that he had been expelled from the SACP Central Committee shortly before these events on account of his tendency to factionalism. He was accused of plotting 'to create little groups in the ANC to attack Kotane, Marks and Tambo and to remove them from the leadership'.[144] Kgokong was one of his alleged accomplices, as was his cousin Ambrose, the former commander at Kongwa. Critics accused Kgokong of having lost his way after he had attended the Party school in Moscow and returned to Africa with an inflated idea of his own revolutionary value, seeing himself as a new Lenin.[145] Whether or not Kgokong and the Makiwanes had really helped write the memorandum, it does appear that Hani had the backing of leading SACP members, including Dadoo and Slovo, as Hani himself said.[146]

Other than Modise and Nokwe, another leader who was often the target of criticism – although he was not named by Hani and his colleagues – was Joe Matthews. 'There was a time in the early 60s in exile when some people in the leadership who had some English knowledge and ability to write well regarded themselves as the all, and an end all in the ANC because at the time the movement had few intellectuals,' John Pule Motshabi recalled,[147] in what appears to be a dart aimed at Matthews, who indeed was one of the most influential figures in the movement. He was one of the few ANC leaders outside Robben Island able to write a text in clear and even elegant English, rivalled only perhaps by Nokwe, a talented legal draftsman. These two ANC lawyers detested each other.

It is said to have been Kgokong who first suggested the idea of a consultative conference to air the issues raised by the Hani memorandum, as announced by Tambo in February 1969. There had already been three consultation conferences since the banning of the ANC nine years earlier. The first was at Lobatse in 1962. The second was 'a consultation conference held in Morogoro at the end of May 1965', in Tambo's description, which took the form of a meeting of the National Executive Committee expanded to include senior army personnel.[148] The third was at Dar es Salaam in 1966. The second and third of these conferences, as we have seen, had been concerned with the question of what should be the proper relation between the ANC and its allies in the SACP and other survivors from the old Congress

Alliance. The new conference, convened to discuss the issues raised by the Hani memorandum, was also to be held at Morogoro. It was scheduled for the last week of April.

Leading figures of the SACP Central Committee had for some years taken the view that the way forward was to open ANC membership to all races.[149] The main opponent of this course of action was Moses Kotane. Prudent as always, he urged his comrades not to take any action that would offend their hosts in Zambia and Tanzania.[150] But in November 1968, just a few weeks after Hani and his comrades had turned up in Lusaka, something happened. One evening as Kotane left his office in Dar es Salaam to get into his car, he was overcome by an attack of vomiting. He had suffered a cerebral haemorrhage, a stroke. He was evacuated to Moscow and confined to hospital. His absence shifted the balance of power within both the SACP and the ANC.

CHAPTER THREE

The Party Triumphant

Morogoro

Delegates arriving in Morogoro for the opening of the consultative conference on 25 April 1969 found the air thick with calumny. Tambo referred to the malicious gossip swirling around him as 'whispering', according to the academic Bernard Magubane,[1] one of the 70 or so people who attended the conference. It was clear that it was going to be a political fight to the death. At stake were individual careers as well as key strategic issues.

The main target of the whisperers was Tambo himself. Chief Luthuli had died in a bizarre accident two years earlier, leaving Tambo as the ANC's acting president. Never having been duly elected, he struggled to impose his authority. Critics accused him of weakness, of being unable to take firm decisions or give clear direction to the movement. Magubane also noticed the venom directed at secretary-general Duma Nokwe. The most senior critics of the leadership were Alfred Kgokong and Tennyson Makiwane, recently suspended on suspicion of having given encouragement to Hani and his fellow dissidents. Some people thought that Kgokong had designs on Nokwe's job.[2]

73

Invited by friends to help draft a document for the conference, Magubane learned that Jack and Ray Simons, like other communists from the minority groups, were urging the ANC to 'merge forces' with the rest of the Congress Alliance.[3] Whites, Indians and coloureds were still in the odd position of being allowed to join Umkhonto we Sizwe, the ANC's armed wing, but not the ANC itself. For four years, Joe Slovo had been arguing in favour of opening ANC membership to all, and this position had been taken up by other leading members of the SACP Central Committee. Nevertheless the SACP as a whole was far from united on the issue, and some of the most dogged defenders of the ANC's traditional blacks-only status were also prominent Party members, like Kgokong and Makiwane. On this issue, the line of cleavage was largely one of colour, the critics of open ANC membership being black South Africans influenced by the Africanist ideas espoused by ruling parties in Tanzania and many other parts of the continent, while the main champions of open membership were the whites, Indians and coloureds in the SACP, led by Dadoo and Slovo. For years, Moses Kotane had played a key role in keeping these disagreements in check and in smoothing relations between the Party as an institution and the ANC. After his stroke, however, there was no one to play this role. It was clear that the conference would have to address the membership issue, as well as consider the allegation voiced by Hani and his colleagues that the struggle had lost direction and that the leadership was out of touch.

In any conference of this nature, half the battle is won or lost in advance. Who is to attend? Who will be in the chair? How is the agenda to be determined? The main organisers of the conference were Joe Matthews and Duma Nokwe, both SACP members, who had been contemporaries at Fort Hare. In the chair was JB Marks,[4] who was also chairman of the Communist Party. The Party was particularly skilled in organisational matters, with a tradition of paying infinite attention to detail and the fine print of resolutions. For the first time at an ANC conference, the Party was to be represented by its own delegates,[5] including 11 from the minorities. Also of vital importance was the presence of a large block of delegates – some sources say as many as 55,[6] although this sounds unlikely – from Umkhonto we Sizwe, where feelings ran high after the Rhodesian campaign. There were also observers from allied organisations and friendly governments.

The first day of the conference gave vent to criticisms of the leadership. Although Tambo, as acting president, was the main target, he was generally regarded as a decent and likeable man. He was not a forceful public speaker, but he could be effective. Now he produced one of his most brilliant performances. Towards the end of a day filled with anger, Tambo made a speech on 'the dangers of whispering' that culminated in him publicly offering his resignation. The conference then broke for the evening, leaving people time to think things over. Even some of Tambo's critics realised that if he resigned, the entire ANC external mission – the only apparatus it had, in effect – was in danger of collapse or a permanent split. The next day, a majority was in favour of his reinstatement as acting president.[7] This was a crucial moment, as the delegates' rejection of Tambo's proffered resignation greatly strengthened his authority and helped clear the air. It was the turning point of the conference. From then on, the Communist Party leadership, which was firmly behind Tambo and had a clear idea of the changes it wanted, had the wind behind it and could proceed to introduce the motions it supported.

Debate on the most controversial item on the agenda began with Flag Boshielo speaking strongly in favour of opening ANC membership to people of all racial groups. He poured scorn on opponents of the proposal, asking why people from minority groups, like Basil February, a coloured man, should be allowed to give their lives for the ANC but not to be members of it. Boshielo's views carried weight among those very ANC traditionalists who were most concerned about the influence of the minorities if they were allowed to join the organisation. In many respects Boshielo was himself the epitome of an African traditionalist, coming from a rural background and being steeped in the knowledge of healing. He had been the first volunteer in the Transvaal during the 1952 Defiance Campaign. He had worked closely with migrant labourers in Sekhukhuneland and had played a key role in the 1950s uprising there. A long-standing Party member, he had been in the first cohort of ANC people to study at the Lenin school in Moscow. In the mid-1960s, after returning to Tanzania and being sidelined on suspicion of espionage, he had subsequently been cleared, and in January 1968 was coopted to the ANC's national executive.[8]

After discussion, the conference reached a compromise: delegates voted to open membership of the ANC to people from all racial backgrounds, although only Africans (here meaning black people) would be eligible for appointment to its governing body, the National Executive Committee. Coloureds, Indians and whites could now formally join the ANC and take positions on its committees, but only at lower levels. However, the effect of this restriction was mitigated by the creation of a new body to direct the armed struggle, to be known as the Revolutionary Council, which would be open to members of all groups. In other words, formal control of the ANC remained with an exclusively black African committee, but control of the all-important army was now vested in a body that included minority groups. For the SACP, this was a particularly sweet arrangement because it allowed the Party to have its hands on the real levers of power while remaining formally subject to an exclusively black body. In the words of the Party's historian, Morogoro 'formalised the process of including other oppressed groups and organs such as the SACP into the liberation alliance under the leadership of the ANC'.[9] The actual effect, however, was to 'strengthen the authority of the Communists' over the ANC, as the East German intelligence service did not fail to note.[10]

A further triumph for the Party was the adoption of a paper, authored largely by Joe Slovo, with revisions by Nokwe and Matthews, known as the Strategy and Tactics document.[11] This set out the political and military means by which the ANC proposed to carry out a revolution, laying great emphasis on the need to involve the African masses. For the first time in ANC policy, the Strategy and Tactics document characterised the urban working class as the leading force in the struggle, although it also reflected the belief that the rural areas offered the best prospects for guerrilla warfare. (Slovo, writing under a pen name on the tenth anniversary of Umkhonto we Sizwe, still advocated the use of rural warfare in 1971.[12]) The Strategy and Tactics document was the first comprehensive strategic guideline for the organisation since Operation Mayibuye, the plan elaborated in 1962–63 that had been seized by the police at Rivonia. It was the first written programme adopted by the ANC since the Freedom Charter of 1955.

The Strategy and Tactics document clearly reflected the influence of the Communist Party's manifesto published in 1962. 'The struggle of the oppressed people of South Africa,' the new document proclaimed, 'is taking place within an international context of transition to the socialist system.'[13] It marked 'the ascendancy of the SACP's theoretical and practical vision of struggle within the ANC', in the words of a later analyst.[14] Some of those present at Morogoro later alleged that the Strategy and Tactics document was never actually discussed there,[15] although a text closely resembling it was surely tabled.

These innovations of Morogoro were completed by an overhaul of the ANC's organisational framework. The existing, 20-person National Executive Committee was dismissed and replaced with a body of just nine members, approved by delegates from a list presented by Tambo. The national executive was also given the power to coopt additional members, which it soon did by adding Joe Modise. He was now known as the chief of operations in preference to his old title of army commander, since formal control of the army now lay with the new Revolutionary Council. Flag Boshielo was rewarded for his stirring speech at Morogoro in favour of open membership of the ANC by being appointed as a member of the slimmed-down national executive and also named as political commissar of the army.[16] Notable among the casualties of Morogoro were the ANC's leading internal critics, Tennyson Makiwane and Alfred Kgokong, who were not included in the new-look national executive, and also Duma Nokwe, who lost the job of secretary-general, becoming in effect the only direct victim of the Hani memorandum.[17]

These changes were widely discussed in the ANC and have been commented on by subsequent writers. Less noticed, however, was another key change that occurred in April 1969, the same month as the Morogoro conference. Moses Mabhida, previously the MK political commissar,[18] was now tasked with setting up a new department of national intelligence and security[19] within the office of the president. It is not clear whether this initiative was taken at the Morogoro conference itself.[20] Mabhida was to be director of this body for the next seven years, during which time the East German government increased the scale of training given to ANC personnel in military and security matters.[21] A later head of security, Sizakele Sigxashe, confirmed that the 'formal foundation of NAT' (the short name of the ANC's intelligence and security organisation) took place in the period 1968–76. He stated that the people who knew most about this development were Tambo, Mabhida and Nokwe.[22]

There is strong evidence that the Party played a key role in the foundation of the new security department, beyond the fact that both Nokwe and his replacement, Mabhida, were senior Party members. Within the SACP there had been a flurry of memoranda on the issue of security in the preceding months. 'To establish an Intelligence, Counter Intelligence and Security Organisation capable of meeting the needs of the South African Liberatory Movement,' one Party document noted, 'we require a basic organisation of full-time trained officers who have an understanding of the nature of what has to be done.'[23] This implied the creation of a security organ controlled by the Party with authority over the whole of the ANC.[24] Papers on this matter appear to have been sent to Tambo on 19 April 1969,[25] less than a week before the Morogoro conference.

The innovations effected at, or simultaneously with, the Morogoro conference changed the balance of power within the ANC significantly. The acting president, Tambo, saw his prestige enhanced, even though his authority remained tenuous. In theory, supreme authority was vested in the ANC's governing body, the new, nine-person National Executive Committee. Actually, though, after Morogoro the new Revolutionary Council became the most important body in the organisation. In principle charged with implementing decisions made by the national executive in the political and military fields, its key asset was control of the army, the most important part of the ANC. It was this body that received the most notable influx of Communist Party heavyweights, with the Revolutionary Council being headed by Tambo, with Yusuf Dadoo as his deputy; Joe Slovo and Reg September were members, as was Joe Matthews, who became its secretary. When Matthews unexpectedly resigned in 1970 (for reasons we will shortly discuss), he was replaced by Moses Mabhida, who held the secretaryship of the Revolutionary Council while also heading the ANC's Department of Intelligence and Security – a powerful combination indeed.

Acutely conscious of the risk of splits, Tambo tended to concur with majority decisions in the various committees that dominated the ANC hierarchy. He was in any case temperamentally averse to confrontation. Over time, with a disciplined SACP group at the core of the ANC's power structure, the tradition of collective leadership, in which the president-general presided with the consent of the National Executive Committee, was subtly altered into a system resembling the Leninist technique of democratic centralism. After a decision had been taken at the top level, every other organ and individual within the ANC was expected to accept it without dissent. Actually, many rank-and-file members were hardly aware of what had taken place. Even five years after the Morogoro conference, comrades in Tanzania were asking: 'Is the C-in-C still recognised? Who is the commissar? Who are the members of the High Command? These are open questions to us.'[26]

The identity of senior office-holders in the ANC was also important in understanding how the Party after Morogoro was increasingly able to win its case in meetings of various ANC bodies. Perhaps the most important single position in the organisation after the acting president, Tambo, was that of the secretary-general, the person with a hand on day-to-day administration and the servicing of committees. From 1958 to 1969 this post was held by Duma Nokwe, a lawyer whom Mabhida used to describe as having a 'golden pen', in spite of the alcoholism that killed him. After Morogoro, Nokwe was replaced by Alfred Nzo, also a Party man, but regarded as rather dull, and therefore unlikely to make trouble. Another senior position, that of treasurer-general, was held by Moses Kotane until 1973, when he was replaced by yet another SACP man, Thomas Nkobi.

Considered alongside the adoption of the Strategy and Tactics document, these personnel and administrative changes amounted to an impressive victory for the Party. It had used the challenge posed by the Hani memorandum, articulating as it did the frustrations of rank-and-file members of Umkhonto we Sizwe, to full effect. By backing the dissidents' complaints, the Party was able to secure the implementation of measures that its leading members had been canvassing since the mid-1960s. Accordingly, the SACP Central Committee reported to a plenary session of the Party in 1970 that the decisions taken at Morogoro would enable the Party 'to provide adequate political leadership and guidance'[27] to the ANC in pursuit of its vanguard role. In plain language, it was now in a position to exercise decisive influence over the ANC, whose national executive was occupied mostly by veterans who had made their name in the Youth League two decades or more previously, while the body with its hand on the ANC's political and military machinery was the Revolutionary Council, where the Party men Dadoo, Slovo and September were said to initiate many decisions.[28] Thomas Nkobi complained that there were many matters on which he, even as a member of the national executive and the Revolutionary Council, was not informed. 'This may or may not be the result of factionalism,' a group of critics wrote, 'but it certainly raises the question of where exactly does power lie in the A.N.C., what and who is the ultimate repository of power.'[29] The SACP was henceforth permitted to set up its own collectives inside the ANC, with the exception of the army, and soon that restriction was to fall away too. It also began to hold formal bilateral meetings with the ANC,[30] creating a situation in which SACP members could influence ANC policy from within but also formally discuss the same matters at ANC-SACP summit meetings. The Party had effectively restored the guiding role it had established in regard to the ANC in the months between the SACP's 1960 decision to create MK and the Rivonia arrests two and a half years later, but now on a higher level of sophistication.

However, the Party's victory in years of infighting up to and including the Morogoro conference had also had a debilitating effect. Visiting the ANC's official headquarters at Morogoro, Mark Shope, one of the most plain-speaking of all the Party's senior members, was alarmed to find that 'our chaps appear – except for John Pule – dead ducks'. He thought the ANC bureaucrats to be 'just a bunch of people who have lost their political direction and purpose … there is something very seriously wrong in our movement'. In a letter to Ray Simons, he insisted: 'we in the left must bear the responsibilities for this, more than any other'. The main problem, in his view, was the appointment of cadres on grounds of loyalty rather than merit, which was producing functionaries with no principles at all, 'ready to dance anything when they think that their bread is buttered on the side they stand'. He mentioned 'the element of corruption' and requested that the Party leadership be made aware of his views.[31]

The SACP's reassertion of its influence within the ANC was made possible only by the absence of Moses Kotane, the cantankerous, tough-minded, immensely cautious SACP general secretary who never recovered fully from the stroke he suffered in 1968. He had had an unfailing instinct for what the ANC as a whole would find acceptable and what it would not swallow. In his absence, the strongest influence within the SACP was what opponents called 'the Yusuf Dadoo/ Joe Slovo clique',[32] based in the Party's London office. Conscious that their own ethnic identities placed them in a delicate position, these two cultivated a new generation of young black communists. Thus, the SACP delegation to the 1969 conference of communist and workers' parties in Moscow chose as its secretary Thabo Mbeki, just 27 years old, who was at that time studying in the Soviet capital, at the Lenin school. The following year, Mbeki and Chris Hani – both the same age, both alumni of Lovedale College and Fort Hare – became the youngest-ever members of the Central Committee.[33] Also elected to the Central Committee at this time were Josiah Jele and Moses Mabhida.[34] The augmented Central Committee meeting of June 1970, the first of its kind to be held in exile, had a slight majority of black members, probably for the first time. In 1971, Mbeki was appointed to be administrative secretary of the Revolutionary Council.[35] It was clear that he had embarked on a brilliant career.

The struggle continues

The way was open to rehabilitate the authors of the document that had been the catalyst for the Morogoro conference, the Hani memorandum. All seven signatories were duly reinstated after their suspension, two being appointed to the commissariat and another to staff headquarters. This, however, provoked an immediate reaction. Within weeks, a group of disgruntled cadres sent a counter-memorandum to the newly created Revolutionary Council, complaining that Hani and his comrades constituted a pressure group that had effectively been rewarded for leading a mutiny. This conflict took on a worrying ethnic dimension, as the Hani group – dominated by Xhosas – faced criticism from a faction rooted in the Transvaal, Modise's power base. There was even a spatial dimension to the conflict in Lusaka, as rival blocks emerged among the MK rank and file based on their places of residence, to the alarm of the Zambian government, which feared disturbances in its capital city. This situation 'gradually developed into an acute political crisis whose dimensions posed a threat to our continued existence in Zambia', the ANC secretariat reported.[36] Things deteriorated to the extent that 'there was a crime-wave perpetrated by some of our men in Lusaka for example there were cases of raping, drunkenness and fighting local residents in bars', the ANC's country representative wrote. Under pressure from the Zambian government, the ANC ordered its cadres out of Lusaka. One group refused to budge.[37] After a year of wrangling, 28 recalcitrants were expelled from the ANC in September 1970.[38]

If disorderliness among ANC cadres was causing the organisation's status in Zambia to come into question, its position in Tanzania was even more at risk. On 19 July 1969, ANC headquarters received a visit from Tanzanian government officials who bluntly demanded the closure of Kongwa camp within 14 days. They pointed out that it had originally been established as a transit camp, but had developed into a permanent settlement that posed a security problem. The Tanzanians accused Kongwa residents of hooliganism and crime. 'The protracted stay of the same cadres in the one place has over the years led to exposure of secrets and generally to a breakdown of security to the serious detriment of Tanzania and the freedom struggle,' they maintained. 'In particular, the enemy has been able to collect, and in all probability continues to receive, detailed intelligence information about Kongwa. In this sense the camp is a lucrative hunting ground for enemy agents. This is inevitable where the morale of the cadres has been severely weakened by years of inactivity and frustration.'[39] This was very strong language indeed. It was said that the hardened attitude of the Tanzanians had a further reason that remained unstated in the official notice to vacate Kongwa, namely, a suspicion that the ANC may have become involved in a coup plan formulated by the ambitious former foreign minister, Oscar Kambona, who had left Tanzania in 1967 and was later tried and convicted *in absentia*. It was alleged that he had discussed a coup with PAC leader Potlako Leballo, who controlled hundreds of armed men in Tanzania. Leballo was by this stage working with the Tanzanian intelligence services, and reported the conversation to them. Kambona was said to have approached Tambo as well, but Tambo had failed to report the matter to the authorities. This was alleged to be the real reason for shutting down the Kongwa camp.[40] Perhaps the wily President Julius Nyerere, fearing the Soviet influence that was transmitted via the ANC, wished in any case to keep the movement at arm's length. It was probably for this reason that the Tanzanian government had years earlier declared Slovo to be a prohibited immigrant.[41] The same factor, as much as anything else, caused the Tanzanian government to continue supporting the PAC as well as the ANC,[42] so as to play off a Chinese-backed movement against a Soviet-backed one, while simultaneously flaunting its own liberation credentials. Faced with the instruction to move its people out of Kongwa, the ANC asked the Soviet Union, its most dependable ally, to house the camp residents temporarily. After some debate, during which a possible transfer of ANC personnel to Sudan was discussed as an option, Soviet officials reluctantly agreed. They sent aircraft to Tanzania to evacuate the troops to the USSR.[43] It was to be another three years before the ANC officially transferred its headquarters to Zambia.

The basic demand of many Umkhonto we Sizwe members remained the same as ever: to be sent back to South Africa to fight. In March 1970, a joint meeting of the military headquarters and the Revolutionary Council in Lusaka agreed that cadres should once again be encouraged to return to South Africa in an offensive operation of some sort. But Tambo vetoed the idea, insisting that any expedition had to be properly prepared. 'Certainly,' he said, 'there should be no suicidal "leap in the dark"'[44] – surely a reference to the Rhodesian campaign. The new army commissar, Flag Boshielo, decided he would simply make his way home anyway, with a few companions. Initially Chris Hani wanted to go with him, but soon the number of those who were to accompany Boshielo was whittled down to four. They kept their plan secret, as 'Lusaka was infested with informers in our ranks, disrupters who sought to undermine every operation of which they had information', Tambo informed the Revolutionary Council, in addition to which 'comrades have developed the habit of talking about anything and everything they saw, observed or heard of'.[45] For this reason, the five would-be infiltrators decided to handle their own logistical arrangements and not to inform other members of MK about their intentions. After postponing their departure a couple of times, they eventually moved south in August. Tambo received a report that the South African authorities knew of the plan, but he was unable to stop the group, now reduced to just four people, from going.

On 31 August, reports arrived in Lusaka that Boshielo and his three companions had reached the Zambezi River and crossed into South West Africa (today's Namibia), a territory under South African control, and had been intercepted. Two were said to have been killed and one captured in a shootout with South African police in the Caprivi Strip, leaving one of the four still at large. The police were said to have been tipped off by a disgruntled boatman, after a middleman, given 140 kwachas to pay for a team to paddle the four over the Zambezi in a canoe, had kept most of the money for himself. Feeling cheated, one of the paddlers had informed the police. Tambo, Motshabi and Modise went down to the Zambian side of the border to investigate but were unable to establish exactly what had happened.[46] The following year, Tambo, perhaps having acquired new information in the interim, alleged in a public speech that Boshielo had been wounded and captured.[47] One of Boshielo's closest friends, who had been due to accompany the group as the fifth man, heard that all four had in fact been shot dead in an ambush without being able to return fire.[48] Many years later, the ANC government awarded Boshielo a posthumous medal. The citation mistakenly stated that he had been captured in Zimbabwe in 1972 and two of his companions shot dead.[49]

While Boshielo's quixotic gesture was a personal choice, it was a reflection of the larger fact that the ANC had got itself into an impossible position. The ANC had elevated armed struggle to a central principle of its existence. It had to be seen to be conducting an armed struggle in order to continue receiving international support. Yet it was unable to engage the enemy. Jack Simons was quick to detect this, writing to a comrade that 'we are involved in some great charade, a play staged for the benefit of the outside world'.[50] The Organisation of African Unity (OAU), for example, at a meeting of its Liberation Committee, in January 1972 in Libya, expressed 'its disappointment and indignation at the rather poor level of progress of the liberation struggle being conducted by the two Movements in South Africa', referring to the ANC and PAC.[51] Although the chronically impecunious OAU never actually gave the two organisations nearly as much money as it promised, its political backing was essential. In other quarters, too, by attracting supporters who expected it to be always militant, the ANC's use of warlike rhetoric reduced its room for manoeuvre. As Reg September noted, 'in wide layers of our Movement there still exists the mistaken idea that we are going to liberate S.A. from the outside. This transmits itself to other movements including solidarity movements and this is dangerous.'[52]

The expectation of militancy was reflected in the ANC's relationship with the USSR. The Soviet government was the ANC's main financier probably until the early 1980s. In addition, the USSR was the main provider of military training[53] and the source of diplomatic support that brought with it further assistance from pro-Soviet governments and left-leaning political groups worldwide. Thanks to the existence of national anti-apartheid movements, very often communist-influenced, the ANC was able to attract support even in capitalist countries from parts of Western populations that would not normally be regarded as part of its constituency. For all these reasons, no ANC leader could afford to get on the wrong side of the Soviet government. It is said that Joe Slovo had long arguments with his wife, Ruth First, about the 1968 Soviet invasion of Czechoslovakia. Towards the end of his life, Slovo told an interviewer that he regretted having supported the USSR in its aggression against Czechoslovakia, and said that he had suppressed his doubts about this action as well as other reservations he may have had about the Soviet system. He kept quiet because to have given voice to criticism would have meant being ostracised within the SACP and also the ANC, almost equally slavish in its defence of the USSR. 'That kind of thing just was not tolerated,' Slovo said.[54] One former Party colleague uncharitably recalled that 'it had always been clear that what drove Slovo was megalomania, straight. Power, man!'[55] Another remarked: 'I have not come across a person on the left who is as self-centred as JS [Slovo]. The centre of the struggle is where he is.'[56]

Expecting some military activity as a return for its investment, the Soviet government became deeply involved in a plan, known as Operation J, to land arms and men in South Africa by sea.[57] This was allegedly named after Joe Slovo, the ANC's leading military thinker, although it had originally been conceived by Arthur Goldreich in the days before Rivonia. Goldreich thought that MK should land operatives by sea on the Transkei coast with a view to setting up bases from which they could connect with the peasantry, as Fidel Castro had done in Cuba. Accordingly, the first generation of MK trainees was regularly told that, once they had returned to South Africa, one of their tasks would be to set up camps in the Transkei and Natal and to look for possible submarine landing sites.[58] Operation J acquired formal status in 1967.[59] Planning was the work not of MK headquarters but of a special group formed by Slovo, Dadoo and Ronnie Kasrils, a Durban communist and founder-member of

MK.[60] In what was to become a distinctive feature of Slovo's work as a guerrilla commander, many of the key operatives were white foreigners whom the ANC had recruited in Europe, in this case Alex Moumbaris and Sean Hosey, respectively Greek-Australian and Irish. The great advantage of such people was that they were unknown to the security police and could blend much more easily into white South Africa than any other type of infiltrator. These were aspects of Operation J that foreshadowed the later and far more sophisticated Operation Vula.

Pushing on with Operation J, the ANC acquired a ship, according to various sources named the *Aventura*, *Adventura* or *Adventurer*, which was to pick up arms in Somalia before landing a group of guerrillas on the Transkei coast. However, the *Aventura* had constant technical problems and failed to make it as far as South Africa. Some operatives already in place inside the country were arrested at an early stage by the security police, who were then able to put in place a sting operation to lure some of the others, as became clear when Moumbaris and others were tried in the Pretoria Supreme Court in 1973. In the end, the whole project was a resounding failure. The price to be paid, apart from the imprisonment of many of those involved, was the displeasure of the Soviet government, signalled by a cut in its subsidy to the SACP.[61]

Quaint though the idea now seems, South Africa's security services took very seriously the threat of infiltration by sea. At the start of the Umkhonto we Sizwe campaign in 1961, it was said that Ghana's President Nkrumah had bought a ship to be loaded with arms in Egypt and sent via Somalia,[62] probably a distant echo of one of the schemes hatched by John Lang and his National Committee for Liberation. Even before then, in the 1950s, 'we believed that the Soviets had deployed dozens of submarines along the coast. These craft only appeared at irregular intervals and were invariably only spotted by a solitary witness,' one police veteran recalled with a touch of irony.[63] These reports were taken seriously enough for the South

African Air Force's 35 Squadron to fly anti-submarine patrols from Durban, with a Special Branch man equipped with a camera waiting to capture one of the elusive Soviet vessels on film.[64] Throughout the 1960s there were regular reports of Soviet submarines having been sighted.[65] This particular phobia seems to have originated during the Second World War,[66] when a Nazi agent, Robey Leibbrandt, really did land in South Africa from an enemy vessel.[67]

But the real significance of Operation J, which became apparent only later, was not its maritime aspect. With hindsight, Operation J can be seen to have been the last effort to implement the early Umkhonto we Sizwe strategy of inciting a rural insurrection. Despite its utter failure, Operation J was the nearest MK came to implementing the strategy that had dominated the first phase of its existence. The Strategy and Tactics document of 1969, in evoking the role of the urban working class, was an early indication of a shift in ANC thinking, and as time went by the idea of an urban-based insurrection was to supplant the older notion of a peasant rising.

Cut off by exile, ANC leaders had little feeling for changes taking place within South African society. This included the emergence of a new generation of thinkers and activists that was developing a Black Consciousness philosophy, particularly influential among students. The psycho-social analysis of the black South African condition developed by Black Consciousness activists had little in common with the increasingly rigid Marxist view that was becoming standard in the ANC. In August 1971, the ANC's national executive met to consider Black Consciousness,[68] which it regarded as a possible threat. A major strike that began in Durban in 1973 indicated the re-emergence of a spirit of collective defiance hardly seen in the previous ten years. Activists of the new stamp often had little knowledge of, or even interest in, the ANC and the popular campaigns in the 1950s or the Rivonia Trial. News, and even historical knowledge, was relatively easy for the government to keep under control, not least because South Africa remained without television until 1976.

A year after the Morogoro conference, an ANC member, unhappy with the movement's lack of dynamism, wrote a memorandum asserting that 'the ANC in South Africa today is almost dead' and drawing attention to the rise of Black Consciousness.[69] The author of this document also noted that the homeland governments established by the South African government now had a real existence. He pleaded for the ANC to adopt a more pragmatic attitude towards the homelands with a view to infiltrating their governments rather than simply condemning them on principle. It was on precisely this issue that a division had opened among the ANC prisoners on Robben Island, with Nelson Mandela and Walter Sisulu being in favour of the ANC's participation in Bantustan politics, and Raymond Mhlaba and Govan Mbeki opposing it.[70] The Bantustans were indeed becoming a reality, particularly KwaZulu under the leadership of Chief Mangosuthu Buthelezi, who in his younger days had been a member of the ANC Youth League and a friend of Nelson Mandela.

While the ANC had been effectively destroyed as an organisation inside South Africa after the Rivonia arrests, there remained many individual sympathisers and former members, a few of whom were able to meet discreetly and discuss political matters.[71] Particularly active were Albertina Sisulu, Winnie Mandela and some former Robben Island prisoners who, as they were released from prison and rejoined society, resumed their ANC activities. There was some concern in MK that the imperious Winnie Mandela was representing herself as having a direct line to the ANC leadership simply in order to bolster her own standing.[72] A handful of white intellectuals, having more opportunities for overseas travel than their black compatriots, managed to make contact with the ANC and SACP in London and to engage in political work underground after their return to South Africa.[73] Current or former students who joined the ANC at this time, like Raymond Suttner and Jeremy Cronin, were more likely to have been influenced by their reading than by stories handed down by veterans of earlier campaigns. In Natal, by 1975 there was a functioning ANC group that included Harry Gwala and Jacob Zuma, both only recently released from Robben Island. In the eastern Cape, too, there were ANC networks led by ex-Robben Islanders. In Soweto a network formed around another Robben Island veteran, Joe Gqabi, and the trade unionist John Nkdadimeng,[74] although MK operatives outside, tasked with making contact with the internal resistance, suggested that the sympathisers in Soweto hardly constituted a cohesive group.[75] There were also ANC networks in Cape Town.[76] Some of the networks and groups inside South Africa were in contact with each other. Together, these small groups of activists were able gradually to form distinct underground networks inside South Africa, devoted more often to study and discussion than any form of action. Communication between these internal elements and the ANC outside was never easy, although some had contact with ANC operatives in Swaziland and Lesotho, where Chris Hani was based from 1974. Hani's deployment was due less to the ANC as such than to the Communist Party, which was keen to capitalise on the wave of strikes that had swept South Africa in the previous year. He was able to communicate fitfully with contacts inside South Africa and sometimes even to venture over the border himself.

The first significant infiltration by trained saboteurs for some years was a group led by Tokyo Sexwale, a young man from Soweto who had joined the ANC in exile. After military training in the USSR, he and his group entered the country in 1976 and made contact with local sympathisers.[77] Sexwale and his colleagues were soon arrested.

Dissidents

The Morogoro conference did nothing to resolve the conflicts that had riven the ANC and that had led even to armed confrontation at Kongwa. In 1970, JB Marks, SACP chairman and a member of the ANC's national executive, asked John Pule Motshabi to help resolve the feud between Ambrose Makiwane and Joe Modise, still simmering after six years.[78] Motshabi set up a four-person commission that duly handed in a report attributing what it called 'a tribal threat and mutiny' – a reference to the Hani memorandum – to Xhosa domination. The report pointed out that there was an ideological aspect to some of the ethnic and personal rivalries within the organisation inasmuch as they were related to the Sino-Soviet dispute. Where the SACP had originally been open to both Moscow and Beijing, it had firmly sided with the USSR in the mid-1960s, and the Party's victory at Morogoro had sealed the victory of the Soviet camp within the Party, leaving the small number of Maoists isolated. In the course of his inquiry into internal divisions, Motshabi found that a substantial number of ANC cadres in Lusaka were 'unwilling to cooperate with all leaders of the movement in Lusaka'. He met personally one such group of as many as 200 in the Zambian capital, and was told that about half that number again were staying outside town. His analysis was that their main grievance arose from the 'tribal onesided administration' mentioned in the Hani memorandum.[79] Motshabi's report was buried by Tambo, whose style of non-confrontation was based on his wish to prevent formal splits at all costs.

In the words of those on the receiving end, the Hani memorandum 'was subsequently used to start a campaign of witch hunt among the A.N.C. leadership'.[80] First in line for retribution were Ambrose Makiwane and Alfred Kgokong, whose most implacable enemies were located in the Central Committee of the SACP. This was not a simple case of communists versus nationalists, since both men had themselves held senior positions in the Party. But, crucially, both had taken a stand against the line taken by the Party's most powerful leaders on the issue of open membership of the ANC, and it was for this that they were to be punished. Having been dropped from the ANC's National Executive Committee, Makiwane and Kgokong were informed by the new secretary-general appointed after Morogoro, Alfred Nzo, that they had been redeployed to junior positions. Both refused to accept, whereupon the National Executive Committee removed them from the ANC payroll.[81] After a partial surrender by the two, the National Executive Committee made a gesture of reconciliation by inviting them to attend an enlarged session of one of its own meetings.[82]

The revenge of the Party on Kgokong and on Ambrose Makiwane, soon to be joined by his cousin Tennyson, has never been entirely forgotten in the ANC, but it has been remembered in an inaccurate manner. Today, for example, the ANC states that the Makiwane cousins and Alfred Kgokong were expelled from the National Executive Committee in 1972,[83] but the archives show that they were in fact suspended three years earlier and never reinstated. In time, the three became inscribed in ANC and SACP lore as the nucleus of a wider group that had impeded the unity of the ANC, their resistance being eliminated by the decisions taken at the 1969 consultative conference. 'It was at Morogoro,' wrote Bernard Magubane, who was close to the ruling group, 'that what came to be known as the Gang of Eight was smoked out.'[84] This name was a parody of a contemporary term, the Gang of Four, applied to a powerful political clique within the Chinese Communist Party. The Gang of Eight eventually became the label used by the SACP Central Committee to designate a disparate group of ANC members identified by their opposition to the open membership principle. In reality, the people who objected to the changes made at Morogoro were far more than eight in number.

Some people thought they could detect the origins of the Gang of Eight in the unofficial intelligence network constructed by Maindy Msimang in the mid-1960s.[85] But while the networks cultivated by the Makiwanes and Kgokong indeed had a history, the notion that there was a handful of dissidents and malcontents lurking in the shadows, who had to be exposed at the right moment, is unfair and misleading. Support for those who criticised the way in which the Party, and within it a cluster from the minority racial groups, was spreading its influence inside the ANC was widespread. The dissidents' opinions, far from needing to be 'smoked out' as Magubane alleged, were often highly public, voiced in open meetings and committed to paper. Their views were actually rather traditional ones inside the ANC, where the fear that the main vehicle for the political expression of black Africans could be hijacked by others through a too-close relationship with the Communist Party could be traced back through the decades. Such an opinion had been expressed in opposition to JT Gumede, the ANC president removed in 1930 on account of his pro-communist views. It was articulated by the Youth League in the 1940s and led to the breakaway by the PAC in 1959.

The move of the ANC's leadership into exile had had a deep effect on a movement traditionally open to all shades of opinion. In exile, the ANC was redefined as a body devoted to conducting an armed struggle for the conquest of state power, labelled a liberation movement by its friends and a terrorist organisation by its enemies. The new-look ANC required a higher degree of ideological uniformity than the organisation had traditionally possessed. At Morogoro, the Marxists within the ANC had succeeded in getting the organisation to adopt a formal programme influenced by the SACP's strategic vision. Some wanted to go further still by having the ANC declare itself a socialist organisation. Many of the dissidents were themselves not at all unsympathetic to socialism, including as they did not only SACP members but also other people who had in the past flirted with Trotskyist ideas, and for that matter still others who had once been close to the Liberal Party. Inasmuch as the dissidents had any coherent ideology at all, it was an idea that black Africans should be given space to organise themselves without undue interference from racial minorities. 'In actual fact,' wrote one of their opponents, 'they were reactionaries who complained about the role of white communists and Indians in the ANC's affairs.'[86]

Within months of Morogoro, some of those unhappy with the conference's outcome were reported to be 'actively attempting to build an organisation in South Africa without the knowledge of the ANC'.[87] Another report claimed that they were trying to set up their own organisation 'within the ANC both in South Africa and among the exiled elements'.[88] Tennyson Makiwane was said to be in contact with seamen who could act as couriers taking messages to sympathisers in South Africa. The SACP Central Committee was particularly concerned about the influential Robert Resha. At a drinks party in London in July 1971, Resha told one SACP member, who was apparently working for the Party's security network, that he was no longer part of the ANC's external mission 'and confided he was now confining his political work to international organisation'.[89] Resha was said to be 'undoubtedly … the central figure' of the dissident network in London. He had substantial funds at his disposal, some of them from 'various wealthy women … because of his charm and sexual attraction for them'.[90] The author of this report named Resha's female admirers but concluded that they could not be the main source of his money, which, the writer speculated, perhaps came from some fraud that Resha might be perpetrating with ANC funds. Another possibility was that the money came from Canon John Collins of the International Defence and Aid Fund (IDAF), with whom Resha and others were in close contact.[91]

By 1972, the dissidents were said to be gaining support especially in Tanzania, but also in Zambia. They were said to have support among ANC members in East Germany too. The main coordinator of their activities was Joe Matlou, one of those charged in the 1956 Treason Trial and once the chief organiser, together with Robert Resha, of the ANC branch that flourished in Sophiatown in those days. The dissidents' meetings were attended by ANC veterans of the stature of Resha, the Makiwanes, Kgokong, Chief Luthuli's son-in-law Pascal Ngakane, MB Yengwa, John Gaetsewe and others. Raymond Kunene and Maindy Msimang were also mentioned as associates. Some people also suspected Mzwai Piliso, one of the nine members of the national executive elected at Morogoro, of 'aligning himself' with the dissident group,[92] although in retrospect one wonders whether Piliso was not acting as a mole on behalf of the SACP Central Committee. Common themes of discussion at the dissidents' meetings were criticism of Tambo's performance as acting president, the stalling of the armed struggle, the negative consequences of the Morogoro conference and the alleged control over the ANC exercised by minority groups. 'Among the general membership of the movement people like Matlou and Ambrose [Makiwane] are bold enough to utter racial statements in which they challenge the participation of people like Slovo and Dadoo in the RC [Revolutionary Council],' a group of Party members reported.[93] John Pule Motshabi, himself a former SACP Central Committee member, agreed with the dissidents that the leadership of the Party was 'always entrusted with our white intellectuals',[94] a category in which he included Yusuf Dadoo and other Indians.

Out of perhaps a thousand ANC members in exile by 1975, probably no more than five percent were from the racial minority groups. The problem was that this small group could be seen to have a disproportionate role in ANC affairs after Morogoro, to a considerable extent, no doubt, because of the much higher average level of education enjoyed by the minority groups. Within months of the conference, it appeared to some ANC members that the London office in Rathbone Street was run by non-blacks. Reg September was now the ANC's chief representative in Britain, with MP Naicker as director of information and Frene Ginwala as head of research. Some black ANC members complained that they did not feel comfortable in an office run by people from ethnic minority groups.[95] The three members of the Revolutionary Council who were based in London were also white or Indian: Joe Slovo, Yusuf Dadoo and Brian Bunting.[96] A series of meetings of black African ANC members held in London in early 1975 stated explicitly the grievances of this community. 'The vast majority of the ANC African members resident in the UK are very critical of, and even profoundly opposed to the workings of the

ANC abroad in the post 1969 Morogoro Consultative Conference era,'[97] one such meeting concluded. Those present were strongly opposed to opening ANC membership to non-Africans. They also criticised 'the open-ended tenure of office by the NEC' and the use of 'secrecy' as 'a cover for inefficiency and undemocratic practice'.[98] If such views were current among ANC members in London, where the Africanist strand had always been at its weakest, one wonders how strong they were elsewhere.

So bitter were the ensuing rivalries that some people went as far as trying to enlist support from the historic leaders of the ANC imprisoned on Robben Island. At some date in the late 1960s or early 1970s – it is not clear exactly when – Alfred Kgokong sent letters to Wilton Mkwayi, the third commander of Umkhonto we Sizwe, denouncing Mabhida, Modise and others. 'I received letters written by [Kgokong] when I was [in prison],' Mkwayi recalled. 'In these letters he was saying: "That Pondoman, *ela Mpondo lisi gxhothile*, has put us aside in the organisation",'[99] a pejorative reference to Oliver Tambo. Kgokong is also said to have described the ANC as having been taken over by boys and *tsotsis*. The latter term was a reference to Modise, the former to Mabhida, who as a Zulu was uncircumcised, making his manhood the object of Kgokong's crude scorn. The Robben Island prison authorities are said[100] to have allowed the letter to reach Mkwayi uncensored, no doubt hoping to encourage conflict inside the ANC. Mkwayi, together with Nelson Mandela and others on Robben Island who had knowledge of this correspondence, rejected these approaches.

The dissidents argued their case with such vigour that the Party felt obliged to defend itself. 'Slanders are spread about the rôle of the Party in the liberation alliance and it is being suggested that the Morogoro Conference was a Party manoeuvre to gain control of the A.N.C.,' noted one text prepared as a pamphlet.[101] The Party claimed that this was inaccurate, on the grounds that 'the Party as a collective neither initiated nor played a dominating rôle in the

Morogoro Conference'. It denied that the Revolutionary Council had become the real locus of power, since this was appointed by the ANC's National Executive Committee.[102] This was an argument couched in the Party's characteristic mode of legalism, always one of its greatest assets. The same pamphlet counterattacked by accusing the dissidents of tribalism.[103]

The Party had some strong arguments at its disposal. Chief among these perhaps was that since Umkhonto we Sizwe had contained non-blacks who had died for the cause (like Basil February) or been willing to face torture and long imprisonment (like the Indians Ahmed Kathrada and Mac Maharaj, the whites Bram Fischer and Denis Goldberg, and many others), it was churlish or even racist to argue that these people should not be properly represented in the ANC, to whose service they had dedicated their lives. They also had a new martyr in the person of Ahmed Timol, who had left South Africa in December 1966 and made his way to London. There Dadoo had recruited him to the Party and sent him for training at the Lenin school. Tasked by the Party leadership in London with distributing pamphlets, he returned secretly to South Africa in February 1970. He was arrested more than a year and a half later, in October 1971. In less than a week he was dead, having allegedly jumped out of a tenth-storey window at the new security police headquarters in Johannesburg during a break between interrogation sessions.[104] An inquest came to the conclusion that he had committed suicide, but he was generally regarded as another victim of police brutality.

A further argument that the Party could make against its critics was that open membership was not so new as they pretended, as minorities had sometimes been included in ANC delegations in the past, such as in 1966 when Dadoo, September and Naicker had accompanied ANC colleagues to a conference in Cuba, where Dadoo had met Fidel Castro.[105] The anti-Party position of Kgokong and the Makiwanes was hardly convincing when they themselves were communists of long standing. The fact that a couple of the dissidents had belonged to the African Resistance Movement (ARM) or had been associated with the defunct Liberal Party meant that they could be regarded as heretics. In short, it was not hard to represent the dissidents as having personal motives rather than standing on matters of principle.

Many of the Party's other arguments displayed its habitual casuistry, such as the allegation that the Party as an institution had not played a leading role at Morogoro. In the narrowest sense this was true, thanks to the skill with which an influential group within the Party, including Dadoo, Slovo and Jack and Ray Simons, had manoeuvred. Their pleas for the ANC to open its membership to people of all ethnic origins did not reflect a formal decision by the Party, but the belief of influential individual members. Their argument was based not only on grounds of equity, but on the calculation that open membership would enable the Party to occupy a position in which it could perform its self-appointed role as a vanguard, able to guide the ANC in the correct path without formally dominating it. In the same way, the Party sometimes pointed out that it had never as an institution had foreknowledge of the Wankie campaign, yet it would be absurd to pretend that the leadership was not fully aware of that initiative. Its legalism was one of the Party's great tactical strengths. Party members were taught to make a careful distinction between actions undertaken on the formal instructions of the Party and those carried out in an informal capacity or while acting as a member of another organisation, in which case the Party as an institution could take its distance. Party leaders could thus encourage members to take positions informally but in the Party's calculated interest, and then dissociate themselves if necessary. Concerning the Revolutionary Council, there can be no doubt that it had indeed become the real centre of power in the ANC, despite the fact that it was formally junior to the ANC's governing body, the National Executive Committee. In fact, the NEC was seriously depleted. Of the nine members elected at Morogoro, by the mid-1970s two (Marks and Boshielo) had died; one (Matthews) had effectively left the ANC; and a fourth (Kotane) was an invalid. A committee set up by the London meetings of ANC members protesting against open membership claimed that only four of the nine NEC members remained active.[106]

The long-suffering Tambo was sometimes close to despair. 'There has been so much mud slung about Xhosas and tribalism and so many of our people have swallowed and been killed by this poison,'[107] he lamented. He is said to have had sight of an SACP document in 1971 that called on Party members not to cooperate with eight named ANC leaders regarded as being part of a dissident faction, including Piliso and Resha. For once, Tambo objected to this blatant interference in ANC affairs, and the Party was obliged to promise not to repeat such behaviour.[108]

Matters came to a head after Resha died in London in 1973. Ambrose Makiwane used the erection of a memorial stone at Resha's grave two years later as the occasion to launch a public attack on the Party and the ANC leadership.[109] A meeting of the depleted National Executive Committee held in September 1975 in Morogoro responded with a unanimous decision to expel eight people associated with this protest.[110] This removed from the ANC some influential people representing a variety of ideological strains that were unacceptable in the new climate. Those expelled included OK Setlapelo,[111] who had been a member of the ARM and various Trotskyist groups, and others who had spoken in favour of China.[112] Temba Mqota (previously better known as Alfred Kgokong) had not supported the Soviet invasion of Czechoslovakia and had opposed the ANC's abandonment of its traditional non-aligned stance and its growing closeness to the USSR.[113] Other than these two, those expelled were Ambrose and Tennyson Makiwane, George Mbele, Joe Matlou and Pascal Ngakane. An eighth person, Thami Mhlambiso, had once been close to members of the Liberal Party. Although named in official documents as one of the dissidents, he does not appear actually to have been expelled from the ANC at this date, as he continued to represent the ANC at the United Nations.

It was in the SACP's pamphlet offensive against them that this group became known as the Gang of Eight.[114] Some of the Eight pointed out the incongruity that they should be attacked by the SACP, notably in the pamphlet entitled 'The Enemy Hidden Under the Same Colour', whereas their fight had been within the ANC. This proved their very point, they said: 'The A.N.C. of Tambo is now simply a front or cover organisation used as a tool to achieve the objectives of the S.A.C.P.'[115] Duma Nokwe in particular – by now rehabilitated after being dropped post-Morogoro – loosed upon the dissidents a stream of abuse, calling the Eight 'imperialist agents', 'anti-communists', 'racialists' and 'tribalists'.[116] He and John Pule Motshabi told the government of Botswana the outrageous lie that the Eight were expelled from the ANC because of their association with BOSS[117] (the Bureau for State Security, set up by Hendrik van den Bergh in 1969). The Eight set up their own organisation called ANC (African Nationalists). The new organisation contacted the leaders of the homelands, put out feelers to the PAC and won limited support from the Tanzanian government. Chief Buthelezi expressed sympathy with the new group, indicating the danger of an anti-SACP movement arising that could make some claim to being a legitimate strand of ANC thinking. Soon, though, the dissidents' new movement petered out.

The expulsion of the Gang of Eight was of very considerable importance. Ben Turok thought it 'the most serious rupture the ANC was to suffer in exile'.[118] Bernard Magubane wrote that the affair 'almost broke the ANC apart'.[119] A similar opinion was held by Rusty and Hilda Bernstein. Rusty pointed out that the ANC's adoption of an open membership policy would probably not have been possible if the organisation had been based in South Africa rather than abroad, and he thought that the expulsions were necessary to achieve this objective.[120] It was clear to him that at the heart of the matter was 'the influence of whites, the influence of communists'.[121] He thought that the affair did not disappear with the expulsion of the Eight, but that it simmered even until the Kabwe conference ten years later.[122] It is notable that, of those named as dissidents in unpublished documents, Maindy Msimang and Mzwai Piliso were to become staunch supporters of the mainstream ANC after the purge. Most others disappeared from view and their revolutionary careers came to an abrupt end.

Struggling to assert his authority over an organisation as quarrelsome as this, Oliver Tambo saw his role essentially as that of an umpire. He had left South Africa in 1960 as the deputy president of an organisation that was only weakly centralised. Appointed to lead an external mission, he was contested by people who had carved out for themselves fiefs in the various countries where the ANC had a substantial presence. In time he became acknowledged as the ANC's acting president, but this title endowed him with only faint legitimacy. Flying from country to country, witnessing at close quarters the politics of military coups and tribalism emerging throughout Africa, wrong-footed in his dealings with the Tanzanian government, aware of the suspicion with which many governments regarded white communists, Tambo was acutely aware that he was not operating from a position of strength. He saw his long-term goal as keeping the formal unity of the ANC, which required constant compromise. Bernard Magubane wrote that 'it was OR's capacity to listen that saved the ANC from the fate of the PAC, which was destroyed by factionalism and corruption'.[123] Joe Matthews thought the same.[124]

Whatever the fine points made by its theoreticians, in practice the ANC relied heavily for its legitimacy on an armed struggle that was failing to materialise. Lurking in the background was a ghost that haunted the organisation. This arose from the manner in which Umkhonto we Sizwe had been formed in 1960–61. Tantamount to a coup within the ANC, it had, as Matthews said, 'resulted in a very dangerous situation, where you had the official policy that was not for an armed struggle and you then had an organisation established called Umkhonto we Sizwe, which embarked on an armed struggle'.[125] Chief Buthelezi, gaining in power through his participation in homeland politics, regularly pointed out that the ANC had never actually voted in favour of an armed struggle. He enlisted the support of Rowley Arenstein, a highly principled man and a staunch SACP member with family links to many senior Party figures.[126] Arenstein chose the Chinese side during the great Sino-Soviet split, and appears to have been expelled from the SACP. He and his wife eventually joined Buthelezi's Inkatha movement, as did Joe Matthews at a later date.

Factionalism

The disputes surrounding the Gang of Eight were a sign that the ANC in exile was absorbed with itself. It was struggling to stay in touch with South African realities and to understand the changes taking place in South African society. There was almost no effective communication between the ANC internationally, with its origins in the external mission that Oliver Tambo had been mandated to establish in 1960, and its few networks inside the country. Abroad, ANC cadres were frustrated and bored. Their leaders were taken up by international work. Some members complained that 'the NEC has become too engrossed in matters of international conferences to the extent that quite often all NEC members are away from headquarters simultaneously'.[127] Leaders gave little information to the membership on the outcomes of their international dealings and the decisions reached in their conclaves. Matters that leaders were happy to discuss with foreign journalists were regarded as security issues when it came to the membership.[128] Whereas the Revolutionary Council established at the Morogoro conference had been intended to reanimate the armed struggle, by the mid-1970s it had been responsible for very little activity inside South Africa, and none that was militarily effective. In the meantime, the Revolutionary Council had developed no fewer than nine departments. The Strategy and Tactics document was a dead letter.

The chief activity of the ANC leadership in exile was factional manoeuvre. Increasingly influential was Joe Slovo, regarded as the ANC's top military strategist after his success at Morogoro. He tried to exercise 'personal control over who could participate in "internal work", that is, work directly related to South Africa'.[129] But his relationship with one of the rising stars of the ANC and the Party, the young Thabo Mbeki, was not developing well. It seems that Slovo tried to discipline Mbeki during the latter's period at the Lenin school in Moscow, and that the proud Mbeki resented Slovo's attempts to patronise him. Like many of the factional disagreements inside the ANC, this one had ideological and political implications.[130] Mbeki pleaded in favour of sending cadres back into South Africa to concentrate on political work rather than risk further heroic failures like Wankie.[131] Slovo, on the other hand, remained intent on organising military activities. He developed a better relationship with another rising star of the SACP, Chris Hani.

While progress inside South Africa was close to zero, the Party could at least be satisfied that it had positioned itself exactly where it wanted, as the guiding influence on an organisation that had an international reputation, still modest at this stage, as the leader of the struggle against apartheid. 'In the last two decades (apart from the few post-Rivonia years) it can on balance be claimed that our organisation played its leading role with effectiveness and in a manner which benefited the whole liberation movement,' the Party secretariat advised members in 1978. 'During this period the leading initiatives taken by our organisation in the prosecution of every aspect of the struggle and the influence which it wielded to encourage the whole liberation movement to adopt policies for greater revolutionary militancy, speak volumes for the way in which the vanguard role was in fact carried out in the best Leninist tradition.'[132] The Party contrived to explain how it could simultaneously be in the vanguard, giving leadership to the whole liberation movement, and yet not dominate it. 'As stated in the Party guidelines adopted in February 1978, the leadership role of the Party should not be understood in the vulgar sense of formally placing itself at the head of the liberation front,' it explained. 'The Party can effectively exercise its leadership role by giving correct guidance to the revolution by strengthening, supporting and collaborating with bodies like the ANC.'[133] What this really meant was that the Party should lead, but not be seen to lead.

There were still other aspects to the settling of scores after Morogoro that attracted less attention than the contest of the senior SACP leadership with the Gang of Eight but that are worthy of note. One was the position of Joe Modise. His performance as army chief had consistently attracted criticism from the mid-1960s. The Hani memorandum had explicitly named Modise as one of those most responsible for the poor state of affairs in the ANC. If anyone could be expected to have taken the blame for the incompetent planning of the Wankie campaign, it would be he. But so adroitly did Modise handle matters that he was out of the firing line in the bitter conflict after Morogoro. He had his own constituency among MK cadres, especially those from urban areas of the Transvaal, who were sometimes derided by others as thugs, largely in reference to Modise's own *tsotsi* background. Yet he was astute enough not to identify openly with the faction, largely composed of Transvalers, that in 1969 wrote a counter-memorandum criticising Hani and his group, eventually getting themselves expelled for their pains. Nor did Modise identify himself with the main dissident group later reviled as the Gang of Eight, which included his foe Ambrose Makiwane. On the contrary, he could rejoice that Makiwane's discomfiture would strengthen his own position in Umkhonto we Sizwe. The fact that Modise was not a Party member played to his advantage here, since it made him irrelevant in intra-Party disputes like that between the dissidents and the Central Committee. In effect, by letting his opponents fight each other, Modise was able to cement his own position and to become an immovable fixture in ANC politicking. There was a further aspect to Modise's position, too, which derived from his success in setting up a network that helped hundreds of people to leave South Africa via what was then the British protectorate of Bechuanaland in the early 1960s. After Botswana's independence in 1966, he continued to control the main networks for smuggling people in or out of South Africa along the same border. This was a network sorely needed by the many people in the ANC leadership whose origins lay in the eastern Cape and the Transkei, who over the years had developed a de facto alliance with Modise. The people most obviously excluded from this arrangement were those from Natal. Their frustration was reflected in the bitter complaints heard from the Zulu cadres at Kongwa.[134]

It is also worth commenting on the position of Joe Matthews. He was a star of the ANC and the SACP from the late 1950s, and especially after his momentous trip to Moscow in 1960, the year he became a member of the Party's Central Committee. On his appointment as secretary to the new Revolutionary Council in 1969, his position seemed assured. But Matthews was losing his stomach for the fight. Being a son of South Africa's first prominent black academic, Professor ZK Matthews, he was one of the few ANC members who could be said to have grown up in relative privilege. The fact that he was well educated and well connected internationally provided him with options that were not available to most people in the movement. In the months after Morogoro he decided to bale out of the ANC. In 1970 he resigned from the secretariat of the Revolutionary Council and got a job in the office of Botswana's president, Sir Seretse Khama, a friend from college days. By mid-1972 he had been appointed to a position as assistant attorney general in the government of Botswana.[135] At the same time, Matthews was shrewd enough to maintain cordial relations by corresponding by letter with the SACP heavyweights Dadoo and Slovo.

Matthews's defection seems to have been motivated largely by his growing doubts about the direction the ANC was taking. Time and experience had tempered him. From being a youthful firebrand he had come to hold opinions that did not fit with a job as secretary to a revolutionary body. He was in favour of rethinking the ANC's radical opposition to the homelands in South Africa, for example, and in this he was not alone. Joe Nhlanhla, a cadre trained in the USSR who was later to rise to a senior position in intelligence, was another person who openly discussed the possibility of ANC participation in the homeland system.[136] It was rumoured that delegations from the ANC and SACP held secret talks in London with Kaiser Matanzima of Transkei and Mangosuthu Buthelezi of KwaZulu in the early 1970s,[137] although this remains unconfirmed. In a remarkable interview in 1974, ANC secretary-general Alfred Nzo said that the ANC's decision to boycott the homelands had been a mistake, since the governments of these quasi-states had attracted the participation of people in the rural areas. 'Finally we were forced to ask ourselves: "Are we not isolating ourselves from a significant sector of the masses by continuing to boycott elections and government-created structures which [a] large number of people participate in?" The answer, we finally agreed, was "Yes",' Nzo said.[138]

Matthews had come to hold views even more remarkable for their revisionism than this, and, having relocated to Botswana, he made these known in public. In early 1976 he resigned from the Botswana civil service to open a private law practice. He spoke freely to a South African journalist who in April 1976 published an article in the Johannesburg *Sunday Times* describing how Matthews was not only well disposed to the independence of the Transkei but was also calling for the ANC to abandon the armed struggle and end its alliance with the Soviet bloc. The quid pro quo he called for was for the government to release Mandela and other political prisoners.[139] Matthews wrote a memorandum setting out these views at more length, pointing out 'that the ANC National Convention had never taken a decision to embark on armed struggle; and that the imprisonment of many ANC leaders on Robben Island was directly attributable to the decision to launch an armed struggle'.[140] In private, Matthews explained that he had lost confidence in the military strategy. Like the Gang of Eight, he was outraged that the ANC's London office was run by non-blacks. He had particular contempt for Duma Nokwe, now making a return in the ANC after his humbling at Morogoro. Matthews told the American academic Tom Karis that he considered Nokwe 'a drunkard and a fool'.[141]

It is striking that Matthews's ideas, heretical among the ANC in exile, are quite close to what actually came to pass in 1990. But in politics, timing is everything. While the ANC had indeed made no headway in the armed struggle, in the 1970s it was still backed by a superpower, the Soviet Union, that believed victory in the Third World was the key to victory in its long contest with capitalism.[142] The 1974 revolution in Portugal briefly offered the prospect of bringing to power a communist party in a western European country. And although this did not transpire, it did result in a promise of independence for Angola and Mozambique under parties long allied to the Soviet bloc, thereby radically changing the situation in southern Africa. The following year, Vietnam was united under a communist, pro-Soviet government after a long and bitter war. These international developments did nothing to encourage compromise on South Africa. On the contrary, they caused friends of the USSR to believe that victory in the Third World was coming closer, with the collapse of capitalism to follow.

In Pretoria, too, these events did nothing to stimulate an atmosphere conducive to moderation. Within the National Party, the imminent independence of Angola and Mozambique served only to fuel debates concerning the succession to Prime Minister John Vorster. None of the pretenders to Vorster's position would have dreamed of negotiating with the ANC. The most hawkish of them all was the Defence Minister, PW Botha, in those days nicknamed 'Piet Wapen' (Piet the Weapon).

The frontline emerges

It is astonishing to think that only 30 years before this time, a South African prime minister, Jan Smuts, had played a significant role in the creation of the United Nations and had been hailed as a leading internationalist. In Smuts's heyday, South Africa's racially-based constitution was not yet a matter of international debate.

This was not a state of affairs that could survive the decolonisation of Africa and the rise of the Third World, an expression first used in 1952. From India's independence in 1947, many newly sovereign countries in Asia and Africa made a point of publicly criticising South Africa's internal arrangements. By the late 1950s the existence of apartheid was considered an outrage by pan-Africanists and Soviet and Chinese diplomats as well as the political and intellectual leaders of newly emerging states in Asia, while liberals worldwide were coming to a similar view. Within days of the Sharpeville killings in 1960, the United Nations passed a motion of censure against South Africa. On 7 August 1963, the UN Security Council passed a resolution calling for a voluntary arms embargo against the country, the first of many official sanctions. Non-governmental groups in some of South Africa's main trading partners called for the boycott of South African goods.

To these challenges, the National Party and its supporters responded with a mixture of defiance and contempt. In regard to sanctions on arms imports, it took just a couple of decades for South Africa to develop a sophisticated arms industry of its own. It never had much difficulty obtaining oil and other key commodities or high technology. But all this came at a price, not only in the premiums paid to oil traders for evading sanctions, but in terms of the siege mentality that developed among the South African public.

Less noticed than its flouting of sanctions, but more damaging to South Africa in the long term, was the corrosive effect on the quality of governance as South Africa's state authorities developed techniques to evade international restrictions. These required making arrangements that were hidden from public view, and even the creation of entire government departments whose existence had to be disguised. Important elements of this hidden bureaucracy acquired a particular importance in the last phase of the struggle to overthrow apartheid. An early manifestation was the creation of the secretive Republican Intelligence Service in 1963, which transmuted into the Bureau for State Security in 1969. Although BOSS's capacity for murder and mayhem was exaggerated by a fabulist, a petty criminal who wrote a book about his work for the agency,[143] there is no doubt that the state indeed developed an offensive capacity for use against its opponents. This was in addition to the ruthless methods adopted by the security police under Vorster and Van den Bergh. In 1972, the SADF and BOSS collaborated to give military training to opponents of the Zambian government as a means of putting pressure on a state that had become the ANC's main host after its expulsion from Tanzania.[144] It was most probably an agent of BOSS, or of the security police, who was responsible for a parcel bomb that killed the ANC deputy chief representative in Lusaka, the Wankie veteran Boy Mvemve, in February 1974.[145] Abraham Tiro, a Black Consciousness leader living in Botswana, was another victim of the same method. When PW Botha became prime minister four years later, he formulated a coherent strategy aimed at mobilising every department of the state, and even the private sector, in a total strategy of counter-revolution. All manner of off-budget funds and off-the-record organisations and front companies were now willed into existence. Spies, money launderers and assassins and their accomplices acquired a significant role in government.

These arrangements reflected changes in the international context. The African revolution, which had been longer in coming than the SACP had foreseen in 1960, seemed to have arrived at last with the collapse of the dictatorship in Portugal in 1974, brought down by the cost of its counterinsurgency wars in Africa. The military men who took power in Lisbon promised independence for Portugal's African territories. This meant that Angola and Mozambique, both of strategic importance for South Africa, would shortly become sovereign states under local ownership. Angola had a long border with South Africa's own quasi-colony of South West Africa, the future Namibia. Even more interesting for the ANC was Mozambique, which shared a frontier with South Africa itself. The ANC had a close relationship with the victorious Mozambican liberation movement FRELIMO, whose forces had occupied a camp next door to the ANC base at Kongwa in Tanzania. ANC leaders had developed a cordial relationship with Samora Machel and other FRELIMO leaders. Both FRELIMO and a leading Angolan movement, the MPLA, had enjoyed Soviet-bloc support for over a decade.[146]

While it was clear from an early stage that FRELIMO would form the government of an independent Mozambique, the future of Angola was less clear. Two rival organisations, the MPLA and the FNLA, both had a real chance of taking power, while a third, UNITA, was also in the contest. Prime Minister Vorster, working closely with his security chief Van den Bergh, and believing that he had the full backing of the US government, rashly decided to send the South African army into Angola to install the government of his choice in Luanda. This was a disastrous decision, as it prompted Cuba to respond by sending a force of its own to back the MPLA. The US, unnerved by the loss of Saigon and its defeat in Vietnam earlier in the year, withdrew its support for the South African venture. This left South Africa with the worst possible outcome: the SADF over-extended, and a Marxist, pro-Soviet government in place in Luanda, supported by troops from Cuba. In November 1975, there were 40 Soviet military advisers in Angola. By 1979, there were 500.[147]

A blunder of this magnitude was bound to have political repercussions at home. There was already an atmosphere of decay surrounding Vorster, a small-town lawyer who had never been outside southern Africa before he became premier and who was out of his depth in international affairs. Senior figures in the National Party, including PW Botha, jockeyed for position. Military chiefs resolved that national security would never again be put in the hands of a political crony such as Van den Bergh, but should be the subject of a coherent strategy to be implemented by professionals. Defence Minister Botha and his military supporters were able to draw political benefit from press revelations in the so-called Information scandal, also called Infogate or Muldergate, when it was revealed that the Department of Information had used government slush funds for various propaganda projects. By selectively leaking material to the press, insiders were able to manipulate information in a way that helped Botha's campaign for the leadership of the National Party in preference to the previous favourite, Information Minister Connie Mulder.

CHAPTER FOUR

New Strategies

On 16 June 1976, schools in Soweto erupted as students headed into the streets to demonstrate. The movement turned into a rising and soon spread to other townships, leading the state to prosecute 2 500 people for sabotage, many of them very young, between 16 June 1976 and April 1978.[1] Hundreds died. A generation had lost its fear.

It was at once obvious that the Soweto rising would put its stamp on South Africa's history. Oliver Tambo sensed its revolutionary potential, confiding to his notebook that the country seemed close to 'ungovernability'.[2] After weeks of battling the police with stones, hundreds of youngsters headed for the country's borders. Most often, they were running from the police. Few of them had more than the vaguest idea that there were guerrilla movements established in exile. What they did know was that there were independent countries on South Africa's borders where they could hope to find refuge and plan their return.

If the South African government was taken by surprise by the June 1976 rising, so was the ANC. Ronnie Kasrils admitted as much when he wrote to a colleague that the ANC and the Party had been 'woefully lagging behind' when it occurred.[3] Many of the angry young men and women streaming out of South Africa were natural recruits for the PAC. But the PAC had been so weakened by corruption and leadership disputes that it was unable to channel many of the newcomers to its camps in Tanzania and unable to retain them when it did. For all its problems, the ANC was in better shape than its rival. It had in place operatives of the stature of Chris Hani in Lesotho and Stanley Mabizela in Swaziland, both Party men. So successful was the ANC in shepherding the young fugitives of the 1976 generation into Umkhonto we Sizwe that by 1980 the ANC's army was estimated by one insider to be 'more than 85% youth and students'.[4] A security police estimate was that in 1978 the ANC had up to 4 000 trained members in total, the vast majority outside South Africa,[5] although there were also lower figures circulating. One of the best studies reckons that by 1981 the ANC had about 5 000 people in Angola alone, most of them MK personnel. Of these, about one third were men and slightly less were adolescent males. There were about 1 000 women and 900 girls.[6]

While the Soweto rising offered a major opportunity for the ANC, it also posed a formidable challenge. The new recruits joining the organisation abroad in such numbers 'still need to enjoy their youth', as one of them put it, 'and are mostly controlled by emotions and quickly get demoralised and lose hope, they somehow become despondent, disgruntled consequently they act as the heart dictates'.[7] They tended to be rash and undisciplined. They knew nothing of the Marxist-Leninist theory and practice that the SACP had instilled into the ANC.

If the newcomers had an ideology at all, it was Black Consciousness. On this matter the attitude of ANC leaders was at best patronising. Francis Meli, one of the ANC's specialists in this field, described Black Consciousness activists as 'surrogates to the ANC'.[8] He thought that 'they were representing the ANC in the sense that there was no public voice of the ANC',[9] implying that they would have naturally gravitated towards his own organisation were it not banned inside South Africa. Meli, who after studying at Fort Hare had obtained a doctorate in history at the University of Leipzig in East Germany, was a diehard SACP member. In his opinion, Black Consciousness was an immature philosophy that would be left behind by new recruits as they were introduced to Marxism-Leninism. This view was widely shared inside the Party. Black Consciousness was useful but dangerous, unless in safe hands, like high explosive. Oliver Tambo later claimed that the leading Black Consciousness thinker Steve Biko, before his tragic death in September 1977, had come to accept the ANC's point of view. According to Tambo, Biko had understood 'that the ANC is the leader of our revolution' and that 'the BPC [Black People's Convention] should function within the context of the broad strategy of our movement'.[10] Biko is said to have had plans to travel outside the country to meet the ANC in 1976 and 1977, but on both occasions he had to postpone his trip.[11] A top security policeman later confirmed that Biko had indeed intended to meet Tambo.[12] Nevertheless, it is by no means clear that he was ready to submit himself to the authority of the ANC, as Tambo asserted. Some of the Black Consciousness activists who joined the ANC after fleeing the country were told repeatedly by their senior colleagues that Biko was a CIA agent.[13]

Before the Soweto rising, the ANC's exiled leadership had had fitful contact with a few groups of activists inside the country, but it did not have anything approaching a serious infrastructure inside South Africa with which to shape the internal struggle. 'At that time we had no organised combat groups inside the country,' an internal document stated, 'and the enemy had broken through most of the internal network of mixed political, recruiting and combat machinery'.[14] The few active groups were led mostly by ANC veterans and ex-Robben Islanders such as Joe Gqabi, one of the generation of militants trained in China. Sent to Robben

Island in 1963, he threw himself into underground work as soon as he was released from prison in 1975. Later, he went into exile in Botswana. Struggling to establish an underground apparatus that could liaise with the ANC leadership outside the country, Gqabi came to believe that a large part of the problem lay at headquarters in Lusaka. 'Each department is jealous about its work and secretive,' he wrote, noting that rival sections of the bureaucracy competed to maintain their own channels of communication with people inside the country. The dangers of this were obvious.[15] When another former Robben Islander, Mac Maharaj, arrived in exile, he too found the movement to be 'bureaucracy driven'.[16] Maharaj's biographer observed that 'within the ANC in exile, like all organisations in which career prospects depended on one's not having made a mistake, inertia was the preferred modus operandi'.[17] The same writer observed that 'the organisational structure of the ANC promoted a climate in which members of the leadership did not criticise one another. A place on the NEC depended on the degree of esteem in which you were held by fellow members and the extent to which you supported its policies and decisions.'[18] When Maharaj was appointed to the Department of Internal Reconstruction in December 1977,[19] he found that its files were empty.[20] In effect, 'there was no political underground'.[21] The Revolutionary Council was disorganised. Senior organs located in the frontline states were private fiefdoms.

Once he had established himself at ANC headquarters in Lusaka, Maharaj assumed the task of creating a real political-military machinery inside South Africa. This was something that just about everyone in the ANC leadership said was important, but concerning which few did much. An official estimate in 1979 was that the formal ANC political underground inside South Africa consisted of between 300 and 500 people[22] located mostly in the cities, but with a larger informal pool of support. An official document on the underground noted in 1983 that 'very few of our units or single operatives work under what we understand as ANC discipline' and that 'qualitative change' was needed 'desperately'.[23]

A problem arose not only from the lack of direction provided by ANC headquarters but also from the macho culture of so many of the few underground operatives that the organisation did manage to send into the country or to station in forward areas in the frontline states close to South Africa's international borders. They often risked betraying themselves through their brash behaviour. 'Experience has also shown that our reputation as a serious revolutionary organisation our security and even the very survival of internal operatives has been threatened by examples of serious personal misconduct – more especially uncontrolled drunkness [sic]', it was stated.[24] 'The picture we get of some of our cadres who supposedly are operating underground but are constantly found in public places such as hotels, bars and other drinking places' was dismaying, wrote secretary-general Alfred Nzo. He continued: 'in their drunken state some have on many instances provoked brawls against local citizens threatening to use and in some cases actually using the firearms that are meant for use against our racist enemy in South Africa'.[25] One such incident involved an Umkhonto we Sizwe commander in Swaziland who ordered his men to punish a Swazi national who had quarrelled with an ANC member, Nzo complained. '[Name withheld] actually led this group and on arrival at this Swazi citizen's shop they fired several shots,' riddling his car with bullets. The incident led to the arrest of ANC members by the Swazi police.[26] Such conduct was by no means exceptional.

The ANC's strategy review

After 1975, it became possible for the ANC to set up bases in Angola and Mozambique. The SACP created a politburo and shifted its headquarters first to Luanda, and later to Maputo and finally Lusaka.[27]

The ANC decided that Angola was the best place to set up camps where it could house the new recruits joining Umkhonto we Sizwe in unprecedented numbers. The first of these new settlements was set up in early 1976, just weeks after the withdrawal of the South African army units that had invaded the country the previous year. The situation in Angola was chaotic, with the new government controlling little outside the main cities.

In March 1977, the ANC opened what for a couple of years would be its most important camp, at Novo Catengue, inland from Benguela. It was located next to Angola's main railway line in an abandoned building adapted to house the hundreds of recruits who were to be licked into shape by a corps of commissars and instructors. The political commissar was the veteran communist trade unionist Mark Shope. Among the political instructors was Jack Simons, formerly of the University of Cape Town, whose enormous enthusiasm was infectious. Both Shope and Simons were remembered by graduates of their courses with real affection. The chief of staff at the camp was a promising young Soviet-trained officer known as Thami Zulu. So successful was Novo Catengue in educating the young recruits that it became known as the University of the South.

The presence of a number of commissars at Novo Catengue was an innovation. Commissars were originally introduced by Lenin during the Russian civil war to dilute the influence of Czarist army officers in the new Red Army. The post of army commissar had existed in MK since the move into exile, but it had never been of major importance. Faced with the influx of raw recruits after 1976, the ANC appointed commissars throughout its units in order to keep ideological control of the newcomers. Within a short time the commissars, who were invariably Party members, were overseeing the whole spectrum of ANC political life. Each unit and department, including student bodies and cultural groups and so forth, acquired its own commissar, extending the Party's influence from the army to other parts of the movement. As a further means of integrating new recruits, the ANC established a youth section, intended as a revival of the Youth League that had flourished from 1944 to 1960. Members of the youth section were encouraged to form links with similar organisations in communist countries and were invited to attend youth festivals from Cuba to North Korea.[28]

As talent scouts, the commissars were also looking for promising candidates for recruitment to the Party. While a handful of senior people – Slovo, Simons, Mabhida and others – were well known to be Party men, membership generally continued to be secret. New members were brought into the Party without any information being made known to ordinary ANC members. The fact that it tended to be the most promising ANC members who were asked to join the Party reinforced its reputation in ANC circles as an elite, a secret society whose initiates were reputed to be the best, the bravest and the most dedicated revolutionaries. They were subject to the Party's own code of discipline, as well as that of the ANC as a whole. Party members were expected to lead exemplary lives, refraining from excessive drinking or sexual misconduct. This rather puritan attitude became a wider rule, so that the ANC, for example, reserved the right to approve marriages by its members in the camps.

Life in the camps was not easy. At Kongwa, there had been reports of widespread same-sex relations between men, and in Angola there were frequent allegations of sexual abuse of women by camp officials. This was no doubt related to the fact that the occupants of MK camps were overwhelmingly young men.[29] As in army camps the world over, boredom and frustration were constant problems. Even at its best, the food was boring. The staple diet was rice, supplemented by maize porridge. Poor quality meat – gristle and bone, really, known to the cadres as 'skop – was occasionally supplemented by tinned meat imported from the USSR or by tinned fish obtained from the Soviet fishing boats that worked in Angolan waters. In rural camps, pigs and ducks were reared for food, although there were often complaints that camp officials kept these for their own consumption while denying fresh meat to the rank and file. Only occasionally did cadres have sugar and condensed milk or milk powder for their tea. By 1982 the ANC had set up stores in several Angolan cities, where it stockpiled supplies chiefly from the USSR, East Germany, Yugoslavia, Cuba and Sweden. These could then be distributed to the camps that by that time existed in various parts of the country. Nonetheless, logistics never ceased to be a problem. While the Soviet Union was in many respects the most important donor, the Swedish state aid agency SIDA became the largest single financial contributor to the ANC, both in Angola and more generally.

The University of the South at Novo Catengue had a special status among all MK camps. Many students experienced genuine intellectual excitement from what they learned there. Youngsters fleeing from police repression in the wake of the 1976 rising felt that here they could breathe the sweet air of freedom, which enabled them to endure material hardships. But Novo Catengue's place in ANC folklore is above all associated with the incident known as Black September. In the early evening of 29 September 1977, the troops returned to the camp from their daytime tasks as usual. Their normal routine was to sit down for dinner before attending evening classes. This evening, however, as they finished their meal, one after another began to suffer violent stomach cramps, vomiting and diarrhoea. By the end of the evening as many as 500 people had been affected, about nine out of every ten of the camp's residents. One of those who lived through the event wrote that the camp sick bay was 'full of people crying and messing their pants, and there was vomit all over the place'.[30] The camp authorities begged for help from a nearby Cuban army base. Cuban medics came to the rescue with tablets and injections that eventually got everyone back onto their feet. No one died.

Word spread that the incident was the work of enemy agents who had put poison into the camp's food supply. In course of time, an official investigation identified the chief culprit as one Vusi Mayekiso (whose real name was Derrick Lobelo). Under interrogation, Mayekiso confessed to having given four poison capsules to one of the camp's cooks, who in turn had put them into the food served in the soldiers' mess. He named no fewer than 64 other enemy agents who were known to him.[31] Mayekiso's name figures on a list given by the ANC to the later Truth and Reconciliation Commission (TRC) of people it executed in the early 1980s.[32] Yet there were some people who never were convinced that the Black September incident was the result of sabotage. Jack Simons thought that it was a case of food poisoning, no doubt resulting from the poor hygiene at the camp and the low quality of the tinned meat provided to the soldiers. Being a vegetarian, Simons did not eat this stuff, and he was one of those unaffected by the poisoning.[33]

Meanwhile, on the other side of the continent, the independence of Mozambique enabled the ANC to move personnel into a friendly country bordering South Africa. At the same time that it established the camps in Angola, where it housed the bulk of its troops, the ANC established a military presence in Maputo and set up an infrastructure to run what it called its Transvaal urban machinery.[34] The older routes for smuggling people into and out of South Africa via Botswana were now being superseded by the development of networks spanning the border with Mozambique, greatly enhancing the strategic importance of KwaZulu and Swaziland. When, in April 1978, an MK unit from Botswana clashed with a combined SADF/ Bophuthatswana Defence Force unit, Pretoria put heavy pressure on the Botswana government and initiated a successful campaign to plant agents inside both ANC networks and the local police in Botswana, causing the country to become less useful as a base for infiltration.

The proximity of Mozambique to the major urban centres of the Transvaal rapidly led Umkhonto we Sizwe in the direction of urban guerrilla warfare. Unlike the earlier strategy that had envisaged infiltrating groups of trained fighters into rural areas to spread insurrection, the aim was now to send soldiers into the country singly or in small groups with a view to launching direct attacks. The first of the new-style actions was by a fighter who tossed a grenade into the cab of a police vehicle at Bordergate in the Eastern Transvaal on 30 November 1976. A week later, a bomb went off in the Carlton Centre, the smartest shopping mall in Johannesburg, causing the deaths of two civilians.[35] This type of activity required operatives to take very high personal risks, with two or three guerrillas being captured or killed for every three attacks.[36] In 1977, Solomon Mahlangu, a young man who had received training abroad, infiltrated the country and carried out a botched operation in which two civilians were shot. He was arrested, convicted and hanged. The ANC hailed him as the first in a new generation of MK martyrs, naming in his honour a crack sabotage unit as well as its school in Tanzania, the Solomon Mahlangu Freedom College (SOMAFCO). The new tactics made it easier than before for the security police to represent the ANC as a terrorist group, intent on causing harm to civilians. Nevertheless, there were also skirmishes between small groups of MK and police or military units that did a great deal to enhance the ANC's reputation among young militants from the Soweto generation.

The new style of military activity indicated that the strategic vision adopted at Morogoro a decade earlier was obsolete. Heartened by the independence of Angola and Mozambique, believing themselves at last to be within striking distance of South Africa, ANC leaders decided that it was time to undertake a thorough review. They arranged to go on a study tour to Vietnam in October and November 1978 to learn from the country's communist leadership exactly how it had managed the extraordinary feat of defeating the mighty USA. The ANC delegation was led by Oliver Tambo, who was accompanied by Slovo, Modise and several others. The group met leading Vietnamese dignitaries including the legendary General Vo Nguyen Giap, military architect of the country's anti-colonial struggle against France and later of its war against the USA. The main lesson drummed into the South Africans by their Vietnamese hosts was the need for military action to be integrated into a political strategy that would eventually develop into a people's war – the mobilisation of the bulk of the population in the war effort. This was at bottom a Maoist approach to guerrilla war, to which the SACP had earlier been unfavourable due to its ideological preference for the Soviet way.

Slovo, the ANC's chief strategist, was mightily impressed by what he saw and heard in Vietnam.[37] He became converted to a view, previously held by Maharaj, that political struggle should be the basis of armed struggle,[38] and not vice versa. It dawned on him that the effort to date had not only been unsuccessful, but that it had encouraged what Slovo acknowledged to be a 'militarist illusion' that the struggle in South Africa would be the work of 'specialist armed fighters' rather than the people as a whole.[39] They had been going 'ass backward', Slovo wrote.[40] To prepare the way, ANC leaders decided that there was a role to be played by 'armed propaganda' in the form of spectacular sabotage attacks that were calculated to attract supporters. At Tambo's behest, in 1979 Slovo set up a special operations unit, originally with just 14 hand-picked members. These included figures who were to become legends in MK, such as Montso 'Obadi' Mokqabudi and Aboobakr Ismail, also known as Rashid.[41]

Returning to Lusaka headquarters from Vietnam, the ANC delegates began work on summarising the lessons they had learned in a form that could be absorbed by the ANC at large. The National Executive Committee considered a report on this matter in late 1978. The same issue was then tabled at a special combined meeting of the national executive and the Revolutionary Council in Luanda, from 27 December 1978 to 1 January 1979.[42] The national executive held a separate meeting with the SACP's politburo.[43] The strategic review was completed in March 1979 in the form of a document known as the Green Book.[44] Oddly, though, the Green Book itself was not made available outside a tiny circle, perhaps for fear that it would fall into the wrong hands. A year later it was noted that it 'has not been circulated to our membership let alone being placed before the masses'.[45] The new programme was called the 'Four Pillars of the Revolution'. In addition to armed struggle and the establishment of underground structures inside South Africa, the other two pillars of ANC strategy were popular mobilisation and the international isolation of the regime.

Following completion of the strategic review, Tambo used the occasion of an extended National Executive Committee meeting that was held in two parts, in May-June and August 1979, to make a major speech reviewing the ANC's position.[46] He noted that this was in fact the first meeting of the National Executive Committee for 17 months, which, he said, 'raised doubts about the very existence of this important organ'.[47] He pointed out that there had been no ballot for the position of ANC president since the re-election of the late Albert Luthuli 21 years previously. Tambo had himself been formally appointed as ANC president-general in 1977, after ten years as an interim leader, but this had been by the National Executive Committee and not as a result of a popular vote. Choosing his words carefully, he called for the convening of a new Morogoro-type conference, with the aim both of renewing the mandate of the ANC's senior organs and of ensuring that the conclusions of the recent strategic review were made known throughout the movement. He noted, too, the need for the 'continuous political education' of cadres, the lack of which meant that unsuitable people were being elected to regional political committees. He was concerned by the number of suicides, which, in his opinion, stemmed from confusion and despair in the ranks. He also expressed his views concerning the risk that a lack of proper guidance might result in what he called a 'third force' emerging, in the sense of an ideological bloc distinct from the apartheid regime on one side and the ANC on the other. Consequently, there was a need for the ANC 'to defeat ideological variation' and to 'guard against enemy moves to infiltrate'. He announced a plan to meet

Chief Mangosuthu Buthelezi, chief minister of KwaZulu and a controversial figure in ANC circles due to his participation in homeland politics. Finally, Tambo revealed his intention to create a planning committee within the Revolutionary Council headquarters, to be tasked with driving the internal struggle. It would be chaired by Moses Mabhida.[48]

The announcement of a planned meeting with Buthelezi, although made only to the restricted audience of the National Executive Committee, shocked the many people within the leadership who regarded the chief minister of KwaZulu as a sell-out. Nevertheless, it was the logical consequence of a quite widespread perception that something beyond a total boycott of the homelands was required. Disagreement with a blanket ban on working with the homelands was one of the issues that had caused Joe Matthews to part ways with the ANC in the early 1970s, and the same issue had caused divisions between the historic leaders of the movement on Robben Island, whose differences on the matter were known to the ANC in exile.[49] In 1977, some of the ANC's leading Zulu members had had a meeting with officials of Buthelezi's Inkatha organisation in which the latter had requested a formal meeting between Tambo and their chief.[50]

The ANC's highly ambivalent attitude towards Buthelezi was part of a more general strategic problem posed by the existence of the self-governing Bantustans, or homelands. The ANC had been firmly opposed to any form of cooperation with these from their inception. Even in the early 1960s, long before any of the homelands became independent, some Umkhonto we Sizwe officers had been prepared to launch murderous attacks on people who collaborated with them, as we have seen.[51] But the fact was that the homelands had drawn millions of South Africans into their orbit, including by means of voting and other political activity. On a purely pragmatic level, infiltrating trained guerrillas into South Africa or bringing activists from inside the country to frontline areas for consultations would be much easier if the ANC had contacts with people planted within homeland governments. It was to secure some degree of understanding on this latter point in particular that the ANC was motivated to talk to Buthelezi.

Of all the homeland leaders, Buthelezi was by the late 1970s the most important. Born into a family that had traditionally supplied prime ministers to the Zulu kings, as a young man Buthelezi had been a member of the Youth League and had sat in Fort Hare lecture rooms with many future leaders of the ANC. His college-mates knew that his family background destined him for high office of some description. Buthelezi seems to have been expelled from Fort Hare for political activity. He had wanted to work as a lawyer, but on being offered the chieftaincy of his clan, he accepted the position after consulting Tambo and other friends within the ANC. After the ANC's banning in 1960, rather than heading into exile Buthelezi had remained in Natal, building a political following in rural Zululand and among migrant workers on the Rand. He criticised the government's homeland policy but participated in the new structures of government to the extent of becoming chief minister of KwaZulu, still discreetly encouraged by his old Youth League colleague Oliver Tambo. In 1974, he launched Inkatha, billed as a national-cultural movement. During these years, Buthelezi was successful in his strategy of developing a domestic power base while continuing to project himself as fundamentally opposed to apartheid, to the extent that it was rumoured that the security chiefs in Pretoria considered deposing him. Yet, from Inkatha's inception, government intelligence structures were intent on grooming it.[52]

Inkatha's status was one of the many aspects of South African politics that changed with the rise of Black Consciousness and the Soweto rising of 1976. Black Consciousness activists tended to despise Buthelezi as a collaborator with the state. He purged members of Inkatha's own youth brigade when they argued in favour of more radical positions. In March 1978, Buthelezi was publicly humiliated at the funeral of PAC founder Robert Sobukwe when hundreds of stone-throwing youths attacked him and his delegation, forcing them to retreat under armed guard.[53] Buthelezi was convinced that this was actually the result of a plan to assassinate him hatched by Dr Nthato Motlana, a prominent Black Consciousness activist in Soweto.[54]

While the younger generation in the ANC leadership had no time for Buthelezi, Tambo remained determined to establish a working relationship with him. On 22 August 1979, the ANC working committee, the body that governed the organisation in between meetings of the national executive, agreed to arrange a meeting with Inkatha. The working committee stipulated that it should be held in secret and that there would be no public statement even after it was over.[55] When the meeting finally took place in London two months later, no fewer than 16 delegates showed up on behalf of Inkatha, led by Buthelezi himself, compared to the eight who were present from the ANC. After an exchange of pleasantries, Buthelezi set out his list of demands. He wanted the ANC to recognise Inkatha as a national liberation movement. He wanted SACTU, the trade union arm of the Congress Alliance, to collaborate with Inkatha. He read out a letter of support from Nelson Mandela, written from Robben Island. Buthelezi complained about his systematic denigration by the ANC, and urged those present to use their influence to counter a plan to assassinate him being hatched inside South Africa that, he hinted, had its origins with the ANC in exile. He revealed that Moses Mabhida had approached Inkatha with a request to allow MK guerrillas to infiltrate South Africa. Finally, Buthelezi warned that the situation in KwaZulu and Natal was close to civil war.[56]

Many senior figures in the ANC who did not know the meeting with Inkatha was being planned were shocked when they heard of it after the event. Chris Hani, for example, wrote from Lesotho that he and his companions were 'a bit confused about the reported meeting in London between Inkatha and the movement. We would dearly love more information.'[57] Buthelezi, officially or otherwise, obtained a copy of the ANC's own minutes of the meeting, and a copy thereafter found its way to the Deputy Minister of Defence in Pretoria, presumably passed on by the Inkatha leader. It now lies among his papers in an archive in Bloemfontein.[58]

The October 1979 meeting was the last real attempt by the ANC and Inkatha to develop a working relationship until the 1990s. The gulf between the two organisations was not only personal and political but also strategic. Having begun its armed campaign in 1961 with the aim of inspiring a rural insurrection, the ANC had now started to concentrate on urban areas, where Tambo was calling for the creation of what he called 'self-defence' groups.[59] The public recognition by Nzo and others in the mid-1970s that work in the homelands was desirable was forgotten amid the euphoria of the new people's war strategy that had been learned in Vietnam. This left Inkatha virtually unchallenged in the rural areas of KwaZulu where its support was strongest.

A key role in the new post-Vietnam strategy was allotted to armed propaganda in the form of spectacular attacks to be carried out by Slovo's special operations unit. The purpose of such attacks was not so much to damage the South African war machine as to inform South Africa and the world that Umkhonto we Sizwe was in business. Demonstrations of the ANC's military style and capacity were to be coordinated with a political offensive designed to spread knowledge of ANC policy and to imbue South Africans with a few basic slogans. Thus, 1979 was declared to be the Year of the Spear in commemoration of the victory of a Zulu army over British redcoats at Isandlwana a century earlier. The following year, 1980, was the Year of the Charter, a theme designed to spread knowledge of the Freedom Charter, then 25 years old but not widely known inside the country. Armed propaganda was also intended to attract new recruits, embodied in the slogan 'Swell the Ranks of Umkhonto we Sizwe'. In the original plan, the short phase of armed propaganda would close with the Year of the Youth in 1981 and be replaced by people's war, on the assumption that a command-and-control infrastructure would be in place by then. The whole strategy was controlled by the Revolutionary Council in Lusaka.

Despite the clarity of the ANC's new insights, it continued to face great problems of implementation. Try as it might, 'the ANC couldn't turn policy into practice', as sympathetic analysts have noted.[60] National Executive Committee members were good at making revolutionary declarations, but they remained jealous of their own positions and suspicious of innovation. Joe Modise, despite having been part of the delegation to Vietnam, 'never saw any need for a change in strategy'. In his view, 'the armed struggle would eventually prevail'.[61] Full stop.

Pretoria's total strategy

Just as the events of the mid-1970s caused the ANC leadership to rethink its strategic approach to the struggle, they had a similar effect on government and security chiefs in Pretoria. The disastrous intervention in Angola in 1975 was a fatal blow to Prime Minister Vorster's standing. Senior National Party figures, sensing the end of an era, positioned themselves for the eventual succession.

Of all the contenders, PW Botha, Minister of Defence and leader of the National Party's Cape Province caucus, showed himself to be the most ruthless political infighter. He made skilful use of press leaks concerning the existence of a secret slush fund designed to pay for propaganda operations that was administered under the authority of his rival Connie Mulder, Information Minister and head of the party caucus in the Transvaal. Revelations concerning the fund discredited Mulder, allowing Botha to secure the premiership for himself.[62] These political events were accompanied by an institutional shift as the generals, concerned by the setback in Angola, determined to implement a strategic defence to counter the hostile forces they saw gathering around the apartheid state. Botha, a lifelong anti-communist who had always insisted on the global nature of the threat facing his country,[63] needed no persuasion. He used the phrase 'a total onslaught' in reference to the challenge facing the state over which he presided. Having cast Hendrik van den Bergh aside, Botha plucked from academia a brilliant young professor, Niel Barnard, whom he appointed interim head of the National Intelligence Service, the former BOSS, in November 1979. Barnard was eventually to become perhaps the most influential political strategist of all on the government side. He was himself conversant with the writings of Mao Zedong and General Giap,[64] the Vietnamese officer who had made such an impact on the ANC.

Many of the security initiatives of the previous two decades had had a homespun look, from the dispatch of police to Rhodesia to learn paramilitary skills on the job to the ham-fisted propaganda efforts revealed by the Muldergate scandal and the disastrous invasion of Angola. Vorster's habit of making policy in consultation with individual ministers and officials rather than in formal committees did nothing for coordination. This amateurism was something that the generals and security experts (soon to be dubbed 'securocrats') despised. Just as the ANC looked abroad for inspiration in redesigning its approach, so did the government's new generation of securocrats. In addition to their exchanges with such traditional allies as the British military and intelligence services and the CIA, they worked closely with Israel on weapons development and looked for expertise on counterinsurgency to Chile and Argentina, then in the middle of their own 'dirty wars' characterised by the use of subterfuge and illegality. An Argentinian officer, one General d'Almeida, took part in an important conference held at Fort Klapperkop in Pretoria in 1979. This conference, which focused on how to counter guerrilla warfare, was convened after the government had learned of the ANC's trip to Vietnam.[65] Another Argentinian, Vice-Admiral Ruben Chamorro, who had headed his country's most notorious torture centre, eventually retired to Pretoria after the military junta in his own country had lost power.[66]

Drawing on other countries' practical experience, as well as on a wide range of academic writing on counterinsurgency, in August 1979 the South African government formally established the National Security Management System (NSMS), designed to integrate the efforts of the entire state, with the SADF, the police and the intelligence service at its core. In March 1980, the State Security Council (SSC), a minor body now upgraded to be a top forum for decision-making, produced its first national strategy plan.[67] Botha and his securocrats, aware of the ANC's intention to use neighbouring countries as springboards for future operations inside the country, were adamant that their first line of defence must lie outside South Africa's borders. 'If we fight on the Limpopo and the Orange river,' Botha told the State Security Council, 'then the enemy can attack our heartland.'[68] It would be far better to begin the battle in Angola, Mozambique and elsewhere.

By the time Botha had established himself as premier, it was clear that his first real test within the region would be South Africa's northern neighbour, the country then being rebranded as Rhodesia-Zimbabwe. Ian Smith's white minority government was failing, and was sure to be replaced by one or other party representing the majority black population. This was a contest in which South Africa had been closely involved from an early stage. Hendrik van den Bergh had planted agents in the Rhodesian intelligence services as early as the 1960s,[69] and it was he who had persuaded John Vorster to send in a police contingent as soon as the two men received news of the ANC's Wankie campaign in 1967. By the late 1970s, there were 500–600 South African police officers working in Rhodesia at any one time.[70] They learned the arts of counterinsurgency warfare on the job, as one of them, Eugene de Kock, later recalled. 'Why keep to the Queensberry rules and fight one boxer when you can kick them in the balls and kill three?' De Kock asked himself.[71] After

working in Rhodesia, De Kock joined the aggressive counter-guer-
rilla unit Koevoet, set up by the South African Police in Namibia on
the model of Rhodesia's Selous Scouts and led by another policeman
with Rhodesian experience. De Kock finally graduated to the command of a police death squad.

South Africa's best hope for its northern neighbour was that the
transition to Zimbabwe would bring to power the anti-communist
Bishop Abel Muzorewa, whom it was secretly subsidising. Needless
to say, the ANC had its own hopes for Zimbabwe's future. Even before the talks at Lancaster House in London that set the timetable
for the country's first (and last) free election, the ANC was discussing
with both wings of the Zimbabwean Patriotic Front 'the need for
our strong presence in the country'.[72] While ZANU reacted to this
suggestion without enthusiasm, the ANC's collaboration with ZAPU
forged ahead. The two organisations had a long-standing association, cemented by their common alliance with the USSR and their
training in Soviet methods, very different from the Maoist guerrilla strategy followed by ZAPU's rival, ZANU. The respective military
wings of ZAPU and the ANC had worked closely together since the
Wankie campaign of 1967. ZIPRA and MK personnel were training
together in Zambia in 1977 or 1978,[73] and it was from ZIPRA cadres
that MK people first learned the toyi-toyi,[74] a military drill that was
to become known all over the world as the war dance of the South
African townships. As it became clear that Zimbabwe was soon to
gain independence under one or other black-majority party, an ANC
military intelligence officer, Keith Mokoape, suggested placing MK
cadres inside ZIPRA units in Zambia with a view to infiltrating them
into the country as the rival guerrilla armies mustered at official assembly points. By the end of 1979, MK had 114 guerrillas secretly
encamped with ZIPRA north of the Limpopo River, poised to move
into Zimbabwe under cover of the Lancaster House agreement.[75]

Knowing that the elections scheduled to take place in Zimbabwe
in February 1980 were sure to enhance the strategic importance

of Mozambique, the SADF top brass studied various Mozambican anti-government groups to see which of them might be of use. The SADF rejected most of them on the grounds that they were interested only in personal gain and were run by Portuguese settlers. The armed forces chief, Magnus Malan, came to the conclusion that the most useful of a pretty poor lot was the Mozambican National Resistance, later known as RENAMO, an outfit originally established by the Rhodesian intelligence services. The SADF simply paid the Rhodesian intelligence organisation for RENAMO's services, effectively buying the whole operation for a mere R2 million.[76] This was in addition to the R400 million that South Africa had already handed out to prop up Rhodesia economically and politically.[77]

In the same spirit of taking whatever military resources it could from Rhodesia as it was transformed into Zimbabwe, the SADF recruited some of the expiring regime's toughest soldiers, black and white. South Africa's special forces chief, General Loots, personally supervised Operation Winter, a mass recruitment of Selous Scouts and other troops, who were incorporated into South Africa's own rapidly growing special forces. Some of the ex-Rhodesians, now working for Pretoria, formed a secretive unit within the SADF called D40, which grew from an operation known as Barnacle. This was intended as a support unit for South African special forces but also had a pseudo-operations capacity of its own. D40 was soon to develop into a general-purpose death squad. In 1980, C section of the security police also established a new unit that was shortly to develop into another hit squad.[78] This was the unit, later known as C10, that was to be headed by Colonel Eugene de Kock.

The Rhodesian experience had a strong influence on South Africa's counterinsurgency forces and their way of making war. But the fact that these arrangements were hidden from the general public was an illustration of a contradiction facing the South African state in its whole approach to the armed struggle. It was almost the mirror image of a strategic difficulty the ANC was facing on its side in regard to the dependence on armed struggle generated by its alliances. In the case of the government in Pretoria, ministers felt that the measures it took to wage war for the defence of the South African state should be kept secret, and yet this very element of secrecy left the white public unaware of the mortal danger that the securocrats believed to be facing the country. Prime Minister PW Botha blamed the press, complaining bitterly that it 'apparently is unaware of the importance of this business and that we are involved in a struggle for survival'. Foreign Minister Pik Botha thought that the public was living in a dream world and that 'they must be woken up'.[79] These remarks were uttered in January 1980 after the police had stormed a branch of the Volkskas bank in the Silverton suburb of Pretoria where a group of ANC guerrillas armed with guns, grenades and explosives was holding 25 people hostage following a botched sabotage attack.[80] The press had responded with less than total support for the way the police dealt with an incident that, according to the two Bothas, was a perfect illustration of the threat posed by ANC terrorists backed by a Soviet government intent on the conquest of South Africa.

The results of the independence elections held in Zimbabwe in February 1980 only added to the paradoxes of the situation. To general surprise, the ZANU party led by Robert Mugabe won a handsome victory. Pretoria was obliged to accept the outcome of an internationally legitimated election while being privately shocked. Initial reactions by the ANC and SACP were almost as negative as those in Pretoria, as they had hoped for a victory for their allies in ZAPU. South African communists were at first inclined to regard Mugabe's victory as 'a conspiracy with international capital'.[81] 'Progressive forces should reject elections,' a Party meeting heard. '[The] slogan of one man one vote is wrong.'[82] The South African comrades soon came to accept the truth, however, which was that ZANU had snatched victory not by collusion with international imperialism, but by a ruthless use of intimidation.[83] Furthermore, ZANU and ZAPU were divided by ethnic tensions rooted in history. These remained largely unspoken within the ANC, which on ideological grounds shied away from frank analysis of the ethnic factor.

By the time of the February 1980 elections, there were reckoned to be about 180 MK personnel in southern Matabeleland. Moreover, the 32 Wankie veterans held in Rhodesian prisons were freed by the new Zimbabwean government. They were soon contacted by Moses Mabhida, who asked them to resume work with the ANC undercover.[84] When ZANU government officials discovered that armed forces allied to their fiercest rival were being deployed without their knowledge, they were livid with anger. They expelled the MK men from the country, although 14 MK cadres who managed to evade detection received orders from Lusaka to set up a secret military hub.[85] From his base in Matabeleland, Thomas Victor Hlabane, also known as Buti Barks or Buti Buks, became the main organiser of MK activity in Zimbabwe.[86]

The ANC appointed one of its most experienced and astute operatives, Joe Gqabi, to be its first official representative in Harare. Pretoria, meanwhile, was recovering from the shock of Mugabe's rise to power to explore the dynamics of the new situation. In June 1980, a South African diplomat met ZAPU leader Joshua Nkomo, who was very pessimistic and said that he expected a civil war. Pik Botha remarked, on receiving a report of this meeting, that a civil war in Zimbabwe was not necessarily contrary to South Africa's interest.[87] The fact that South Africa was able to recruit agents in Zimbabwe's intelligence apparatus at the same time as it offered employment to ex-Rhodesians who had moved south gave it great scope to exert its influence on its northern neighbour. On 31 July 1981, agents employed by South Africa murdered Gqabi with machine-gun fire as he was reversing his car out of the driveway of his suburban home at 19 Eves Crescent in preparation for an evening out. This was an early action by D40, the ex-Rhodesian unit that was a direct forerunner of the later special forces death squad, the Civil Cooperation Bureau

(CCB).[88] Gqabi's killer was Graham 'Gray' Branfield, a former deputy inspector of police with Bulawayo's Special Branch, who was himself to meet a violent end many years later while working as a mercenary in Iraq. Reconnaissance for the Gqabi murder was done by a local spy ring recruited on behalf of Pretoria by two ex-Rhodesians, one of whom worked for South Africa's intelligence services, the other for special forces.[89]

The Gqabi killing was an early glimpse into the world of duplicity and violence now pervading South Africa's neighbours. Every party, liberation movement and army in the whole southern African region harboured secret units and hidden factions. South Africa's military, intelligence and police establishments, now including substantial numbers of ex-Rhodesians with continuing contacts inside Zimbabwe, were soon in their element manipulating the abysmal relations between ZANU and ZAPU,[90] to the extent that South Africa's State Security Council was informed on 30 July 1983 that 'the cauldron of internal conflict in Zimbabwe is subtly being maintained at the simmering point'.[91]

The securocrats had foreseen the emergence of this sort of deadly contest of wits and were determined that it should be fought as far as possible beyond their borders. On 12 February 1979, the State Security Council adopted guidelines authorising five different kinds of external operation by South African forces.[92] The five types ranged from those that required long-term planning and formal approval by the SSC to ad hoc covert operations that would not be reviewed in committee but that required authorisation at the highest level. The SSC adopted detailed strategies for Angola, Mozambique and Zimbabwe. With regard to Angola, the immediate goal was to divide the country and support the effective secession of the south. With Mozambique, the goal was to build a clandestine capacity. When South Africa first took a close interest in RENAMO, it had only about 900 trained men living 'a beggarly existence'. It grew after the SSC had approved, at Malan's request, the principle of launching

clandestine operations against Mozambique.[93] By early 1980, REN-
AMO, now under the complete control of the SADF, had grown to
about 4 000 people.[94] The whole operation was now headquartered
in South Africa.[95] An ultra-secret directorate of special tasks was set
up within the SADF to provide support to proxy armies throughout
the frontline states, of which RENAMO was only one. Its headquarters
were in an office building at 119 Proes Street in Pretoria.[96] One of
the consequences of Botha's promotion of the policy of destabilisation was the great power it gave to the Chief of Staff (Intelligence) of
the SADF. This position attracted ambitious officers since it provided
direct contact with the prime minister (later, the state president). By
the same token, it gave Botha his own personal security apparatus,
rather as Vorster had had BOSS.[97] Botha, like a medieval king, surrounded himself with favourites who competed for his attention.

As for the ANC, while its relationship with Zimbabwe remained
under constant strain due to its prior history with ZAPU, it enjoyed
a much better rapport with the governments of newly independent
Angola and Mozambique. The bulk of the ANC's army now being
based in Angola, in 1979 Ronnie Kasrils signed a secret agreement
on behalf of the ANC with the chief of military counterintelligence
of the Cuban forces in Angola on intelligence sharing and on provision for training by Cuban personnel.[98] In Maputo, the ANC was
able to establish facilities from which it could organise infiltrations
directly into South Africa. The city was home to the elite special operations unit led by Slovo. Having previously specialised in running
operations from London, using white cadres especially, Slovo was
now closer to his target and able to send people in by land. For work
of this type, the ANC enlisted the help of the Irish Republican Army
(IRA), at that time perhaps the world's most sophisticated urban guerrilla force. The ANC's representative in Ireland made contact with the
IRA via the Irish Communist Party, which put him in touch with the
Sinn Fein politician Gerry Adams,[99] an extraordinary development
in view of the Irish Communist Party's distrust of the Provisional IRA.

In due course, IRA men set up a bomb-making school at a safe house in Luanda.[100] The IRA connection was one of the ANC's most closely guarded secrets, although rumours reached the ears of the South African Broadcasting Corporation, which in 1977 reported that ANC guerrillas were being trained 'by a powerful group of IRA experts who have made their appearance in Tanzania since the middle of March in order to direct a training programme'.[101] This information apparently originated with a Rhodesian source – oddly enough, since the ANC/IRA collaboration actually started only in 1978.

On 1 June 1980, the MK special operations unit launched a spectacular attack on a Sasol facility in South Africa that caused millions of rands in damage and underlined South Africa's dependence on imported oil, then a matter of great sensitivity due to the recent revolution in Iran, the country's leading supplier. The sabotage team was led by Motso Mokqabudi, who had trained in rocketry in the USSR before honing his bomb-making skills with the IRA men in Luanda. South African intelligence soon learned the identities of the Sasol saboteurs, and when Mokqabudi was detained by security police in Swaziland some months later, Pretoria offered the Swazi government a $1 million ransom for him. The Swazis, realising they had detained someone too hot to hold, preferred to hand him over to the ANC in Maputo. In Lesotho, the South African security police planned the assassination of Chris Hani, who was known to have built up an effective intelligence structure. The agent charged with the job, a young Lesotho national, blew himself up while handling his own bomb.[102]

At this stage, Pretoria was probably nervous of the international consequences of taking too-strong action against countries that gave sanctuary to MK at a time when the world was still savouring Zimbabwe's independence and while Jimmy Carter, who had gone to some lengths to achieve it, was still in the White House. It was only towards the end of the year that the government received its first piece of really good news on the international front when, in November

1980, Ronald Reagan was elected President of the United States. This followed the election in Britain the previous year of another ferocious anti-communist, the redoubtable Margaret Thatcher.

The Reagan government was soon to demonstrate its commitment to something more than the traditional US policy of containing the USSR. It wanted to go on the offensive against pro-Soviet regimes worldwide, seeking local allies wherever it could. This was welcome encouragement for Pretoria. The South African government, firmly under the control of PW Botha and his security chiefs, could now go full speed ahead with its plan to confront the armed opposition inside the neighbouring states in the knowledge that if the ANC and SWAPO developed military facilities in these areas, the result would be infiltration deep inside South Africa and Namibia.

It was just days after President Reagan's inauguration that, on 29–30 January 1981, a force of SADF reconnaissance commandos attacked three ANC bases in the Maputo suburb of Matola. Reconnaissance for the attack was carried out by ex-Rhodesian soldiers, now working for South African special forces, who had accurately identified three buildings used by the ANC. One was used by the special operations unit to plan attacks inside South Africa, including the Sasol bombing and the Silverton bank siege, and another was an office for the South African Congress of Trade Unions (SACTU). The strike force was led by Garth Barrett, the former commander of the Rhodesian SAS, one of the many Rhodesian soldiers to have joined the SADF.[103] The attackers drove to Maputo in vehicles camouflaged to look as though they belonged to the Mozambican armed forces along a main road that passed right in front of FRELIMO headquarters. They assaulted all three targeted buildings, claiming to have killed 24 ANC personnel and one Mozambican, shot by accident.[104] The ANC at first claimed to have counted just 12 dead, but later admitted to having lost 16 of its own. The accidental casualty was actually a Portuguese national.[105] Among the dead were the former Robben Islander William Khanyile, a cousin to ANC warlord Harry Gwala and recently trained at the Higher Trade Union School in Moscow,[106] and also Motso Mokqabudi, who had commanded the Sasol attack seven months earlier. The South Africans did not at first realise that they had also killed Mduduzi Guma, a lawyer and rising star of the SACP known for having translated the Party's manifesto into Zulu. The attackers lost three of their own, two of them former members of the Rhodesian SAS. In the aftermath of the raid, the US government was eloquently silent, signalling the Reagan administration's sympathy for the muscular anti-communism of its opposite number in Pretoria. The Mozambican government accused the CIA of having collaborated with South Africa and expelled a number of agents from the country, damaging its already poor relations with the US.

In Angola, late in 1980, the SADF launched Operation Protea, one of what became almost annual campaigns involving conventional military units. There were a few more spectacular actions by MK, including a daring rocket attack on the military base at Voortrekkerhoogte, outside Pretoria, on 12 August 1981. This too was the work of the special operations unit.

Throughout all of what were now known as the frontline states bordering South Africa, the government in Pretoria was exerting enormous pressure in pursuit of the strategy of destabilisation. Sometimes this took a diplomatic form. On 17 February 1982, King Sobhuza II of Swaziland signed a secret agreement with South Africa binding both parties not to allow 'any act which involves a threat or use of force against each other's territory' and calling for 'action individually or collectively as may be deemed necessary or expedient to eliminate this evil'.[107] Other attacks were against individuals. In December 1981, two members of the ANC's special operations unit were ambushed and killed in Swaziland. On 17 August 1982, the communist intellectual Ruth First – Joe Slovo's wife – was killed by an explosive device delivered to her office at the university in Maputo. On 9 December 1982, the SADF attacked no fewer than 12 houses in Maseru, Lesotho, killing 30 South Africans and 12 local citizens, in an effort to wipe out the entire ANC command structure in the country. The attackers impudently phoned the Lesotho security forces, telling them to keep out of the way. Among the dead were two former Robben Islanders: Jackson Balsani Tayo, suspected of having murdered two Transkeian policemen in August the previous year, and Zola 'Bra Ned' Nqini, the ANC representative in Lesotho.[108] Such was the paranoia in ANC ranks that one of the few survivors, Tokyo Sexwale's elder brother Peter, was questioned as to how he managed to escape the fate of his comrades.[109] He was expelled from Lesotho and later detained by ANC security in Tanzania. Unlike on some previous occasions, the brazenness of this particular raid did not go without rebuke by the US government, which supported a UN resolution condemning the attack. The ANC responded in its own way on 20 December, the very day the Maseru victims were buried, by exploding three bombs at South Africa's Koeberg nuclear power station, then still under construction. This time, the attack was not the work of the MK special operations unit, but was carried out by a lone saboteur, a white left-winger who worked at the plant and had had to struggle to convince the ANC of his good faith.[110]

Even the distant Seychelles were subject to destabilisation from Pretoria. In November 1981, a group of mercenaries, many of them ex-Rhodesians who had signed up with South African special forces, attempted to take over the island state. Failing in their attempt, they hijacked an Air India passenger jet to fly home, to South Africa's great embarrassment. Officially, the whole venture was represented as the work of a private group. In reality, it was planned and supported by the authorities in Pretoria.[111]

Sanctions

A major aspect of ANC strategy was a move to isolate South Africa internationally. Economic sanctions had been mooted in India as early as 1944 in protest against the South African government's treat-ment of people of Indian origin.[112] The number of countries willing to announce at least symbolic trade restrictions against South Africa grew steadily as former European colonial territories in Africa and Asia gained independence: confronting South Africa was an excel-lent way of demonstrating their new political profile, not least be-cause in many cases it was virtually cost-free. The closer the new states were to South Africa, the harder they had to think about the wisdom of a total boycott.

A key date in regard to sanctions, as to so much else in South Africa, was 1960, the year of Sharpeville and of what Harold Macmillan called 'a wind of change' that propelled so many new states into existence in Africa. The same year witnessed the launch in Britain of the Anti-Apartheid Movement. Within two years of Sharpeville, the UN General Assembly had set up a special committee on apart-heid. A year later, it was calling for non-mandatory sanctions. And so it went on, year after year, with a gradual build-up of pressure resulting in the adoption of more stringent sanctions against South Africa, formal and informal, mandatory or voluntary. True to their self-image, successive National Party governments responded with defiance. More practically, they soon began making discreet arrange-ments to evade sanctions.

Of all the boycotts that were applied over the years, the most damaging from a psychological point of view was in regard to sport and culture. This reinforced white South Africans' sense of isolation and eventually deprived whites of their beloved international rugby. From a strategic point of view, the most important sanctions were probably those in respect of arms and oil. Sensing at an early stage how vulnerable it was on the oil front, in 1964 the government set up the Strategic Fuel Fund, tasked with designing a counter-strategy that would include storing large reserves of crude oil in disused coal mines. After Arab countries had decided to apply official oil sanc-tions in 1973, South Africa became heavily dependent on Iran. The overthrow of the shah and the installation of a radical Islamic government in Iran in 1979 came as a shock. Policy-makers in Pretoria were close to panic, paying premiums as high as 70 percent on crude oil purchases from traders with oil to sell.[113] By 1986, South Africa was reckoned to have paid over $22 billion in premiums necessitated by the oil embargo.[114] Scenting vulnerability, international scoundrels and fraudsters descended on the country. In December 1979, the Strategic Fuel Fund paid over $30 million for a supply of oil it had bought from one such gang. The oil was transported on a decrepit old tanker, the *Salem*, which after leaving Durban headed to West Africa, where it sank. When the ship's owners filed a claim for compensation from their insurance company, it emerged that the oil delivered in Durban had actually been sold twice over, to South Africa and to the Shell oil company, and that the *Salem* had been deliberately scuttled in an insurance fraud. In the end, the $30 million was paid by the South African taxpayer.[115] Among the sleazy characters arriving in South Africa at this time was the Italian Marino Chiavelli, who had previous experience working with his own country's state oil company to generate commissions for Italy's notoriously corrupt politicians. In South Africa, Chiavelli pocketed a cool $7.5 million per month for arranging deliveries of overpriced oil but neglected to pay tax on his income, and eventually left the country owing between R30 million and R60 million in unpaid taxes – a huge sum at that time.[116]

The king of all the oil brokers was the legendary Marc Rich. On 12 April 1979, Rich signed a long-term contract with the government for the delivery of oil.[117] Although later to become a fugitive from US justice – until his controversial pardon by President Bill Clinton on his very last day in the White House – Rich was no fly-by-night con artist, but a serious trader who understood the value of trust and reputation in his business. Over the next decade, he became South Africa's most important oil supplier, importing about one third of its oil needs and making vast profits in the process.

Lesser importers included the Greek trader, Tony Georgiadis. The crude oil supplied by Rich and others came mainly from Saudi Arabia, the United Arab Emirates and Oman, but also from Iran, the very country that had cut off supplies in 1979. There were other oil-exporting countries, too, that had imposed official sanctions against South Africa but which, in need of foreign exchange, were willing to supply the country, using Marc Rich as an intermediary. Such suppliers included Angola, Nigeria and the USSR.[118] The USSR also had discreet contacts with the apartheid government and with the De Beers corporation for the marketing of commodities in which both countries had vital interests, notably diamonds.

Although the parastatal oil company SASOL experimented success-fully with manufacturing oil from coal, the hard fact was that South Africa would always remain dependent on other countries for the bulk of its oil. It was in regard to weapons, the other key strategic sector, that self-sufficiency appeared more feasible. In 1964, the government set up a production board to oversee the supply of arms for the SADF, and the following year it established the Atlas Aircraft Corporation to work on military aviation. These initiatives were fol-lowed by the creation of the armaments company Armscor. Within a couple of decades the country had built up a weapons manufac-turing industry that made the country virtually self-sufficient in the type of equipment it needed to fight its wars. South Africa became a major weapons exporter and, with significant assistance from Israel, even acquired its own nuclear weapons.[119] There was one field, how-ever, where domestic manufacturers were unable to compete, and that was in new-generation military aircraft. This was eventually to prove crucial as the SADF in Angola was eventually confronted by the latest Soviet aircraft and by sophisticated anti-aircraft defences that the Angolan government was able to afford thanks to its oil wealth.

It was largely to fund measures to combat international sanctions and boycotts that the government established or expanded its secret funds. At the end of the 1960s, secret state funds included, notably, the budget for military intelligence, which was drawn from the overall defence budget; provision for the security police, part of the police budget; and money for the new Bureau for State Security, which was funded from the prime minister's budget. Among the secret funds was a special procurement fund for military procurement known as the Defence Special Account.[120] Previously in existence but rather unimportant, it was revived by Defence Minister Botha in 1973.[121] A law introduced in 1974 specifically removed secret funds from scrutiny, even by the auditor general.

In an atmosphere of increasing threat, it was to be expected that secret funds would be used for purposes other than those formally designated, and so it was from the Defence Special Account that the funds were drawn to finance the ambitious propaganda projects initiated in the mid-1970s and exposed in the Muldergate scandal of 1977. The way these projects were financed was as follows: funds for the Department of Information were passed by the Minister of Defence to the Bureau for State Security, which in turn passed them to Volkskas or the Reserve Bank, bypassing the usual accounting systems. In effect, these monies could be allocated unaccountably by the Minister of Defence, generally acting in conjunction with the Minister of Finance. According to the director of the Department of Information, Eschel Rhoodie, interviewed in 1987,[122] vast sums of money from this fund simply disappeared. He estimated the amount at R200 million per year, a very large sum at that time. The emergence of a major sector of state activity that was designed to avoid public and even parliamentary scrutiny brought with it possibilities for fraud. It drew state officials into direct contact with major international networks of corruption and subterfuge from which South Africa had previously been relatively immune.

The rapid growth of covert state activity came at a time when global factors were combining to transform the scale and nature of international corruption generally, very often in ways that were not widely discerned at the time. The dismantling of the European

colonial empires in Africa and Asia and their replacement with national states over the previous two decades had caused the directors
of companies doing business on a global scale to think hard about reorganising their affairs in this new context, especially as some newly
independent states were threatening them with nationalisation and
stringent rules on repatriating their profits. The world's biggest companies revised their operating techniques in order to adjust to new
realities. They took to lobbying governments all over the world with
a view to shaping legal structures that would allow them the protection they required. Even as the British empire was disappearing from
the political map, financiers in the City of London were finding ways
of retaining their international influence in a new guise, turning
London into an offshore banking centre and trading in vast quantities of the world's paramount currency, the US dollar, thereby maintaining London's place at the heart of global financial transactions.
City bankers and lawyers discovered the legal possibilities offered by
Crown dependencies with archaic jurisdictions, such as the Channel
Islands and the Isle of Man, and by colonies like the Cayman Islands
and Hong Kong.[123]

In this new phase of financial globalisation, the US possessed a
unique asset by reason of the dollar's status as the world's reserve
currency. International commodity sales were routinely priced in
dollars. Faced with paying for its war in Vietnam, the US administration under President Richard Nixon hit on the simple idea of
delinking the dollar from gold, which it did in August 1971. The US
government could now print dollars to pay its bills at reduced risk
of domestic inflation, since so much of its money supply was being
exported for international transactions. When the Organisation of
Petroleum Exporting Countries (OPEC) drove up the dollar price
of oil in 1973, the US government responded by encouraging the
country's banks to lend money abroad, making dollars into an instrument of diplomacy in a more direct sense than ever before.[124] The
former US Secretary for Defense, Robert McNamara, transformed

the World Bank during his presidency, which lasted from 1968 to 1981, turning it into a machine for recycling petrodollars in the form of development loans. This was a powerful tool for reconciling Third World countries with international capitalism. Developments in information technology were also revolutionising the speed and ease of international transfers.

This financial revolution took place in the middle years of the Cold War, when competition between superpowers armed with nuclear missiles made the threat of all-out war too terrible to consider. Aiming to enhance their power without running the risk of a nuclear holocaust, the US and the USSR and their respective allies engaged in wars by proxy in places like southern Africa, where they could supply local allies with weapons and diplomatic support in a bid to assert their regional influence. During the 1960s, Soviet ideologues and propagandists had been quite successful in arguing that their government was a natural ally of national liberation movements in Africa against a capitalist bloc that was on the defensive, struggling to defend interests linked to the disappearing colonial order. It was this very logic that caused the USSR to support the ANC. However, the new style of financial globalisation brought with it exceptional possibilities for the capitalist powers, and these were to become a key factor in the Cold War contest. The greater fluidity of financial transactions, combined with the development of offshore banking, made it easier than before for secret services to generate funds beyond those officially granted by their political masters in government. They could extend patronage to professional criminals or other lawbreakers in return for payments that could then be ploughed into supporting their own proxies, or they could themselves commit fraud or other forms of crime that could be justified on grounds of political necessity. They could even share the illegal proceeds with their political masters, always hungry for campaign funds. In their southeast Asian wars, the US intelligence services discovered that they could fund anti-communist insurgencies by allowing local allies to trade heroin.[125] On the communist side, the East German intelligence service supplied counterfeit rands and dollars to ANC operatives in southern Africa. On balance, the massive circulation of petrodollars and the growth of financial globalisation turned the Cold War contest in America's favour.

When Ronald Reagan was elected president in 1980, his entourage included a core of Cold Warriors who had realised that they could turn the rhetoric of national liberation to US advantage, especially in light of the recent Soviet occupation of Afghanistan. President Reagan promised a renewal of American power and self-confidence after the setbacks of the 1970s – failure in Vietnam, the resignation of Richard Nixon under threat of impeachment, and revelations of earlier undercover operations by the CIA. Reagan gave a cabinet seat to his Director of Central Intelligence, Bill Casey, a veteran of Second World War secret operations who also had wide experience in the business world. Rather than putting all his faith in the CIA, which had been demoralised by internal purges and emasculated by legislative oversight, Casey set up an elaborate parallel system of secret diplomacy and paramilitary activity, persuading a string of governments and wealthy individuals to effect the strategic arrangements necessary for his global offensive against communism.[126] Seeking to break the left-wing near-monopoly on the concept of national liberation, the Cold Warriors of the Reagan administration aimed to support insurrectionary movements in countries aligned with the USSR wherever they could find them. Their main focus was on backing anti-Soviet guerrillas in Afghanistan and anti-Sandinista forces in Nicaragua, but southern Africa also figured on their map of world counter-revolution. South Africa exported its excellent artillery pieces to both Iran and Iraq for use in their war, receiving Saudi oil in return. It also supported UNITA in Angola, and even provided arms[127] to the Nicaraguan contras and pilots to fly supplies to them. For the Botha government, the chance to be America's point man in southern Africa was a wonderful opportunity. The only drawback was that South Africa's role was disproportionately in the realm of covert activity rather than in that of formal diplomacy, where American support was constrained by the stigma of apartheid.

Quite separately from their American alliances, South African secret servants were creating their own schemes. The SADF, deeply embroiled in Angola, set up a network for smuggling ivory and rhino horn from Angola and central Africa to Johannesburg and Durban, from where it was shipped to East Asian consumer markets. The same networks were used for smuggling diamonds, hardwoods and possibly other commodities as well. An official inquiry[128] was eventually to establish that the SADF chief, Magnus Malan, had given approval for these activities in 1978, but it was never established who pocketed the money generated by this large-scale smuggling venture.

After the establishment of the financial rand in September 1985, it became possible for South Africa's covert warriors also to make money from currency trafficking. The financial rand system provided for two exchange rates, one for current account transactions, another for capital account transactions for non-residents. This made it quite easy for anyone having the support of the Reserve Bank to generate a profit, since the Bank could turn a blind eye to currency being exported at one rate and imported at another in contravention of the law. As the South African economy went downhill, private sector companies also undertook increasingly desperate efforts both to evade sanctions and to get their money offshore, often using illegal methods.[129] A later investigation carried out by the British company Ciex, headed by a distinguished former MI6 officer, estimated the theft or misappropriation of public funds during the apartheid era at no less than R200 billion.[130]

The people who ran South Africa's off-the-record secret establishment had a useful asset that enabled them to make complex smuggling and payment arrangements while preserving their country's record of financial respectability. This lay in the existence of purportedly independent homelands, which, being outside South African law, could serve as locations for the registration of banks, airlines or other companies that were in fact working for some branch of the secret services. Bophuthatswana, with its famous casino at Sun City, became a centre of money laundering.

At the heart of many cases of officially sanctioned fraud were the Reserve Bank and favoured commercial banks, notably Volkskas and Trust Bank and their eventual successor, Absa. Losses made by these banks were made good by secret subsidies from the Reserve Bank, which, when publicised, were described as a 'lifeboat' needed to stabilise the banking system as a whole. Pervading these networks was the Broederbond, which had had a strategic influence on the financial sector for many decades, and by some accounts[131] was increasingly used by individual members for their personal enrichment rather than for the original purpose of furthering the emancipation of the Afrikaner *volk*. White-collar criminals, like the Pretoria lawyer Albert Vermaas, developed close relationships with leading politicians and secret servants whom they helped to organise the legal and financial aspects of front companies active in banking and transport.[132]

By the late 1980s, a general atmosphere of *fin de régime* had set in. It became known among South African secret servants that the government was opening contacts with the ANC abroad and that, in effect, preliminary negotiations concerning a change of regime were taking place. In the private sector, major firms, afraid of the future under a new government, contemplated disinvesting from South Africa in search of more promising locations. Some were tempted to use illegal means to get their money out.

Many observers might agree with the economist Sampie Terreblanche, who has written: 'With the wisdom of hindsight, we now realise that the structural corruption that took hold in the public sector and in the dealings between the public and private sector in the 15 years before 1994 was far more serious than was appreciated at the time and the long-term effects were extremely damaging.'[133]

CHAPTER FIVE

The Grinding Stone

The official body tasked with oversight of ANC security, established under Moses Mabhida in 1969, went by various names. Sometimes it was listed as the Department of Security and Intelligence, and sometimes as the Department of Intelligence and Security. Among ANC officials it was generally known as NAT. (This was apparently short for National, but no one seemed very sure.) Years later, a senior official casually remarked: 'maybe it is time we ascertain the exact name of our department'.[1] According to an official document the department 'came into being through evolution … It was not planned nor was its birth a subject of discussion'.[2] In 1976, when Mabhida was replaced by Simon Makana, NAT's core management was said to consist of just three people,[3] situated within the office of the ANC president.[4]

So it was that when the first camps were set up in Angola to house the 1976 intake, known as the June 16 detachment, they were equipped with little in the way of a security or counter-intelligence capacity.[5]

Security, bureaucracy, ideology

It was on account of the new demands created by the influx of young recruits that ANC leaders decided there was an urgent need to expand the scope of the security and intelligence department. In 1976, the East German government offered to provide an intensified programme of training.[6] This was followed in May 1978 by the signature of a cooperation agreement between the ANC and the Socialist Unity Party, as the East German Communist Party was known.[7] The standard course offered to ANC security personnel by trainers from the East German state security service, or Stasi, aimed to instil a highly ideological view of security, as training manuals show.[8] Those selected for instruction were taught that security depended on respect for what were termed 'states of real socialism', among which the USSR occupied the prime position. Trainees learned to regard failure to subscribe to this ideology as prima facie evidence of disloyalty or even espionage. They were told that '*Unrühestiftung*' (causing unrest) and '*Gerüchteverbreitung*' (spreading rumours) were among the signs by which 'hostile elements' could be identified.

With the benefit of training from probably the world's most pervasive intelligence and security service – and one of its most efficient – NAT 'began to take shape', in the ANC's own words.[9] 'In the mid- to late 1970s,' wrote an MK cadre who witnessed the installation of the new security department in the Angolan camps, 'it was reorganised and greatly expanded with young men who had been trained in the Soviet Union and East Germany. These [became] a law unto themselves.'[10] Many NAT operatives were very young, a few of them barely teenagers. Cadres took to calling the beefed-up security apparatus Mbokodo, a Xhosa word used to designate the stone used by women for grinding mielie meal. Some even referred to it as 'BOSS', in reference to the apartheid intelligence service.

The new-look NAT began to make its presence felt in the aftermath of the 1977 mass poisoning at Novo Catengue camp, an event known as Black September. A close reading[11] of documents produced by the ANC in southern Angola in the late 1970s shows how a vocabulary of treachery and espionage crept into standard descriptions of operational matters. Conditions at the Angolan camps were very trying, as the food was poor, the facilities were minimal, and there were many administrative shortcomings. All of these were increasingly described as being the result of sabotage by enemy infiltrators. The 1977 poisoning was soon being routinely described as a 'mission performed by enemy agents in the ANC',[12] even though not everyone was convinced that the incident was more than a bad case of food poisoning. Some of the brightest students at the University of the South, the popular name for Novo Catengue, were now being labelled as 'dissidents' for expressing opinions of their own. Officials came to regard all manner of minor offences as crimes against the movement.[13]

At first, punishments inflicted under the new security regime were relatively mild. In late 1977, 14 cadres who were refusing to follow orders unless they were allowed to go and fight in South Africa were despatched to Quibaxe camp, some 200 kilometres northeast of Luanda, pending a decision on what to do with them. Eventually the 14, who included the former lightweight boxing champion of the Transvaal, Ben 'TNT' Lekalake, were brought before a tribunal appointed by Joe Modise and chaired by the chief representative in Angola. The 14 were sentenced to short periods of detention, of up to two months.[14] Two years later, a similar incident took place at Fazenda, 'when about fifteen cadres demanded to go to the front, refused to be disarmed, and fired shots at night'. The dissidents 'wanted to go to Luanda to meet the ANC leadership to demand immediate deployment'.[15] They also made allegations of tribalism, complaining that the people in charge of the Natal machinery were not themselves from that province.[16] When the ANC failed to send them back home to fight, they tried to resign from the organisation, but their resignations were not accepted.[17] This time, the incident was repressed more severely. According to the ANC's own account, 'this "mutiny" was solved politically by Mzwai Piliso and Moses Mabhida, who talked to the cadres'.[18] However, this bland description appears inaccurate, as three of the Fazenda protestors gained the dubious distinction of becoming the first occupants of a new prison built by the ANC specifically to house security suspects.[19] Officially called Camp 32, and described as a correction centre, a rehabilitation centre or a special camp, this was the prison that became generally known as Quatro. Other Fazenda protestors were sent to Zimbabwe as part of the Umkhonto we Sizwe contingent tasked with mingling with ZIPRA.

A further incident – the most serious yet – that was attributed to enemy agents occurred at Novo Catengue on 14 March 1979. At about 7.15 in the morning the camp was bombed by five Canberra jets of the South African Air Force, causing three deaths and several serious injuries in an attack lasting just two minutes.[20] The relatively low number of casualties was because camp personnel had taken the precaution of sleeping outside the perimeter, allegedly because the ANC had received information about a possible enemy attack. However, there had been previous air attacks on SWAPO and ZIPRA installations in southern Angola and South African prime minister John Vorster had made a broadcast speech threatening to attack Novo Catengue in similar manner.[21] In any event, the camp itself was so badly damaged that the University of the South had to be abandoned. The air raid was immediately considered by ANC officials to be the result of information passed to the enemy by an infiltrator, despite the fact that the Novo Catengue camp was located in view of Angola's main railway line and could quite easily have been reconnoitred from the air or on the ground without inside help. Investigation of these incidents in southern Angola became an assignment for the new-look NAT. The ANC's national commissar, Andrew Masondo, told an interviewer that the security people from an early stage regarded both the 1977 poisoning and the 1979 bombing as subjects of a single inquiry, on the grounds that both resulted from a leak of information from inside the ANC.[22]

The strengthening of the security department was only one of a range of measures taken to improve the control of the rank and file by the hierarchy. A further step was the construction of Camp 32, described in January 1980 as being 'almost ready'.[23] In the same month, the ANC's National Executive Committee discussed establishing a four-person tribunal, to include one official from NAT, to deal with security and disciplinary problems in Angola.[24]

These measures were accompanied by a campaign to assassinate high-profile people considered as traitors to the movement. An SACP document of the time stated that 'the process of dealing with traitors has at last begun and has had a most stimulating effect both within our ranks and amongst the people'.[25] Patrick Abel 'Giraffe' Mthembu, one of the original China trainees, who had been arrested in May 1963, had broken under torture and been made to act as a state witness at the Rivonia Trial, was shot dead at his Soweto home in April 1978.[26] Mthembu's son, one of the thousands of youngsters who had left South Africa after the Soweto rising, said he was approached by Mzwai Piliso with a request to kill his own father. He refused,[27] but evidently someone else was found to do the job. Another victim of the assassination campaign was the Wankie veteran and former Soviet trainee, Leonard Nkosi. Having been the only person to make it from Wankie unaided all the way home to South Africa, he had served as a state witness in several trials and joined the KwaZulu police. He was shot dead in September 1977[28] at his home in the Durban township of KwaMashu while he was in bed with his wife.

Of all the killings of those classified as traitors, the most shocking was the murder in June 1980 of Tennyson Makiwane. A former classmate at Fort Hare of many people now senior in the ANC, Makiwane had named his eldest son after his friend and relative Mzwai Piliso. Makiwane had been a leading member of the original

ANC external mission and was one of the most important of the eight members expelled in 1975. After his expulsion, ANC leaders continued to monitor Makiwane's movements. They were alarmed to learn that he had established contacts with Joe Matthews in Botswana,[29] whom the National Executive Committee also came close to expelling at the same time as the Gang of Eight.[30] Senior figures in the ANC are said to have intervened with the United Nations to prevent Makiwane from getting a job there. Close to destitution, he made his way back to his birthplace in the Transkei. There, he was offered a job by the homeland government, and his old colleagues in the ANC became convinced that he was passing sensitive information to the authorities. In 1979 the ANC working committee received a report that Makiwane was 'active anti CP [and] anti ANC'. It further noted that two comrades were proceeding to Transkei.[31] These brief committee minutes acquire a rather sinister significance in the light of Makiwane's murder in the Transkei in June 1980. The ANC's publicity department boasted of his death, holding him up as an example of a traitor who 'should never be left to live a minute longer'.[32] According to one ANC source, he was killed on the orders of Chris Hani by a hit man using the pseudonym Charles Bronson.[33] One David Simelane, an ANC member, later applied for amnesty for this murder, among others.[34]

The security regime was further tightened as a consequence of a policy initiative from the very top of the ANC. On 5 February 1979, secretary-general Alfred Nzo copied to all units a memorandum that had originally been submitted to him by the regional political committee in East Africa. This text asserted that levels of discipline within the movement had been 'falling catastrophically in recent years'. As examples it listed the theft of ANC property, drunkenness, dagga smoking, fighting and the abuse of women.[35] Citing such cases as justification for tough action, the National Executive Committee insisted on the need for strict personal discipline among the rank and file. Cadres who treated vehicles without due care and who spent money on alcohol and nightclubs – as many did if they got half a chance – were now held to pose not just a disciplinary problem but a security risk.[36] Nzo delivered his warning just five weeks after the special combined meeting of the national executive and the Revolutionary Council in Luanda that had taken a hard look at the ANC's strategy and received a report-back on the study trip to Vietnam. As we have seen, later that same year Tambo called on the national executive 'to defeat ideological variation' in the ANC and to 'guard against enemy moves to infiltrate'.[37] At more or less the same time, the organisation suspended members of a Trotskyist group known as the Marxist Workers' Tendency that included the eminent historian and theoretician Martin Legassick.[38] He was later formally expelled from the ANC.

The ANC's governing body held regular discussions on security matters throughout 1979. It arranged for existing security personnel to be sent on refresher courses in East Germany and the USSR.[39] Reorganisation of the beefed-up security and intelligence department was entrusted to the Fort Hare graduate and Party stalwart Sizakele Sigxashe. At Tambo's suggestion, Sigxashe was moved from the Department of Information and Publicity,[40] where he had previously worked alongside Thabo Mbeki. On 25 August 1980, the ANC's governing body proceeded to appoint officials to head the six internal departments of the new-style NAT.[41] Three weeks later, this body was promoted from the status of a directorate to that of a headquarters committee, 'the highest organ of the department'.[42] According to the ANC's own description, one of the aims of this reorganisation was to eliminate the 'significant overlap' that existed 'between MK and NAT structures, particularly in Angola',[43] by ensuring that the security service was rigorously separated from the army. Mzwai Piliso was appointed in general charge of all camps in Angola and in 1980 was also made head of NAT,[44] taking over from Simon Makana. The security branch now had comprehensive control of the Umkhonto we Sizwe rank and file. The way was clear for the launch of a counterespionage campaign, dubbed by some of its victims the 'internal-enemy-danger-psychosis'.[45]

Some cadres regarded the rise of the security department within the ANC as nothing less than a 'coup', which 'changed almost the very nature of the army'. They listed 'some unfortunate mishaps' associated with the new-look security organ. These were as follows: '1. Cadres disappeared without trace at the hands of the security. 2. Individuals would kill without any accountability. 3. Beatings to death became rife. 4. Members of the security assumed enormous powers.'[46] But this description of the enhanced role of the security department as a coup is misleading, since it was the result of an SACP initiative and the security department remained largely under the control of the SACP, strengthening the grip taken by the Party at the 1969 Morogoro conference. For years, leading Party members had been urging the ANC to set up an efficient, centralised security apparatus to replace the small department established in 1969 and the informal 'James Bond' networks existing before that. Some, like Jack Simons, believed that the Party should have its own security apparatus tasked with gathering information for transmission to the Party hierarchy, 'which would then decide whether or not to pass the information on to the ANC'.[47] His Party cell, based in Lusaka, passed a recommendation along these lines up the chain of authority via John Nkadimeng,[48] in conformity with standard procedure. Eventually Simons and his Party colleagues in Lusaka received a considered response to their suggestion. The SACP leadership rejected the idea of creating a security organ belonging to the Party alone 'because it might cause confusion and friction'. Simons's SACP cell was told that Party members' task was 'to raise [the] level of political consciousness of security personnel',[49] implying that Party leaders preferred to keep a grip on a security organ that was formally part of the ANC rather than to create an independent unit. From 1978, Moses Mabhida, NAT's founding director, had a leading role in Party affairs following the death of Kotane. In 1979, he was confirmed as the SACP's general secretary.

With the rise of the security apparatus came the hardening of ideological positions that Tambo had demanded.[50] This was the real significance of the training imparted by East German experts: the propagation of a highly ideological view of what constituted disloyalty. The drive to maintain ideological purity, on pain of being accused of treachery or espionage, even made itself felt among the leadership. In this respect, a distinctive position was occupied by Thabo Mbeki, who had excelled at the Party school in Moscow before being appointed to the SACP Central Committee. He was soon at odds with the Party's leading theoretician, Joe Slovo, and also with Party chairman Yusuf Dadoo. Among their points of disagreement was the question of whether the ANC should officially describe itself as a socialist organisation.[51] In the course of 1979, rumours began to circulate connecting Mbeki with the CIA, apparently based on nothing more than his willingness to give interviews to US journalists.[52] Rumours that the South African police had planted a spy at a senior level of the ANC had existed for years,[53] giving rise to permanent speculation about various individuals. Mbeki's status, however, was such that colleagues came to his rescue. The allegations were discussed by the ANC's working committee and dismissed with a decision that 'SG [secretary-general Nzo] would write a statement on behalf of WC [working committee] to clear Thabo'.[54] Similar relief was not given to people of lesser standing, who remained defenceless against accusations of espionage. Mbeki's untouchable status was assured by the eminence of his family, his relationship with Tambo and the quality of his friendships within the Party. In its inner councils he could rely on support from people such as his old college-mate Aziz Pahad, a fixture at the London office, from Jacob Zuma, and from his young protégé Joel Netshitenzhe,[55] even as he clashed with Slovo. After Mbeki had taken up the top job at Information and Publicity, his frequent contacts with foreign journalists and diplomats provided him with sources of information that he was able to put to good use in the permanent factional disputes that were a feature of ANC life. When he was re-elected to the SACP politburo in 1984 after being dropped three years earlier for missing meetings, he was in the odd position of being in the seat of power while remaining semi-detached.

Party strategists were concerned to make the SACP's position inside the ANC so secure that it would not be at risk in the event that the ANC ever came to power. They were keenly aware of what had happened in Egypt and Algeria, where nationalist revolutions had ended with the military retaining power for themselves and leaving their communist allies out in the cold. 'The Party should for example start working within the army,' one discussion concluded in early 1980.[56] Later that year, the SACP leadership stated that 'our central task at this stage' was the establishment of its own area committees, composed of three to five people, membership of which would not be known to officials of MK. These committees were to liaise with commissars inside the army.[57] Secrecy was vital for the success of these measures. Each SACP unit was in principle self-contained, and had no horizontal connections to other units. Just one member was authorised to report to the next step upwards, at regional level, and each region in turn reported once every two months to the Central Committee.[58] The full composition of the Central Committee was not disclosed even to Party members.[59]

The grip of the SACP, reflected in the role of the revamped security department, led to a change in the nature of MK camps. While life at Novo Catengue had been austere, the high quality of instruction in the camp's heyday combined with the excitement of taking part in a collective revolutionary enterprise to generate real enthusiasm. This changed. There were reports from several camps of staff enjoying separate facilities and different food, eating fresh meat that was not available to the rank and file. Camp officials often had cigarettes and were able to drink alcohol when it was available, even as they inflicted severe punishments on cadres caught drinking. A particularly widespread complaint was that 'people in administration use their positions to seduce women comrades', even married ones. 'The boy-friends are harassed and if need be, transferred to other camps,' a later inquiry found.[60]

As the Party took steps to secure its influence within the ANC with the long-term aim of ensuring that it would remain in a position to determine events when the day of freedom eventually dawned, the ANC leadership steadily developed – to borrow a Russian word – a *nomenklatura*, a self-perpetuating and closed elite of people deployed from one position to another. Many were Party members. Some insiders detected a 'certain tendency towards stagnation in the ANC which became especially marked around 1980'.[61] When Alan Brooks was summoned from London to advise on setting up a research department, he was shocked by what he found in Lusaka. In March 1980, he wrote a critical report declaring that 'the present situation is unhealthy. It would not be an exaggeration to describe it as a crisis.'[62] He described the state of affairs in the Department of Information and Publicity as 'messy' and 'unhealthy', criticising both Sigxashe and Mbeki, former and current senior departmental officials. In a more general critique of affairs in Lusaka, he referred to staffing problems, alcoholism, a 'lack of leadership' and 'lack of collective discussion', as well as 'idleness and corruption'. Brooks was so appalled that, on returning to England, he resigned from the SACP after 18 years of membership to join the British communist party instead.[63]

One cadre summoned from a camp in Angola to work at headquarters in Lusaka was struck by the intensity of the infighting he found there. So vicious was it that he dubbed ANC headquarters 'the animal kingdom'.[64]

Corruption

Brooks was not the only person to bracket corruption along with other forms of malaise. The word 'corruption' was often used by cadres to refer to malpractice by camp commanders who neglected those under their command or otherwise abused their office. But there were also allegations of financial corruption, in forms more sophisticated than the casual misuse of ANC property, that were increasingly a target of attention by the security department.

Chris Hani and his six comrades had explicitly condemned high-level corruption, in the form of illicit moneymaking, in the famous 1969 memorandum that the Party had used so adroitly. By the late 1970s, the most serious reports of commercial corruption concerned car smuggling. Some ANC members in the frontline states were in contact with car thieves inside South Africa, taking delivery of stolen vehicles once they had been driven over the border. Some staff at ANC headquarters were known to receive cars that had been driven through Botswana (and, after 1980, through Zimbabwe) and on to Zambia. The recipients could either keep the cars for their personal use or sell them for profit.

In the early stages, the car-theft racket is said to have had the tacit blessing of the ANC hierarchy, which saw it as a way of obtaining the cars that it needed and of raising funds for operational purposes. By 1980, according to a paper written by Alfred Nzo, car smuggling had reached such a scale as to be unacceptable. 'It is clear to everybody,' he wrote, 'that the evil of car smuggling is threatening our very healthy body in this region.'[65] In July 1980, the ANC's highest day-to-day authority, the working committee, was provided with the names of members involved and details of stolen cars.[66] No action seems to have been taken against those named, although the National Executive Committee directed NAT 'to handle [the] question of car-smuggling and Economic sabotage'[67] along with other security concerns.

There was clearly a degree of institutional collusion in car smuggling, as some ANC members were abusing the permission given by the Zambian government to the ANC to import cars duty-free for its own use. Profiteers were tapping this facility to import cars, ostensibly for use by the movement, but in fact in order to resell them, thereby perpetrating a simple customs fraud.[68] The ANC's treasury department was formally implicated insofar as it had the authority to permit individuals to import cars duty-free in conformity with the privilege granted by the Zambian government. The ANC treasurer-general, Thomas Nkobi, did nothing to prevent abuse of this right. At a meeting of treasury department officials to discuss the issue it was simply 'agreed that it is not the Treasury that is smuggling cars into Zambia, and it recommends that the A.N.C. should investigate car smuggling by members'.[69] Nkobi did not propose to take any remedial action himself. Nzo decreed that individuals would no longer be allowed to own cars at all and that they could only use vehicles from the ANC's car pool.[70] This directive was ignored, and Nkobi continued to assist individuals in importing cars for private use in the ANC's name. There were rumours that Nkobi was accumulating property in Zimbabwe,[71] his country of origin. By the early 1980s, the contraband routes were said to extend as far as Luanda, with the Angolan branch being under the control of a high-ranking NAT official; smuggling convoys were escorted by regular MK troops.[72]

'Corruption was rampant,' one cadre recalled.[73] Dealing in cars that were stolen or imported under false pretences was accompanied by other forms of personal enrichment. 'Some ANC leaders were using ANC personnel and facilities to indulge in illegal activities such as drug smuggling, car theft and illicit diamond dealing,' the same person reported.[74] Money given by Scandinavian governments for the welfare of the movement as a whole is said to have been stolen.[75] One internal document referred to corruption, racketeering and drug-smuggling and sexual abuse of women as problems 'throughout our structures from the leadership to the last cadre in the section'.[76]

In the late 1970s a new word entered the vocabulary of corruption. This word was Mandrax, the name of a tranquilliser that was at the heart of the most lucrative rackets linking Zambia and South Africa. This substance originated in an accidental discovery in 1951 by scientists in India doing research on malaria, who found that the chemical methaqualone had mild hypnotic effects. Pharmaceutical companies researched its properties further, and in course of time began to manufacture methaqualone as a safe alternative to barbiturates, introducing it to markets in Europe, North America and elsewhere. In 1965, Roussel Laboratories developed the chemical into a popular brand sold under the name Mandrax, which was widely prescribed by doctors as a sedative. Some consumers, however, discovered that swallowing Mandrax with alcohol could produce a pleasant sensation of drowsiness, often countered at parties by dancing to stay awake. They also found that Mandrax was an aphrodisiac. Little by little, medical authorities became worried by the extent to which people were using methaqualone in the form of Mandrax purely for recreation. Eventually it was made illegal in Western countries. Manufacturers, unable to sell their product in Europe and North America, sought outlets in other parts of the world, including South Africa. There, some consumers, previously accustomed to mixing glue or other chemicals with marijuana to give an extra kick to their smoke, took to crushing Mandrax pills to a powder and adding it to dagga to produce what was known as a 'white pipe'. Mandrax was made illegal in South Africa in 1977.[77]

As so often with the banning of drugs, declaring Mandrax illegal instantly created a new criminal market, generating profits for smugglers. There was now big money to be made by importing Mandrax manufactured in India, legally or not, into east and southern Africa and from there to consumers in South Africa. The fact that Mandrax was not made illegal in Botswana until the early 1980s made transportation almost risk-free for several crucial years, and in 1981 official seizures by the South African police topped one million tablets.[78] Ministers and top officials in Zambia developed interests in the trade. International criminals homed in on it. Probably the biggest Mandrax smuggler in the world at that time was a West African, one Cissé Fodé, who worked out of Nairobi.[79] Another foreigner involved was an Indian businessman, Vijay Giri 'Vicky' Goswami. He entered Zambia for the first time in 1987, according to the authorities,[80] and his first arrest for Mandrax smuggling came two years later.[81] Goswami was a particularly significant figure on account of his connection to Ibrahim Dawood, the legendary Mumbai gangster who in the 1980s moved to Dubai and built himself one of the world's most important criminal empires, spanning the Indian Ocean.[82]

As an illustration of the profits to be made from smuggling Mandrax into South Africa, we may take the case of a seizure by Zimbabwean customs officers in 1984 of 201 000 tablets in transit from Zambia. The confiscated pills were supposed to be destroyed by the Zimbabwean police, but some of the consignment mysteriously resurfaced in South Africa, suggesting that someone in the Zimbabwean police service had kept the Mandrax and sold the stock to associates who took it south.[83] This series of transactions had begun with the purchase of Mandrax manufactured in India at a price of just one US cent per tablet. By the time the tablets reached Zambia, they were worth about R2.50 each. When they transited through Zimbabwe, there was no local market for them, but they continued to have a resale value as an export product. The South African taxi drivers who were the main retail dealers sold the tablets at between R10 and R20 each, at a time when the rand had a high international value. Thus, in the case of the 201 000 tablets intercepted in 1984, the manufacturer in India had received some US$2 010 for his goods. The Zambian middleman could sell the whole cargo for export at US$502 500, making a profit of half a million dollars. A South African distributor could benefit from a street price of R15 to make some R3 015 000. By comparison, the cost at that time of a house in the upmarket Johannesburg suburb of Bryanston was about R75 000, and a family hatchback car cost about R6 000.

Furthermore, the profits from trading Mandrax could be enhanced by evading the official controls on movements of currency that were in force throughout southern African countries in the 1980s. These restrictions made many national currencies effectively worthless outside their borders, with the notable exception of the rand or global currencies such as the dollar. Like legitimate businessmen, smugglers moving goods between the frontline states and South Africa had to settle debts owed to their suppliers, but moving large quantities of rands abroad with a view to paying bills connected to illegal activities would attract the wrong sort of attention from the police and the banking and tax authorities. The ideal solution was therefore to export a product made in South Africa to a value equivalent to the amount of Mandrax imported into the country, plus rands in cash to fill any funding gap. Consequently, South African smugglers hit on the idea of using cars stolen inside their country, stuffing currency into the door panels, and driving them north to deliver as payment to the people sending Mandrax in the other direction. Some criminals were able to develop contacts inside car companies, notably BMW and Mercedes, which enabled them to steal brand-new cars with zero mileage on their clocks from inside company car pounds. By driving a stolen car north and giving it to a Mandrax supplier, the trade circle could be closed, keeping the traders at both ends happy while generating maximum profits.[84]

To be sure of success, smugglers needed to enjoy a degree of immunity from arrest, usually obtained either by bribing police and customs officers or by attaching themselves to someone with the political clout to keep them out of prison. The ANC, the PAC and other liberation movements in the region had perfect qualifications to enter into this business, as their activities brought them into contact with politicians all over the region and their own clandestine activities in smuggling guns and people over borders endowed them with an excellent network of underground contacts.

It is therefore unsurprising that some ANC officials developed interests in the Mandrax business in the late 1970s. By mid-1980, the ANC Working Committee was specifically concerned about drug smuggling by members of the organisation, which it listed as a concern alongside 'violation of security', embezzlement, and what it called 'racket with ANC tickets', referring to frauds perpetrated with airline tickets.[85] In September 1980, the Working Committee established a subcommittee to look at the corruption issue in general. One of the three persons appointed to this body was Joe Modise.[86] This was ironic, as Modise had time and again been denounced for his association with corruption. In relation to the smuggled car racket, he was 'widely spoken of amongst those who knew the ANC's Lusaka operation'.[87]

Modise's resilience in the face of persistent allegations of corruption was remarkable. In his youth in Sophiatown, according to one of his friends from those days,[88] he used to organise gambling games in the street. He had been addicted to fashionable clothes, a hallmark of the *tsotsi* style, and sometimes mugged American tourists in downtown Johannesburg specifically to steal their shoes or another article of clothing that appealed to him. In the late 1950s, Modise is said to have become associated with the notorious gangs of Alexandra, the township on the north side of Johannesburg.[89] Thomas Nkobi and Alfred Nzo, by the 1970s respectively the treasurer and the secretary-general of the ANC, are said to have been among his associates in the Alexandra gang world of that time,[90] and they had kept faith with Modise over the years. His control of strategic networks vital to the ANC's leadership, added to his propensity for violence and his skill as a political infighter, allowed Modise to preserve his position inside the movement. Time and again, Tambo defended him against critics in the knowledge that any attempt to remove Modise from the leadership of Umkhonto we Sizwe risked opening up a damaging conflict with ethnic and regional overtones.

As the years went by, the accusations against Modise became ever more damning. 'For the last 8 years nothing took place,' one group of cadres complained in the early 1980s, in reference to Modise's failure to turn Botswana into an active military zone. They said that constant changes in personnel disrupted planning. MK cadres stationed in Botswana seemed particularly liable to arrest and were plagued by faulty weapons, they stated. 'The man in charge is Joe Modise when told about this he defended, and insisted those cadres who said something were taken to the West [Angola],' his critics noted,[91] implying that he was determined to stop any effort to redress the situation. To cap it all, he was said brazenly to use smuggling networks, intended to further MK's cause, for no purpose better than shopping in Johannesburg. 'He personally sent a comrade home to buy Johnson and Murphy shoes,' his detractors charged.[92] His enemies even hinted that he might have a relationship with the South African police, accusing him of having 'shot a comrade in defence of an enemy agent'.[93] Some of Modise's closest MK associates in Botswana were deeply involved in car and drug trafficking between Botswana and South Africa.[94] After Zimbabwe's independence, he became one of the few ANC leaders to cultivate a good relationship with members of the ZANU government, particularly the army commander Rex Nhongo (also known as Solomon Mujuru),[95] himself reputed to have interests in Mandrax smuggling. In ANC terms, Zimbabwe became Modise's fief, an extension of his existing barony in Botswana. He spent ever more time there despite the fact that the ANC's army was less active in Zimbabwe than in any other frontline state.

It was in Botswana that Modise was arrested in March 1982 and charged with the illegal importation of weapons and cash. Although he was convicted by a magistrate's court in Francistown, the case was referred to the presidency due to its political sensitivity.[96] ANC intelligence sources reported[97] that the arrest came as the result of a tip-off to the Botswana police by a South African agent and that the MK chief of ordnance, Cassius Make (real name: Job Thabane), was held on the same occasion. The two are said to have been caught in possession of two unregistered pistols and over R60 000 in cash and illegal diamonds. Importantly, they also had with them a plan for

MK military operations for the coming year that they were taking to a meeting with operatives from inside the country. There is documentary proof that Modise was held in Botswana for some weeks.[98] The arrest was much discussed within the ANC,[99] and it was quite often speculated that Modise may have been visited by members of the South African police while he was in prison in Francistown, especially as Pretoria was known to have agents inside Botswana's Special Branch. Perhaps, it was often surmised, the South African police made a deal with Modise in his cell. The South African security forces do indeed appear to have accorded some degree of immunity to Modise after this date, as the military archives in Pretoria contain a list of possible assassination targets drawn up by South African special forces that explicitly mentions that Modise 'must be removed from the general target development list', together with Thomas Nkobi, although the same document states that they nonetheless 'must be seen as targets'.[100] This formulation, although ambiguous, supports the view that Modise, and possibly Nkobi too, were regarded by the state security forces as belonging in a special category.

Certainly, South African state intelligence agencies were well aware of corruption inside the ANC. A 1983 state document records that 'intelligence at hand shows conclusively that the ANC-SACP alliance is involved in motor car theft and Mandrax drug smuggling syndicates operating in the RSA out of several neighbouring states. There are also indications that the ANC-SACP alliance is involved in the distribution of East German manufactured counterfeit South African currency.'[101] This latter reference concerns another important criminal activity, which must have been sanctioned by the ANC at the highest level of its security service. The East German intelligence authorities, enjoying access to the services of a security printer, gave the ANC forged rands of the highest quality.[102] The ANC insisted that these be given only to operatives in forward areas, to be used inside South Africa and not in the region as a whole.

In 1986, the Johannesburg *Sunday Times* carried an article quoting government intelligence sources who alleged that senior members of Umkhonto we Sizwe had interests in drugs, car theft and bank robberies, with Joe Modise at the heart of the operation. An ANC spokesman rejected the charges as 'a pack of lies'.[103] To this day the ANC remains silent about smuggling networks in which military logistics and personal profit had become hopelessly mixed.

Shishita

After the 1977 Black September incident at Novo Catengue, it became an article of faith in the ANC that the organisation had been heavily infiltrated. In the opinion both of the security department and of some leading individuals outside it, this was directly related to the arrival in exile of the 1976 generation. John Nkadimeng, a respected figure in the ANC, the Party and SACTU, thought that the security problem arose when 'large numbers of students came into our ranks; most were BCM [Black Consciousness Movement], not ANC or P[arty]'.[104] Similarly, the security department, NAT, reckoned that infiltration by enemy agents 'started with the rise of BCM'.[105]

The 1976 recruits, steeped in Black Consciousness thinking, typically underwent a rather bewildering variety of experiences in rapid sequence when they went into exile. There was the excitement of going abroad, the exhilaration of initiation into a revolutionary army, the fear and confusion of seeing comrades denounced and punished for disciplinary offences. For some new recruits, their first formal lessons in Marxism were mixed with other messages indicative of the political climate inside the ANC. One such person recalled that it was during his stay at the ANC facility in the Maputo suburb of Matola that he first learned of democratic centralism and the need for 'an infallible leadership'.[106] In December 1980, he wrote a petition on behalf of a group of his comrades frustrated by being shunted from Matola to one or other location in Maputo rather than being deployed inside South Africa.[107] Other cadres wrote similar letters and memoranda expressing their views. Generally top of the list of grievances was a demand to be allowed to go and fight at home.[108]

So strong were feelings of this nature that in late 1980 the National Executive Committee invited the two age cohorts in MK – the members of the Luthuli detachment, who had joined in the early 1960s, and the June 16 and Moncada detachments, who had left the country after 1976 – to draw up a list of their thoughts and mandate one of their number to present it on their behalf. The older generation, known as *mgwenya*, chose Zola Skweyiya as their spokesman. The younger ones chose Sidwell Moroka, one of Tambo's bodyguards, with Timmy Zakhele to represent the Moncada detachment. Moroka was the first to make his presentation to the National Working Committee. He complained about embezzlement and about corruption, especially the abuse of women. He also mentioned the lack of focus of the struggle and the absorption of the leadership in tribalism and infighting. For his pains he was called a 'rabble-rouser' by Thabo Mbeki. The next person to present was Skweyiya, who covered roughly the same points.[109] In the opinion of the ANC's National Working Committee, the expression of such views was symptomatic of an 'alarming disciplinary situation'.[110] The committee decided to extend the consultation process it had set in motion by holding a series of meetings with cadres 'from all sections of our organisation'.[111] Before this decision could be implemented, though, a disaster occurred: on the night of 29–30 January 1981, the SADF launched its daring raid on ANC houses in Matola,[112] the district of Maputo that housed the MK and SACTU offices concerned with work inside South Africa.

In the wake of the Matola attack, panic gripped the ANC leadership. It was decided that the way to regain the initiative was through a show of firmness that would emphasise the virtues of loyalty and discipline. The internal purge that had been in preparation for many months, signalled by Tambo in his May 1979 speech to the National

Executive Committee calling for the elimination of ideological deviation and enemy infiltrators, was now initiated. 'What ensued was a massive purge throughout the entire ANC, based on the claim that enemy agents and ANC traitors had worked with the SADF to make the Matola attack possible,' one MK man recalled.[113] This purge was called *Shishita*, from a word in the ci-Nyanja language spoken in Lusaka, meaning 'to sweep'.

The campaign began with a speech by Moses Mabhida that was delivered in Luanda, tape-recorded and circulated. Former director of NAT and former army commissar, secretary to the Revolutionary Council and now installed as SACP general secretary, Mabhida was one of the most powerful individuals in the movement. He was also a very forceful orator. The speech that was played throughout the Angolan camps was calculated to make listeners' blood run cold. Mabhida called for dagga smokers to be shot, and made terrifying threats against idlers and anyone straying from the rules.[114]

Following Mabhida's visit to Angola, Tambo himself led a leadership group on a round of visits to the Angolan camps. He warned cadres that there were spies in their midst.[115] On 5 March 1981, the working committee formally decided to reintroduce corporal punishment in ANC camps.[116] On 26 March 1981, Joe Modise delivered to the same committee a verbal report concerning 'progress on work on suspects and traitors'.[117] Groups of security officers were working closely with camp commanders to investigate breaches of discipline, reporting directly to the chief of their department, Mzwai Piliso, who issued crude threats against suspects, saying in Xhosa that he would 'hang them by their balls'.[118] Among the first to be purged were some of the cadres who had returned after months of being embedded with ZIPRA in Zimbabwe,[119] whose recent experience seems to have made them into objects of suspicion, perhaps partly because of ZIPRA's toleration of dagga consumption. It was particularly ironic that abuse of alcohol should have been a target of the crackdown, as at more or less the same time a member of the Party's

Central Committee was unseated for offences that included criticising the drinking habits of chairman Yusuf Dadoo;[120] Francis Meli was repeatedly sent to East Germany for treatment for his alcoholism at the same time as lowly cadres were beaten for drinking alcohol procured in Angolan villages. One ANC official reviewing the purge at the end of the year stated that 'the movement acted with speed, [and] almost suspended every activity in favour of this operation'. The enemy, he thought, 'has succeeded in infiltrating us very deep', and was 'drunk with its successes', notably in destroying the ANC's Matola bases.[121]

The most common punishment for alleged offenders was a beating, often very severe.[122] Some of those targeted were tied to trees or poles, beaten, and left for days, a treatment known as *mbophelele esihlahleni* (tying to a tree). This punishment was much in evidence when Tambo visited Pango camp at the height of the Shishita purge. One witness has left an account of the ANC president making his way to the administrative building along a path lined with the 'bloodied and filthy' victims of beatings 'hanging from trees'.[123] The same person noted that the Shishita campaign was accompanied by the promotion of 'a Tambo hero cult', with cadres being 'required to sing his praises in a reverent manner as though sacred hymns were being sung'.[124] Altogether, at least six people were beaten to death in 1979–81, according to the ANC itself,[125] although many memoirs suggest the number of deaths was higher. Among the victims was one Joel Mahlatini, a talented musician, who died after a beating ordered by his camp commander, Kenneth Mahamba.[126] The number beaten or otherwise maltreated was probably in the hundreds.

Within weeks of the purge being launched, NAT informed the ANC working committee that it had detained a number of probable spies.[127] The committee decided that these suspects 'should be studied to observe patterns, method etc of the enemy in infiltration'.[128] These arrests caused a sensation because of the seniority of the key suspect, Elliot Mazibuko, known as 'Piper'. His real name was Pule

Moses Malebane. A member of the 1976 intake, he had worked as an instructor at the University of the South in Novo Catengue.[129] His talent had caught the attention of Party leaders to the extent that in 1978 he was one of a group of six sent to the prestigious Lenin school in Moscow,[130] where he stayed for two years. Groomed for higher things, he was invited to an enlarged meeting of the SACP Central Committee in East Germany.[131] After his return to Africa, he became unguarded in his conversation, 'showing contempt for our security forces' and criticising the use of torture in Angola.[132] According to Mac Maharaj, Piper 'was in a group of six people being prepared by me for deployment inside the country and in the forward areas'.[133] However, after the unleashing of the Shishita purge, he was judged to have engaged in 'loose conduct' and consequently was ordered to proceed to Angola, the usual dumping ground in such cases. One source claims that his actual offence was to have discussed with a Russian instructor the recent invasion of Afghanistan by the Soviet army.[134] Rather than submit to exile in Angola and hope for eventual rehabilitation, Piper contacted an ANC protocol officer, one Godfrey Bosigo Khumalo, known as 'Oshkosh',[135] with a request to help him leave the region. Both men were arrested. It was Piper's attempted flight that caused ANC security officials to suspect him of being an enemy agent. As a result of his interrogation, Piper was duly identified as a 'sleeper', an agent recruited by the security police, trained, smuggled into the movement and ordered to lie low for many months before becoming active. His interrogators found that his handlers had assigned him the task 'to strive to get to the top leadership, up to the point of effective decision making'.[136] He was said to have stayed in regular communication with the security police office at Krugersdorp.[137]

Piper's arrest reverberated throughout the ANC. So shocking was it that the Revolutionary Council took direct control of the ensuing spy hunt. Those overseeing the work were 'Joe Modise, Peter Dlamini, who was also in NAT ... [and] others'. Peter Boroko, head of

NAT at the Revolutionary Council and a Party man of long standing, took day-to-day charge of the hunt for spies.[138] Specifically within the SACP, many people were disturbed by what they considered 'extensive enemy infiltration into [the] NLM [National Liberation Movement]'.[139] Jack Simons, for one, did not doubt that the ANC had been infiltrated by enemy agents 'at high level'.[140]

The arrest of Piper, Oshkosh and others was officially described as the start of a 'counter-offensive by the movement [which] began the process of disrupting enemy plans'.[141] The security people now pounced on Simon Faru Nogale, also a former political instructor. He had been regarded as a troublemaker for some time already on account of instigating what was dubbed an 'anti-leadership group' that organised discussions among MK cadres in Lusaka.[142] This activity had brought him to the attention of the ANC's working committee two years earlier.[143] Once Faru was subject to formal investigation, his interrogators deduced that he was an enemy agent and that 'the overall objective of Faru's mission ... was to create political confusion in the ranks of the organisation through wrong interpretation of its aims and objectives, the creation of an anti-communist spirit', and so on.[144] He was said to have received two weeks' training in social psychology and mass communication from his police handlers, in addition to small arms training.[145] NAT interrogators required Piper and other detainees to provide the names of accomplices.

According to a submission by the ANC to the later Truth and Reconciliation Commission, an equally sensational case of espionage was revealed after Kenneth Mahamba, the commander of Quibaxe camp in Angola,[146] had ordered the detention of Joel Mahlatini, previously mentioned, causing his death. It was while NAT was investigating this abuse that it determined that Mahamba was an imposter, planted in the movement by the enemy.[147] However, there are also other versions of how Mahamba came to be classified as an enemy spy. The ANC national commissar Andrew Masondo told the Truth and Reconciliation Commission that he personally arrested Mahamba after the latter had crashed a car belonging to the ANC, which in terms of the new disciplinary crackdown was considered an act of sabotage. According to Masondo, it was while he was being questioned about this that Mahamba confessed to having been recruited by the security police and to having left South Africa in company with the aforementioned Faru.[148] Others said that Mahamba got into trouble when he was denounced by Piper. All the major suspects named alleged accomplices and fellow-spies or other suspicious people. Mahamba provided 40 names and Faru 52.[149]

A full inquiry was instituted to study the matter in all its complexity. After a tribunal had submitted its report to the National Executive Committee, Mahamba was executed with three others in 1982.[150] One of these was Vusi Mayekiso (aka Derrick Lobelo), the person found to have been responsible for the Black September incident at Novo Catengue five years earlier.[151] Another was Justice Tshabalala (real name: Isaac Ditso), a Sowetan rated as the best soldier of the June 16 detachment when his class graduated at Novo Catengue, but subsequently found to have been one of the Black September poisoners. Later, four other members of the same alleged spy network were also executed after a similar process,[152] one of them a participant in the 1979 protest at Fazenda camp. However, concerning the fate of Kenneth Mahamba, once again there exist other accounts. One former detainee testified that he saw Mahamba at a detention facility just before his death. He described him as having been beaten very severely. Mahamba said: 'Tell them anything they want to hear.' He subsequently died as a result of his treatment.[153] Some former prisoners allege that this occurred in the Quatro prison camp, where Faru, Oshkosh and others also expired.[154] Mahamba, whose real name was Timothy Seremane, was a brother of the former Robben Islander and PAC firebrand Joe Seremane.

Executions of alleged enemy agents continued throughout 1982.[155] The purge could sometimes affect whole families. For example, Gordon Moshoeu was one of the hundreds who left South Africa after the 1976 Soweto rising and joined the ANC, where he was known as 'Grenade' on account of his soccer skills. He was sent for training in Angola and Bulgaria, rising to become a camp commissar. Moshoeu was one of those arrested after Moses Mabhida's notorious death-to-dagga-smokers speech in early 1981. After his arrest, Moshoeu was sent to Quatro on the orders of Andrew Masondo. Quite possibly his real fault was originally to have left South Africa in company with Derrick Lobelo,[156] the man NAT identified as responsible for the Black September mass poisoning. Whatever the precise allegations concerning Moshoeu, he was very badly treated, spending 18 months in solitary confinement and being held at Quatro from 14 February 1981 to 23 September 1984.[157] Having lost news of her son, Gordon's mother, at home in South Africa, sent his brother Gabriel to look for him in Botswana. Under the nom de guerre of Rodgers Mayalo, Gabriel Moshoeu was one of those sent to infiltrate ZIPRA in Zimbabwe, and is reported to have been court-martialled on a charge of having had contact with the enemy. He was also named by Faru as having had relations with an alleged police handler in South Africa.[158] Mayalo was executed by the ANC in 1982 or 1983, in company with 12 others.[159] Mrs Moshoeu had now lost a second son, although Gordon was fortunate eventually to get back home.

As more and more people fell into the net of suspicion, NAT investigators claimed to have made 'a major breakthrough with the discovery of an extensive network of infiltrators in a number of countries, some of whom were linked not only to Pretoria, but also to the intelligence services of some Western powers'.[160] They believed that some were reporting to the security police, some to the National Intelligence Service, and others to the CIA.[161] Faced with reports of such massive penetration, many senior officials concluded that the best way forward was to press on with arrests and root out the whole nest of traitors. One top SACP man, former MK ordnance chief and Revolutionary Council member Jacob 'Mavili' Masondo, expressed his concern that 'the clean-up operation is losing momentum. Weakness is shown in the handling of traitors and saboteurs'.[162] He thought that the spy problem had arisen in part because the ANC was too passive in its attitude to recruiting new members. 'We wait for people to come forward to join us,' he complained. 'Most of them who do are policemen.' The solution, he believed, was to get tougher still. Some SACP units once more urged the Party to create its own intelligence and security organ. Failing this, they urged their comrades to redouble their efforts to persuade ANC colleagues of the need for security structures. 'There is need to educate the general membership on the vital importance of having the intelligence and security organs in our movement. This will eliminate negative attitudes regarding the security people as "spies" and "policemen"', one Party cell in Lusaka thought.[163] The issue was later debated at the Party's sixth congress, held in Moscow in November 1984. However, there were also Party veterans who thought that conditions in the Angolan camps were now so bad that they 'resemble those in Kongwa days when some comrades received SA prison treatment'.[164] Indeed, some people with experience of being detained by both the ANC and the South African state said that the latter was preferable.[165] In fact, the name Quatro used by prisoners held in the ANC's Camp 32 was a reference to the Number Four prison in Johannesburg.

The Shishita campaign certainly intimidated the rank and file of Umkhonto we Sizwe, but at a high cost. NAT became feared and hated, but so too did the commissars, whose chief was Andrew Masondo. They became regarded as 'protectors of corruption and autocracy'.[166] Many cadres who fell under suspicion were sent to the MK camps in Angola and grounded there. The lucky ones were in due course deemed to have been rehabilitated and were appointed to normal positions, in some cases even as commissars, but many were left in a limbo as uncleared suspects, sometimes for years. This had a debilitating effect both on the people concerned, unsure whether they might be called for further questioning at any time, and also on the ANC as a whole, as it spread uncertainty and demoralisation. Some committed suicide. The atmosphere of intolerance spread as far as Cuba. One ANC student who was on bad terms with Alex La Guma, the ANC representative in Havana, was deported to Mozambique and dumped with others in the remote province of Nampula. Left without resources, he and others undergoing similar banishment survived by working in the fields, sometimes even without shoes. Only in 1983 were they rescued after a visit by a commission of inquiry.[167]

Hoping to draw a line under the proceedings resulting from Shishita and to restore some measure of harmony, in September 1982 Tambo instructed all army units to make proposals regarding the way forward. Cadres in the large transit camp at Viana, just outside Luanda, were invited to submit their ideas in writing. Known as the Viana papers,[168] the documents produced were supposed to be presented to the annual meeting of the ANC's National Executive Committee for consideration. Many cadres undertook this task with some enthusiasm, thinking that at last the leadership was ready to listen to their grievances. A call commonly heard was for a consultative conference of the whole ANC where the issues could be thrashed out. Would-be reformers thought they could see a virtuous calendar ahead: the leadership would consider their submissions and produce a response at the annual meeting of the National Executive Committee, due to be held in January 1983. Perhaps this would be followed by the announcement of a conference. The more cautious cadres, though, regarded the whole exercise as a ruse to identify potential dissidents.

In the event, the reformers' hopes were dashed. 'The outcome,' according to of one of those involved in drafting the Viana papers, 'was a mixture of cosmetic changes and madness.'[169] Rather than accepting the documents, leading officials pronounced themselves dissatisfied with the views expressed. The national commissar, Andrew Masondo, toured the camps with the message that the president, Oliver Tambo, found the ideas sent to the leadership unacceptable and even scandalous.[170] Masondo was already unpopular, as he was held responsible for the excesses of political commissars throughout the movement. He publicly referred to the Mbokodo security officers as 'his boys, the red ants'.[171] Supporting the campaign of repression, Modise, Hani and other heavyweights visited ANC camps in Tanzania with the message that they should create their own detention facilities. John Nkadimeng told cadres at Mazimbu in Tanzania that they should 'try and eradicate bad tendencies'. Modise was more explicit, saying that 'not only undisciplined elements but enemy agents also have to be dealt with'.[172]

When the National Executive Committee gathered in January 1983, Tambo too vilified the Viana papers.[173] Rather than address the complaints of the membership or announce the holding of a conference to air the issues further, the ANC's governing body decided that the way forward was to find work for the army cadres to do. They would be sent into battle against UNITA, the enemy of their Angolan hosts and an ally of both Pretoria and the US. In the following weeks, Umkhonto's base camps emptied as troops were transported to Malange province, UNITA's eastern front.[174] A further element of the National Executive Committee's response to the grievances of the rank and file was to announce an overhaul of ANC management structures. The National Executive Committee coopted some new members. Above all, the Revolutionary Council, which since 1969 had had formal control of the armed struggle, and which had exercised hands-on control of the Shishita purge, was now replaced by a body called the Politico-Military Council (PMC). This committee was charged with coordinating the armed struggle with activity on the political front, as some of the ANC's most sophisticated thinkers, and most notably Mac Maharaj, had long been urging. The PMC's first secretary was Joe Nhlanhla, an SACP member whose organisational skills had caught Tambo's eye. The intention was for the PMC to oversee the work of regional politico-military commands in the frontline areas, to be created in the next few months. But this never

quite transpired. The power that was supposed to be concentrated in
the PMC in fact drained on the one hand towards the military headquarters, dominated by army commander Joe Modise, and on the
other hand towards the political headquarters, run by the triumvirate
of Nkadimeng, Maharaj and Josiah Jele, Party men all three. These
two nodes of power competed to install their own loyalists in the
new structures in the frontline areas.

The establishment of the Politico-Military Council failed to en-
thuse the disillusioned cadres. NAT, its force demonstrated by the
Shishita campaign, remained a menacing presence. Security officials
analysed their notes on the 'scores of agents' they claimed to have
uncovered and drew general conclusions.[175] They noted that almost
all the suspects netted in the Shishita purge were black people. In
regard to the social background of suspected or confessed enemy
agents, many were gangsters, drug smugglers or car thieves. Piper,
Faru, Mahamba and the other key suspects, though, did not fall into
this category, being among those with what was termed a 'petty
bourgeois' class background.[176] In terms of their mode of operation,
the infiltrators were deemed to fall into distinct categories. One was
'squads for assassination'. These were said to consist of small cells of
enemy agents who waited for an opportunity to kill, such as had occurred in the notorious Black September mass poisoning (although
it did not actually result in any deaths). A second category was 'the
THIEVES who are destroying our logistics'.[177] NAT seems to have
believed that enemy agents were more often saboteurs and assassins
looking for opportunities to strike rather than spies who patiently
sought out information for transmission to their handlers, although
these were thought also to exist. One suspect, interrogated in mid-
1985, confessed to having been a member of an enemy network for
six years and even gave the name of his handler, one Lieutenant
Coetzee from Protea police station.[178] The counterintelligence chief,
Peter Boroko, wrote to Tambo describing in detail a complex ring
of agents, allegedly run by the same Coetzee, that had penetrated

ANC networks in Botswana to great depth.[179] This ring was uncovered while the security people were on the trail of a man who undoubtedly was an enemy agent, Joe Mamasela, whom they never apprehended.[180] A professional car thief, born in 1955, Mamasela had agreed to work as a police agent in exchange for an exemption from prosecution after being arrested for a criminal offence. He joined the ANC in Botswana, where he was detained by ANC security during the Shishita purge. He managed to escape, returning to South Africa where he was formally enrolled in the South African Police in February 1982.[181] He later became a member of a notorious police death squad.

Studying the results of numerous interrogations, senior NAT officials believed they could detect a chronology and a method in the enemy's operations. It seemed that many spies were people who, having fallen foul of South Africa's criminal justice system, were recruited by the police while they were in prison. Others had been recruited by other means. NAT believed that in 1976–1977 the security police had put prospective agents through brief training courses, and that since 1979 training had become more sophisticated, with newly recruited spies following courses lasting as long as a year. According to NAT, espionage training centres of this sort existed inside South Africa at Lenz, Hammanskraal and elsewhere. As a result, 'the enemy has voluminous information about the ANC in all our operational areas'.[182] In similar vein, an ANC propaganda leaflet maintained that most spies were 'trained in the South African police barracks and the fascist army bases after which they are infiltrated into the ranks of the ANC with the aim of collecting information and to cause whatever damage'. Spies were also trained to poison food and 'to damage the fighting spirit of our cadres by encouraging drug addiction'.[183] To this day, no information from state archives has come to light concerning the existence of any such schools for training spies.

Even a person as senior as 'Mavili' Masondo, who fully supported the counterespionage campaign, was vulnerable to the spycatcher-in-chief Peter Boroko. After an argument with Boroko, Masondo was exiled to the ANC farm at Malange in a remote part of Angola, where he died in late 1983 as a result of his diabetes.[184] It was also Boroko who was responsible for the detention of Pallo Jordan, one of the few people in the ANC with the stature and the independence of mind to take on the SACP elite. Jordan was the son of a famous intellectual couple, who had himself studied up to Master's level at the University of Wisconsin. In June 1983, Jordan was working at the ANC's Department of Information. Suspecting − correctly − that a couple of his colleagues there were secret informers working for Mbokodo, he mockingly referred to them in the presence of others as 'amapolisa'. Furious, the two reported the matter to their boss, Peter Boroko. The latter hauled Jordan into the Green House, Mbokodo's headquarters in Lusaka. There, Jordan was detained and questioned, being made to write his autobiography again and again in the manner the security people had learned from their Stasi mentors. He is said to have almost died from lack of water.[185] No one really thought that Jordan was a security threat, but his arrogance annoyed some people, and his lack of a popular following made him an easy target. When security officials met to discuss his case, one of them remarked: 'eli intellectual lase Merika lisijwayela kabi' (This American-trained intellectual is uppity). This, in the opinion of one of those present at the meeting, 'seemed to capture the essence of the entire saga'.[186] Jordan's detention was unjustified on any security ground, but had clear ideological overtones. His American connection made him suspect to young Mbokodo officials brought up in an atmosphere created by the SACP in which everything associated with America was reviled.

The cases of Masondo and Jordan illustrate the changes wrought in the ANC by the Shishita campaign. At the outset, the reason given for the purge by secretary-general Nzo was a decline in standards of discipline. Whether discipline in the army had actually got worse, as he maintained, is not clear, since similar problems had been evident at Kongwa 15 years earlier. What had undoubtedly happened was that the ANC, led by the generation that had founded the Youth League in the 1940s and taken part in the mass protests of the 1950s, had been shaken up by the influx of thousands of new recruits in the aftermath of the Soweto rising. The newcomers generally knew nothing of ANC history and, on arrival, had no understanding of the Soviet style of Marxism-Leninism imbued in the organisation by the SACP. As we have seen, the SACP was the driving force behind the reorganisation of the security department, NAT, as the liberation movement braced itself to absorb this new cohort.

In a report on the Shishita purge, NAT stated: 'In the area of our investigation, it is clear that there was, in fact, a campaign promoted by enemy agents, within and outside our ranks, for discrediting the leadership of the African National Congress on "grounds" of "corruption", "in-efficiency" [sic], "money-making", "too old to lead", etc.'[187] It placed much of the responsibility for spreading such views about the leadership on two senior figures, the trade unionist Mark Shope and the former Robben Island prisoner Albert Dlomo. Shope in particular had been plain-spoken in his criticisms of the ANC leadership from the early 1970s, as we have seen.[188] At Novo Catengue he had encouraged equal frankness in his young colleagues, who included 'Piper' Mazibuko. Apparently on these grounds, NAT concluded that 'objectively these comrades [Shope and Dlomo] are playing the role of enemy agents or provocateurs despite the fact that they were never formally recruited'.[189]

This is the language of Stalinism. The adjective 'Stalinist' is rather overworked, but it retains a precise technical meaning. This pertains notably to the method used by the Soviet communist party to kill and imprison vast numbers of people in the purges of the 1930s, and to the ideology associated with it.[190] Those who ordered the purge in the ANC were steeped in a Marxist-Leninist tradition that regarded the historical achievements of the late Soviet leader Josef Stalin with admiration. Those who implemented the campaign had

been trained in East Germany in a tradition of ideological intolerance little changed since Stalin's death in 1953. Their lecturers spoke
admiringly about the Bolshevik secret police, the Cheka.[191]

A classic technique of Stalinism was for the leadership to identify
an ideological or political enemy and classify that person or group as
treacherous by reference to a purportedly scientific method. This resulted in people being labelled as 'objectively' belonging to a specific
sociological or political category already identified as undesirable.
If necessary, torture or coercion could be used to secure supporting evidence. This was precisely the method used in the Shishita
campaign. Anyone who criticised the leadership, complained of corruption, or called for a conference was regarded as undermining
the tried and tested leadership of Oliver Tambo and others. Since
this served the interests of the enemy, they were 'objectively' enemy
agents and deserved to be treated accordingly. This was so even if
they were not actually aware of being agents. Mark Shope and Albert
Dlomo were placed in this category and were lucky to escape with
their lives. Others were less fortunate. As Mac Maharaj noted, the
Shishita purge 'made us insensitive to grievances that were real'.[192]

A further aspect of the Stalinist heritage is worth commenting
on. Just as Stalin weakened his own army by purging many of his
best generals in the 1930s in the interests of political and ideological
conformity, so too did the ANC undermine Umkhonto we Sizwe
by creating two hierarchies of command, one proper to the army
itself, the other consisting of security officers. Cadres were no longer
sure which of two lines of command to follow. The real function
of Umkhonto we Sizwe was henceforth not to aspire to the highest military standard, but rather to serve the political purpose of the
leadership. Some of the most able and original thinkers in the ANC
were distrusted by the SACP/Mbokodo senior command precisely
because of their unpredictability. MK was hamstrung by the exclusion
of some of its most talented members.

Mkatashinga

Despite the difficulties it was experiencing with its new entrants, the ANC leadership was determined to press on with the next phase in the implementation of people's war, as prescribed by its 1978 strategic review.

As ever, the ANC could rely on the staunchest support from the USSR, its Warsaw Pact allies and Cuba. In addition, Sweden had become a particularly generous donor, especially after a visit to Stockholm by Tambo in May 1983 had resulted in the Swedish government increasing its grant to the ANC by no less than 550 percent.[193] The ANC was also making steady progress in winning public support in many capitalist countries, thanks to the success of the Anti-Apartheid Movement. Its greatest concern was the frontline states: Angola, Mozambique, Lesotho, Swaziland and Zimbabwe were all subject to Pretoria's campaign of destabilisation and some of them were feeling the pressure very acutely. At the very time the Shishita campaign was in full spate, there was a flurry of diplomatic activity throughout the region, including the first speculation by informed observers concerning a possible release of Nelson Mandela as part of a comprehensive diplomatic settlement.[194]

The Cold War intruded. CIA chief William Casey took quite a close interest in southern Africa as a theatre of the struggle against communism and Soviet imperialism, and he sensed that the Mozambican government especially might be ready to moderate its wholehearted support for the ANC. In late 1982, Casey met South African government leaders and urged them to show restraint towards Mozambique. Probably unknown to the ANC, the Mozambican security chief Jacinto Veloso entered into secret talks with US and South African officials about normalising their relationship.[195] Negotiations on Angola were also taking place. As for Zimbabwe, its government was increasingly consumed by concern about its rival ZAPU, a historic ally of the ANC. It was not difficult for South African intelligence and military officials to turn this hostility to their advantage. These were elements that led to the tragic Gukurahundi, the ZANU government's anti-Ndebele initiative of the mid-1980s. Amid almost complete silence from international diplomats and the press, Prime Minister Robert Mugabe launched the largest genocide seen in southern Africa since the German colonial campaigns against the Herero at the start of the twentieth century.

It was in this international context that the ANC's national executive sent an entire brigade of its army into battle against UNITA in August 1983. Even some detainees from the penal centre at Quatro were sent to the battlefront. The ANC's units in the field were led by Chris Hani, newly appointed to the position of MK political commissar, Lennox Lagu, a veteran of Wankie and Operation J who had also worked with FRELIMO inside Mozambique, and Timothy Mokoena. While the troops were at first glad to see action, they lost heart when they began to take serious casualties at the same time as they witnessed at first hand the demoralisation of their Angolan military allies and reflected on the pointlessness of their own deployment. By the end of the year, the mood among the ANC rank and file in Malange province had turned ugly. The return to base of one unit that had faced UNITA while going without food for three days is said to have tipped the balance.[196] On the ANC's national holiday of 16 December, a gun salute at MK's forward base in Kangandala got out of hand, with sporadic shooting continuing for many minutes. Troops acquired the habit of shooting in the air at almost any time, creating a menacing atmosphere.

Knowing that an important meeting of their army headquarters was scheduled to take place at Caculama, the main Umkhonto we Sizwe base in Malange, just 80 kilometres away, frontline troops at Kangandala decided this was the opportunity to confront their leaders. When, on 12 January 1984, Tambo arrived at Caculama with a delegation from the National Executive Committee, the troops sent a message demanding an end to operations against UNITA and the opening of a campaign in South Africa instead. Further demands included the suspension of NAT and an investigation into Quatro. Finally, they wanted Tambo to come and talk to them. Many soldiers had the idea that, like a good king surrounded by bad courtiers, Tambo himself was unaware of the true conditions experienced by the rank and file. Another reason for them to believe that there were some at least in the leadership who might be disposed to listen to their grievances was an article recently published by Joe Slovo in the *African Communist* that emphasised the political element in a people's army,[197] which some readers interpreted as 'a call for active involvement into the solution of our problems'.[198] The appointment to a prominent position of Hani, the hero of Wankie and himself once the bold leader of a protest against a failed leadership, was another reason for hope. When the restless troops finally met Hani at Kangandala, they presented him with 'a package of demands'[199] for Tambo and the national executive, gathered just a couple of hours' drive away. But the National Executive Committee paid no heed, and Tambo headed off to Luanda without meeting any of the fractious troops. Instead, ANC leaders called for intervention by the Angolan and Cuban forces in the region, in vain.[200]

Determined to present their grievances directly, the protestors now commandeered vehicles and headed towards Luanda with the intention of laying siege to the ANC leadership. Rather than going into the city centre, which would surely provoke the intervention of Angolan government forces, they stopped at the transit camp at Viana, some 15 kilometres from the centre. Hundreds of angry soldiers bearing arms were now gathered in close proximity to the Angolan capital. It is estimated that up to 90 percent of Umkhonto we Sizwe members in the region may eventually have associated themselves with the protest.[201] The ANC again asked the government and the Cuban garrison to intervene, but both refused.

For the first time, Umkhonto we Sizwe cadres found their collective voice, holding a series of mass meetings that culminated in a gathering of perhaps as many as a thousand people. Speaker after speaker lambasted three people in particular: Joe Modise, the army commander; Andrew Masondo, the national commissar, head of the corps of commissars; and Mzwai Piliso, the head of NAT, who had personally supervised the beating of suspects during the Shishita campaign, as he later admitted to a commission of inquiry.[202]

The MK regional commander, Timothy Mokoena, addressed the dissident troops. He urged them to remember what had happened to the PAC in Tanzania a couple of years earlier, when government forces had opened fire on rebellious cadres.[203] He advised them to elect a committee to present their grievances, and on 6 February the hundreds of angry soldiers in Viana duly put forward names until they had assembled a ten-person committee. It had no chairperson, but rather a convenor, Bongani Matwa, a member of the June 16 detachment who had studied with Mark Shope and Jack Simons at the University of the South and was one of the few political commissars to enjoy popularity. The secretary to the committee was Zaba Maledza. The real name of this cadre, a graduate of the University of the North at Turfloop, was Ephraim Nkondo. Few of the troops assembled at Viana knew him personally, but he was popular due to his broadcasts on Radio Freedom. He had the prestige of having studied at the Lenin school in Moscow. He came from a prominent struggle family, one of his brothers being Curtis Nkondo, the Soweto schoolteacher and Black Consciousness intellectual, and another being head of the ANC radio station in Lusaka. Maledza had himself been detained in Quatro from 1980 to 1982 after a disagreement with the military leadership.[204] Maledza and some others elected were travelling to Viana camp during the day and returning to Luanda in the evening. A third member of the committee was the MK district commander Sidwell Moroka, who was not actually in Viana when he was nominated, but at his post in Luanda itself.

Following these events, Angolan president José Eduardo dos Santos decided to intervene after all, apparently after receiving a phone call from Tambo. On 7 February 1984, troops from the elite presidential brigade encircled the Viana camp before dawn, provoking a brief exchange of fire with the dissidents. There was one death on each side. A more serious confrontation was avoided only by the intervention of the committee elected by the dissidents.[205] Bongani Matwa headed to Luanda to enlist the help of Maledza and Moroka, who realised that if the dissidents did not give up their weapons they would simply be wiped out by the Angolans. Maledza, Moroka and two other members of the Committee of Ten, Sipho Mathebula and Moss Thema, met the chief of the Angolan force, Colonel António França 'Ndalu', and proposed a deal: if they persuaded the mutineers to surrender their weapons to Ndalu, then he would hold the weapons and not pass them on to Mbokodo. Ndalu agreed to this proposal, and the committee duly persuaded the mutineers to give up their arms. But Ndalu did not keep his promise. Having taken charge of the mutineers' weapons, he handed them over to ANC officials who had stayed loyal to the senior command.[206]

Transcripts of radio messages sent from ANC leaders to their headquarters reveal the drama almost from hour to hour. On 8 February Modise radioed from Luanda to Oliver Tambo, now back in Lusaka, that the situation was coming under control. He reported three deaths, one among the dissident troops in Viana, and two at the propaganda unit in Luanda.[207] The latter was a reference to two radio staff murdered by Mbokodo while on their way to a studio to broadcast news of the events at Viana.[208] The following day, Hani reported three more deaths, including one suicide.[209] Later, he radioed that he had received news from Timothy Mokoena that the situation further north among the cadres remaining in Caculama was 'deteriorating', and that 30 more had left the camp without permission. Hani thought that what he called the 'counter-revolution' was spreading. He recommended 'firm and decisive action', which would entail sending loyal troops to strengthen the northern front.[210] A further report revealed that the politburo of Angola's ruling party, the MPLA, had instructed the country's interior minister to liaise with the ANC on this most delicate and dangerous matter. On 9 February, Mokoena estimated the number of dissidents at 250, but believed that the situation was 'calm and under control' as they had followed his advice in electing their own spokespersons. He reported having met a representative of the group in the morning and said he would be seeing the entire Committee of Ten later that day.[211] However, just four days later, on 13 February 1984, Lusaka received a message from Lambert Moloi intended for his chief (and later relative by marriage), Joe Modise. 'Had decisive meeting with rebels yest[erday],' Moloi reported. 'Dissolved so-called Committee of Ten, installed Interim Administration.' He went on to report that 'Chris [Hani] left for Malange to help improve the situation there as Lennox [Lagu] and Tim [Mokoena] not coping well.'[212] Hani confirmed that the Committee of Ten had been dissolved on Modise's orders.[213] The Committee of Ten and a couple of dozen other dissidents were arrested and taken to Luanda's maximum-security prison under Angolan military escort. By this time, all the Viana protestors had been disarmed.

On the very same day, Monday 13 February, the working committee of the ANC appointed a commission of inquiry chaired by James Stuart, which flew to Luanda and went straight to work. During the next three weeks, members of the Stuart Commission 'visited and interviewed practically all the occupants of Viana Transit Camp', as well as the other camps affected. It also interviewed the 33 cadres, including members of the Committee of Ten, who had been detained by Angolan government forces.[214] Some 300 people who had been present at Viana were bussed to MK camps at Quibaxe and Pango and dispersed.[215] On 17 February Thabo Mbeki, in Maputo, reported to Tambo that the 'troublesome group' had been 'brought under control' with the assistance of Angolan government forces.[216]

The crisis was not over. In mid-March, several of the prisoners being held in Luanda went on a hunger strike after their female colleagues were included in the beatings meted out by Mbokodo personnel. The strike ended when security officials transported 11 of them to Quatro prison.[217] Meanwhile, the protestors from Viana who had been sent to Pango were officially deemed to be following a six-week reorientation course, but what they actually experienced was a punishment regime administered by Mbokodo personnel acting with more than usual brutality.[218] Detainees at Pango who continued to show defiance were separated from their comrades and moved to a separate section of the camp that they dubbed 'Pollsmoor'. The hardliners held at Pollsmoor began discussing how to arm themselves. This dangerous situation continued for some weeks until an incident on 12 May. On that day one of the dissidents, 'Stopper' Nyembezi (real name: Mandla Reuben Jele) returned to Pango after having been to Luanda without permission. He refused to give up his weapon and was forcibly disarmed. On the next day he was due to be punished for insubordination, at which point some 21 inmates of the Pollsmoor section mutinied. Led by one Ronald Msomi, they stormed the camp's outer guard posts 'with clear mission to fight, kill and capture weapons', according to an official report.[219] It was also apparent that they aimed to wreak revenge on members of the security department. They shot six of the camp staff, including camp commander Zenzile Phungola, who was badly wounded; the mutineers finished him off the next day. The mutineers then proceeded to open the camp armoury and distribute weapons to at least 37 of their comrades.[220] Their goals were described by loyalist officials as being to restore 'so-called order', to attract the attention of the leadership, to secure the release of the Committee of Ten and others detained after the original protest at Viana, to demand immediate publication of the Stuart Commission report and to force the leadership to convene a national conference of the ANC. The mutineers also demanded a meeting with officials of the United Nations and the Organisation of African Unity. There were said to be nine main plotters, while 19 other people had had prior knowledge of the takeover of Pango camp.[221]

The mutineers held on for less than a week. On 18 May, an assault force assembled by Timothy Mokoena stormed Pango camp and re-took it after a pitched battle in which some 16 people died.[222] Dead rebels were thrown into the same pit that they themselves had dug to dump the bodies of the people they had killed. By this time the camp resembled a slaughterhouse.[223]

A military tribunal was immediately established, composed of Lennox Lagu and five others, with instructions 'to look into the problems that led to the pinnacle of counter-revolution at our camp on 13th of May 1984', and 'to take appropriate measures by meting out justice'.[224] The tribunal began work on 22 May. After taking testimony from 66 people, it found that 'a clique of reactionary elements within our ranks' had taken control of Camp Number One at Pango, killing five and injuring four others. Of the 66 people it heard, seven were sentenced to be executed immediately, and eight others at a later date. Another person condemned to death succumbed to malaria while awaiting execution. Fourteen others were recommended for demobilisation from the army, and 29 were referred to the camp disciplinary committee to face minor charges.[225]

The first batch of seven people was executed by firing squad on 24 May in the presence of other inmates of the camp.[226] It is said that among those forced to watch was the father of one of those executed.[227]

Two ringleaders of the Pango mutiny, Wellington 'Philosophy' Sejake and 'Bazooka' Mbulawa, remained at large among a group of some 17 mutineers heading towards the Zaïrean border.[228] The group soon ran out of supplies and sought asylum at an Angolan army base where Soviet advisers were present. Their hosts turned them over to the ANC, which detained the whole group. They were tortured, but saved from death by the intervention of Gertrude Shope, head of the ANC women's section.[229]

The protests and the mutiny of 1984 became known in the ANC as *Mkatashinga*, from an Mbundu word said to refer to the burden carried by a soldier. The leader of the mutiny, Ronald Msomi, was among those publicly executed on 24 May 1984.[230] The mutineers are said to have chosen him on account of his exploits fighting against UNITA. His real name was Cekiso Hoyi. He was the son of Inkie Hoyi, the Ciskei headman whose house in the East London township of Duncan Village had been attacked by MK in 1962, resulting in the first fatality it ever inflicted.

There were further deaths. Ephraim Nkondo, considered by many to be the pre-eminent figure in the Committee of Ten, which had been established at official behest and which had negotiated the disarmament of the Viana dissidents, was officially said to have hanged himself in an isolation cell at Quatro with a strip of blanket in the early morning of 28 May.[231] But many people doubted this version of events. A couple of days before Nkondo's death, he had been summoned by the prison commander, informed about the mutiny at Pango, and told that he was being held responsible. One of those present in the camp reports that his death actually took place on 27 May, a day before it was officially reported, and that when Nkondo's corpse was dragged away from his cell, it had around the neck a rope, not a piece of blanket.[232] It is hard to believe that Nkondo could have obtained a rope unless it was either given to him by guards, with a suggestion that he use it, or he was actually lynched by prison guards who then reported his death as suicide. Later in the year, when a member of the Nkondo family learned of Ephraim's death, she wrote to a senior official at ANC headquarters in Lusaka that 'nobody will believe he committed suicide because he was a brave and courageous person'.[233] Early in 1985, Nkondo's brother Gessler wrote to Oliver Tambo complaining about the time taken to inform the family of Ephraim's death. 'According to a Luanda source,' he observed, 'Ephraim died on May 28, 1984 somewhere in Angola, but [younger brother] Zinjiva received telegraphic notice about October 26, 1984 and by December 14 had not been furnished with any details about the suicide. The delay is an absolute outrage against

ABOVE LEFT: Oliver Tambo (1917–1993), pictured before going into exile. He struggled to impose his authority on the ANC's external mission. He was confirmed as ANC president only in 1977.
(Photo: UWC-Robben Island Museum Mayibuye Archives / Eli Weinberg)

ABOVE RIGHT: Ray Simons, veteran communist militant and trade unionist, born Latvia 1913, died South Africa 2004.
(Photo: UWC-Robben Island Museum Mayibuye Archives / Eli Weinberg)

LEFT: Tennyson Makiwane (1933–1980), a leader of the ANC external mission sidelined after 1969. In 1980 he was assassinated by the ANC itself.
(Photo: UWC-Robben Island Museum Mayibuye Archives / Eli Weinberg)

LEFT: Moses Kotane (1905–1978), general secretary of the SACP from 1939 until his death. He suffered a stroke in 1968, crucially changing the balance of forces inside the Party and the ANC.
(Photo: UWC-Robben Island Museum Mayibuye Archives/Eli Weinberg)

BELOW LEFT: Duma Nokwe (1927–1978), ANC secretary-general 1958-1969, one of the founders of the intelligence and security service.
(Photo: UWC-Robben Island Museum Mayibuye Archives/Eli Weinberg)

BELOW RIGHT: Patrick Molaoa (1925–1968), last president of the ANC Youth League before its banning in 1960, killed in action in Rhodesia, 1968.
(Photo: UWC-Robben Island Museum Mayibuye Archives/Eli Weinberg)

Robert Resha (1920–1973), former gold miner and street fighter. Resha resisted the South African Communist Party's takeover of the ANC after the 1969 Morogoro conference, provoking a major power struggle.
(Photo: UWC-Robben Island Museum Mayibuye Archives/Eli Weinberg)

Joe Matthews (1929–2010), a key insider throughout the 1960s, became disillusioned with the struggle and went to live in Botswana. His 1976 interview in the *Sunday Times* sent shock waves through the ANC.
(Photo: UWC-Robben Island Museum Mayibuye Archives/Eli Weinberg)

Reg September in 1976. The first coloured person officially permitted to join the ANC after the 1969 Morogoro conference, his appointment as head of the London office offended many black ANC members. *(Photo: Hans van den Bogaard)*

Umkhonto we Sizwe troops in training, somewhere in Africa. Bayonets were of no use against the SADF, but this type of training helped instil a sense of military discipline. *(Photo: Internationaal Instituut voor Sociale Geschiedenis)*

Umkhonto we Sizwe soldiers drilling. *(Photo: Internationaal Instituut voor Sociale Geschiedenis)*

Mac Maharaj, 1978. A former Robben Island prisoner, he was one of the masterminds of people's war and Operation Vula. *(Photo: Bert Zijlma)*

Moses Mabhida (1923–1986) at a conference in 1978. He was one of the most powerful men in the ANC: former director of the security department, secretary of the Revolutionary Council, general secretary of the SACP. He launched a brutal purge in 1981. *(Photo: Zenzo Nkobi)*

Alfred Nzo (1925–2000), pictured in 1978. He was ANC secretary-general from 1969 to 1991. *(Photo: Zenzo Nkobi)*

Jacob Zuma sitting behind Oliver Tambo, Maputo, 1978. *(Photo: Zenzo Nkobi)*

Patrick Mosiuoa 'Terror' Lekota, a Black Consciousness firebrand, converted to ANC membership on Robben Island. The arrival of the Black Consciousness generation transformed the ANC. *(Photo: Unknown)*

Solly Smith, ANC security officer and double agent working for the South African state, pictured in 1979. The ANC became aware of Smith's treachery but allowed him to serve as chairman of the party's Northern Free State region from 1991 to 1992. Branch members were not informed. *(Photo: Jan Stegeman)*

Zola Skweyiya in 1980. A lawyer, he acted as spokesman for the Luthuli detachment during hearings in 1980. He later chaired an inquiry into human rights abuses inside the ANC. *(Photo: Eduard de Kam)*

Joe Gqabi (1929–1981), Umkhonto we Sizwe founder member, pictured in 1979. After his release from Robben Island, he became one of the ANC's most effective underground operators. His family was left widowed and orphaned after his murder in Harare. His killers were ex-Rhodesians working for the South African armed forces. *(Photo: UWC-Robben Island Museum Mayibuye Archives / Eli Weinberg)*

LEFT: Bobby Tsotsobe was part of a military unit active in the PWV region. After his arrest, he was made to point out weapons caches. *(Photo: Historical Papers, William Cullen Library, University of the Witwatersrand)*

RIGHT: He was condemned to death in 1981, but his sentence was subsequently commuted. In 1996, he was pictured standing proudly in front of his house. *(Photo: Andrew Mohamed)*

One of the three ANC houses in Matola, Mozambique, raided by the SADF in January 1981. The attackers were led by the former head of the Rhodesian Special Air Service (SAS), now working for South Africa. *(Photo: Historical Papers, William Cullen Library, University of the Witwatersrand)*

Andrew Masondo (1937–2008), pictured in 1982 when he was ANC national commissar. Massively unpopular, he was removed from his post but finished his career as a general in the South African National Defence Force. *(Photo: René Bouwman)*

Houses burned in the Gukurahundi campaign conducted by Robert Mugabe's Fifth Brigade, 1983. This was the worst genocide in southern Africa since the early twentieth century. *(Photo: Zenzo Nkobi)*

First lady Elize Botha with Mrs Tshabalala, wife of the mayor of Soweto, 1984. In the early 1980s, the government's attempts to win over black opinion failed. *(Photo: Paul Weinberg)*

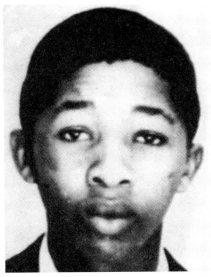

Montso 'Obadi' Mokqabudi, Umkhonto we Sizwe explosives and rocketry expert. Trained in the Soviet Union and by the Irish Republican Army at a safe house in Luanda, he led a spectacular attack on the SASOL complex at Secunda. He was killed by the SADF in the raid on Matola, Mozambique, in January 1981. *(Photo: Security Branch of the South African Police)*

Derrick Lobelo. Joined the ANC in exile in 1977, and in 1979 was accused of poisoning the personnel at Novo Catengue camp in the incident known as Black September. Executed by the ANC, 1982. *(Photo: Security Branch of the South African Police)*

Alfred Kgokong (real name: Temba Mqota). Head of information and publicity of the ANC's external mission, he fell out with the leadership in the late 1960s and was one of the leading members of a dissident group expelled in 1975, known as the Gang of Eight.
(Photo: Security Branch of the South African Police)

Lefoshie Glory Sedibe, known as Comrade September, was related by marriage to Joe Modise. The Umkhonto we Sizwe intelligence chief for the Transvaal region, he was captured by the security police and 'turned', later working for SADF military intelligence. After 1994, he was negotiating his return to the ANC when he died mysteriously.
(Photo: Security Branch of the South African Police)

Thami Zulu (real name: Muziwakhe Ngwenya), a rising star of the Communist Party and of Umkhonto we Sizwe, was tipped to become chief of staff. He was arrested on suspicion of espionage in 1988, but was later cleared. After a year in detention, he died of poisoning just days after his release. His death led to a continuing feud inside the ANC, pitting the army command against the intelligence and security service.
(Photo: Security Branch of the South African Police)

Ronald Msomi (real name: Cekiso Hoyi). Leader of a mutiny of Umkhonto we Sizwe troops at Pango, Angola, he was condemned to death by an ANC military tribunal and executed by firing squad on 24 May 1984. *(Photo: Security Branch of the South African Police)*

Bongani Matwa (real name: Norman Phiri), convenor of the Committee of Ten at Viana, 1984, lifetime democracy activist, Quatro prisoner. Pictured here in happier times. *(Photo: Phiri family)*

Zaba Maledza (real name: Ephraim Nkondo), secretary of the Committee of Ten elected by ANC protestors at Viana, Angola, in February 1984. Maledza/Nkondo was found hanged in a cell at the ANC's Quatro prison in May 1984, probably murdered by his gaolers.
(Photo: Security Branch of the South African Police)

Landmine blast on a farm near Musina, 1985. This was the start of a campaign directed against farmers and farmworkers. *(Photo: Historical Papers, William Cullen Library, University of the Witwatersrand)*

Thomas Nkobi (1922–1994), pictured in 1987. ANC treasurer-general from 1973 to 1994, he was one of Joe Modise's key allies. *(Photo: Inge Goyaerts)*

Marius Schoon (1937–1999), pictured in 1987. A Stellenbosch graduate and ex-political prisoner, he was one of the few Afrikaners in the ANC's external mission. His wife and daughter were killed by the security police in 1984. *(Photo: Pieter Boersma)*

Life in exile was not all struggle: the ANC farm at Chongela, Zambia, March 1988. *(Photo: Pieter Boersma)*

LEFT: Maindy Msimang in 1988. A former clerk at the Mandela and Tambo law practice, founder of an early intelligence network, and later treasurer-general of the ANC.
(Photo: UWC-Robben Island Museum Mayibuye Archives / International Defence and Aid Fund)

BELOW: Pallo Jordan, ANC intellectual and critic of Stalinism, detained by the ANC security service. Pictured in 1989.
(Photo: Pieter Boersma)

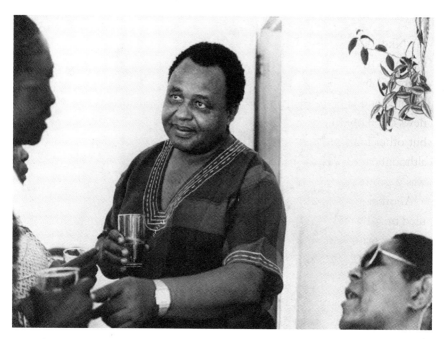

Joe Modise (1928–2001), the most unpopular man in the ANC, pictured in 1990. Former commander of Umkhonto we Sizwe, appointed Minister of Defence in 1994, he was one of the architects of the 1998 arms deal. *(Photo: Pieter Boersma)*

Chris Hani (1942–1993), the hero of the ANC insurrectionists, pictured in the Transkei in 1990. *(Photo: Pieter Boersma)*

the Nkondo family.'[234] Gessler Nkondo demanded a postmortem. In response, he was invited to Lusaka. He was also informed, in words approved by the ANC's governing body, that Ephraim had been 'a devoted and talented cadre of our people's struggle'.[235] Not only was news of Nkondo's death withheld from his family for several months, but other branches of the ANC were also left uninformed of events, although rumours abounded. In distant Tanzania, for example, there was 'a growing feeling of unease'.[236]

Another detainee, Dumile Yokwe (also known as Selby Mbele) died on 3 December 1984 of rheumatic fever contracted in Luanda's security prison.[237] Yokwe had for some time been the boyfriend of Nkosazana Dlamini, who was later to marry Jacob Zuma and to occupy a series of senior positions in the South African government. Twenty-two-year-old Phillip Makou, also known as Ben Tibane, died seven days later, also in an Angolan prison. A leading Mbokodo official described him as 'a confessed enemy agent'.[238] As a result of these deaths, by the end of the year the ANC was under pressure from the Angolan government to charge or try detainees who were being held in Angolan prisons.[239]

When Oliver Tambo eventually gave a public account of the Mkatashinga tragedy, years later, it was blatantly dishonest. Accounting for his period of tenure to the first ANC conference after the ANC's unbanning, in Durban in July 1991, he stated that 'in 1984 enemy agents managed to start a mutiny in our camps in Angola'.[240] Those held for interrogation reported that Mbokodo officers were intent from the outset on proving that the protests had resulted from a plan designed to unseat Oliver Tambo.[241] But this was not the finding of the Stuart Commission, which had investigated the initial stage, up to the dissolution of the Committee of Ten at Viana, and whose fair-minded report had been suppressed. Moreover, the ANC had explicitly absolved the most prominent leader of the dissidents, Ephraim Nkondo, of disloyalty in the letter it had written to his brother.[242] To this day, survivors of the Viana protests risk being tainted by the innuendo that they were government agents when there is no evidence to support this beyond an unsubstantiated allegation by one of the most brutal Mbokodo officials against one of the hundreds of Viana protestors, Phillip Makou. Really, the protests that culminated in the mass meetings at Viana are not accurately described as a mutiny, although soldiers were refusing to follow orders. It is an odd sort of mutiny in which the rank and file demand to be sent into battle against the enemy. It is better labelled a pro-democracy protest, with the bloody events at Pango conforming more closely to the description of a mutiny.

It was remarkable how little of all these events was reported in the press. News of Mkatashinga certainly reached Pretoria, as within months the anti-communist journalist Aida Parker wrote an article in her newsletter referring to 'the celebrated mutiny of dissidents in the ANC's armed wing'.[243] In 1988, a short account appeared in the newsletter *Africa Confidential*, based on interviews with serving members of the ANC.[244] Even this short report caused alarm among ANC leaders.[245] The first substantial published account appeared only in 1990, when a sharp-witted international journalist stumbled on a group of survivors of the events in Kenya and gave sympathetic attention to their story.[246] Former SACP member Paul Trewhela phoned them from England and discovered that the group had written a memoir about the Viana protests and the Pango mutiny. This they sent to him, and their story was published in a small-circulation journal edited by Trewhela and the Trotskyist ex-political prisoner Baruch Hirson.[247] The ANC released the Stuart report, which covered only the initial disturbances and not the mutiny at Pango, only later. One of the survivor group, Amos Maxongo, made his way to England and met Nelson Mandela during the latter's visit in 1991, giving him a first-hand account of the Mkatashinga episode.

Infiltration

The ANC has never made public its archives concerning either Shishita or Mkatashinga, although it supplied some valuable documents to the Truth and Reconciliation Commission and a few scattered papers are to be found in public archives.

The allegations contained in these documents concerning alleged spies have never been tested in an inquiry that conforms to internationally accepted standards or even publicly aired, and it is therefore almost impossible to say whether any given suspect really was a government agent. As the ANC should be the first to acknowledge, confessions made under torture cannot be taken at face value. Nevertheless it is necessary to inquire whether infiltration by government agents was as extensive as the ANC's own Department of Intelligence and Security believed, and what the consequences may have been.

The most famous/infamous government spy ever to inveigle his way into the ANC in exile was not actually associated with MK or with any of the camps in Angola. He was Craig Williamson. Born into an English-speaking family in Johannesburg in 1949, Williamson had attended the University of the Witwatersrand and joined the National Union of South African Students (NUSAS). His background was typical of a white liberal in many respects, although, unusually, he had chosen to do his national service in the police rather than the army. While Williamson was still at university he was in fact secretly commissioned in the police and allocated to section four of BOSS. Taking an increasingly left-wing stand in student politics, in due course Williamson went into exile in Europe, posing as an ANC supporter while secretly reporting to both BOSS and the police.[248] He obtained a job with an international organisation that provided scholarships for ANC members. Through the connections he was able to make, Williamson succeeded in meeting many senior ANC officials, fooling some but not others as to his real identity, before it became clear he was about to be unmasked. At this point, Williamson returned to South Africa and his role as a spy was made public. After his return to South Africa in 1980, Williamson was appointed to a succession of key posts in the security police that allowed him access to the most sensitive information in the possession of the South African state concerning the ANC. In the early 1980s Williamson was as well informed about the ANC and the SACP as anyone in the security establishment. A report written on the basis of his debriefing therefore reveals much about the quality of police intelligence on the ANC at that time.

In his debriefing, Williamson explained that, contrary to an opinion frequently heard among South African government supporters, there was no fundamental divide in the ANC between communists and non-communists or nationalists. A police report written on the basis of information supplied by Williamson stated accurately enough that 'the SACP is part and parcel of the ANC and cannot be differentiated from the ANC because of its power and control ... The two are intertwined.' This document went on to describe how the SACP leadership had 'infiltrated and influenced virtually every anti-apartheid body outside the RSA', controlling the British Anti-Apartheid Movement and the International Defence and Aid Fund. The report went on: 'It must be stated that we have very little information on the SACP, and we know even less about its membership, its methods of operating and its cells within the RSA.'[249] In other words, the security police did not know the names of members of the SACP Central Committee. The security police were capable of insightful and accurate analysis of the ANC, but fell far short of having the sort of information that would have been at their disposal were they to have had a spy operating at the very highest level, as was so often rumoured. Years later, long after the demise of apartheid, this was confirmed by a former operations chief of the National Intelligence Service when he told an interviewer that state intelligence agencies had achieved 'quite considerable' penetration of the

ANC but 'not the very top people'.[250] This seems to be a reasonably accurate description.

Regarding the few available NAT dossiers on the spies arrested during the Shishita campaign in 1981, the best that can be said is that the evidence they contain is unconvincing. The case against Piper Mazibuko boils down to a perception that he was over-ambitious, seeing himself as ANC leadership material. 'His main aim was to work towards promotion,' his interrogators reported.[251] Tellingly, he had worked at Novo Catengue under camp commissar Mark Shope, who had been open in discussing the corruption and the shortcomings of the leadership and who encouraged others to express their views. Faru Nogale seems to have been guilty chiefly of criticising the leadership. The Black September incident was quite likely a case of food poisoning, although at least two people were executed for it. On all these matters the few details contained in those official ANC interrogation reports that are available are shot through with contradictions. The alleged Piper network of spies consisted largely of people from the Mafikeng area who had known each other back home. It is most unlikely that the security police would have allowed individual agents to know one another's identities, thereby contravening a basic rule of espionage tradecraft. It seems far more likely that after the first few suspects had been forced to confess, they simply gave to their tormentors the names of anyone they knew, often their friends and former classmates. It is well established that Mbokodo used torture to extract confessions. Joe Modise used the Shishita campaign as a pretext to send into Angolan exile some of his old enemies from the time of the Rhodesian campaigns.

Yet, there is no doubt that the ANC in exile really was infiltrated by security police agents. This appears to have been predominantly at a low level although, as we shall see in due course, towards the end of the ANC's period in exile the security forces may have had informants at mid-level or even higher. One government spymaster admitted that some people who lost their lives at Quatro were indeed security police assets.[252] Former ANC security officials are today adamant that many of those arrested really were government agents, and that it was only through their interrogations that NAT was able to learn the names of their security police handlers. One of the main suspects, Kenneth Mahamba, in his capacity as a camp commander had himself cast doubt on the loyalty of several talented cadres, whose careers were becalmed as a result.

As far as is known, the idea held by ANC security officers that the police had special training institutes where would-be infiltrators were instructed for long periods was unfounded. Even in regard to low-level penetration, it is hard to escape the impression that Mbokodo officials greatly exaggerated the state of affairs. When Craig Williamson's handler, General Johan Coetzee, head of the security police, boasted to an American journalist that he had agents 'all the way to Moscow', Tambo commented: 'He was right!'[253]

According to former Soviet official Vladimir Shubin, the Shishita campaign resulted in about 60 people confessing to contacts with the South African intelligence services, and still more coming under suspicion.[254] An opinion widespread among cadres in Angola was that up to about 80 percent of those arrested and questioned during the Shishita operation were in fact innocent.[255] We have noted that some suspects – most probably under torture, in many cases – named dozens of alleged accomplices. It seems that literally hundreds of people in the early 1980s were suspected of being possible government spies in an ANC community of no more than a few thousand. Dozens of people were executed. It was small wonder that an atmosphere of paranoia became widespread. General Coetzee may have been correct in suggesting that the ANC had become crippled by the knowledge that the more people it recruited, the higher its chances of being penetrated.[256]

One area in which Mbokodo was correct was in detecting the important role played by petty criminals in regard to infiltration. There are several convincing accounts of low-level criminals being pressured by police officers to leave South Africa and join the ANC.[257] A person caught in the act of stealing a car, for example, might be offered a bargain in which they would be released without charge in return for going abroad to join the ANC. Many who agreed to such a proposal probably kept quiet and hoped never to have further contact with the security police. In theory, a person forced by the police into becoming an agent could make a clean breast of their relationship with the police as soon as they reached an ANC office in the frontline states, but that required considerable nerve, as anyone making a confession ran the risk of being tainted with the smell of treachery from the outset. This was hardly an attractive option when the ANC was using the most brutal methods against anyone with the slightest hint of suspicion attached to them. Political activists could be coerced in a similar way. This seems to be exactly what happened to the ANC youth leader Peter Mokaba at the very end of the period in exile. According to John Nkadimeng, among others, Mokaba agreed to work for the security police to secure his release from detention.[258] By that stage quite a few ANC people and security police officers were trading information with each other, as we shall shortly see.

Using techniques they had learned in Rhodesia, the security police made systematic use of askaris, captured guerrillas who were then forced to work for the police. An askari could either be sent back to the ANC as a double agent or forced to work undercover inside South Africa on assassination and sabotage duties. Many were told to visit township shebeens on the lookout for any MK infiltrators whom they might recognise from their own time in exile. Often, askaris were forced to carry out the murder of an ANC member in order to ensure that they could never find a way back to the organisation. They became mainstays of the main police death squad during the 1980s.[259]

The dirty war that evolved from the mid-1970s in various countries of southern Africa included legions of unfortunate people who were lured or coerced into working for one military or security unit or another, or even for several in succession. For example, South Africa's military archives contain information concerning a Zimbabwean man who was drawn into the war when he joined the Rhodesian African Rifles to fight for the Smith government. After independence, he went on to serve in ZANU's Fifth Brigade, responsible for the genocidal anti-ZAPU campaign in Matabeleland. In 1982, he deserted and headed for South Africa. In October 1983, he was recruited into 5 Recce, an SADF unit containing many former Rhodesians, black and white, and many Mozambicans. He participated in commando attacks in Mozambique, Lesotho, Angola, Zambia and Botswana. He eventually deserted again, returning to Zimbabwe.[260] More unusual was the case of Ronald Bezuidenhout, a white South African who left the SADF to join the ANC and was then detained for 14 months in Zambia on suspicion of espionage. When he eventually returned to South Africa, he was recruited by the police as an askari, perhaps the only white ever to acquire that dubious status.[261]

The ANC, like the police, made occasional use of professional criminals for operational purposes. Perhaps the most graphic example was the car bomb detonated to devastating effect by Umkhonto we Sizwe outside the headquarters of the South African Air Force in Church Street, Pretoria's main artery, on 20 May 1983. One of those found to have planted the bomb was a criminal hired for the purpose by the number two in MK's special operations, Chris (also known as Victor) Mnisi, also known as Jackson Diba. Mnisi himself had been forced by the police to work as an askari after being arrested in 1981. However, in 1982 he had defected to the ANC, carrying with him information he had gleaned during his spell working with the security forces, notably concerning a top-secret military intelligence facility at Poynton.[262]

The mixing of crime and political warfare went much deeper than the opportunistic use of the underclass of losers, paupers and petty criminals that Karl Marx called the 'lumpenproletariat'. From the

1950s onwards, the ANC had recruited in the *tsotsi* milieu of the townships. 'Quite a lot' of township hard men had joined at that time, especially through the Youth League, 'those who were known as street fighters and things like that', Tennyson Makiwane recalled.[263] Several leading figures from such a background, of whom Joe Modise was the most eminent, had come to occupy senior posts in the organisation. After the start of the armed struggle, there were occasional cases of hardened professional criminals becoming converted to politics on Robben Island, like Sinatla Matome,[264] or Joe 'My Baby' Zungu, formerly a member of a notorious gang of armed robbers called the Big Five. He joined the ANC while he was imprisoned on the Island and later became head of Mbokodo in Lusaka.[265] In view of the fact that, during the 1950s, the police had also made use of crime gangs or vigilante groups to work against political activists, the skeins of crime, activism and security were particularly complicated.[266]

It is a standard technique of police work all over the world to cultivate professional criminals with a view to gleaning information from them. In this way, South African police officers had connections with the rings of criminals smuggling luxury cars northwards to Zimbabwe as well as with the Mandrax traffickers sending drugs in the other direction.[267] Relations of this sort easily became reciprocal, in the sense that while criminals might pass information to police officers eager to identify their networks, the same criminals might also pay police officers for protection, forming relations of collusion and corruption. Sharif Khan, known to be one of Johannesburg's biggest Mandrax smugglers, appears to have had good relations with both the SAP and the ANC, and there were allegations in the press that he was paying off police officers.[268]

Once the security police learned that there were people inside the ANC and the PAC with interests in Mandrax trafficking and car theft, they realised that there was advantage to be gained by infiltrating smuggling networks with a view to getting close to the guerrilla armies. Smugglers of all descriptions tended to use the same routes and to depend on the same intermediaries, whether they were criminals acting purely for profit, revolutionaries in the service of a cause, or, indeed, security officers. The most successful criminals secured protection by paying off corrupt politicians or police and customs officials, facilitating their movements across national borders.

In the cases of Zambia and Zimbabwe, some of the most notoriously corrupt politicians were those with responsibility for security matters, which brought them into contact with the liberation movements. It was the security officials in the ANC who often came the closest to colluding with their opposite numbers in the security police. Officials named in this regard by some veterans of the Mkatashinga were said to be favourites of Mzwai Piliso.[269] But the most glaring example within the ANC was Joe Modise.

Indirect relations between security officers, guerrilla fighters and criminals could turn into a closer relationship as time went by. This was ironic, as these same security people were also required to be the most resolute of all the participants in the dirty war.

CHAPTER SIX

War Among the People

'He was very irritable, bad-tempered,' one of PW Botha's many foes, the parliamentarian Helen Suzman, said of him.[1] 'He was not enormously intelligent.'

Botha was nevertheless an excellent organiser. Within a short time of his elevation to the premiership, Botha had imposed his authority on the various security services, always prone to squabbling over budgets and areas of responsibility. He turned the State Security Council into the pinnacle of a bureaucratic apparatus, the National Security Management System (NSMS), that could oversee every aspect of defence and offence, and shifted the prime responsibility for fighting insurgency from the police to the military.

The principle around which government was reorganised was Botha's notion that white South Africa was the target of a total onslaught. Combining the post of Prime Minister with that of Defence Minister until 1980, Botha gave the 'securocrats' – the generals and security specialists who acquired such influence under his premiership – the space they needed to implement their strategy. This was based to a large extent on a simple inversion of Maoist principles of insurgency. Umkhonto we Sizwe aimed to develop bases in neighbouring states from which to attack South Africa and eventually to institute a people's war. The securocrats' primary aim was to prevent this by applying such pressure to the frontline states that they would deny sanctuary to the ANC or other guerrilla armies. They were prepared to recruit or sponsor local armies of their own for this purpose.

Botha and his securocrats knew that keeping their military enemies at arm's length was not enough. They had to find a way to move South Africa from the apartheid system to a new dispensation that would be more acceptable to the black population and the rest of the world and yet that could also satisfy the white electorate. This was a conundrum for which there was no obvious solution, but politicians and strategists in Pretoria were beginning to appreciate the extraordinary character of Nelson Mandela, under lock and key for many years already, paying close attention to his opinions on a variety of issues.[2] Mandela was in occasional communication not only with his comrades among the ANC leadership in Lusaka, but also with others, including Chief Mangosuthu Buthelezi.

Government advisers searched the literature of political science, sociology and law in search of a formula. The best they could come up with was a timid proposal for sharing power between different sections of the population still based on the notion that South African society was divided into distinct communities defined by race. Even this was too much for some on the right of white politics, who would tolerate no dilution of racial supremacy. In the international field, the country's reputation went from bad to worse.

Meanwhile, South Africa's dynamic business sector was identifying black people as a new consumer market. Television arrived in 1976. Billboards advertising drinks and cigarettes were increasingly likely to depict groups of whites and blacks enjoying life together. Government strategists believed that better welfare provisions and rising living standards might help reconcile black South Africans to National Party rule. Viewing these developments from Lusaka,

Oliver Tambo believed that the government was trying to buy off the radicalism of the people by nurturing in them what he called 'capitalistic expectations'.[3]

With these factors in mind, some in the South African government saw the outlines of a possible breakthrough emerging in 1983–84. On the domestic front, the government passed legislation that would create a new constitution, featuring a parliament composed of three separate chambers, one each for whites, coloureds and Indians. Its hope was that if coloured and Indian voters could be reconciled to National Party rule, then in the fullness of time a way would also be found to allow representation for blacks at national level. In the meantime, a new Local Authorities' Act would provide for local elections in black townships.

This was a serious misreading of South Africans' mood. Opponents organised a patchwork they called the United Democratic Front (UDF) to mobilise protest against the proposed new constitution. Known ANC supporters such as Archie Gumede (son of a former ANC president) and Albertina Sisulu (Walter's wife) became patrons of the UDF. They were joined by veteran ANC members coming out of prison, like Steve Tshwete, who had been part of the first generation of MK militants in the eastern Cape 20 years earlier. The ANC representative in Berlin told the East German government that all 11 members of the UDF executive were actually members of the ANC.[4] It was a sign of the times that some activists who had gone to Robben Island as Black Consciousness devotees, like Mosiuoa 'Terror' Lekota, re-emerged as ANC supporters. More than anything else, this was due to the statesmanlike role of Nelson Mandela. Having long discarded his SACP membership, he had taken his distance from the SACP ideologues on Robben Island, led by Govan Mbeki.

Among the frontline states of southern Africa, Mozambique was proving the weakest link. Withering under the effect of Pretoria's destabilisation, its FRELIMO government was ready to reach terms. In March 1984, President Samora Machel arrived in a Rolls Royce at the border town of Komatipoort to sign a non-aggression pact, known as the Nkomati Accord. This was an agreement by South Africa to cease helping the RENAMO insurgency if Mozambique's government denied sanctuary to the ANC in return. Prior to the Nkomati Accord, the ANC had had 'many hundreds' of its people in Mozambique.[5] After the signature of the agreement, only ten people were officially allowed to man the ANC office, and there were probably only about 150 ANC people left in the country in total.[6] In Angola, the MPLA government was close to collapse. East German observers estimated that UNITA had become 'a real political-military force' that seriously threatened to overthrow the government. SWAPO entered into secret talks with the South African government, and the Angolan authorities were pushing the ANC to do the same.[7] Botha, State President of South Africa in terms of the country's new constitution, basked in his achievement, telling the State Security Council in March 1984 that his total strategy was one 'which is perhaps not perfect, but which works'.[8]

Within six months such hubris was to evaporate, as popular protests erupted over rent increases and other local issues in the Vaal Triangle at the very moment the new constitution was being implemented. For the first time, the army was deployed in the townships as the police lost control. It was a perfect illustration of the dictum that the most dangerous moment for an authoritarian government is when it starts to reform.

The township risings

Much like the student rising eight years earlier, the township risings of 1984 presented the ANC with a golden opportunity.[9] The Vaal Triangle disturbances provided perfect cover for the organisation to put in place the command-and-control networks necessary to develop a people's war. But it was above all the UDF that made use of the opportunity as the rising spread, enabling the political sophisticates who had organised the UDF to reach a wide popular constituency protesting mostly over local issues. In some townships, gangs of youths known generically as 'comrades', armed with sticks, stones, homemade weapons and petrol bombs, attacked government targets. They rooted out police informers, developing in the process a horrible new weapon, the 'necklace', a petrol-filled tyre used to burn victims to death. The security police intelligence system dried up. But there were also many townships where none of these things happened. Local patterns formed a national mosaic. Most rural areas remained calm, although there was a pro-UDF movement in Sekhukhuneland, where young comrades targeted especially chiefs, elders and alleged witches.[10]

The media played a crucial role. South Africa became the setting for a global morality play in which public opinion in many countries sympathised with opponents of apartheid. All over the world, television viewers saw images of angry crowds confronting armed policemen. The suffering of unarmed civilians became the ANC's most valued currency. Journalists, South African and foreign, often saw themselves as actors in this great drama, and many wrote their stories in a way sympathetic to the UDF. The UDF leaders argued that they represented an essentially nonviolent movement, despite their connections to activists who in some cases burned people to death or used other atrocious methods. Conservatives in the US, Britain and elsewhere were alarmed at the sight of white South Africa apparently crumbling under the pressure of forces of lawlessness backed by international communism, but they found it hard to convince Western publics who were disgusted by racism and had increasingly less sense that communism posed any impending threat to themselves.

It was in the ANC's interest to portray South Africa as a country starkly divided into those who were for the system and those who were against it, knowing that the majority of the population was likely to side with the opposition to apartheid if it were forced to take sides. By this logic, there was no room for any other body of organised opinion, and after the liquidation of the Liberal Party of South Africa in 1968 there were indeed few organised alternatives. In 1982, Tambo was describing those who opposed the government but did not support the ANC as 'a third force'[11] – a phrase he had been using for some years already. (The concept of a 'third force' in South African politics can actually be traced back to 1960.[12])

The ANC's exiled leadership was particularly hostile to Inkatha, and this made it increasingly difficult for Buthelezi in his attempt to navigate between the two massive forces that were the state on the one hand and the ANC and its surrogates on the other. Inkatha was obliged increasingly to rely on the government for support. Buthelezi publicly questioned the legitimacy of what he persisted in calling the 'external mission', implying that the ANC's core leadership lay inside the country. Equipped with an intimate knowledge of the ANC's history, and having his own line of communication to the imprisoned Mandela, Buthelezi pointed out that the ANC had never held a national convention to decide on an armed struggle, that it had gone behind the back of its president, Albert Luthuli, to form Umkhonto we Sizwe, and that Oliver Tambo and the rest of the National Executive Committee had never been chosen by any internal formation. These subtleties were lost on most South Africans, since government censors had prevented them becoming acquainted with the history of the ANC in the first place. Rather, the ANC and the SACP enjoyed a mystique by reason of the very fact that they were absent. Like God, their very invisibility made them all the more powerful. The names of Oliver Tambo and other exiled leaders were sung at demonstrations and funerals.

In the initial stage of the rising, ANC leaders in Lusaka tried to assert their authority over restive township youth through propaganda and by targeting symbols of apartheid. In his presidential address of 8 January 1985, described by his biographer as 'the most dramatic in Tambo's career',[13] the ANC president emphasised the concept of 'ungovernability'. Lacking a pervasive apparatus inside the country, to assert its control the ANC was heavily reliant on broadcasts by Radio Freedom and on the role of those people who were able to communicate with the external leadership and were also connected to the UDF. By these means, ANC leaders in Lusaka could spread their ideas about what they called 'liberated areas' and 'alternative structures'.[14] Individuals claiming some connection to Lusaka, or enjoying prestige as ex-political prisoners, acquired authority in the ANC's name without actually forming part of a real chain of command. It was not hard to find links between the UDF inside South Africa and the ANC outside. In a series of major trials, government prosecutors painstakingly built a case that sought to prove that the UDF was no more than an instrument of the banned ANC. In the end, every such prosecution failed. There was an indeterminate space between the ANC outside the country and the activists of the UDF and, increasingly, the trade unions who gave their allegiance to the ANC but had no direct connection to it. The ANC name functioned as a franchise, allowing local groups to use it in whatever way suited them. That this franchise was formally, and to a large extent actually, non-racial in nature was due to the influence of the SACP over previous decades.

In some respects, it hardly mattered whether or not the ANC gave orders to the UDF. As a senior security policeman wrote, the fact was 'that they were both so-called "Charterist" organisations, endeavouring to achieve the same objective, namely the destruction of the existing order'.[15] 'Charterism', in the Cold War context of the time – referring to the 1955 Freedom Charter – meant a non-racialism derived ultimately from the SACP, as distinct from the radical populism offered by organisations that had absorbed the influence of Black Consciousness. A brutal conflict between the UDF and AZAPO and related groups was a real manifestation of this.[16]

In reality, the ANC hierarchy was often quite suspicious of the UDF. Security chief Mzwai Piliso considered it too legalistic in its willingness to use the courts and to collaborate with other institutions inside the country. He thought it was being run by factions of doubtful loyalty. He identified a group he called the Cabal, which he named as including Archie Gumede, Paul David, Yunus Mohammed and Pravin Gordhan, 'which is seen to be determining policy'. He thought the UDF in Natal owed its strength to the Indian constituency especially.[17] Tambo, too, was concerned by the UDF's tendency to use the existing system to its own advantage. He urged the necessity to 'abandon all illusions of legality', and not to entertain hopes 'that the apartheid regime will allow us to defeat it through mass legal pressure'.[18] It was the violent overthrow of the apartheid regime that the ANC sought, not a negotiated solution.

The ANC's attitude to the township rising of the mid-1980s was still related to the idea that it had held since the early days of Umkhonto we Sizwe, derived from Che Guevara's concept of *foco* (Spanish for 'focus'), namely, that properly organised revolutionary forces would become poles of attraction for popular discontent. Applying this idea from the 1950s to the situation in the townships, the ANC thought that making South Africa ungovernable would allow the establishment of ANC-friendly institutions in places where the apartheid police and local councils had been driven out.[19] The resulting liberated zones would then become enclaves of people's power that would draw in the wider population. In some areas, such as the eastern Cape townships organised by the remarkable Matthew Goniwe, a schoolteacher by profession, this actually happened. Something very similar to the M-Plan that Nelson Mandela had devised 30 years earlier was put into effect in Goniwe's home town of Cradock and elsewhere in the region.[20] ANC apparatchiks in Lusaka tracked as closely as they could the emergence of what they called 'organs of people's power', meaning the committees and the kangaroo courts that emerged where the police and town councillors no longer existed. Nevertheless, 'we were not able to work out the linkage between structures of the underground and the OPPS [organs of people's power]', one ANC document noted.[21] Even where liberated zones were created, their link to the ANC leadership was tenuous at best.

The concept of an alternative system of power assumed the collapse of the administrative and coercive power of the apartheid state.[22] This in fact came about in only the most radical townships, and these were largely isolated from each other. The government remained in full control of the cities and of the national infrastructure of government, particularly after it had declared a state of emergency in 36 magisterial districts in July 1985. Alternative structures never acquired a proper source of funding, and this almost inevitably led to the emergence of strongmen who could extort money by force. The rhetoric of people's power was accompanied by tactics that were unacceptable to many people, of which the most atrocious was the burning to death of people regarded as local supporters of the apartheid system. According to the police, between September 1984 and December 1989 there were 406 deaths from necklacing in South Africa, and 395 from burning.[23] ANC officials in Lusaka sometimes hinted that necklacing was an acceptable method of ridding the townships of collaborators, and some ANC members, such as the increasingly embarrassing Winnie Mandela, were more explicit still. This risked tarnishing the ANC's international image as an essentially moderate organisation.

For ANC leaders in Lusaka, many of whom had personally suffered at the hands of the police in the 1960s, and all of whom had spent decades denouncing the apartheid state, the township risings could hardly fail to excite. The ultra-militant Mac Maharaj later recalled how he had 'gloried in the spectacle of eight-year olds standing up with sticks and stones against Saracen and Hippo tanks'. Yet he also professed to being 'deeply concerned and shaken by what this would mean for the next generation'.[24] Not all ANC members and sympathisers had even this modicum of concern for the future, so intoxicated were they by the thought of imminent liberation. Ideologues produced slogans such as 'Liberation before Education' that were based on an assumption that a new dawn lay just around the corner.

The cold reality was that school boycotts condemned a generation of mostly poor South Africans to almost no education at all, which did not aid their material chances of earning a decent living in the future, nor improve their sense of self-worth.

The ANC was poorly equipped to respond to the internal situation in any practical way. Its cumbersome bureaucratic apparatus, 'drowning in structures',[25] was not able to install an underground network of operatives inside the country that could make a direct link with internal activists.

Marius Schoon, one of the few Afrikaners to serve the ANC at a fairly senior level, who had lost his wife and daughter to a parcel bomb sent by the security police, was struck by the poor quality of officials he found at an ANC facility in Tanzania in 1986. 'I am continually surprised at the reliance and trust placed upon people here that I would not trust either politically or personally,' he reported to the Lusaka headquarters. 'To my mind [there follows a list of names] are all small people with closed minds. They are arrogant, authoritarian, almost paranoiac in their distrust of foreigners and exhibit a very marked degree of racism.'[26] He reported that ANC security personnel had recently beaten one of the comrades to death. An official had been charged with murder by the Tanzanian authorities. 'Increasingly our law enforcement group are knocking on doors after midnight and subjecting comrades to drunken harassment,' he wrote,[27] behaviour that reminded one of Schoon's comrades, an East German, of Nazi practices. 'I discern a pattern of increasingly arbitrary action and violence, a leadership which is seemingly accountable to nobody (least of all the rank and file), and a large measure of racism'[28] was Schoon's scathing conclusion. Elsewhere, there were continuing accusations of tribalism.[29]

Attitudes like those described by Schoon, identified among middle-level officials, formed the sinews of factionalism among those higher up in the ANC. At Lusaka headquarters, some of those showing 'a clear recurrence of the exclusivist (African) attitude towards comrades of non-African origin' were aligned with senior figures in the movement.[30] On being asked about this, two officials of the Internal Reconstruction Department said that their chief, John Pule Motshabi, had a particular dislike of Mac Maharaj and Reg September, respectively Indian and coloured. Among a group of anti-whites at headquarters in Lusaka were several Lenin school graduates who were in the habit of drinking together, quite often at Motshabi's house. In their cups, they also complained of what they called the ANC's 'torturing machine' in Angola. One member of Motshabi's department was fond of spreading rumours that CIA agents were active inside the senior leadership 'despite the fact that an order was given to stop such dangerous allegations'.[31] This appears to be a reference to the scurrilous gossip aimed at Thabo Mbeki for years already.

The SACP, meanwhile, had its own distinctive take on the situation inside South Africa. Believing that liberation was approaching, the Party was concerned to position itself so that a future ANC government, whenever that might come about, would not be able to turn against its communist ally. By 1982, the SACP had its own units inside Umkhonto we Sizwe. But it still had very little presence inside the country. '[O]ur members inside are few and far between,' Ray Simons wrote. 'They are not organised in a meaningful way or linked to the Centre in a chain of command. Our units in the front line areas depend on spasmodic contact to receive directions and give reports.' Moreover, since the death of Moses Kotane in 1978, 'the African Party leaders are faceless', she added.[32] This was perhaps unfair to Moses Mabhida, certainly not a weak or retiring figure, who formally took over as general secretary of the Party in 1979. Nevertheless, according to Jack Simons, the impression persisted 'that revolutionaries among the minority groups express their leadership through the Party and that Africans do so through the ANC'. Communists had to remain on their guard because 'within the top echelons of the movement exists a lot of anti-communist sentiments'.[33] Seeking to strengthen its own influence within the ANC, the SACP recruited agents via the method known in espionage circles as 'false flag', whereby a target is persuaded to work for an organisation in the unwitting belief that he or she is actually working for someone else. Thus, an agent named Bheki was recruited and serviced by a Party area committee but 'was not told that he was being serviced by the Party. He would have been under the impression that he was being handled by the ANC.'[34]

At this stage, there was no hint of any reduction of support from the USSR to either the Party or the ANC. The ANC budget amounted to as much as $100 million, half of which was for an armed struggle that was financed by Soviet bloc allies, much of it in kind, while non-military spending came overwhelmingly from the UN and Scandinavia.[35] A former KGB officer has left a graphic description of how the Party chairman, Yusuf Dadoo, used to visit the Soviet embassy in London and receive bundles of cash. In the second half of 1982, Oleg Gordievsky claims to have handed to Dadoo £54 000 for the SACP and £118 000 for the ANC. He noted how Dadoo's thin frame filled out with banknotes as he stuffed money into his pockets before wandering out into the London streets, apparently unafraid of muggers.[36]

Kabwe

Oliver Tambo recognised at an early stage that the logic of the ANC's 1978 strategy review implied holding a conference to put a stamp of legitimacy on it. Yet several people detained in the 1981 Shishita purge were accused of having called for a conference, as the Viana Committee of Ten also did three years later: in the view of the security department, such calls emanating from the rank and file were evidence only of subversive intent. NAT, faithful to the principles of democratic centralism its officials had imbibed in East Germany, regarded demands to hold a conference as legitimate only when they had the support of the leadership. Otherwise, they were regarded as prima facie evidence of disloyalty and even treachery.

In September 1983, the SACP Central Committee decided to press for what it called a 'Morogoro-type conference' of the ANC.[37] The issue was discussed by Party units[38] in advance of the SACP's sixth congress, to be held in Moscow in November 1984. Only when the Party had worked out its position on this could it place its full weight behind the convening of an ANC conference, confident that there was no risk of it being hijacked by another body of opinion. Thereafter, it was simply a matter of making the necessary arrangements.

Accordingly, the ANC's first consultative conference since 1969 took place in the Zambian town of Kabwe in June 1985. It was attended by some 250 delegates, more than three times the number present at Morogoro, a reflection of the ANC's improved fortunes in the interim. Although by this time South Africa had risen to a top place on the agenda of international journalists due to the drama of the township uprisings, only the tamest of journalists were allowed to attend. Well-informed critics, like Mwezi Twela, a former member of the Committee of Ten elected by the dissidents at Viana, claimed that delegates were vetted by the secretary-general's office and by the chief of security, to make sure that no dissenting voices would be heard. 'The Mbokodo attended the conference as journalists or catering staff,' he claimed. 'They ended up voting even though they had no mandate to do so.' By these means, the conference avoided examining the issues of corruption and accountability that Twela and hundreds of others had raised over the years. He went on to recall how security officials 'would gloat that the purpose of the conference had been subverted'.[39] There are indeed documents recording that some delegates were prevented from attending the conference by order of headquarters.[40] Numerous officials attending ex officio were given voting rights, ensuring that the leadership retained control of conference decision-making. The Stuart report, a fair and balanced assessment of the Viana protests of the previous year, was not tabled at the conference and remained under wraps. The largest voting block was the army, expertly organised by Chris Hani to ensure that it voted for positions caucused by the Party. The cantankerous John Pule Motshabi complained bitterly that he was muzzled.[41] He circulated a pamphlet known as 'the green document' in which he argued in favour of keeping the ANC's National Executive Committee closed to anyone other than black Africans. He pointed out the preferential treatment accorded to non-Africans in the ANC. Most ANC members in Zambia, he wrote, lived in Lusaka townships, whereas the whites and Indians were to be found in the comfortable suburbs of Roma, Kabulonga and Woodlands. The small number of whites in MK almost invariably did their training in Europe or at special camps in Angola run by Cubans and Russians. He also alleged that the ANC was dominated by Xhosas.[42]

The most lasting achievement of the Kabwe conference was the abolition of all racial distinctions in the ANC, which meant that whites and other minorities could henceforth sit on the National Executive Committee for the first time. This had been the strategic aim of most white and Indian SACP leaders for 20 years. It was notable, therefore, that prominent among those who opposed the motion put to the conference on this issue was Party veteran Brian Bunting. He argued that there was still a need for the ANC to reflect an exclusively black African identity, and that this was an issue that should not be resolved until the movement was back in South Africa. Bunting's expression of his personal opinion is a sign that no decision had been made by the SACP as an institution on this issue. Bunting received support from Johnny Makatini, head of the international department, from Ruth Mompati, from the SACTU and MK veteran Eric Mtshali and others. They were overwhelmed by other speakers in favour of the motion including, perhaps oddly, Joe Modise, the leading non-communist in the ANC other than Tambo himself. Modise supported the proposal to open the ANC completely to all races. This put Modise in the same camp as Joe Slovo.[43] The motion on open membership at all levels was duly carried.

From now on, the ANC was officially colour-blind. Joe Slovo, Ronnie Kasrils and other senior SACP members from the ethnic minorities became members of the ANC's governing body, reinforcing the Party's grip. A Party document recorded that 'the entire politburo of the Party, except Josiah Jele, were elected to the NEC' at Kabwe.[44] Jele too was coopted onto the same body just a year later, by which time well over two thirds of the ANC's governing body were Party members. Tambo was the perfect frontman, since he was not a communist, his manner was disarmingly mild, and he could generally be relied upon to deliver whatever speech was put in front of him by his aides, of whom Thabo Mbeki was the most important. While journalists and diplomats often engaged in a contest to identify the communists in the ANC leadership, their estimates were usually wildly inaccurate. The US State Department came close to the truth in calculating that 'roughly half'[45] or even 'as many as 21 of the 30 members of the ANC's executive committee also belong to the Party',[46] although this was still an underestimate. The South African government was also wide of the mark, since it reckoned that 19 out of 30 were communists,[47] or, in another estimate, 23.[48] Shortly before Kabwe, the fanatically anti-communist Aida Parker thought that only seven of 22 NEC members were communists.[49] Lack of information on the SACP's real composition was a measure of the Party's extraordinary success in keeping its inner workings secret even from its own members. This was key to its ability to exercise – in the Party's own words – a vanguard role, despite its tiny membership. According to the Party's historian, in 1989 the SACP had a mere 340 members in 48 units. Adding on probationers, members in prison and members at the Party school, this came to 494 in total.[50] These numbers seem very low, however, especially in the light of estimates made without benefit of access to Party archives suggesting a total membership in the low thousands.[51] This would be consistent with an authoritative statement that the Party had some 15 000 members by September 1991.[52]

The opening of membership of the national executive to people of all ethnic groups, which had been steered through the Kabwe conference by the Party, provoked widespread criticism. Many of the most forthright critics, both at the conference itself and subsequently, were Zulus. This added to the ethnic tensions caused by Hani's blatant championing of Xhosa-speakers. Within the army command, there was continuing rivalry between Joe Modise, the army commander, and Chris Hani, the commissar. Modise could count on support from the 'Joburgers', a group of his contemporaries, many of them from Alexandra, who had cut their teeth in the ANC's campaigns of the 1950s. They included Thomas Nkobi, Alfred Nzo, Josiah Jele and others. They looked down on Hani as a *moegoe*, a rustic who had been a mere schoolboy when they began their militant careers. They competed to recruit the new influx of cadres after the latest township uprisings, Hani building his personal following among exiles from the militant eastern Cape townships and Modise among those from Sharpeville, Mamelodi, Soweto and Alexandra. The resulting factions were based on both age and ethnicity. Hani 'adroitly manipulated the young cadres' instinctive Xhosa loyalty', one of his lieutenants recalled. 'Modise countered by mobilising the Tswana constituency.'[53]

For the international public, the main point of interest emerging from the Kabwe conference concerned military targets. Oliver Tambo was careful to tell a post-conference press conference only that 'the distinction between hard and soft targets is being erased by the development of the conflict',[54] but ANC publicity material was more forthright, noting that the Kabwe conference 'has been described as a Council of War precisely because it charted the way forward to the intensification of the armed struggle. It decided that the distinction between "hard" and "soft" targets should disappear.'[55] Some six months later, MK for the first time began laying land mines in border areas of the Northern Transvaal with the apparent intention of killing white farmers. After the first incident of this kind, when two people were injured in separate mine blasts near Messina (now Musina), the ANC's Radio Freedom, on 28 November 1985, described the mines as a 'sign of the intensification of the struggle', warning white South Africans that similar attacks would soon become 'the order of the day'. In January 1986, Radio Freedom effectively acknowledged ANC responsibility for further blasts in which six white women and children and at least one black farm worker were killed. By the end of the year, the ANC was justifying its landmine campaign by reference to the fact that many farmers had been integrated into security networks. 'White men, women and youths are part and parcel of the military and paramilitary units of the SADF,' it charged. It went on to claim that the white farming community had 'a slave-owner mentality' that made it a legitimate target, suggesting that farmers and their families could be targeted on racial and ideological grounds. Casualties among black farm workers were collateral damage.[56]

By this time, there was a low-level civil war in Natal and in areas of the Rand where Zulus had come to live as migrant workers. This was partly the consequence of the deterioration in relations between the ANC and Inkatha since the 1979 meeting in London, as well as the result of local tensions. In Natal itself, support for the ANC and the UDF in mostly urban areas led to friction with Inkatha, whose bedrock support was the system of chieftaincy rooted in the countryside. Numerous bloody clashes degenerated into a cycle of revenge killings. Buthelezi himself believed – with apparent justification – that the ANC planned his murder. ANC officials in Lusaka 'made no secret' of their wish to kill Buthelezi.[57] He requested the government to provide him with bodyguards. In response, the SADF established a secret project to give both defensive and offensive military training to some 200 Inkatha members at a base in the Caprivi Strip.[58] This was known as Operation Marion. The Caprivi trainees were led by a defector from the ANC, Daluxolo Luthuli, who had earlier undergone military training in the USSR, had taken part in the 1967–68 Rhodesia campaign and had served a long sentence on Robben Island. Emerging from prison, he had decided to join Inkatha rather than go back to the ANC. Upon graduating from the Caprivi course, he became the leader of the SADF-trained Inkatha death squad.

Inkatha became a plank in the state's politico-military programme. In April 1986, the State Security Council endorsed guidelines for a strategy of counter-revolutionary war emphasising the use of 'anti-revolutionary groups such as Inkatha … as well as the ethnic factor in South African society'.[59] This was an example of the state using revolutionary tactics in reverse in pursuit of its strategy: if the ANC wished to develop a people's war by inciting people in black communities to violence and by distributing weapons among them, the state would reply in kind. In April and May 1986, a series of high-level decisions in effect licensed the security forces to wage counter-revolutionary war inside South Africa using techniques similar to ones they had applied in Zimbabwe, Mozambique and elsewhere. On 9 May, members of the State Security Council received a document signed by the Minister of Law and Order informing them that consensus had been reached on establishing 'a special capacity' to 'set up counter-revolutionary actions'. Three days later, President Botha told the Council that members of this new force must be prepared to be 'feared' and that entrepreneurs of violence 'can be countered with their own methods'.[60] This was quite similar to the blurring of the distinction between hard and soft targets decided by the ANC at Kabwe.

In regard to the ANC, the more it incited people to take up arms in the service of a people's war, the less clear it was in its statements about who exactly the enemy was – in disregard of the dictum that in war 'the first principle is to identify your enemy accurately'.[61] Tambo himself hinted on occasion that whites in general were potential targets inasmuch as they tacitly supported the state and the National Party government and many white men were part of the SADF military machine. But not all whites voted for the National Party, and the SACP provided living proof that some whites were actually ANC supporters. From 1985, some were even members of the ANC's own governing body. In June 1988, two of the most radical, as well as the most senior, officials of MK, Chris Hani and Steve Tshwete – whom Hani had placed in the number three position in the MK hierarchy in the teeth of internal opposition – gave a series of interviews in which they threatened all white South Africans and proclaimed their readiness to turn the country into 'a waste land'.[62] These two ultra-militants knew that a rival faction inside the ANC was talking to supporters of the regime, and their aim was probably to signal their disapproval of the negotiations taking place. They actually lacked the means to make good their threat to lay waste to South Africa. The pair were soon slapped down by Tambo, in an unusual display of firmness. He fired Tshwete from his post as MK commissar, and the National Executive Committee issued a statement affirming that the ANC did not target civilians.[63] On other occasions, the ANC seemed to suggest that the target of its violence was not whites, but supporters of the apartheid regime in general. But what did that really mean? It surely meant soldiers and policemen, but for the most part MK could not get near them. Were all government employees, even tea ladies, legitimate targets? Alfred Nzo told at least one journalist that 'collaborators with the enemy' had to be eliminated. He and others seemed to support the terrible method of necklacing. In the same interview, Nzo said that if people 'decide to use necklacing, we support it'.[64]

In practice, the choice of targets was made by militants inside the country over whom Lusaka's control was tenuous in the extreme. An internal unit operating in Durban in the months after the Kabwe conference caused a bomb explosion that, one member wrote to his colleagues, 'was not well received by our leadership'. He went on to discuss what sort of targets were henceforth permissible. 'Firstly soft targets are white adult civilians who are hostile towards us – basically meetings of NP [National Party], CP [Conservative Party], Broederbond etc. School children is definitely out … If there is a massacre of black school kids in our area, our retaliation must be accompanied by well thought out propaganda … We must not hit soft targets at any time, but it must be determined by the situation.' He went on to advise that 'misplaced attacks' could be 'referred to as the casualties of war'.[65] Bombings of shopping malls, cafés and other non-military targets were embarrassing to Lusaka but were nevertheless carried out by some units. Years later, the ANC explained that MK members who bombed fast-food restaurants 'believing they were acting in accordance with ANC policy, carried out operations not in line with ANC policy'.[66]

Whether attacks were carried out by trained guerrillas sent into the country or by local sympathisers, ANC headquarters in Lusaka made great capital out of operations inside South Africa, implying that they demonstrated the ANC's capacity for military escalation. In the period from 1976 to April 1990, 1 400 acts of terrorism were officially catalogued, nine tenths of them perpetrated by ANC members.[67] The ANC itself registered 250 operations inside the country in 1987, an increase on the 240 in 1986 and the 150 in 1985.[68] The security police noted the appearance of what it regarded as genuine combat units inside the country, at Mamelodi in February 1986 and Gugulethu a month later.[69]

Yet in spite of the spread of support for the ANC inside South Africa in the 1980s, and the growing difficulties faced by the police and other authorities, by 1989 the ANC had still not put in place the system of command and control necessary for the implementation of people's war. 'When our movement called on our people to form organs of people's power, our people responded,' the Department of Internal Affairs maintained.[70] Some internal units were reckoned to have a potential for growth, but 'in virtually every instance, effective lines of communication do not exist', ANC headquarters noted.[71] The Internal Political Committee headed by Ruth Mompati reckoned in early 1989 that the total number of personnel 'involved in the underground' was no more than 222, compared to 386 two years earlier, the decline no doubt being a result of government repression. She identified eight networks and five units with potential for growth, nine of which were composed of black South Africans. Most were involved in propaganda work rather than armed activity.[72] Many ANC personnel inside the country were isolated individuals rather than members of units, and their numbers diminished as the state of emergency bit – first the partial emergency of 1985, and then a blanket measure in 1986. Tens of thousands of people were detained. Some townships came under military occupation. The security forces had virtual free rein to act as they liked. From 500 in 1984, the number of MK infiltrators diminished to 156 in 1987 before recovering to 222 in 1988.[73]

Whether trained abroad and infiltrated into South Africa or consisting simply of local enthusiasts claiming allegiance to the ANC, with perhaps a minimum of in-country training in the use of weapons, activists inside South Africa often had precious little connection to Lusaka. Lines of reporting were confused. Some people liaised with Lusaka, some with London and some with ANC officials stationed in the frontline states. As much as ever, armed guerrillas entering South Africa from neighbouring countries faced almost certain death or detention. Yet such was the ANC's mystique that many internal activists believed that the organisation had a clear policy line that they should follow. They grasped for direction by interpreting known ANC slogans, Radio Freedom broadcasts, and scraps of information gleaned by UDF or trade union activists who had met ANC officials outside the country. Most contacts between insiders and outsiders were so fleeting that the internal activists had no clue of the real situation at ANC headquarters. One activist and prison graduate who spent only a brief period in exile, Jeremy Cronin, summed this up when he observed: 'Everyone used to say "Lusaka says, Lusaka says" and later I discovered that well, this one's connecting with Mac Maharaj, this one's connecting with X,Y and Z. A lot of the factions we [in the internal movement] had back then were really just different personalities sitting in Lusaka.'[74]

Another person who became part of the SACP and the ANC internal underground in 1980, the journalist Gavin Evans, during ten years of fitful contact with outside only slowly came to detect the existence in Lusaka of 'an unpredictable blend of fervour and obfuscation frequently revealing no more than bewildering incompetence'.[75] When he eventually took part in a meeting that included Joe Nhlanhla, he was astonished to witness the ANC's security chief deliver a speech that was 'literally, senseless – verbless sentences full of sound and fury signifying nothing'. On making further inquiries, he found that ANC people 'acknowledged [Nhlanhla's] reputation for incompetence and talking nonsense'.[76] This was perhaps a harsh judgment: Nhlanhla had a reputation for administrative efficiency, and a charitable explanation often used by his colleagues was that his brain worked faster than he was able to formulate his words.

Evans realised that a number of purported activists that he and many others in anti-government circles in South Africa suspected of being police agents, including two women, Olivia Forsyth and Joy Harnden, had infiltrated the ANC. The pattern was similar to that of Craig Williamson a decade earlier, and the even earlier Gerard Ludi: establish a reputation among the South African left as a radical, then go abroad and infiltrate the ANC in exile. The organisation was remarkably lax in dealing with Forsyth and Harnden in spite of many warnings from inside the country. It was after experiences like this that Evans 'started to realise there was seldom a coherent ANC "line" on any issue and that rivalry between various ANC leaders and power centres was intense'. When he met Chris Hani in 1987, he found that Hani's main concern was to find links between his bitter rival Thabo Mbeki and a particular UDF faction that Hani opposed.[77] Evans concluded that there was 'a culture of sycophancy and of placing hierarchy before considerations of competence or even honesty' that was 'deeply ingrained'.[78]

The insouciance with which the ANC initially embraced spies such as Forsyth and Harnden, in spite of warnings about them from inside the country, was an indirect consequence of the township risings of the mid-1980s. Just as after the Soweto rising, there were again large numbers of new recruits heading for the frontline states. This posed once more the question of how to screen them. 'The enemy always squeezes a few of its own people into such groups,' the ANC representative in Dar es Salaam, Stanley Mabizela, wrote to Joe Modise. 'I think it would be advisable for you to consult Comrade Mzwai [Piliso] so that a sizeable part of people of his department are brought to Tanzania. How about sending some two or three tough guys from your department?' he asked.[79] In April 1986 the Department of Legal and Constitutional Affairs sent a message to Mzwai Piliso expressing concern 'about the rumoured excesses of our NAT in East Africa, particularly in Mazimbu and Dakawa'. Piliso replied only that 'he and the President are aware of the problems in that region', which were sufficiently serious for the Tanzanian government to arrest three NAT officers.[80]

Clearly, the Mkatashinga episode had not inhibited the security people. Nothing had been said about it at the Kabwe conference. Yet another commission was set up, this time to look into implementation of the Stuart report, but in essence NAT was free to carry on as before. In June 1986, Chris Hani told an East German diplomat that he was flying to Luanda to interrogate personally four alleged enemy agents who were said to have had no less than six months' training before being sent to infiltrate the ANC.[81] It is not known who these four unfortunates were, but it is striking that Hani should have intruded so clearly on the terrain of the security department. Hani, Tambo and other dignitaries also visited Quatro detention centre, where conditions were appalling. But little or no action was taken until late 1987, when there was a flurry of correspondence concerning the need to do something about Quatro, formally known as Camp 32.[82]

The new international context

PW Botha 'had enough sense', said Helen Suzman grudgingly, 'to realise that change would have to come because the black resistance was gearing up considerably and the opposition of the international community was growing very strong'.[83] He told National Party voters, in a striking phrase, that they must adapt or die. He and his generals were well aware that the ultimate solution to South Africa's problems had to be a political one, and that military power alone could not resolve the issue. Even in the early 1980s, they were considering Mandela's release, sensing that he had a key role to play.

Botha's main attempt at political reform, the promulgation of a new constitution in 1984, was an abject failure. What it did do was to open a political space that was seized by the UDF and the new trade union organisation, COSATU. Thereafter, not wanting to deal with anyone from a position of weakness, Botha devoted his energy to crushing the township uprisings of the mid-1980s. Only when he felt that a state of emergency and the use of exceptional (and often illegal) counterinsurgency measures had restored control was he prepared to invite Nelson Mandela to tea at his Cape Town office in 1989. In the meantime, occasional contacts were taking place between white South African academics and businessmen and ANC exiles. In 1984, Botha offered via an intermediary to open talks with the ANC.[84] In 1986, the chairman of the Broederbond, Pieter de Lange, met Thabo Mbeki in New York.[85] Botha ran out of time for any more political initiatives, suffering a stroke in January 1989 that caused him to lose his grip. Later that year, he was deposed inside the

National Party by his Cabinet, which rose in rebellion and replaced him with FW de Klerk.

ANC leaders generally understood the political dynamics in Pretoria rather poorly. Most believed that the rise to prominence of the generals was evidence of a silent military coup that could result only in a government more obdurate still. They underestimated the degree to which Botha, a career politician, remained in charge until his health failed, and behind him the National Party. Nevertheless, as early as January 1986, Oliver Tambo set up yet another of the ANC's endless committees, this one tasked with investigating the outline of a future constitution. It was manned by the ANC's top legal brains, Albie Sachs and Kader Asmal, and by social scientist Jack Simons, SACP members all three. It was not clear to them whether they were seriously being asked to draft a constitution for a future South Africa or whether this was just a tactical ploy, a document 'for use if we are "forced" to negotiate'.[86] Simons himself believed in 'a prior seizure of power by revolutionary forces',[87] and most people in the ANC probably held similar views, in many cases dreaming that they would one day ride into Pretoria on the top of a tank, as Fidel Castro had entered Havana. The only figure of note intent on pursuing the path of negotiation was the urbane Thabo Mbeki, head of the international department and chief aide to Tambo. The security police were probably correct in their assessment that Mbeki had come to detest the militarists within his own organisation.[88] Mbeki became the main contact person for the delegations of white South Africans who by the late 1980s were regularly making their way to meet the ANC abroad. Many were impressed by Mbeki, who had the ability to turn on the charm in small meetings. 'I remember the trail of white South African notables from Lusaka, successfully seduced after late night drinking sessions with this genial pipe-smoker,' recalled Gavin Evans. 'Time and again I would hear comments from previously cynical or antagonistic businessmen and Afrikaner *oorbeligtes* along the lines of "if I knew Thabo would take over, I'd have no trouble supporting the ANC".'[89]

In many ways, the changes most decisive for the future of South Africa were taking place not in the region but in the USSR. Yuri Andropov became general secretary of the Soviet Communist Party in 1982. Being a former chief of the KGB, Andropov knew the regime's secrets, including just how dire was its economic situation. It was stuck in an aggressive strategic posture based on an ageing heavy industrial sector, spending too much of its wealth on a huge military machine that was unusable in the nuclear era. Andropov urged on his colleagues the need to review commitments in the Third World, where the Cold War contest with the US had become ruinously expensive and also self-defeating, since it entailed support for such embarrassing allies as Ethiopia's murderous Mengistu Haile Mariam. Andropov died in 1984 before he could undertake the reforms to which he was committed. After being followed by another septuagenarian who lasted just 13 months, Andropov was succeeded in 1985 by the man he had groomed, Mikhail Gorbachev, at 54 a mere youth by Soviet standards.

While Gorbachev's reforms held the world's attention, the USSR continued to provide military support to the government of Angola, whose oil wealth allowed it to pay for Soviet arms and to acquire sophisticated air defence systems. In 1987, Angolan government forces launched an offensive against UNITA from a base in the town of Cuito Cuanavale. The attack was so heavy as to require the intervention of the SADF. Rushing to UNITA's help, the South Africans halted the government offensive at the Lomba River before pursuing the retreating Angolan troops back to where they had come from and laying siege to Cuito Cuanavale.[90] Fearing the complete rout of its Angolan ally, the Cuban government took a huge gamble by pouring in fresh troops and equipment, to the extent that it left its own country nearly defenceless: had the US, for example, wanted to depose the Cuban government at this juncture, it could have done so quite easily. The Cubans and Angolans together succeeded in holding Cuito Cuanavale until the SADF's withdrawal in March 1988.

President Castro then increased his gamble by ordering some 1 000 Cuban troops to advance towards the Namibian border at the moment the SADF was withdrawing, strengthening Cuba's negotiating position but leaving it dangerously exposed.[91]

The international players in the Angolan war all now had incentives to seek a negotiated solution.[92] Diplomatic contacts gained in intensity. The top Africanist at the US State Department, Assistant Secretary of State Chester Crocker, became the architect of what he called 'a road show that would run non-stop', an eight-month series of international conferences that opened in London. There, in Durrants Hotel, in a quiet square off Oxford Street, 80 US, Angolan, Cuban and South African officials gathered in May 1988 for the first in a marathon series of meetings,[93] at precisely the moment Cuban troops were moving close to the Namibian border. The stakes were very high; if fighting continued, hundreds or even thousands of Cuban troops, with dangerously long supply lines, risked being stranded. The Cuban advance was essentially a bluff; according to their East German allies, the Cuban army half-expected a further South African counterattack.[94]

With international attention focusing on the game of diplomatic poker now in progress, hardly anyone noticed the visit to South Africa of the German politician Franz Josef Strauss, the premier of Bavaria. A right-winger of robust character, who had fought on the Russian front in the Second World War, Strauss was one of the very few foreigners whom PW Botha trusted. It was he more than anyone else who convinced Botha that the world really had changed, and that the Soviet government was earnest in seeking a solution in southern Africa.[95]

Cuba's President Castro was being urged by Moscow to reach an agreement and withdraw from Angola. The South African government, which was spending perhaps 25 to 30 percent of its budget on security and defence by 1987–88,[96] had been close to bankruptcy since 1985, when Chase Manhattan Bank became the first in a string of banks to refuse to extend existing loans, signalling a loss of confidence. South Africa had by now lost its air superiority, meaning that it would have to invest in a new generation of high-performance jets if it were to continue fighting indefinitely. President Botha told his State Security Council that the public would not stand for further casualties in Angola.[97] Pretoria was under intolerable pressure to withdraw from Angola and also to give independence to Namibia, the former UN Trust Territory that it was occupying illegally. The series of complex, multi-sided negotiations between diplomats from many countries moved on to Cairo, New York, Cape Verde and Geneva, where a protocol was signed. It was then on to Brazzaville, and back to New York and Geneva before going to Brazzaville again to sign more documents in December 1988, before signing the final documents in New York. By chance, at almost the same moment, Gorbachev announced the withdrawal of half a million Soviet troops from Eastern Europe, an indication of the momentous changes taking place worldwide.

The diplomatic deed was now done. Cuba would leave Angola, and South Africa would leave Namibia, allowing the country to become independent. Everyone claimed victory. Chester Crocker hailed the agreement as a triumph for US diplomacy. The official Soviet press agency referred to what it called 'the new political thinking in international relations'.[98] South Africa claimed it had won, since it had secured a Cuban withdrawal and defeated the communist threat, obliging the ANC to close its bases in Angola. Cuba boasted of its military success and prepared to bring its armed forces home. Its victorious general, Arnaldo Ochoa Sanchez, a hero of the original Cuban revolution, was now the most powerful man in his country, with the exception of the Castro brothers, Fidel and Raul. This was presumably why he was subjected to a show trial and executed by firing squad in July 1989.[99]

The ANC was humiliated by its inability even to secure a place at the negotiating table, and by its expulsion from Angola. Desperate for a propaganda victory, it hailed 'the crushing defeat suffered by the apartheid war machine at Cuito Cuanavale',[100] implying that the set of agreements finalised in New York represented the demise of the SADF. For good measure, it claimed that MK had 'raised our armed offensive to higher levels of intensity'.[101] Anticipating the outcome of talks, the ANC had closed its prison at Quatro in November 1988. Detainees regarded as hardcore were sent to a new detention centre under construction in Uganda. Those who were freed were made to sign a document promising that they would not tell anyone of their experiences. They were informed that they had been officially reha- bilitated, before being transported to camps in Tanzania. The mass of MK cadres from the Angolan camps were also dispatched to Uganda and Tanzania. After the ANC's expulsion from Mozambique in 1984, and from Lesotho after a military coup in 1986, its great trek contin- ued. Its armed forces were now as far from South Africa's borders as before the Portuguese coup of 1974.

The aim of ANC policy ever since the 1978 policy review had been to build an underground command inside South Africa that would become the nerve-system of a people's army. Ten years later, it had made little progress. 'What is immediately apparent in an ex- amination of the functions of each unit/contact' inside the country, according to a report by Ruth Mompati in 1989, 'is that in virtually every instance, effective lines of communication do not exist'.[102]

Unknown to Mompati and many others even in senior positions, however, was the existence of the ultra-secret Operation Vula and a parallel operation, known as Bible, aimed at recruiting sources inside the state's own security apparatus.

Operation Vula

The origins of Operation Vula can be traced as far back as the SACP's sixth congress, held in Moscow in November 1984, where the Party decided to expand its activity inside South Africa.[103] Vula itself was initiated by a secret decision of the ANC's national executive in 1986.[104] The organisation's governing body mandated Tambo and Slovo to supervise the operation, dispensing them from any obligation to report back: Vula was to proceed on a strictly need-to-know basis. Although headed by Tambo, Vula's management was otherwise in the hands of leading SACP members. Elaborate measures were taken to hide Vula's existence from other ANC members, and when Mac Maharaj disappeared from Lusaka to go underground inside South Africa, the story was spread that he had gone to Eastern Europe for medical treatment. Many senior operatives believed that so many parts of the ANC were riddled with informers that a successful operation required a special apparatus. Above all, Joe Modise was kept strictly in the dark.

The first Vula operatives entered South Africa in 1987.[105] Their aim was to set up a single, secure channel for communication between internal operatives and an externally based leadership group known as the president's council.[106] Vula's internal wing was commanded by Maharaj, Kasrils and Siphiwe 'Gebuza' Nyanda, with the new ANC intelligence chief, Jacob Zuma, also playing a key role after an important reshuffle that we shall examine shortly. The senior committee outside was manned by Tambo, Slovo, Ivan Pillay and Archie Abrahams.[107] Communications were conducted through a sophisticated computer-based system, and some key logistical aspects were managed by friends of the ANC from European solidarity groups.[108] The fact that the security police had no inkling of Operation Vula until they stumbled upon it in July 1990 was testimony to the efficiency with which it was managed. It was the most effective and impressive project ever mounted by the ANC – or perhaps by the Party, as the ultimate ownership of Vula remains unclear to this day.

Operation Vula, run by SACP insurrectionists, posed a clear challenge to Thabo Mbeki's plans to push on with negotiations. Mbeki was regarded by the more radical of his colleagues as being too close to the Swedish social democrats who were such staunch support-ers of the ANC.[109] Mbeki was instrumental in getting Tambo to is-sue a declaration of principles on negotiation known as the Harare Declaration.[110] But thanks to his senior position in the Party, Mbeki did this in the knowledge of Vula's existence. He played his hand masterfully after his re-election to the SACP politburo at the Party's 1984 congress, giving enough attention to Party work as to chair the seventh congress of the Party, held in Havana in 1989[111] and attended by 49 people. The Havana conference produced a new manifesto, 'The Path to Power', that was strongly influenced by Slovo's in-surrectionist thinking. This document, written less than six months before the fall of the Berlin Wall, included mention of 'more and more peoples taking the path of social progress' – a clear allusion to Marxism – and 'the growing instability and internal crises of modern capitalism'.[112] It hardly reflected Mbeki's views, but his high-profile role at the conference helped him to keep his negotiations show on the road.

Hardliners within the Party were worried by the speed of events, as several confided to East German intelligence officers on sepa-rate occasions. Chris Hani told an East German security contact in March 1989 of his concern that if the government released Nelson Mandela any time soon, it would catch the ANC unprepared.[113]

The security question

The ANC's failure to reformulate security policy after the Mkatashinga episode, such as by open debate of the report produced by the Stuart Commission, was debilitating. Gavin Evans recalled how, as a result of his repeated trips to the frontline states, 'it gradually dawned on me that far from being a unified movement, the exile-based ANC was riddled with divisions and awash with spy rumours'.[114] The security and intelligence department, he came to realise, was itself 'spy-infested, incompetent and vindictive'.[115] At one and the same time it persecuted rank-and-file MK members yet took no action in cases where there was considerable evidence of collusion with the apartheid security police, such as with the youth leader Peter Mokaba.[116]

Hundreds of cadres were living a life of permanent uncertainty due to their status as non-cleared security suspects. Paranoia about infiltration increased the already intense factionalism that had become characteristic of the ANC as a whole. Perhaps the most notorious single case of the late 1980s concerned Muziwakhe Ngwenya, born in 1954. His parents were both teachers who became school principals in Soweto, where they were widely considered to be pillars of the community. Living in the melting-pot of Soweto, their son grew up with little experience of Zululand, where the family had its roots. Muziwakhe was sent to boarding school in Swaziland, where he did well enough to aspire to study engineering at the University of the Witwatersrand. When this proved impossible, he instead enrolled at the university in Swaziland.[117] He left university in December 1975 to join Umkhonto we Sizwe, where he adopted the name Thami Zulu. Trained in the USSR and joining the SACP, the man henceforth known as Thami Zulu served as chief of staff at Novo Catengue. After Party chieftains Chris Hani and Joe Slovo had spotted his potential, he was invited to attend an extended meeting of the SACP Central Committee in East Berlin in 1979.[118] On his return to Angola, he became a camp commander. In 1983, he was appointed by the military leaders Modise and Hani to be commander of the MK's Natal machinery, based in Swaziland. His appointment to this key post was said to have been strongly opposed by Moses Mabhida and Jacob Zuma.[119] Both Zulus, they apparently lobbied for the appointment of someone from Natal rather than a Sowetan.

The command that Thami Zulu inherited was a difficult one. The person who held the position immediately before him had been assassinated by the South African security police under circumstances suggesting he may have been betrayed by a colleague.[120] This was just one incident out of many in the Swaziland and Natal areas suggesting that the security police had an extensive network of informers inside the ANC's structures in the region. After the Nkomati Accord of 1984 had resulted in the virtual closure of Maputo as a base of MK operations, Swaziland became more important than ever, housing the MK machineries for both Natal and Transvaal urban, South Africa's industrial heartland in the Pretoria-Witwatersrand-Vereeniging region. The Swazi police deported hundreds of activists who had arrived there from Maputo after being expelled as a result of the 1984 Nkomati Accord. This left Thami Zulu with a depleted staff while having to contend with scheming against him by internal rivals determined to exert their own control over the Natal machinery. Zulu attended the 1985 Kabwe conference, where he chaired an important commission. He was earmarked by Chris Hani as a possible future chief of staff of Umkhonto we Sizwe.

The rivalries surrounding Thami Zulu were part of a wider power struggle involving the status of the intelligence and security department, NAT. The Stuart report into the 1984 Angolan disturbances, which had clearly identified NAT as a factor in the troops' discontent, had been buried. After failing to table the report at the Kabwe conference, ANC leaders had set up yet another committee, this time chaired by Alfred Nzo, to report on the implementation of the Stuart report. Nzo's commission recommended redeploying some of the most fearsome NAT officials, in particular the counterintelligence chief Peter Boroko, a long-standing Party member, and his number two, Ulysses Modise. Boroko pushed back. Claiming that the reshuffle was a Xhosa plot, he secured the support of some National Executive Committee members, including Ruth Mompati, known for her propensity to defend anyone whom she thought to be the victim of a Xhosa faction in the ANC leadership. Nevertheless, in January 1987 the entire security organ was dissolved and a new leadership brought in, with Joe Nhlanhla as security and Jacob Zuma as the new intelligence chief.[121]

Under Thami Zulu, the Natal machinery continued to suffer one disaster after another, losing dozens of operatives. One MK cadre working in Natal, Thabo Mahlopo, travelled to Swaziland to report to his superior officers. On returning to his post in Natal, he was arrested by the police. His interrogators coolly showed him a copy of the report he had just given, demonstrating just how well connected they were. Mahlopo was subsequently sentenced to 20 years in prison. Another operative, Phila Ngqumea, was similarly shown a full report delivered in Lesotho.[122] A senior MK official, Ebrahim Ismail Ebrahim – a close friend of Jacob Zuma, with whom he had been imprisoned on Robben Island – was abducted by the security police in Swaziland on 15 December 1986. He had been betrayed by the former intelligence chief of the Transvaal machinery, Glory Sedibe, known as Comrade September, who had himself been abducted in Swaziland and retained as an intelligence source first by the security police, and later by military intelligence. September was a relative by marriage of Joe Modise.[123]

Once the new NAT hierarchy had been established in January 1987, Joe Nhlanhla and one of his officers, Abbey Chikane, set about investigating the Swaziland debacle. On the basis of their information, Thami Zulu's number two, Ralph Mgcina, also known as 'Fear' or 'Cyril', was hauled in to Lusaka for questioning. Under interrogation, he admitted to having been recruited by the security police. Shortly after making his confession in May 1988, he died,[124] according to varying accounts choking on his own vomit, poisoned or beaten to death. His wife, Jessica, was also detained on suspicion of espionage. Her case was shocking as she was a Party member, with the distinction of having been the only black woman to attend the 1984 SACP conference, shortly after graduating from the Lenin school. She had charmed those present by singing a popular song in Russian so beautifully as to move some of them to tears.[125]

Mgcina's arrest did not solve the security problem associated with MK's Natal machinery. The disasters continued, with nine MK operatives being killed in two separate ambushes in June 1988 while infiltrating from Swaziland. The security apparatus, now headed by Zuma and Nhlanhla, summoned Thami Zulu to Lusaka and held him for questioning. Modise and Hani immediately interpreted this as a factional ploy. 'The two commanders made furious demands inside the ANC National Executive to know the basis of Thami's detention and to have access to him,' a journalist wrote.[126] They did not succeed. Thami Zulu's parents in Soweto heard of their son's detention and phoned ANC headquarters to find out what was happening.[127] In December 1988, Zulu's father visited Lusaka and met senior NAT officials. They were friendly, and allowed him to see his son, who was fit and healthy. They politely told Mr Ngwenya that they had not found any compromising material regarding Thami, and that he would be released shortly.[128]

But he wasn't.

Zulu's parents complained to the Reverend Frank Chikane, secretary of the South African Council of Churches, who took up their case. Frank Chikane was a brother of Abbey Chikane, one of the security men who had investigated the Swaziland situation. It is unclear whether this relationship had an effect on Frank Chikane's decision to intervene, but in any case he expressed his concern about the case directly to Oliver Tambo.[129] This had no effect. By July 1989, Thami Zulu was still under house arrest, and his father again travelled to Lusaka, but this time was not allowed to see his son. It was probably at this point that Thami Zulu wrote a five-page manuscript, acknowledging some mistakes he had made in his leadership, but certainly not confessing to treachery.[130] Zulu was now transferred to a NAT facility in Lusaka known as the White House. At one point he was able to phone his parents, telling them that he had been tortured. He also managed to get word to Modise and Hani 'that he feared for his life'.[131] In November 1989, he was finally released from detention in an emaciated condition. Within five days he was dead. Years later, his father reportedly said that he held three people responsible for

Thami's death.[132] Two of the three, Nzo and Nhlanhla, are now dead. The ANC's national executive, as was its habit, established a committee of inquiry. The inquiry team found that there had been reasonable grounds to detain and question Zulu in the first instance, but that no real evidence of wrongdoing had been found against him. It also concluded that he had been suffering from AIDS and tuberculosis, but that these were not the cause of his death. He appeared to have been poisoned with an organic phosphorous pesticide called Diazinon. He had ingested several doses of this substance, dissolved in beer, in the hours before his death. The commission of inquiry suggested, without any evidence, that this was perhaps the work of South African government agents.[133] In fact, it made no attempt to inquire into who may have administered the poison.[134]

When Zulu was buried in Swaziland in November 1989, a graveside eulogy signed by both Chris Hani and Joe Modise was read out to the mourners. His death became the subject of a feud between the army and NAT, the organisation considered responsible for his demise.[135] Gavin Evans, visiting Lusaka shortly after Zulu's death, noted that 'the underground and the Party hated'[136] the top intelligence and security people. Thami Zulu's seniority within the military had not protected him from the security department. The enmity between these two institutions dated back to the Shishita campaign eight years earlier, which had set up a dual command structure that left military commanders competing with security officials for control of the army. In the interim, a power struggle had taken place inside the security and intelligence apparatus, displacing the old guard and bringing in Jacob Zuma. For the remainder of his political career, this experience in charge of intelligence was to be Zuma's key institutional base.

Gavin Evans wrote that 'everyone I know who worked with Zulu was convinced he was innocent'.[137] According to Chris Hani, Thami Zulu was a victim of 'paranoia and hysteria about the ability of the regime to send in agents'.[138] The ANC's national executive stated that

Zulu, 'before these unfortunate incidents, had a distinguished career in Umkhonto we Sizwe and the ANC'.[139] Elsewhere it paid more extravagant homage, implicitly clearing Thami Zulu of treachery.[140] Pallo Jordan, just about the only senior ANC leader with a substantial record of objecting to the abuses perpetrated by the security department, and himself one of its victims, later wrote that 'we have never offered a credible explanation' for Zulu's death.[141] Yet, just a few years later, NAT stated categorically, without offering any additional information or explanation, that Zulu had been an agent run by the government's National Intelligence Service.[142]

Thami Zulu's death was not an isolated incident. A few weeks later, NAT security officers beat to death one of his associates, Thabo Twala, in their Lusaka prison known as Sun City.[143] Other friends of Zulu's in Lusaka went into hiding, dodging the attentions of security personnel as the new regime inside NAT flexed its muscles. Unrelated cases of abuses by the security department included the persecution of Sipho Mbeje, who was assaulted by NAT officials several times between 1987 and 1989 before being abducted by security officers on 5 August 1989, together with three other ANC members.[144] In yet another incident, a NAT officer, Zakithi Dlamini, who was investigating the embezzlement of a very large sum of money by people within the ANC, was killed by a bomb at Andrews Motel, just outside Lusaka. Although the leadership, inevitably, blamed South African agents, it is most likely that this was an inside job, carried out to prevent Dlamini from fingering fraudsters inside his own organisation. The ANC tried to pin the blame on Sipho Mbeje, who was tortured by NAT officers in Lusaka.[145] Mbeje's real offence seems to have been his general insubordination. One intelligence officer said that he was accused of having said that the ANC was sending comrades to their deaths for propaganda purposes only.[146]

The security men were out of control. Earl McCann, one of the 1976 generation who had himself served in NAT for 12 years, tried to resign after his wife was accused of espionage and declared by Joe

Nhlanhla to be 'a threat to the ANC'. The real reason, McCann said, was that another comrade had tried to rape her and also to enlist her in a drug and stolen car racket 'for the good of the ANC'.[147] McCann had once been a bodyguard to Oliver Tambo and had resigned with others in protest against corruption. He and his wife now sought refuge in Kenya.[148] Another security man, Jackie Mabusa, died of poisoning while investigating corruption in the National Executive Committee.[149] When the government released the first batch of Rivonia trialists in 1989, and Walter Sisulu and his comrades went to Lusaka, they were astonished by the anger directed against Alfred Nzo, not least because of his reputation for stealing other men's wives.[150] Nzo confirmed his reputation for incompetence by reading out the wrong speech at a public event, giving a frank account of the ANC's weaknesses that was intended for internal use only.[151]

Even before the ANC was forced to close its camps in Angola in early 1989, causing thousands of cadres to seek new places to live, an ANC committee in Lusaka had reported that 'we have hundreds of people in the region whose job is to sit at home, sleep, eat and roam around town aimlessly'.[152] After the expulsions from Angola, the number of ANC members in Lusaka swelled even more. Even the ever-optimistic Ronnie Kasrils noticed their listlessness. After addressing a meeting in Lusaka in August 1989, he wrote: 'I must say that this was the most dispirited group of cadres I have met in a long time.'[153]

The ANC facility at Dakawa in Tanzania was also swollen with cadres transferred from Angola. Many felt only bitterness towards the ANC leadership. One wrote that they 'believed that no democratic formula was possible … We were slaves of the ANC/SACP alliance, as we were not permitted to resign.'[154] Among those transferred to the region in late 1988 was a batch of former detainees from Quatro prison, including some survivors of the 1984 Viana protests. They were all the more popular with cadres because of their history of standing up for their convictions. Two veterans of the Committee of Ten elected at Viana were voted first onto a youth committee in

March 1989, and later onto the Regional Political Committee. One of the two, Sidwell Moroka, had spent almost five years in Quatro, despite having played no role in the Viana events other than persuading the protestors to give up their weapons. When he and a third veteran of the Viana Committee of Ten, Mwezi Twala, were voted onto the Regional Political Committee in Tanzania, the election was annulled on orders from Lusaka. A new chief representative who arrived in Dar es Salaam at this time wrote concerning the annulment of the election that 'the main reason was that the people elected to senior positions of the RPC' were the wrong choice.[155] The new chief representative reported that the ex-dissidents from Angola continued to constitute an organised group. He had no doubt of their popularity with the rank and file, and was sure that if the election were re-run, the same people would be chosen again.[156] Chris Hani and Stanley Mabizela were sent to Dakawa to dismantle the elected committee. This was a clear demonstration that, in the ANC, the leadership tolerated elections only as long as voters chose the right people. 'I realised that the communist monster had devoured the true idealism of the original Luthuli ANC version,' a veteran of these events wrote.[157]

While NAT officials scoured Lusaka for suspects and ANC leaders cancelled elections that resulted in the 'wrong' people being chosen in Tanzania, people actually known to be spies were left in place. One person definitely established to have passed information to South African intelligence was Allan Wellington Madolwana, better known as Francis Meli. Born in 1942 in East London, Meli lost his parents at an early age and was brought up by an uncle and in an orphanage. Despite his difficult childhood, Meli managed to get a decent education. After graduating from Fort Hare, he left South Africa in the early 1960s and settled in East Germany. He wrote his PhD thesis at Leipzig on the history of the Comintern. Meli's communist orthodoxy earned him a post as a political commissar in one of the Angolan camps, and he was also elected to the Central Committee of the SACP. In 1977 he was appointed editor of *Sechaba*, although editorial colleagues found that his heavy drinking made him inactive for much of the time. He published under the names Phineas Malinga and Nyawuza. By the late 1980s, Meli was living in London and had become a hopeless drunk. He was beset with personal problems. His wife left him for a younger man. 'I am writing this note here in London in misery and loneliness,' he wrote to a girlfriend overseas. 'I hope you will expedite your coming to join me ... I miss you ever so much.'[158] Lonely, alcoholic, short of money, Meli was easily duped by a charming Ghanaian who, unknown to the ANC, was working as an agent for an NIS officer based at the South African embassy in London. The Ghanaian, a former army major named Kojo Boakye-Djan, ran a newsletter as a front activity that enabled him to meet Meli, whom he befriended and offered a flat where he could stay for free, saying that it belonged to a friend who was away for a few months. Meli accepted, and Boakye-Djan simply gave to his handler a set of keys to the flat.[159] It was child's play for South African intelligence operatives to enter the apartment when Meli was out, and peruse and photograph documents at leisure. It was through the papers copied in Meli's flat that security police intelligence back in Pretoria acquired details of negotiations between the National Intelligence Service and the ANC.[160] Meli, meanwhile, was recalled to Lusaka and subjected to a humiliating investigation but otherwise left unpunished.

South African agents also recruited the ANC's London representative, Solly Smith, whose real name was Sfofane Samuel Khanyile, a Soviet-trained intelligence officer. He actually owned a share of the company set up by the NIS to publish Boakye-Djan's bogus newsletter as a front for his espionage activities.

Both Meli and Smith died rather mysteriously after their return to South Africa, Meli in 1990 and Smith a couple of years later. Information about their treachery emerged only in the two years following.[161]

Quite why the ANC failed to act against proven spies at such a senior level remains a matter of speculation. An ANC Cabinet minister confided: 'there are people at the top of the organisation who are scared their own links with the enemy might be exposed if anything is done'.[162]

CHAPTER SEVEN

Homecoming

The factional disputes that destroyed Thami Zulu reflected a deep strategic shift.[1] When the first ANC recruits left the country for military training in the early 1960s, they most often went via what was then still the British protectorate of Bechuanaland, which became Botswana on gaining independence in 1966. Smuggling people from Johannesburg into Botswana was largely the work of Joe Modise.[2] His cross-border networks made him an important asset in the early years of the armed struggle. Military recruits from the Cape especially, speaking none of the local languages of the Transvaal and with few personal networks there, were reliant on his Botswana connection when they went abroad for military training. As Modise cemented his position as the ANC's army commander in the mid-1960s, he cultivated a following among recruits from the Transvaal townships, most of them Tswana and Sotho. The underlying logic of the situation favoured the alliance between Modise and his friends and protégés and the Xhosas who predominated in the leadership.

The logic underlying the alliance between Modise and the Xhosa element changed over the years. The Botswana government was careful to maintain workable relations with Pretoria, being prepared to arrest anyone who carried weapons without a permit. Moreover, South Africa's security police built up an extensive informer network among ANC people in Botswana in the late 1970s and were said to have agents inside Botswana's own Special Branch, crippling attempts to infiltrate from that direction.

In the meantime, South Africa's eastern borders became an easier site for penetration after the independence of Mozambique in 1975. Maputo became the operational centre of MK activity until the Nkomati Accord of 1984. Just as Modise's Transvaal networks and his contacts in Botswana had previously been of vital strategic importance on the northwest border, now it was the turn of the east, where Zulu was the common language and many of the key networks ran through Natal. This was a significant part of the issue between the ANC and Inkatha, for Buthelezi had refused a request from Moses Mabhida to allow guerrillas to transit through his territory of KwaZulu.[3] Control of the Umkhonto we Sizwe networks on South Africa's northeastern border was of the greatest strategic importance as this was in striking distance of the Witwatersrand, the country's industrial heartland.

In appointing a Sowetan, Thami Zulu, to be the commander of the Natal machinery based in Swaziland, Modise, Slovo and Hani, the triumvirate running the military headquarters, were attempting to assert their control over the eastern border region. It is no coincidence that the resistance was led by two Natal men, Moses Mabhida and Jacob Zuma, who wanted this key post to be controlled by one of their own people. Underlying the dispute was the ethnic composition of the people running the ANC. Mabhida died in 1986, leaving Zuma as the pre-eminent Zulu leader inside the ANC.

Thami Zulu was caught up in machinations that pitted not only NAT against the army, but also that affected the balance of ethnic and regional forces.

Towards civil war

This strategic shift coincided with other profound changes that resulted from the spectacular economic growth experienced by South Africa in the late 1960s. A booming economy sucked people from the rural areas towards the cities and towns, yet one of the mainstays of apartheid was the principle that black people should remain rooted in the homelands and should stay in town only as long as they had employment. In effect, the rapid economic growth in the 1960s and early 1970s, while hailed by the National Party, was also apartheid's undoing since it was accompanied by a soaring growth in the black population and it created a greater need for a city-dwelling black workforce.

Both the National Party government and the ANC sensed the enhanced political importance of the black urban population. After its 1978–79 strategy review, the ANC concentrated its efforts at propaganda and infiltration increasingly on urban areas, where the black population was growing so fast as to make the pass laws unworkable. On the government side, the growing political weight of the black urban population was one of the reasons for introducing a new constitution in 1983–84. While denying political representation to black people at national level, new legislation gave them voting rights in regard to local government in urban areas, recognising that they were in town to stay.

The social fact of a permanent and growing black urban population underlay the struggle for control in apartheid's final years. The ANC encouraged what it called 'ungovernability' in the hope that areas where municipal government and local services had collapsed, where police informers had been driven out, and the security forces could not penetrate other than in battle order, would become liberated zones. These would then be the building blocks of a new revolutionary power. It was a vision whose antecedents could be traced back to the M-Plan masterminded by Mandela in the 1950s, originally as a way of rooting the ANC in black communities, now as a way of ridding those same communities of apartheid control.

By 1985, the government had accepted that its new constitution was a failure. It realised that it had lost control of some large townships, particularly in the Vaal triangle and the eastern Cape. At the start of the year the State Security Council considered an important new propaganda initiative in 'strategic communication'. Guidelines for what the securocrats came to call Stratcom specified that the state was engaged in 'an unconventional struggle', which could not be conducted with 'conventional and limiting methods' against 'an enemy without rules'.[4] Stratcom was to develop into a key concept of the counterrevolutionary effort. On 18 March 1985, the State Security Council approved a document presented to it by its secretariat on the revolutionary climate in South Africa. Approving a plan to arrest key leaders of the agitation on a selective basis, President Botha said he was concerned that the impression was being given 'that the state's authority is being undermined and that action is not being taken in a sufficiently focused way'.[5] At the council's next meeting Botha announced that he wanted to meet privately with 20 to 22 senior officers of the security forces to talk to them 'about how to fight the revolutionary climate'. He added that the government would meanwhile continue with its reforms, but that there was no question of conceding one person, one vote.[6] A police general who attended the subsequent meeting reported that 'PW gave us hell', and that 'he told us we must take the gloves off'.[7] A document approved by the State Security Council in August 1985 stated that 'there is consensus over the view that the unrest has developed into a revolutionary struggle', although it noted that it would be unwise for the government to state as much in public.[8] The following month, the State Security Council considered an important memorandum from its new secretary, the aggressive Lieutenant General Pieter van der Westhuizen. He informed his colleagues that they had underestimated the reaction of black South Africans to the constitutional changes introduced in 1983. 'The impact of their exclusion cut much deeper than what was foreseen or generally realised,' he stated. He also noted that the total onslaught had been wrongly defined as limited to the communist bloc, and did not take sufficient account of the socio-economic impact of Western hostility to apartheid, the latter a clear reference to the shock of Chase Manhattan refusing to roll over its loans to the South African government and the crisis in financial relations that underlay the debacle surrounding Botha's infamous 'Rubicon' speech. Van der Westhuizen concluded that the council needed to help empower local communities to act against intimidation.[9]

It was in this context that the State Security Council's secretariat opened a file with the title 'third force'.[10] What it meant by the term 'third force' was rather innocuous in the light of the sinister undertones this phrase later acquired. The expression was used by the State Security Council to mean the creation of an autonomous paramilitary unit resembling a gendarmerie, that would be more heavily armed than the police but, unlike the army, would be dedicated to internal security. When this proposal was introduced, the SADF responded by arguing that a 'third force' capacity already existed within its own ranks in the form of the special forces and the Special Tasks Directorate under the Chief of Staff (Intelligence).[11] These units had been very active in the destabilisation of the frontline states. In similar vein, representatives of the police noted that their force also had an existing paramilitary capacity, with experience in Rhodesia and Namibia. It is significant that one of the main police representatives in staff meetings on the formation of a third force was Brigadier JJ Viktor, the founder of the police death squad based at Vlakplaas, a farm outside Pretoria. Traditional rivals, the police and the army could agree only that there was no need to create an autonomous new force. In the face of their opposition, the original proposal to create a new entity was dropped. However, both the police and the army were in time to create units, or adapt existing ones, to carry out the job of internal repression of the robust nature the government required.

Throughout the first half of 1986, the security establishment, headed by the State Security Council, adopted a steadily more aggressive approach to counterinsurgency. In May 1986, the Civil Cooperation Bureau, incorporating special units of Rhodesian origin and structured as a commercial company, was launched as a front organisation for the special forces. In June, the head of special forces received an order to deploy his men in support of the police, using what were termed 'unconventional and revolutionary methods'.[12] The Chief of Staff (Intelligence) set up Operation Marion to train paramilitary personnel for Inkatha, and an attempt was made to create a similar force in the Transkei and Ciskei. Also in June, the government extended the existing state of emergency to the whole country. Three months later, President Botha ordered a treatise on counterrevolutionary warfare written by General Charles 'Pop' Fraser, a veteran of the Burma campaign in the Second World War and former head of the army, to be translated into Afrikaans and circulated to senior officials. This seminal work noted that the type of war that South Africa was experiencing was fought among the people. It argued that the style of revolutionary warfare being waged against the South African state could be effectively countered only by using the same techniques in reverse. Botha wrote a foreword in which he expressed the wish for officials to assimilate and apply the principles in Fraser's short book.[13] It became the single most influential text used by the military top brass.

The events of the mid-1980s introduced a *logique de guerre* into a confrontation that had existed for at least two decades already.[14] The ANC was encouraging township youth in particular to render their areas ungovernable, and was striving to deliver weapons to them. The security forces were stepping up their support for anti-ANC groups wherever they could find them. Having helped UNITA and RENAMO in Angola and Mozambique to wage war as proxy forces, they were now applying the same technique to South Africa itself, arming potential allies among the black population to fight the pro-ANC comrades who had taken control of some townships.[15] The securocrats who headed the National Security Management System divided the whole country into zones under the supervision of local management committees that could supervise the state's policy right down to street level, just as the ANC aimed to install a command-and-control infrastructure of its own. Both sides were stoking the fire of civil war in the hope of ultimate political gain.

The ANC's urban strategy left Inkatha unchallenged in swathes of rural KwaZulu.When Mangosuthu Buthelezi had originally assumed the chieftaincy of the Buthelezi clan, in 1953, accepting thereby a role in the apartheid system of local government, he did so with ANC support. He continued to have a relationship with Tambo personally until 1979 and never lost his friendship with Mandela. However, the social changes that were making South Africa's townships into such political hotbeds were also having their effect on Buthelezi.The new generation of young urban radicals associated with the Black Consciousness Movement tended to despise him and his movement.

Like every other political organisation in South Africa, Inkatha had to decide where it stood in regard to a bulging youth population that, in the towns at least, had little of the traditional respect towards elders. Since Inkatha was so closely linked to the chiefs who were guardians of Zulu conservatism, there was only one position it was likely to take in this matter.When a Durban lawyer and former Robben Island prisoner, Griffiths Mxenge, collaborated with the ANC on one of its propaganda campaigns, Buthelezi insulted him in public. Mxenge was close to the exiled ANC, having been at school and university with Hani and many others.[16] He was murdered in November 1981[17] – it was later revealed at the hands of a police death squad. After the launch of the UDF in 1983, Mxenge's widow, Victoria, became one of its leaders in Natal before she too was murdered.Violence became frequent between UDF-supporting students at the University of Zululand and in some of Natal's biggest town-ships on the one hand and Inkatha on the other. Inkatha was an ethnic party, its strength greatest wherever there were Zulus from the rural areas, not only in Natal but in the migrant hostels and mining towns of the East Rand. It had taken on many of the attributes of a single ruling party. It was intolerant, obliging people to buy a party card if they wanted a government job.

The fighting in Natal was about more than ideology, or even poli-tics. Cannabis was widely grown in Natal, usually by peasant farm-ers who paid their chiefs for permission to cultivate the crop, since chiefs were responsible for land allocation. In KwaZulu, most chiefs were Inkatha members and required their subjects to support the same organisation. These factors became combined with taxi wars, as chiefs liked to own or control their own taxi companies, which they could use to transport guns. In order to control the roads they hired hitmen.[18] After the training in Caprivi of its 200-strong hit squad in 1986, Inkatha enjoyed a military advantage. UDF supporters in Natal took to robbery solely to steal weapons.[19] Control of the KwaZulu police was assigned to General Jac Buchner, another Rhodesia vet-eran and an acknowledged specialist in counterinsurgency warfare.

Crooks and spooks

In 1984, when the SACP was planning its sixth congress to be held in a wintry Moscow, a world away from the heat of Natal, the people's war strategy was high on the agenda. This was the period before Gorbachev, when the USSR was still run by old men who spoke of glorious socialist revolutions and victorious workers.

In preparation for its Moscow congress the SACP circulated its members with a request to submit their views on its people's war strategy. One of the suggestions sent by Party members to the Central Committee was 'that it may be necessary to increase our work among the "tsotsis", gangsters, etc., also the unemployed, to prevent them being used by the enemy'.[20] As we have seen, both the ANC and the police had worked with criminal gangs in the Johannesburg townships during the 1950s. This practice had resulted in the emergence of ANC leaders with gang backgrounds, and it had developed in the police the habit of regarding criminals as potential allies against political opponents.

The SACP's sixth congress took a decision to expand work inside South Africa, anticipating the secret decision taken by the ANC's national executive in 1986 to launch Operation Vula. Once Vula was up and running, its operatives made use of specifically criminal techniques of financing by means of front companies and dummy bank accounts that brought them into the field of white-collar crime. 'The Vula communications read like a banker's guide to double-entry accounting,' one writer has observed.[21] Particular skills were required to perform the technical tasks necessary to run this project. In this regard, an important role was played by Durban's Shaik family, with Schabir Shaik arranging some of the complicated financial operations necessary to fund Vula in the field.[22] A second project run alongside Vula, and often intertwined with it, was Project Bible, the ANC's campaign to cultivate informers in the security police. In charge of Project Bible inside South Africa were Schabir's brothers Mo and Yunus.[23] They reported to Jacob Zuma, head of ANC intelligence and also a prominent Vula operative. Mastery of the intricacies of operations Vula and Bible appears to have been the start of a close and enduring relationship between the Shaik family, Jacob Zuma and Mac Maharaj, all of them with roots in Natal.

In conformity with the advice garnered from Party members by the SACP Central Committee in 1984, one of the techniques used by ANC operatives was to cultivate crime bosses. One person approached in this way was Cyril Beeka, a hard man from the Cape Flats who controlled the supply of bouncers to nightclubs in Cape Town and who, like many crime bosses, also had an extensive network of contacts among the police.[24] An astute criminal entrepreneur like Beeka, with control over territory and businesses, could strengthen his position by cultivating relations with both ANC underground operatives and people from the state security organs.

The security police had been thinking along lines very similar to the Communist Party strategists. They knew that ANC officials were deeply involved in smuggling Mandrax, diamonds and cars. Detectives in South Africa's police force – like all the world's police forces, probably – routinely cultivated professional criminals as informants, and the officers of the narcotics bureau knew very well the identities of Johannesburg's top drug importers and distributors. The fact that some people inside the ANC were involved in smuggling gave a political complexion to this knowledge. 'We proceed from the assumption that the security police often recruited into their networks elements from the underworld,' noted one crime researcher.[25] This was because security policemen were seeking intelligence on political opponents in the first instance, not on criminals. So intent were the police on tackling the political opposition that they had almost no criminal intelligence capacity until an organised crime unit was established in 1993, staffed by officers from the Security Branch. The priority given by the police to politics over crime was an important cause of corruption in South Africa in later years.

The police realised that, by monitoring the smugglers and illicit goods that entered South Africa from neighbouring countries, they could better understand how people evaded border controls, whether professional criminals or political militants. By persuading or forcing some smugglers to act as agents, they could not only amass information about criminal activity as such, but could at the same time acquire intelligence about the movements of ANC personnel. Perhaps they could even blackmail some ANC people into working for them as informers.

When the SADF's formidable special forces set up the Civil Cooperation Bureau (CCB) in 1986, it was with the intention to provide a civilian front for unconventional activities related to the counterinsurgency effort. This initiative was in conformity with the overall strategy of fighting fire with fire; if the revolutionaries were using the population to wage revolutionary war, the army was going to do the same in reverse, using murder, blackmail or any other technique necessary. And if the ANC was ready to use professional criminals, the CCB would do the same. The CCB was not restricted to South Africa. On the contrary, it had a mandate to fight the enemies of the state worldwide. For that purpose it was divided into a number of autonomous regions, each corresponding to a country or area of importance in the armed struggle. Each CCB region outside South Africa was under the control of an officer from the SADF, but there was a formal understanding that internal activities were the terrain of the police, and not the military. Accordingly, the CCB's Region Six – South Africa itself – was run by the Security Branch and military intelligence jointly rather than by the SADF alone. In practice, it was run largely by former members of the notoriously corrupt Brixton Murder and Robbery Squad, and was headed by a member of that squad, 'Staal' Burger. The main purpose of CCB Region Six was to use the police's extensive networks of criminal contacts, that extended even inside prison cells, in order to infiltrate the ANC.[26] One of those who worked as an agent for the CCB, for example, was Cyril Beeka, the Cape Town crime boss.[27] But Beeka was also working for Operation Vula. He was playing both sides at once. He was not a career intelligence officer or even a political activist. A karate black belt, he had made his money as an entrepreneur specialising in the violence associated with organised crime. By 1990, the CCB was said to have some 190 conscious members (and many who did not realise who their real employer was) and some 200 projects.[28]

To coordinate its international activities, the CCB had a planning section that functioned via a front company called Longreach.[29] This was an off-the-shelf company created by an anonymous lawyer, inactive until it was acquired by Craig Williamson, the security policeman who had infiltrated the ANC abroad and had subsequently become the police's expert on the ANC in exile. He liked the name Longreach. At the time the police and the military were reorganising for counterinsurgency war at home, in 1985–86, Williamson publicly resigned from the police and told newspaper reporters that he was going into business. He even made an unsuccessful attempt to become a Member of Parliament and was appointed to a presidential advisory group. What he did not tell the press was that he was secretly commissioned in military intelligence, with the rank of colonel.

Williamson was not the only civilian to be commissioned in this way. One veteran special forces officer described the new brand of military intelligence operator as follows:

> Most of them are civilians, you see. They get a degree, and so on, and he joins the Defence Force and he puts on a uniform and now he's a colonel, or he's a major, or he's a brigadier, or he's a corporal, or whatever. But now he's got status … Being Intelligence they are always secret. And when you are secret you can do all sorts of weird and wonderful things without anybody knowing what you are doing.[30]

Longreach's board of directors included several people with foreign expertise, including a former Selous Scout from Rhodesia with interests in the ivory trade and a former officer in Britain's Royal Marines. Longreach purported to be a business intelligence and risk consultancy. Its company logo, displayed on its business letterhead, was a globe pierced by a dagger. Longreach enjoyed a special relationship with the Seychelles, where, little noticed by the rest of the world, the South African intelligence and security services had developed a close relationship with one Giovanni Mario Ricci, an Italian heroin smuggler who had developed such a remarkable grip over the Indian Ocean republic that he more or less had the Seychelles' president in his pocket. Ricci was connected to some important figures in Italy's own penumbra of organised crime, state security, right-wing militias and political finance.[31]

In 1986, Williamson announced that, having resigned from the police, he would become managing director of Ricci's flagship company, called GMR after the Italian's initials.[32]

For some time, both outfits, Longreach and GMR, worked out of the same office in northern Johannesburg, even using the same phone number. In effect, they were two shop windows for a single operation run by the covert warriors of the CCB. Ricci became one of the CCB's financiers.[33] There is, therefore, a likelihood that the SADF's leading death squad was being financed in part with money from the heroin trade. It may also have received money from the sophisticated financial swindle known as Masterbond.[34] By 1994, when the CCB had been officially disbanded but still had an afterlife, it may even have been using the cars-for-drugs smuggling racket as its main way of financing itself.[35]

As the war among South Africa's people grew more intense, both the ANC's revolutionary struggle and the counterrevolutionary resistance were making greater use of the criminal underworld than ever before. The CCB agent Ferdi Barnard, himself an ex-policeman, an ex-convict and a crack addict, was ordered to infiltrate criminal groups on behalf of the security forces, on the grounds that MK and APLA were working with criminal syndicates.[36] Scientists working for the SADF in laboratories set up to produce chemical weapons took to manufacturing Mandrax. One of the SADF's chief scientists, Wouter Basson, claimed the Mandrax pills he handed to security operatives were placebos, to be used in infiltrating ANC drugs-for-arms smuggling, but a CCB agent testified that Basson had offered him Mandrax tablets to sell for profit.[37] It seems that the secret services had themselves become drug pedlars. The head of CCB operations inside South Africa, Staal Burger, was close to one of Johannesburg's top Mandrax dealers, the owner of a couple of hotel-cum-brothels in the city's seedy Hillbrow district. The CCB used these hotels as a base where they could meet underworld figures from all over southern Africa. Burger's hotelier friend had been deported from Zambia in 1986 during a clampdown on Mandrax-traffickers that had also implicated one of President Kaunda's own sons.[38]

After the SADF's covert-war specialists had been unleashed inside South Africa in 1986, military intelligence operatives applied to their own country all the skills of destabilisation they had honed in neighbouring countries. Yet some state security officers were also working as double agents for the ANC, since, according to Nelson Mandela himself, Operation Bible 'managed to infiltrate the government's intelligence apparatus at a number of levels'.[39] On the ANC's side, the Mbokodo security officers who were so vindictive in punishing minor offenders were also among the most corrupt people in the organisation. Many of them gave up on political activity entirely. 'There are people who have made it a practice that they don't take part in the political life of the movement,' the ANC's Regional Political Committee in Zambia reported. 'The main culprits here are the comrades belonging to the Security department and certain heads of departments at Headquarters.'[40]

As each side in the war tried to infiltrate the other, and both tried to use South Africa's township underworld for their purposes, exceptionally interesting possibilities opened up for intelligent and ambitious criminals. They could gain influence in the security services of the apartheid state and also in the networks of the ANC, the organisation that might be in power in the not-too-distant future. Politics, state security and crime did more than rub shoulders. They went drinking and whoring together. Policemen ceased simply to monitor criminals, but even went into business with them. Relationships of this sort could become extremely complex as all these factors acted in combination.

The patterns of illegality throughout southern Africa became wider as the SADF took to waging covert and clandestine wars following its decision to go into Angola in 1975. After its failure to

prevent the MPLA taking power, the SADF concentrated on supporting its rival, UNITA. To compensate for the arms and other help it
gave, the SADF wanted something in return. UNITA had diamonds and
control over some of the wildest country in Africa, thick with game.
This was how the SADF got into the business of importing ivory
and rhino horn from animals poached in Angola mainly, but also in
Mozambique. Once military intelligence had set up the front companies to transport these cargoes, independent ivory traders made
use of the same network, so that by the late 1970s Johannesburg
had emerged as the wholesale hub of this criminal trade.[41] It is said
that some ANC people smuggled rhino horn out of Zambia that was
marketed down the same channel,[42] meaning that, indirectly at least,
they were doing business with the SADF.

The SADF's covert-war specialists and their colleagues from other
departments of state collaborated with civilians to set up dozens or
even hundreds of front companies that conducted business in a variety of sectors, legal and illegal. They drew into their orbit large
numbers of both state employees and workers in the private sector
– truck drivers and aircraft pilots, but also accountants, lawyers and
bankers. Their networks spread into the frontline states and even
overseas.

In the context of the complex dirty wars being fought in various parts of southern Africa, the smuggling of high-value, low-bulk
goods such as drugs, currency and diamonds, or of cars, easily trans-
portable by their nature, became the medium wherein professional
criminals, sleazy politicians, corrupt guerrilla leaders and policemen
all developed common interests, as did those who gave strategic direction to the armed struggle and counterinsurgency. A police detective later recalled: 'we all used the same routes, the smugglers, the
South African intelligence services all of them together and the ANC.
They used to smuggle their weapons on those routes, your smugglers
would obviously bring in the drugs and stolen vehicles in the night
and we used these routes to, you know, catch up on them.'[43]

A few operators from leading international criminal networks took up residence in some of the nominally independent homelands, where they could do business with apartheid spies and sanctions-busters outside South African jurisdiction and away from the attention of journalists, who rarely paid much attention to goings-on in Mmabatho or Bisho. Bophuthatswana became home to the Russian-Israeli gangster Shabtai Kalmanovitch, who became a close associate of President Lucas Mangope. Kalmanovitch had emigrated from the USSR to Israel in the 1970s and retained contacts in Soviet intelligence as well as with leading underworld figures in many countries.[44] He had smuggling interests in diamonds and heroin, and later gained the dubious distinction of being convicted in Israel of spying on behalf of the KGB. After serving his sentence, he returned to Moscow, where he was murdered in 2009. Another major operator attracted to the homelands was the convicted money launderer Vito Palazzolo, an Italian national jailed in Switzerland in the wake of the infamous US 'pizza connection' heroin case. He absconded from prison, was brought to South Africa by a South African politician and introduced to Lennox Sebe, President of Ciskei, who offered him a post as a government representative. Palazzolo began working for a bank in Bisho in 1986.[45]

In Lusaka, 'the involvement of our people, as reported by the security comrades with drug peddlers and car racketeers goes unabated', the ANC's Regional Political Committee reported.[46] The same committee proposed launching an anti-corruption campaign but found that the office of the treasurer-general was uninterested, as was NAT.[47] Even mid-level ANC people could see that 'the free and uncontrolled trafficking of drugs and car racketeers' was flourishing within their organisation. Pretoria's top expert on the ANC, Craig Williamson, wrote a mischievous book chapter noting that the ANC was 'suffering from ideological inertia, corruption, financial mismanagement, disillusionment, abuses of human rights (especially sexual)'. He also observed that 'many MK cadres spend much of their time smuggling

Mandrax and stolen cars'.[48] This was quite accurate, and he was well placed to know. But it was a cynical observation, as Williamson, being a director of Longreach, was himself deeply involved in crime in the guise of covert operations.

By the late 1980s, many people in the state security sector were preparing for the power shift that clearly lay ahead. At the strategic level, it has been reported that, in 1988, the NIS chief Niel Barnard presented a paper to the secretariat of the State Security Council out of which a two-pronged strategy emerged. The ANC would be unbanned and negotiations would begin. At the same time, the ANC would be subject to destabilisation.[49] Seasoned apartheid operatives, who had seen the change from white to black rule in Mozambique, Angola, Zimbabwe and now Namibia, were looking for niches where they could at least guarantee their own personal future. Some became intent on building up their own bank accounts. Some developed lines of communication with the ANC. Rivalry between the various state security forces, always latent, became sharper as operatives scrambled to assure their own interests.

Immediately after his ascension to the top job in 1989, the new State President, FW de Klerk, authorised the National Intelligence Service to spy on the military.[50] A senior NIS official made the extraordinary claim that it was only at this point that it discovered the existence of the Civil Cooperation Bureau,[51] so jealous were rival services of their turf.

Ever since 1948, successive heads of government had been associated with one or other of the rival security forces. Vorster had had the security police and BOSS. Botha had the military. De Klerk gave a leading role to the NIS, arguing that he needed to exert some control over the security networks spawned by his militarist predecessor. This further stoked turf battles between rival networks at the very time they were in any event being privatised.

South Africa was the home of so many networks, agencies and factions, spying on each other and spinning information for private or public consumption, that it was impossible to be sure in any given context precisely who was manipulating whom. It was a wilderness of mirrors – to use a phrase coined by the legendary CIA counter-intelligence chief James Jesus Angleton, a friend of South Africa's own Hendrik van den Bergh.

Unbanning: the war's climax

When De Klerk succeeded Botha as State President in September 1989, he immediately came under pressure from the US, at that point the world's only remaining superpower, to take further steps to dismantle apartheid. Two months later, the Berlin Wall came down. De Klerk was quick to see the opportunity this created. He calculated that he could catch the ANC by surprise by declaring it legal, and, by releasing Mandela, buy himself acres of political space with this daring move.

When the ANC was duly unbanned and Mandela released from prison in February 1990, the attention given to South Africa worldwide was unprecedented. De Klerk was admired on every continent. The ANC no longer had a superpower sponsor. It was under huge pressure to respond with a big gesture of its own, perhaps by calling for the lifting of economic sanctions or announcing the end of its armed struggle. Yet there were many in the ANC who were appalled by any such suggestion. The Vula operatives working in the shadows were hardline insurrectionists. They reasoned that the possession of an armed force on the ground remained essential, since at the very least it would provide protection for ANC communities against aggression by the security forces and Inkatha. For the Vula people, negotiating and making war could go hand in hand.

Since some of the ANC's most senior people did not even know of Operation Vula's existence, it came as a great embarrassment to the organisation when Vula was uncovered by the police in July 1990.

This came about by pure chance, when a police askari in Natal spotted a known MK guerrilla, causing the police to investigate and to find documents with details of the underground network. They arrested some leading Vula figures, including Mac Maharaj. To Maharaj's disgust, the ANC leadership kept its distance and left him in the hands of the security police.

The embarrassment resulting from Vula's exposure pushed the ANC into signing, in August 1990, a document known as the Pretoria Minute, formally suspending its armed struggle. An ANC leader with the difficult task of explaining the suspension of hostilities to an uncomprehending public told a meeting that 'we decided to unilaterally suspend [the armed struggle] on condition that all obstacles were addressed'. He added that, in international circles, persisting with the armed struggle was seen as 'an obstacle on our side'.[52] The ANC was in considerable disarray, as Mandela, Thabo Mbeki and others were leading negotiations even while some of their colleagues were holding out for a military outcome, the surviving Vula operatives remaining intent on arming units in the townships. Joe Slovo, for example, was both a negotiator and a Vula operative. Chris Hani, meanwhile, on his own initiative established himself in the Transkei homeland, where he had been born and bred, and was busily recruiting new blood for MK and sending people for military training in Tanzania, Uganda and Ethiopia. Some of the new recruits are said to have been used to fight for the Ugandan government against rebel forces, just as an earlier generation had fought for the Angolan government against its domestic enemy. Chris Hani 'is extremely popular with the rank and file of the MK', the security police reported, 'and particularly with the young MK officers, who hero-worship him'.[53]

It was in these circumstances, after an escalation of fighting in the Natal Midlands in March 1990 and a spate of random shootings in the Vaal area and later on the East Rand and killings on trains running between Soweto and Johannesburg,[54] that Nelson Mandela first made public mention of what he called a 'third force'. He hinted that a mysterious third party, distinct from the ANC and the National Party but presumably including members of the security forces, lay behind much of this violence. President de Klerk denied Mandela's allegations,[55] but occasional evidence of collusion by members of the security forces in popular violence chipped away at De Klerk's international standing, especially when a former security policeman revealed that the police were giving secret help to Inkatha.[56] Mandela's massive international prestige inclined many people outside South Africa to take all his accusations at face value. It was not long before the government side was in only slightly less disarray than the ANC, with some military men worried that De Klerk was relaxing his guard and livid that they were being spied on by the NIS. As the months went by, De Klerk slowly lost his sheen. The government's position grew weaker. Many police officers became bitter that De Klerk hadn't pressed for a blanket amnesty for them when he still had the power to do so.

In later years, many former security chiefs came to believe that De Klerk played his hand badly by failing to use his trump card – an army that remained intact and coherent – to maximum political effect. To this day, many white South Africans wonder what happened exactly to cause the National Party to misplay a hand that had been quite strong when formal talks began in 1990. Above all, De Klerk had failed to take account of two major factors.

The first major development that De Klerk did not foresee was that, once he had signalled that there were to be free elections for the whole adult population within the foreseeable future, his government was seen to be on the way out no matter how much it protested that it could still put together a winning coalition. Having announced that it would be superseded by something else, it lost much of its authority. When the National Party entered on the period of transition, the inclination of many of its strategists – although perhaps not De Klerk personally, for whom speed was a key asset – was to play a long game, hoping gradually to wear down the adversary while basking in their own new-found international respectability. But the balance of forces changed in 1991 and 1992 in ways that National Party strategists, informed by the analysts of the National Intelligence Service and the Broederbond, had not expected. South Africa seemed to be slipping into anarchy as the security forces were obliged to loosen their grip of steel. Many international observers were inclined to believe the ANC's claim that the government was itself complicit in the violence. Particularly after the murder of Chris Hani in 1993, the country was perilously close to the edge of a deep canyon of violence.

Increasingly, what kept the country going until it reached the safety of its first truly national election in 1994 was the moral authority of Nelson Mandela. He functioned as an unofficial head of state alongside the legal one, FW de Klerk. Mandela faced a huge task in overseeing the ANC's negotiations while also striving to keep the country as a whole intact. One young man recalled going to see Mandela speak for the first time in 1990, at a time when 'young people ran riot, killing and necklacing in Mandela's name. That year, 1990, I had seen a young woman, whom we all knew as a comrade in my township, being forced to drink petrol, doused with it and then set alight because someone had seen her inside a police Casspir and therefore identified her as an informer.'[57] To his disappointment, he heard Mandela lecture his young listeners on the importance of education and order them to go back to school. When this particular radical got to university, he and his friends were outraged by Mandela's concern to allay the fears of white people about their future. They thought that national reconciliation was 'meaningless to black people'. They swore that once Mandela was out of office, they would shake up the liberation movement and 'reverse the rot and corruption we saw setting in'.[58] They were restrained only by respect for the old man, Madiba.

In view of the ANC's problems, including its difficulty in justifying its negotiating position to some of its more radical supporters, it is at first sight puzzling that the outcome of negotiations should have been so unfavourable to the National Party, which still enjoyed overwhelming military power.[59] It seems that the Nationalists, accustomed to being in government, overestimated their ability to manage the process. As the political scientist Stuart Kaufman writes, this was simply a reflection of demographic reality: 'In an age of mass politics, no racial or ethnic minority can rule indefinitely over an excluded 85%.'[60]

A second development that De Klerk apparently failed to foresee was that one of the consequences of the collapse of communism was to remove any impediment to the US government transferring its support to the ANC. When Mandela visited the US in 1990, America simply fell in love with him. He instantly became the world's favourite politician. More than ever, the ANC acquired a saintly image in the US, where it seemed like a replay of the civil rights movement, with Mandela standing in for Martin Luther King, Jr. Not just that, but Mandela became a hugely successful fundraiser for the ANC. Pop stars, celebrities and businesspeople would pay a fortune for a photo op.

In the early years of the transition, many international commentators and some South African ones thought of the process of transition as an extended political negotiation led by two honest men, De Klerk and Mandela, that risked being sabotaged by the mysterious third force, assumed to consist of right-wing zealots bent on sabotaging the political progress. This was consistent with a view of the demise of apartheid and the liberation of South Africa as an uplifting story of the triumph of reason over violence and fanaticism. It translated well into television sound bites. It was the underlying assumption of the Nobel committee that awarded its annual Peace Prize to the two men in 1993. It is implicit in the excellent accounts of the transition published by journalists who followed the peace talks closely.[61]

Looking back, it is perhaps more striking now than it seemed at the time how, as in many late-twentieth-century wars, negotiations and fighting continued at the same time. In fact, while the years from 1990 to 1994 witnessed a political transition from apartheid, it was also the most violent period of the whole conflict, with some 14 000 South Africans losing their lives in politically-related violence. The war for South Africa, previously fought most ferociously outside the country's borders, now enveloped South Africa itself.[62] For four anguished years, hardly a week went by without a new crisis. 'It is our conviction,' Chris Hani wrote, 'that the National Party government is pursuing a twin-track strategy. This strategy involves negotiating with its major political opponent, the ANC and allies, and at the same time deliberate destabilisation, including violent destabilisation of our forces.'[63] Occasional revelations seemed to bear this out. Exactly the same charge could be made against the ANC. As one journalist close to the ANC noted, 'a thesis has evolved in ANC ranks arguing for the negotiating process itself to be used to gradually but consistently strip the apartheid government of its control over the institutions of state and over society generally, rather than expecting Pretoria to hand over power in one go at the conclusion of the negotiating process.'[64] After the public revelation of the Vula project in 1990, many Vula operatives remained undiscovered. They concentrated on arming what they called 'self-defence units' in the townships. Mandela himself later confirmed, in regard to Vula, that 'we did supply armed and political support for the protection of our communities'.[65] Most of these self-defence units were ill disciplined, and some were indistinguishable from criminal gangs. The ANC's National Executive Committee is reported to have held an inquiry that revealed the involvement of some units in crime,[66] as was confirmed by Tokyo Sexwale, ANC chairman in Gauteng.[67] One self-defence unit led by a member of the ANC Youth League was said to be sending some of its robbery proceeds to ANC headquarters at Shell House.[68] On the government side, the police colonel Eugene de Kock and other counterinsurgency specialists were involved in similar activities, distributing weapons especially to Inkatha.[69] The institutional organisers of violence claimed that they were simply helping people defend themselves against the other side. In the present state of research, it remains unclear which of them was on the offensive at any given moment, and how high up the political hierarchy the responsibility went.

There was an uncanny symmetry about developments in both the ANC and the state forces during the last decade of the war. This is unsurprising, as opposing forces in all wars end up resembling one another if only because they have to find a common ground on which to fight. The aim in the long struggle for South Africa was to win the will of the people. Increasingly, the key was control of the major centres of black population, which lacked a long history of stable government. No doubt this was the reason that contending sides in the struggle consistently sought allies among the criminal milieu in the townships. By the mid-1980s, many black areas were under the effective control of local strongmen variously identified as revolutionaries, crime bosses and warlords, whom strategists on each side of the war believed they could use to advantage to swing local populations to their side. Operation Vula began life at almost exactly the same time that the State Security Council began its search for a third force and launched the CCB. They both made contacts in the same criminal milieu, sometimes even with the same individuals.

Security men on each side were sniffing each other, like dogs in search of a mate, before the politicians had begun formal talks. Even before the transition process had officially started, each was recruiting agents in the other's camp. Each side had the means to blackmail the other. The most dangerous moment in the transition came with the murder of Chris Hani in 1993, when a full-scale race war briefly threatened. An ANC security asset codenamed Ramon is reported to have heard rumours of the Hani murder plot beforehand, and to have informed SADF military intelligence; not only was 'Ramon' in touch with multiple agencies, but he was also the son-in-law of none other than Sharif Khan, the legendary Mandrax king of Johannesburg,[70] who died in 1995. A former CCB operative, Eugene Riley, also gave warning of the impending assassination. He was murdered soon afterwards.[71]

Reconciliation of a special type

While secret policemen and their sworn enemies in the ANC swapped information in search of tactical advantage, by this very action they were also building new strategic relationships that were to endure and even flourish in the new South Africa.

There are numerous examples of how the security men from both sides got together in often the most surprising ways and were joined by figures from the netherworlds of corruption and organised crime. In 1986, Martin Dolinchek, a security operative who had worked for BOSS and its successor organisations before being arrested in the Seychelles for his part in a coup attempt, joined the ANC.[72] He was among the first of a steady stream. After 1994, the new government renamed its domestic security organ the National Intelligence Agency (NIA), merging some 2 000 personnel from the apartheid-era NIS (itself the renamed BOSS) with 400 from the ANC's NAT and others from old homeland agencies or the PAC.[73] This brought old enemies together en masse. Former death squad commander Dirk Coetzee, another who sought refuge with the ANC, was one of those who went on to work for the post-apartheid NIA before leaving to join a company run by Cyril Beeka.[74] Riaan Stander, a CCB man, also joined the NIA and worked with a former Umkhonto we Sizwe official to run a special unit established to track down the millions of rands reportedly stashed away in overseas bank accounts by apartheid apparatchiks fearful of the future. After two men described as NIA special agents but disavowed by the NIA appeared in court in Johannesburg on charges of stealing nearly R100 million, Stander's partner was suspended pending further investigations.[75] The journalist who got this story, a woman, later married the former head of one of the CCB's overseas regions.

A high-ranking NIA operative, the general manager of the organisation's surveillance unit, was a former commander of the Quatro camp where ANC dissidents had been tortured in the 1980s. In 2000, the ghost of Timothy Seremane, the camp commander known as Kenneth Mahamba arrested at the height of the Shishita purge, briefly resurfaced. His brother Joe, a leading figure in the Democratic Alliance, accused this NIA chieftain of being implicated in the death of his brother at Quatro.[76] The NIA man was reported to be under investigation in connection with the use of money from a special account to pay for luxury cars, some of which were registered in the name of a soccer administrator alleged to have extensive underworld connections. The self-same soccer boss is said to have been a key player in the Mandrax trade while he was living in Lusaka in the 1980s. Meanwhile, some of the old SADF front companies, originally set up to smuggle ivory and rhino horn, remained in business after 1994 importing Mandrax from Zambia and, increasingly, cocaine from Brazil through networks that had become thoroughly privatised. Cape Town had reportedly become a useful outpost for the Sicilian mafia, where fugitives from justice could hide out in a congenial environment.[77]

The former Operation Bible operator Mo Shaik was another cloak-and-dagger man who went on to higher things, becoming head of the foreign intelligence service under Jacob Zuma. He had retained from his Operation Bible days a computer disk of possible security moles that could still be of use to embarrass people.[78] It was used to considerable effect.

The list of possible examples of security officers from rival formations who embraced each other is endless. In the 1980s, they had infiltrated each other's organisations and betrayed their new acquaintants, prepared to lie and to kill, but increasingly they had also tended to collude with one another. Security elites, once bitter rivals, assimilated each other. Former enemies became colleagues and even friends or business partners. As a senior security policeman is said to have remarked in 1989 on receiving secret intelligence of talks between his own government and the ANC, 'are we supposed to make love to these people or kill them?'[79] In the original Afrikaans, the expression is likely to have been more earthy.

A similar principle applied to the international businessmen who had made fortunes breaking sanctions against South Africa. Many of them made a seamless transition to working with the ANC. Marc Rich continued doing oil business. One of his protégés who went on to head Glencore, the corporate successor to Marc Rich & Co AG, was a South African. Another former oil sanctions-buster, Tony Georgiadis, is alleged to have played a role in the infamous ANC arms purchases of the late 1990s[80] even as his wife was transferring her affections to former president De Klerk, whom she married. In 2010, Georgiadis accompanied President Jacob Zuma on a business mission to the United Kingdom.[81] Bantu Holomisa, former homeland leader turned Deputy Minister of Tourism, produced detailed evidence that the ANC had accepted political donations from the Sun City casino magnate Sol Kerzner in return for dropping bribery charges against him.[82] This was just one of a series of damaging allegations of corruption made by Holomisa.

Some military intelligence projects initiated under the apartheid government acquired a life of their own as private sector companies. GMR was taken over by PW Botha's former private secretary, a naval officer, who turned it into an arms-trading outfit. He sold a large quantity of arms to Rwanda that were used in the 1994 genocide.[83] By the late 1990s, GMR had apparently mutated into a company selling pharmaceuticals to the Zambian health service. Aid donors regarded it as dubious, and questioned a contract made by GMR to provide services to the Zambian government.[84] Among the ranks of ANC security and military operatives, some who had started out with small-scale rackets before graduating to stolen cars were now in the big league. In June 1999, the ANC intelligence man Bheki Jacobs was approached by some former colleagues who told him how Joe Modise 'and other leaders' of the now-defunct MK were planning to turn South Africa into a hub for international criminal activities.[85]

It is easy to be outraged by revelations about the afterlife of covert projects run for private gain. But indignation alone misses the point. Apartheid South Africa and its main enemy were seeking to reconcile with one another, and reconciliation implies forgiveness for past offences. And if an offence has been forgiven, then there should be no impediment to people doing business together. An ethical problem arises less from reconciliation as such than from a slightly different issue, namely, that the security forces on both sides had developed habits of unaccountability that had spun out of control. When these operatives began working together, whether in the security agencies run by a new South African government or in the private sector, they shared a culture of cynicism and contempt for law. During the decade from the mid-1980s, a merging of politics, security and crime took place in a shadow world whose contours, or even whose very existence, were unknown to many South Africans. When they caught glimpses of this netherworld, ordinary citizens often misunderstood it, believing it was the province either of James Bond-like spies or of professional criminals without any political complexion. Actually, it was the domain of a new breed, with antecedents in both espionage and crime, but also in other types of activity.

With the homecoming of the ANC came the Mandrax traders they had known in Lusaka. Several drug smugglers who had been based in Zambia in the 1980s retained the friendships they had made with ANC people at that time, who had now become South Africa's rulers. One such was Vicky Goswami, who arrived in South Africa in 1993 after being threatened with arrest in Zambia. By the time he was arrested in Dubai three years later, he had become one of the top bosses in the criminal empire of the Indian gangster Ibrahim

Dawood; it is generally thought that the Dubai authorities pounced on Goswami in order to disrupt Dawood's influence in their city, forcing him to move his headquarters to Karachi.[86] Another former Mandrax specialist, who had 'harboured ANC comrades when he was in exile in Zambia in the 1980s', became a business partner of a former chief of one of the post-apartheid intelligence services.[87] When the later intelligence chief Mo Shaik arrived at the ANC's historic national conference in Polokwane in 2007, he was accompanied by none other than Cyril Beeka. After Beeka's gangland murder four years later, Shaik denied that Beeka had been acting as his bodyguard. 'The truth of the matter is that Cyril Beeka gave me a lift to Polokwane. He was my friend,' he said.[88] The same Polokwane conference, which brought the former Vula operative Jacob Zuma to power, was notable for the extent to which the factions in evidence there had roots in Operation Vula and in the late 1980s reorganisation of the ANC's intelligence and security organ that had seen Zuma rise to the top of the apparatus.[89]

Many of the weapons distributed by both sides were never collected. Even after President Mandela had been sworn into office, members of an ANC self-defence unit were happy to be photographed carrying firearms they had originally received from the ANC.[90] One of the most notorious self-defence units was led by Colin Chauke, who went on to become an armed robber while also serving as an ANC town councillor in a Pretoria suburb until his arrest in 1998.[91] While on the run from the police he went to parties with senior ANC officials, including Peter Mokaba.[92] The abundance of arms goes some way to explaining the 465 bank robberies in South Africa in 1997. That same year, 45 000 members of armed self-defence and self-protection units formed during the previous decade and some 15 000 former armed combatants from MK and APLA were unaccounted for, meaning no one knew officially where they were or what they were doing.[93] According to the government itself, some were being hired as strong-arm men by criminal gangs.[94] Former

MK bomber Robert McBride, who had directed ANC armed units on the East Rand in the 1990s, was arrested in Mozambique with a large quantity of dollars on suspicion of gun-running, yet he held a succession of appointments in the police and security services.[95] He appeared to be working with former struggle comrades as part of a syndicate. Charges in relation to McBride's Mozambique arrest were later quashed, and there was a press report that he had been the victim of a set-up. In 2006, McBride was convicted of drink-driving and defeating the ends of justice after he had tried to cover up a drunken driving offence, at a time when he was the head of a regional police unit. He was subsequently sentenced to seven years in prison.[96]

Outside South Africa, even in 1991, ANC people were still disappearing in Zambia.[97] A key witness to alleged murders by Winnie Mandela was sent to Lusaka and placed in 'preventive detention' by the Zambian government at ANC request in order to ensure that he could not give damaging testimony at any criminal trial.[98] 'The ANC cannot afford to pretend that these things are not happening,' wrote Pallo Jordan, secretary of the information department, to NAT chief Joe Nhlanhla, in June 1991.[99]

In Uganda, ANC detainees continued to rot in prison on suspicion of espionage until at least 1992. They included Jessica, the woman who had sung so beautifully to entertain delegates at the sixth SACP congress in Moscow eight years earlier, suspected of espionage on account of her marriage to the late Comrade Ralph, the former deputy to Thami Zulu. At the same time, the ANC received some confirmed spies and turncoats back into the fold. Samuel Khanyile, better known as Solly Smith, the self-confessed spy and NAT operative who for years had occupied a strategic position in the ANC's London office, returned to South Africa in 1991. Information concerning his treachery was suppressed, and he served as chairman of the ANC's northern Free State region from 1991 to 1992 without branch members knowing of his past.[100] Glory Sedibe, the former guerrilla who had lured MK men into ambushes in Swaziland, a relative by marriage of Joe Modise, met ANC people to discuss rejoining the organisation.[101] He died mysteriously, possibly poisoned to stop him talking about corruption inside SADF military intelligence.[102]

Most alarming of all was the appointment to the Defence portfolio of Modise himself, the most corrupt and unpopular man in the ANC. 'It has been commented by some MK members,' the security police wrote in 1990, 'that it would be advisable for some of the more notorious members of the NEC (Joe Modise, in particular, was mentioned as one) to stay in exile for a long time – because they stand the risk of being attacked by those who have suffered in exile at their hands.'[103] Modise went on to play a leading role in the notorious 1999 arms deal. As Modise lay on his deathbed two years later, President Mbeki personally decorated him with the Grand Cross (Gold) of the Order of the Star of South Africa. After his passing, his money disappeared along with Puso Tladi, a former MK district commissar and protégé of Modise in the drugs and stolen car racket in Botswana,[104] the great ANC crime highway of earlier times.

Sipho Phungulwa, a former bodyguard to Chris Hani who had been detained by the ANC security department and had been part of a group of ex-detainees that had spoken to the press about their experiences, was murdered after his return to South Africa while on his way from a meeting at the ANC office in Umtata in June 1990.[105] As late as 1996, ANC security men were still prepared to kill to keep people silent. One of those lucky to escape was Gordon Moshoeu, who had been arrested in the Shishita purge and been held at Quatro. He was the target of a murder attempt in 1996, motivated, he believed, by his announcement of his intention to testify to the Truth and Reconciliation Commission.[106] Mwezi Twala, who was detained for five years at Quatro, dared to write a book about his experiences. Known as Khotso Morena in Umkhonto we Sizwe, he had accompanied ZIPRA forces in Zambia and had been deployed in Mozambique before serving on the Committee of Ten that represented the protestors at Viana camp. After returning to South Africa, Twala was persecuted by the self-defence units in his home town of Evaton, reportedly sent to hunt him down by Chris Hani and others. Seeking protection, he joined Inkatha and ended his life a member of the Democratic Alliance.[107]

While old feuds continued, and individuals sought revenge for old offences, the logic of the exile years changed in 1990. Within the core of the ANC leadership, old differences shifted to issues like backing Thabo Mbeki or Cyril Ramaphosa for the succession. A former MK man commented: 'Those are the people who delivered the deputy presidency to Thabo – the old exile Mafia. That's why Thabo defended them.'[108]

Overawed by Nelson Mandela's personality and by the heart-warming narrative of reconciliation in a country long regarded as doomed to undergo a horrific race war, the world paid little heed.

CHAPTER EIGHT

Perspectives

The long struggle between the ANC and the police and armed forces of the South African state, which lasted from 1961 until the early 1990s, did not involve two armies facing each other on a battlefield. In this respect it resembled many other violent conflicts in the late twentieth century. As PW Botha's favourite military theorist wrote, 'the objective for both sides in a revolutionary war is the population itself'.[1] The point was not so much to destroy the enemy as to win political support. In a contest of this nature, innocent bystanders are sometimes killed not just accidentally, but deliberately, as a way of sending a message to the general public or some part of it.

To be more precise, for more than three decades there was a prolonged confrontation between the apartheid state and a substantial part of the South African population. The ANC, the SACP and some other organisations sought to turn this confrontation into a war that would be fought among the people, by bringing in trained soldiers from outside. They had strictly limited success in this endeavour, but some communities in South Africa were in any event disposed to engage in violent protest on their own initiative, notably in 1976 and after 1984. Furthermore, from 1975 the SADF was simultaneously fighting an old-fashioned conventional war in Angola using all the expensive equipment required. Both contests, the conventional war and the war among the people, were inscribed in the global confrontation known as the Cold War.

The ANC was transformed in the course of this long struggle. Before the Defiance Campaign of 1952, in the words of the former Cape Town professor Jack Simons, the ANC 'consisted of a rather weak central committee, stronger provincial leadership, an annual conference meeting in Bloemfontein, and a membership of perhaps 10 000 subscribers. It had neither the organisation nor discipline expected of a party.'[2] By the time of its banning in 1960, the ANC had somewhere around 100 000 or 120 000 members.[3] Towards the end of its exile, Simons continued, the ANC had become 'a centralised party with a code of conduct, enforced by severe sanctions, a distinct ideology and a well defined programme'.[4] The ANC had turned itself into a liberation movement. The essence of this transformation took place very quickly. Rusty Bernstein thought that by the time he left South Africa in 1964 the ANC had already become what he called 'a sect', as the Communist Party, in his opinion, had been for years already.[5]

Nelson Mandela played a key role in the process, even though he was arrested at an early stage, in August 1962. In the nine months after the March 1960 killings at Sharpeville, he emerged as the ANC's most decisive leader. This seems to have been the moment that he decided to throw in his lot with the Communist Party, whose leading members he had come over the years to know well and to respect. Forced to operate clandestinely, the ANC had a great deal to gain from association with the SACP, which had long experience of survival underground. After the SACP, by this time including Mandela in its Central Committee, had taken a decision in December 1960 to create a guerrilla army, the communist connection offered to the ANC the financial, military and political patronage of a superpower. An alliance with the communist bloc also brought with it a global infrastructure for propaganda by way of an alliance with international communist parties. Ben Turok, surveying the whole period of the struggle, described the extent of SACP influence over the ANC as 'probably a system without precedence [sic] in the history of national liberation movements and arguably no [communist] party has managed to insinuate its presence and influence on such a scale'.[6]

Through a series of colossal tactical blunders, the National Party government made a major contribution to driving the ANC and the SACP together, and, for that matter, other components of the Congress Alliance too. These blunders included, notably, the Treason Trial and the banning of opposition organisations in 1960, which provided every incentive to opposition forces to unite against the government.

The consummation that took place within the ANC between African nationalism and communism was one that ANC leaders dared not reveal. The ANC's alliance with the Communist Party was an affront to black pride at the dawn of modern Africa's independence, as presidents and ministers in several African countries forcefully pointed out to Mandela during his 1962 tour of the continent. It also offended the international universe of generally liberal and social-democratic white well-wishers, in Britain in the first instance, who formed the second tier of global support for the ANC after Sharpeville, the first tier being the Soviet Union. For anyone to have given a frank account of Mandela's actual relationship with the SACP at that time, or for decades afterwards, would have compromised the whole political project. This was the reason for Mandela's own double-speak and evasions and his deception of the overwhelming majority of his black as well as white admirers whenever he was asked about his Party membership.[7]

When the ANC set out its stall as a liberation movement with Umkhonto we Sizwe's public declaration of war in December 1961, it did so without a clear plan to seize power. It formulated a real plan of action in this sense only at the Morogoro conference in 1969. In the same year, it also established a security service that was able to enforce ideological discipline, leading to the purge of the so-called Gang of Eight. The ANC became militarised, as was expected of liberation movements at that time, in faint imitation of the Bolshevik original. The imposition of military-style discipline meant that orders could not be questioned and individual infractions would not be tolerated. This military culture was brought into politics. As Rusty Bernstein noted, 'the acquisition of state power by force was never the aim' of the ANC until after it had created an army.[8]

Soviet thinking influenced the ANC deeply. For South African communists, the USSR was a guide to thought and action to the extent that one of them described it as 'a kind of pro-Soviet hysteria'. The USSR's mere existence gave South African communists the sense that 'we were on the side of history in the struggle for a better future'.[9] One Party member described Brian Bunting, prominent in Party affairs throughout the period, as having 'almost religious devoutness towards the Soviets'.[10] The Party imported to the ANC this loyalty to the USSR and all it stood for.

Waging war

The founders of Umkhonto we Sizwe began their work with a campaign of sabotage designed primarily for political effect. They intended their activity to grow into a wider insurrection that, starting with the insertion of trained guerrillas into rural areas, would inspire a popular rising and overwhelm the state in the same way that revolutionary forces in Cuba had done just a few years previously. This ambition was clear in the Mayibuye plan, a document confiscated by the police at Rivonia. In fact, Umkhonto we Sizwe never got anywhere close to this. The nearest it came was the near-suicidal

Rhodesian campaign of 1967–68 and the Operation J fiasco of the early 1970s.

Frustration and failure resulted in a change of approach that also reflected major changes in South African society as the country's economy boomed. About halfway through the exile period, the ANC changed its strategic orientation. The process began with the 1969 Morogoro conference. Seven years later, the 1976 Soweto rising alerted the ANC to the revolutionary potential of urban youth. Following its leaders' 1978 visit to Vietnam, the ANC aimed to instigate a 'people's war' based in the urban areas, rather than the rural insurrection it had originally envisaged. To get to this stage, it first had to create inside the country the command structure needed to direct a politico-military struggle that was rooted in individual communities. While the ANC was now infiltrating more trained fighters into the country than before, it never really succeeded in putting such a command structure in place. 'We regarded the ANC's military capacity with disdain,' one of the state's top intelligence officials, Maritz Spaarwater, recalled years later. 'Most of the people they infiltrated were caught and very often shot before they could do any damage.'[11] A more clinical way of saying this was offered by an analyst sympathetic to the ANC who wrote that 'the objective conditions for people's war in the Vietnamese sense did not exist … the ANC was dragged into the fray, responding to what was happening rather than fomenting or controlling it'.[12]

For all their militarist ambition, the leaders of Umkhonto we Sizwe realised that any repeat of the Rhodesian operation, risking troops in battle with the SADF or any similar force, would result only in their army's annihilation. This was why they consistently refused demands by the rank and file to be sent into action inside South Africa. Umkhonto we Sizwe lost almost a hundred soldiers in battles not against the South African state, but against UNITA in Angola.[13] Only very late in the day did the ANC devise an effective means of waging revolutionary warfare in the form of Operation Vula, which,

in the opinion of a South African police chief, 'was to come closest to the actual implementation of proper guerrilla strategies'.[14] It
was the most sophisticated operation ever mounted by the ANC – or
perhaps one should say by the SACP, since Operation Vula was almost
entirely a Party affair and seems to have been designed to further
its agenda above all. But Vula was too late to have a major effect on
the strategic balance, being implemented just as formal talks opened
with the government.

The strategic plan elaborated by the ANC after its Vietnam visit
envisaged the physical overthrow of the state. Some of the ANC's
most prominent leaders – Chris Hani, Joe Slovo and Mac Maharaj –
remained insurrectionists into the 1990s, 'dubious about the chances
of a negotiated solution and worried where it might lead', as recalled
by Gavin Evans, who worked in the underground in the 1980s and
played a minor role in Vula.[15] Until the mid-1980s, the insurrection-
ist line had the full support of the ANC's leading ally, the USSR.
The only ANC leader of high standing who seems to have had many
doubts about it at that stage was Thabo Mbeki, who emerged as the
ANC's leading diplomat and advocate of negotiation at more or less
the same time Mikhail Gorbachev came to power in the USSR.
While differing on important matters with many leading members
of the SACP, Mbeki was astute enough to maintain his place in the
Party's top rank. This was essential to his position in the ANC, since
at that time, as another prominent South African communist said,
'it was useful to be a Communist in Lusaka because it gave you
another caucus and another place to sort of feel the pulse of the
movement'.[16]

Thus, in the Gorbachev period, divisions at the top of the SACP
mirrored those within the Communist Party of the Soviet Union,
with most South African communists being on the side of the
Kremlin old guard in their commitment to militarism. As the Soviet
government's new political thinking in international relations began
to produce effects, the ANC's insurrectionists were left with dwindling

international support. Mbeki's power increased accordingly, and his early advocacy of negotiation put him on the same wavelength as Mandela when the latter was released from prison.

In the early days of the armed struggle, in the 1960s, there had indeed been no reason to think that the apartheid state would dissolve peacefully. At that time, advocates of insurrection were to be found not only in the SACP and the ANC but in a swathe of public opinion, including those liberals, socialists and Trotskyists who formed various sabotage groups and, most importantly, the PAC. Had significant figures within the ANC not opted for violent struggle at that time, it is most likely that their organisation would have been eclipsed by the PAC. However, nearly all of this first generation of militants, whether from the ANC, the SACP or some other organisation, misjudged the political-military situation in South Africa. Nelson Mandela seems to have been almost alone in grasping at an early stage that the ANC would never be in a position to wage anything approaching a conventional war. He wrote: 'in our circumstances, the aim of a people's war was not to "win", but gradually through a process of attrition to bring the government to the realisation that we could not be defeated and the government could not win'.[17] Although Mandela wrote these words only decades later, at least one witness of high standing confirms that this really was Mandela's position in the early 1960s.[18] After the Rivonia arrests and the flight into exile, the ANC's strategy soon came to reflect the views of the SACP's hardcore insurrectionists who retained the inflexibility that was characteristic of their ideological lodestar, the USSR. 'It is a pity,' Moeletsi Mbeki observed, 'that the leadership of the ANC and the SACP never delved into the mysteries of how a conventional war between states differed from an armed insurrection within a state, or how these two differed from intensified political protest.' The reason for this oversight, in his opinion, lay in the Communist Party's allegiance to 'the blinkered vision and schematic formulae of the Stalinist period'.[19]

Not only did the SACP remain committed to a military strategy that was based on an inaccurate understanding of the strength of the South African state, but the Party's political ambition of controlling the ANC had an adverse effect on its ability to realise its military aims. The effectiveness of any army is closely associated with its command and control mechanism, yet MK did not have a united command structure, since it owed loyalty to two political authorities, the ANC and the Party. Many field commanders learned to play these two masters against each other. Figures of the stature of Slovo, Hani and Cassius Make were keen to expand the armed struggle but were distracted by having another aim, that of controlling the ANC politically. This channelled energies that could have gone into the armed struggle towards another objective. The strife between Joe Modise and Chris Hani at the head of the army resulted in the two men seeking to neutralise key MK commanders, units and operations that were thought to belong to the other camp. The security and intelligence department, a Party fief from the outset, contested the military hierarchy to the point that, by the time of Thami Zulu's death, these two components of the ANC had become bitter rivals.

As pressure to negotiate increased in the late 1980s, even the most militant leaders of the ANC were forced to consider exactly what Umkhonto we Sizwe had achieved up to then. In January 1990, just days before the ANC's unbanning, Chris Hani, acknowledging the ANC's military weakness, described Umkhonto we Sizwe as 'a military wing which can't be compared to the SADF'. He added: 'but the fact is, it is a military wing which attracted into the struggle thousands of people'.[20] This was true enough, but it was a point that had never been made to the rank and file of MK cadres in their foreign camps or to ANC militants inside the country. No one ever told them that the main purpose of maintaining a guerrilla army that did its best to resemble a conventional force, with soldiers trained to parade Red Army-style wearing military uniforms and steel helmets, was not to do battle with the enemy but only to win over public opinion. It is no surprise that the rank and file of MK cadres, and of ANC activists generally, remained fixated with a stirring image of military victory and that they failed to appreciate subtler points about the struggle's political nature, since their leaders failed to explain core strategic realities to them. Already in the early 1970s there were some ANC leaders who noticed that the organisation's militarism was sending a wrong message about the essentially political character of the struggle.[21] The militaristic message continued to prevail even after the late-1970s strategy review.[22] The ANC carried on encouraging people to leave South Africa with a view to joining their comrades abroad with the slogan 'Swell the Ranks of MK'. Yet the ANC had no military need for new recruits outside the country. On the contrary, one of its biggest problems was what to do with the military cadres it already had. Thousands of them needed to be housed and fed, and their morale had to be kept up. Difficulties in doing this led to several uprisings over three decades, most of which were really pro-democracy protests. There was only one genuine mutiny, at Pango in 1984. The mismatch between the ANC's military posture and the changing needs of the struggle echoed that in the USSR itself, committed as it was to maintaining a massive industrial army that was increasingly unusable and poorly adapted to the emergence of war among the people as a paradigm in the late twentieth century.[23]

What the existence of MK actually achieved, then, was to provide the ANC with the profile of a militant revolutionary organisation. As Jack Simons detected at an early stage, it needed this in order to maintain support from the USSR and other allies, at least until the late 1980s, when the Soviet government began seeking a negotiated solution to wars in southern Africa and throughout the world. The maintenance of a revolutionary army gave the ANC prestige among radical opponents of the government inside South Africa, who were in fact starved of information about the ANC and about the international situation generally, not least as a result of South Africa's diplomatic isolation. The real point of MK's existence was not to win the war, but to allow the ANC, its parent body, to remain a player in the game. The ANC derived political advantage from its armed struggle almost in spite of itself.

What the ANC most needed, in order to project the revolutionary image it sought, was a constant supply of heroes to show that it was in business. Even better than heroes were martyrs, because they brought with them sympathy merging into a victimhood that was an important part of the ANC's international image. It is said that one of the offences committed by Sipho Mbeje, the MK man detained and tortured by ANC security officers in Lusaka in 1989, was to have expressed an opinion that leaders were sending cadres to their deaths purely in order to make propaganda.[24] He had put his finger on a sensitive spot. Even in the 1960s there were cadres who thought that some of their comrades were sent on expeditions not for military purposes but in order to eliminate them from internal factional contests – like Patrick Molaoa, who died in Rhodesia.[25]

To be sure, the cultivation of martyrdom and victimhood has been quite common in wars among the people since the late twentieth century. Its ultimate expression is the suicide attack, which is usually designed less to incapacitate the enemy than to achieve a political effect, magnified through the media, by demonstrating courage, dedication and nobility of purpose. So it was with the ANC in exile. The audience for this theatre of struggle and suffering – the 'great charade' described by Jack Simons[26] – was as much foreign as domestic. From the moment the ANC established itself in exile, it had to play to an international gallery in order to survive. In the programme adopted after the 1978 policy review, international isolation of the regime was described as one of the four pillars of the revolution. The international arena was actually the area in which the ANC was most effective.

This raises the question how the ANC managed to portray such an attractive and coherent image internationally despite its constant factional infighting and its administrative limitations. In the first place, the ANC could benefit from an almost global dislike of apartheid. It seems that people in many countries thought that rule by a racial minority was intolerable. More than this, they simply did not want to know. As time went by, the ANC gained overwhelming support as apartheid's best-known adversary, despite the claims in Africa itself of the PAC and the attempt by Chief Buthelezi to present his Inkatha movement as a strategic alternative. The ANC's London-based media operation, in which the Anti-Apartheid Movement and the International Defence and Aid Fund played a crucial role, used this asset skilfully. It was this same public relations machine that turned Mandela into an icon while he was still in prison.

While journalists in many countries were well disposed to the ANC, and were prepared to overlook its shortcomings primarily because of the nature of its enemy, they were for the most part genuinely unaware of its intense factional problems. Conflicts within the organisation rarely came to the attention of journalists and, through them, the international reading and television-viewing public. The ANC was remarkably successful in keeping the laundry door closed when it was washing its dirty underwear. The only significant exception during the exile years was the so-called Gang of Eight affair, which resulted in the publication of press releases and other documents in which each side publicly berated the other.[27] Fortunately for the ANC, this occurred before the Soweto rising, when not much attention was given to sectarian squabbles in what was, at that time, still a relatively obscure organisation. Later, when the ANC had become world famous, although the government in Pretoria was aware of the Mkatashinga episode and of the existence of Quatro prison, neither was known internationally until the very end of the 1980s, and even then only to small numbers of people.[28] Crucial to the suppression of information on internal matters was the ANC's security service, NAT, which could remove dissenters from view. But probably more important still was the London propaganda operation, which represented any information critical of the ANC, true or false, as being objectively pro-apartheid and racist. Decades after the death of

George Orwell, the great writer on totalitarian thinking, the ANC's international supporters just did not want to read or hear anything negative about the organisation they idolised.

The habit of strategic deception, as the ANC hid the true extent of its communist allegiance, of its factionalism and of its internal repression, came at a price. It created an atmosphere inside the ANC that, to say the least, was not conducive to debate. Ordinary cadres who voiced critical or even just unusual opinions were liable to be detained and even killed. Only people who were exceptionally well connected could get away with the expression of dissent. The repression of criticism meant that corruption could run unchecked. In fact, the worst corruption was associated with senior levels of MK and with NAT, the security and intelligence service. Furthermore, NAT appears to have been more prone to infiltration by enemy agents than any other part of the organisation. But it remained untouchable. Perhaps this was why the South African government chose not to divulge the information it had on Mkatashinga and Quatro – it actually suited the securocrats to have NAT in such a strong position since that had the effect of diminishing the ANC's military effectiveness.

The lack of free speech inside the ANC meant that the official analysis of the struggle and of the South African condition made by the organisation's National Executive Committee, guided by the SACP in its role as a vanguard party, could not be seriously questioned throughout the period of exile. The doctrinaire line developed by the SACP was strongly influenced by experiences in Europe. During the entire history of communism in South Africa, at least until 1990, a remarkable number of the Party's leading theorists were first- or second-generation immigrants from Europe, many of them Jewish, who brought with them world-views formed in the old continent. As a sympathetic journalist noted at the funeral of SACP veteran Violet Weinberg, their passion for politics 'had its roots in the *shtetl*, in the Bund's battle against the Tsar'.[29] (The Bund was a secular Jewish socialist party in the Russian empire, active from 1897 to 1920, that later merged into the Communist Party of the Soviet Union.) In the middle of the twentieth century, the many South African communists with roots in the Jewish communities of Eastern Europe were distraught by news of their families and home villages being wiped out during the Nazi occupation. Many of them, admiring the USSR and accustomed to formulating their ideas in conformity with Marxist-Leninist ideology, equated the apartheid they saw in South Africa with the Nazism that had devastated Europe. On an emotional level, this is easy to understand. But apartheid was not the same as Nazism, in spite of points of resemblance,[30] and the course of South African history was different from that of Germany.

Viewing South Africa through an ideological (and Eurocentric) lens, SACP theoreticians persistently misunderstood the South African condition. Communist Party documents from the whole exile period are striking for their apocalyptic tone, representing not just apartheid but world capitalism as on the point of collapse. The revolution was always just around the next corner. In the 1960s, Party strategists seriously underestimated the state's resilience, and the declaration of war against the state in 1961 deprived anti-apartheid politics of its most capable leaders, who were thrown into prison or went into exile. Thereafter, a principled refusal to compromise with what it considered a fascist enterprise caused the ANC, under Marxist-Leninist influence, to miss many opportunities for furthering its political influence inside the country. The ANC in exile failed seriously to address politics among the more than half of the population that lived in the rural areas, which was one of the reasons that Buthelezi and his Inkatha movement were able to establish such strength. It became increasingly evident that apartheid did not represent a remnant of colonialism, as the ANC had learned from the SACP, so much as 'an increasingly streamlined and expanding system of sophisticated dominance'.[31]

Meanwhile, real struggles against apartheid were taking place on the streets and in the workplaces of South Africa, led during the 1980s by the UDF and the trade unions but involving activists from many other organisations, such as the Azanian People's Organisation (AZAPO) and even Inkatha, and including some white voters, all of whom enjoyed some space for dissent and self-expression. The UDF, the most inclusive social project in South Africa's history, became a political forum in its own right, inspired by the ANC while having only fitful contact with it.[32] UDF militants listened to Radio Freedom, picked up a few slogans and otherwise were guided by what they took to be ANC policy but without detailed direction. When the ANC returned to South Africa, UDF leaders soon joined it, dissolving their own organisation and leaving behind something of a vacuum.

What South Africa itself experienced in the late twentieth century, then, was a civil war, fought among the people. It arose from a prolonged confrontation and occurred simultaneously with a conventional war in Angola to which it was connected via a system of alliances. Yet the main protagonists preferred to portray South Africa's civil war in Cold War terms as a revolutionary/counterrevolutionary struggle waged throughout southern Africa. 'The notion of civil war is less familiar,' Jack Simons wrote. 'Members of the movement usually query its existence and prefer the old notion of resistance against "Colonialism of a Special Type".'[33]

Inside South Africa, actual fighting was restricted to certain zones, generally a relatively small number of townships plus Natal and KwaZulu. The patterns taken by the civil war naturally reflected the complexity of South African society. As the state lost control of individual communities to forces that were sympathetic to the ANC without being under its direct control, its response was to fight back by indirect means, notably by arming sectors of the population it knew to be opposed to the ANC or its local surrogates. The result was a series of intensely local struggles, often defined by relative wealth, by ethnicity, age, status and personal factors. By the late 1980s, the ANC and the state security forces were both arming sectors of the population with a view eventually to determining which of them would control the state. The climax of the conflict was the early 1990s, when a compromise was reached that produced the election of 1994 and the constitution promulgated in 1996.

Some 20 000 people died in political violence in apartheid's final decade, making this a civil war of significant size. It is estimated that half these deaths occurred in the KwaZulu homeland or in the Natal province that surrounded it, whereas this area contains only a quarter of South Africa's population. Much of the rest of the violence occurred in the PWV area, quite often in districts where there were high concentrations of Zulu migrant workers.[34] Political violence declined after the April 1994 election, but remained at over 1 000 deaths per year until 1996 or 1997.[35] The very high proportion of civilian casualties was unusual even by the standards of late-twentieth-century guerrilla wars. The reason was simply that there were few clashes between armies. As in most civil wars, a great deal of the violence 'was not part of any major side's strategy or intent, and sometimes had very little relation to the political issues'.[36] Civilians, once armed and primed for violence, could settle personal scores or simply commit criminal offences for personal gain. Some ANC and Inkatha groups turned into warlord bands or criminal syndicates, as often happens in similar circumstances.[37] An important role in ending the war between the ANC and Inkatha was played by Daluxolo Luthuli, the Wankie veteran who had served a prison term on Robben Island before joining Inkatha and heading its hit squad. Knowing both the ANC and Inkatha from the inside, he sought out the ANC's highest-ranking Zulu official, Jacob Zuma, who pursued negotiations to a successful conclusion.[38] Zuma was later to reap his political reward with an influx of new Zulu members into the ANC, as it absorbed many former Inkatha supporters.

An added layer of complexity consisted in the fact that South Africa's war was related to other wars throughout the region, and of course to the Cold War. As the government strove to defend itself outside its borders in the first instance, the most intense fighting occurred in Angola, where the SADF and its UNITA ally were pitted against the Angolan and Cuban armies, helped by Soviet advisers. This campaign reached its climax at Cuito Cuanavale, where the SADF withdrew without achieving its aims – an important strategic reverse, but very far from an annihilation. The SADF achieved its major goal of not allowing the ANC or its Angolan and Cuban allies or SWAPO any conventional presence in Namibia or South Africa itself.

Characteristic of the world from the mid-twentieth century until today has been the existence in many regions of confrontations that are timeless, in which the strategic use of force is unable to impose a strategic decision as it could in the old days of industrial war.[39] So it has been in Palestine from the 1940s, Korea from the 1950s until today, Afghanistan from the 1970s, Iraq from 1990, and in Cyprus, Kosovo and many other places. In the case of South Africa, many people hoped and believed that the 1994 settlement might bring an end to a long confrontation generally interpreted as pitting a racist state against an organisation representing the mass of the population. The continuation of political violence in KwaZulu-Natal even into the present century[40] and more or less violent expressions of popular discontent since 2000 may cause us to wonder whether the confrontation did not simply mutate in 1994 rather than come to an end. South Africa's confrontation increasingly appears to be re-emerging as one based on social class, as a rapacious new bourgeoisie, growing wealthy on plundering the state rather than on capitalist production, distances itself from the general population.[41]

Interpreting the past

In the euphoria of liberation after 1994, ANC supporters saw no need to engage in retrospection. The prevailing spirit was one of triumph. The former trade union leader Jay Naidoo recalls how 'we had our hands on the levers of power, money in a budget, staff, resources, and the conviction that this government by virtue of its democratic election was the only legitimate representative of the aspirations of our people ... any criticism of the government was a criticism of the revolution'.[42] The leaders who had returned from exile and who dominated the ANC's first government were complacent beyond measure. One commentator, although sympathetic to the ANC, remarked cuttingly of the exiled ANC that 'the leadership of black South Africa's struggle for freedom [had] convinced itself that it could better serve the cause by absenting itself from South Africa. It was an armchair revolution.'[43] For someone like Naidoo, who had participated in the internal struggle throughout the 1980s, it was galling to be told by people returning from exile that 'guys like you and Cyril Ramaphosa have not been being brought up [sic] in the ANC tradition ... You have not been schooled in the revolutionary theory of our liberation struggle.'[44]

During President Mandela's tenure of office from 1994 to 1999, actual policy-making was largely the work of his deputy president, Thabo Mbeki. An economist by training, Mbeki adopted a free-market economic strategy in the probably correct belief that the financial markets and leading capitalist governments would have punished him severely for making any other choice. But embrace of the free market did not make Mbeki a convert to political liberalism. In regard to the ANC itself, he retained the style of democratic centralism he had learned in the Communist Party. In a notorious outburst, Pallo Jordan once described the characteristic traits of the Party as 'a spirit of intolerance, petty intellectual thuggery and political dissembling'.[45]

Mbeki did, though, embrace pan-Africanism, believing that the liberation of South Africa marked a turning point in the history of Africa or even the entire planet.[46] His presidency was marked by quixotic gestures of solidarity intended to show commitment to a Third World that no longer existed, such as taking off to Haiti to celebrate the bicentenary of the Haitian republic and handing R10 million to its president,[47] or humouring his troublesome neighbour, Robert Mugabe.

True to his Marxist training, Mbeki believed that South Africa was undergoing a bourgeois revolution, and he did everything to encourage the growth of a black bourgeoisie in conformity with his understanding of this historical phase. Notwithstanding Mbeki's tendency to lecture people on world history and many other matters besides, liberation became largely reduced to its crudest material aspect. For many South Africans, it came to mean aspiring to the standard of living that was formerly the preserve of whites.

Almost immediately, liberation was actualised as a drive for conspicuous consumption. According to the sociologist Deborah Posel, 'blackness was, in part, a judgment about being unworthy of certain modes of consumption. Surely there is a logic to the position which finds freedom in the power to acquire?'[48] Among the more affluent people living in townships, it created veritable cults of consumption, an exotic example being frenetic Saturday-night parties where dancing culminates with the burning of expensive name-brand clothing and shoes. 'People respect you when you dress expensively and stylishly,' Thulane, a member of the Reflection Destructor Crew, a hiphop outfit that animates Saturday-night street parties in Soweto, told a journalist. 'It brings you fame and fame brings you the girls.' He added that this was the reason that government ministers had to drive top-of-the-range cars. If they did not, they wouldn't be respected.[49] The ANC youth leader Julius Malema became the political epitome of this radical-chic style.

To journalist Allister Sparks, the chronicler of the transition, it had become apparent by 2011 that the ANC, 'steeped in a socialist ideology throughout the struggle years', had seen 'its entire intellectual universe ... collapse just as it came to power'. It was 'pitched into a globalised free-enterprise environment it didn't understand and was reluctant to accept'.[50] Seeing itself as a revolutionary movement representing a whole society, the ANC easily considers political opponents not just as representatives of constituencies with their own particular views and interests, but as counter-revolutionaries. Those who expose misgovernance and corruption are reactionaries.

It is apparently due to the tension between this self-image and its actual evolution since 1994 that the ANC has not wanted to encourage detailed examination of the real history of South Africa's late-twentieth-century confrontation and the conflicts that arose from it. At the same time, it constantly invokes the history of militancy that justifies its tenure of power as the organisation that liberated South Africa. It propagates what one writer calls a 'battle-centric' view of the struggle in which a special place is allotted to Cuito Cuanavale as the point at which apartheid was defeated.[51] This is a fantasy or a delusion. A myth concerning the armed struggle has percolated throughout black South Africa. (A short appendix to this book goes into more detail about the relationship between myth and history.)

In conformity with the myth that has grown up around the history of opposition to apartheid, the claim to have participated in the armed struggle gives people 'the power to activate certain claims in the present'.[52] But the truth is that many former MK cadres who sat for years in miserable camps in Angola are today destitute. Meanwhile, many former township youths who got hold of a weapon only in the last months of apartheid, or who simply threw stones, now claim to have been part of MK, the people's army. Such is the power of the image of South Africa being liberated by a people's war that they might actually believe they really were members of MK.

The rapid arming of civilian groups by the security forces in the 1980s, and by the Vula operatives in the 1990s, put guns into the hands of some people of dubious political loyalty.[53] The most trenchant critic of people's war, Anthea Jeffery,[54] is correct in contending that this strategy damaged the fabric of many already ragged communities, although her analysis is one-sided in that it underestimates the aggressiveness of Inkatha and denies the very existence of a third force in the sense of an active element drawn from the state's counter-insurgency experts in the special forces and the security police. Jeffery is one of several writers associated with the South African Institute of Race Relations[55] who claim that the people's war and the ungovernability encouraged by the ANC in the last century are the main reason for many of the social ills afflicting the country today. This view is ridiculed by former leaders of the struggle such as Mac Maharaj, who wrote that Jeffery's book had him 'oscillating between laughter, tears, anger and irritation'.[56] Yet in 1991, Maharaj himself expressed his concern about the effect of ungovernability on the younger generation and 'the quality of what emerges from our struggle'.[57] ANC leaders have not addressed, let alone refuted, the argument that, by calling on people to render their country ungovernable, as they did in the 1980s, at a moment when the government was in any event losing its grip, and in the absence of any other system that could regulate the tensions and conflicts in society, they played a significant role in shaping the social unrest of the current century. Jeffery suspects the ANC of the basest cynicism in calling on township youth to make their society ungovernable and using the resulting chaos as leverage in the acquisition of state power. While a charge of cynicism might be true in the case of some ANC leaders, probably more numerous were those who were so taken up by the struggle that they simply gave no thought to the longer-term consequences. This is an allegation that can also be made concerning the state's counterinsurgency experts.

Probably the most numerous of all, among the ANC, were those who believed their own propaganda. They may honestly have thought that the comrades doing battle with the police and with Inkatha would stop and go back to school once they had been liberated. For many years after 1994, Thabo Mbeki, in particular, was scathing about anyone who complained about the high levels of crime in South Africa or the lamentable state of its education system, implying that these things were purely temporary problems or even figments of a racist imagination. Only in the present century did it seem to dawn that these were deep problems of South African society that were not going to disappear just because the party of liberation was now in power.

The mystique created around the ANC during its years in exile turned it into something very different from a conventional political party. The ANC has retained traits of Soviet political behaviour, including a distaste for an independent media and judiciary, added to an idea that it is destined to rule until the end of time. As Irina Filatova has pointed out, many governments around the world have followed a similar course independently of any Soviet connection, such as Zimbabwe, but 'decades of admiration for the Soviet system could not but play a role in entrenching these trends'.[58] Many South Africans seem to consider the ANC almost as a family, to which one retains a residual loyalty even when it is dysfunctional. Even voters utterly frustrated by the ANC's performance in office seem reluctant to vote for any other party. Many MK veterans retain an idealised image of the ANC as it might have been, attributing all its many lapses to malign influences from outside. One man from the 1976 generation who spent almost eight years in the appalling Quatro prison said that the abuses he suffered were 'a creation of forces other than the African National Congress', implying that it wasn't the real ANC that was responsible, but the spies that had infiltrated the organisation.[59] Other people explain the ANC's shortcomings in office by reference to the opportunists who joined the organisation only after February 1990, when it was on its way to power. There could be some truth in this analysis, but such an interpretation takes no account of the contempt for real politics that was the result of enforcing revolutionary discipline. Really, attributing all mistakes to traitors and malicious infiltrators amounts to no more than a theory of witchcraft dressed up in the language of scientific socialism.

It is relevant to note how completely the ANC has written out of the historical narrative all the other organisations that contributed to the overthrow of apartheid, including not only the UDF but most particularly the Black Consciousness Movement. Black Consciousness played an enormous role in motivating the 1970s generation. Importantly for today's South Africans, it placed great emphasis on psychology, arguing that true liberation could come about only by liberating the mind in the first instance. Liberation in this sense is sorely lacking today. In its place is a vulgarised Marxism that leads people to believe in a science of revolution that does not in fact exist. It is very common in South Africa to hear ANC supporters, their mouths full of clichés, exalting the national democratic revolution and asserting that true socialism will arrive if only the right structures are put in place and the correct measures taken. This is a measure of how deeply the ANC was affected by the SACP in exile, even though the latter has had little influence within the alliance for the last two decades.

The Marxist-Leninists hammered into the ANC the notion that South Africa was a colony of a special type. It follows that if it is a colony, then the first task is to seize power from the colonial rulers (in this case, white South Africans). Since this is merely the first part of a two-phase revolution, the next step is to expropriate the existing bourgeoisie. Since bourgeois wealth is obtained through exploitation, the bourgeois who are expropriated deserve what they get. This is not a science of revolution; it is an apology for plunder.

Explanations

The apartheid state and its enemies in the ANC were so intent on the integrity of their quarrel that they failed to understand the shifts in

world affairs at the time the Cold War was ending. They did not realise that various branches of criminal activity were not the same as the
type of crime they had known previously, but part of a globalisation
of the shadows that was new. Worldwide, the spread of light weapons
from the 1970s, the privatisation of intelligence and covert warfare
by the US and others, and the emergence of financial globalisation
were all combining to produce a blurring of the frontiers between
the criminal underworld, underground economies, the grey zone of
government and the legitimate business world. The collapse of the
Soviet bloc and of the USSR itself encouraged professional criminals
to make alliances with thuggish political entrepreneurs who had no
ingrained respect for law.[60] The groups resulting from these fusions,
often referred to rather vaguely as 'mafias', deal in a toxic mixture of
politics and crime. All of this went largely unnoticed in South Africa
even as security specialists themselves participated in the process.

Financial globalisation and the flood of petrodollars after 1973,
followed by financial deregulation, resulted in most parts of the
world in huge politico-financial payoffs that made earlier corruption
scandals appear small.[61] The French-Norwegian judge Eva Joly, who
investigated the vast Elf Aquitaine corruption scandal in France in
the 1990s, has written of her conclusion that the global market in
corruption underwent a transformation in size and in nature in the
final quarter of the last century. She believes that this poses a threat
not only to democracy, but even to the system of state sovereignty
that developed in Europe from the seventeenth century and that is
the basis for international relations.[62] In this light, the many so-called
'failed states' in the world may be understood not as temporary lapses
but as part of a world system in formation. This is a matter of particular importance for a country located on the southern tip of Africa,
the continent with the highest number of 'failed' states.

The ANC in power has remained little interested in understanding the world as it is or has become. This insouciance seems to be
one of the reasons why it prefers to peddle a comforting myth that

it overthrew apartheid largely through its armed struggle. In fact, more important was the international isolation of South Africa that brought about the regime's bankruptcy, added to the collapse of the Soviet imperium and the end of the Cold War. The decision of Chase Manhattan Bank in 1985 not to roll over a loan was probably of more consequence than the battle of Cuito Cuanavale,[63] even though it hardly figures in the new official history. To a far greater extent than the ANC likes to think, the end of the apartheid state was determined by changes in the international arena. If they are to understand the forces shaping the world, politicians need to understand what actually happened in the past, not just what they would like to have happened.

The fundamental point at issue in rival accounts of the ANC's exile period is how and why apartheid and the National Party government eventually collapsed, submitted or were overthrown. This is an important matter even today because the relationships that were forged or re-forged during the period of transition became the political basis on which South Africa presently resides. These relationships are underpinned by the founding myth of the new South Africa.

Historic settlements between mighty political blocs always generate a myth. And here is the nub of a major South African problem: for some people, the settlement reached between the ANC and the National Party in the early 1990s was a historic compromise allowing former enemies to live together in harmony. This is the myth of the negotiated revolution and the rainbow nation. For others, however, the negotiated settlement of the late twentieth century was simply a milestone on a continuing revolutionary journey, not a sacred covenant. Their understanding of the foundational myth of the new South Africa is quite different. Their version is that the ANC and the SACP liberated South Africa by their armed struggle, inspiring a mass following that grew to such size that in the end the National Party was forced to negotiate its own demise. For them, history came to a stop in 1994. The clock was re-set to zero. The ANC's historic duty is to make South African society anew, either quickly or gradually according to taste. The ANC will rule throughout time, 'until Jesus comes again', as Jacob Zuma once said.

Whichever version of the founding myth of the new South Africa may seem the most convincing, there are many grounds for nuance.[64] It has been apparent for many years that the negotiated transfer of power, at first hailed as a triumph of politics in the purest sense, was underpinned by more brute force than was generally acknowledged, including that perpetrated by the apartheid military and police units known as the third force. According to Frederik van Zyl Slabbert, the popular risings of the 1980s were not primarily inspired by the ANC's vision of a people's war but were the actions of people who simply 'refused to acquiesce in their own destruction'.[65] In the opinion of Mamphela Ramphele, 'ours was not a freedom won through the barrel of the gun ... [It] was won by citizens who refused to be cowed by the might of an oppressive government.'[66]

Van Zyl Slabbert also made the more questionable statement that 'apartheid self-destructed because of a massive crisis of delivery'.[67] This stresses the technocratic failure of the National Party rather than the political dead end to which apartheid had brought it. One merit of this interpretation is that it throws light on what has happened subsequently, at a time when popular protests are routinely described by the government as motivated by deficiencies in service delivery. It suggests that there is a stubborn continuity between the South Africa of the 1980s and the South Africa of today in the shape of a government that insists on regarding the politics of the poor not as real politics, but as a series of technical problems to be solved by bureaucratic action. Failing that, it is a job for the police.

These alternative interpretations of the demise of apartheid throw further light on the ANC's tendency to mythologise by hinting that the ANC acquired this habit partly from the National Party, as explicitly stated by Slabbert in a sentence that forms the epigraph to the present book. That this degree of continuity between the apartheid state and its successor became possible was due to the circumstances in which power changed hands.[68] The South African government in the 1980s could defend itself against the efforts of Umkhonto we Sizwe almost indefinitely, but it was facing such widespread domestic opposition that it could no longer hold its ground politically. Not least, it could not finance itself under an indefinite siege. In effect, the government faced bankruptcy when foreign bankers realised this, lost confidence and declined to make new loans after August 1985.

During the late apartheid period, South Africa, like its near-neighbours Angola and Mozambique, became embroiled in a Cold War contest that shaped the struggle, even though the country's fate was never close to being the chief preoccupation of decision-makers in either the US or the USSR. At the time, in the 1980s, it was fashionable among people opposed to apartheid both inside South Africa and abroad to regard the obsessive anti-communism of PW Botha and Magnus Malan as pure invention, despite the obvious relevance of the Cold War context. The National Party's anti-communists had a rather simplistic understanding of the Cold War, failing to see that clients of the superpowers could often manipulate their patrons. There were senior officers in the SADF who were more subtle in their views, such as the former military intelligence chief who said of the total onslaught 'it wasn't total, and it wasn't an onslaught'.[69] But this was not what President Botha wanted to hear. Itself an inveterate maker of myths, in the end the National Party was unable to realise the claims it had always made for itself. Its official view collided with a hard obstacle called reality.

Failure to understand fully the international context has been an abiding feature of both politicians and analysts in South Africa. They have tended to think of South Africa as though it were an island, only weakly connected to the African continent yet a significant player in world events in its own right. In this regard, it is extraordinary to reflect that many in the National Party during the era of African decolonisation insisted in regarding their top strategic priority as the assertion of a true sovereign independence that would escape the clutches of the old imperial power, Britain. They apparently could not see that Britain was in decline and that South Africa's rulers would be better advised to adapt themselves to the new political realities of the African continent, including the aspirations of the black majority in their own country (although there were heated debates on this matter at the heart of the Broederbond that have been largely forgotten[70]). On the left, the SACP had its own exceptionalist view of the South African condition, which it labelled Colonialism of a Special Type, which was taken up by the ANC.

Having, during the course of the struggle, persuaded the world that South Africa was a moral problem for everyone, the ANC has blithely continued since 1994 to suppose that the rest of the world still has special regard for the ANC as the bearer of a moral torch.

In reality, this has long ceased to be the case. Although Hollywood makes sentimental films about Nelson Mandela, in other respects South Africa does not have a special place in the calculations of foreigners. It is just another country.

APPENDIX

A Note on Method

M any facts concerning the history of the ANC during its exile
period are well known. Some of them, every writer regards
as landmark events – the Rivonia arrests, the Rhodesia campaign, the Morogoro conference, the 1990 unbanning, and so on. In
that regard, this book is no different from the many histories of the
struggle that have been published before.[1]

Yet the story I have written is rather unusual. This book contains
a good deal of information about the history of factionalism in the
ANC, for example. Why not choose a more uplifting subject? Why
write about those aspects of the story that do not present the ANC
in the best light?

There are two main answers to these questions, one short and
the other slightly longer. The short answer is that in the last twenty
years a great deal of new information about the ANC's and SACP's
period in exile has come into the public realm via official archives,
private papers, the press, the work of the Truth and Reconciliation
Commission and an exceptionally rich seam of published biographies
and autobiographies and recorded interviews concerning many of

the leading figures in the ANC and SACP. There are also memoirs by some of the footsoldiers of Umkhonto we Sizwe, which generally provide a version of events significantly different from that narrated by ANC and SACP chieftains who were later to become Cabinet ministers and parliamentarians. The archives of the Soviet Union have been partially opened and have been consulted by Russian-speaking scholars, although many of these records now seem to be inaccessible once more. Also partially open are the archives of East Germany's Stasi, the pervasive security and intelligence service that worked closely with the ANC and the SACP before 1990. All these new sources of information enable us to know more than before about the ANC's past and to see familiar events in a new light.

The more complicated answer is that I have tried to write a history of power, centred on the ANC in exile. Who held power in the organisation, how they acquired it and the use they made of it is the main thread throughout the story told in this book. It interprets events of the past in the light of our present knowledge, as all histories do. Thus, the story of the ANC in government since 1994 has inevitably caused me, as it causes others, to ask new questions about its past, or to place new interpretations on events that may previously not have seemed significant. These are all points that arise in narrating the story of the ANC in exile.

The historical narrative also touches on other issues of importance for the present day that this book cannot treat other than in passing. Among these, two stand out. One is the damage caused to South Africans by colonialism, segregation and apartheid, not only in material and political terms but also in psychological and spiritual ones. This is an issue that the ANC has consistently overlooked,[2] since it has assimilated the Communist Party's rigorously materialist view of the world. By contrast, the psychological aspect of domination was the main concern of the Black Consciousness Movement, which had such a profound impact on South Africa in the 1970s. For Steve Biko, the most influential advocate of Black Consciousness, the central point was that the 'psychological and cultural liberation of the mind of black people was a precondition for a successful struggle for political freedom'.[3] At that time, the ANC saw Black Consciousness as a potential rival, and the risk of this ideological heresy gaining a foothold in the ANC was one of the main reasons for the Communist Party to play the lead role in the construction of a security service that ruthlessly suppressed internal dissent, killing or torturing dozens of ANC members in the process. Today, official versions of the struggle, fixated with justifying the ANC's present claims to power, pass over the history of Black Consciousness almost entirely.

A similar issue concerns corruption. South African newspapers, some political insiders and many foreign observers seem to believe that South Africa's government has become increasingly corrupt since the late 1990s, with the notorious 1999 arms deal being a key event in the process. Yet the National Party government in its last years was also corrupt in significant ways. Because corruption cannot be exactly measured or even defined, it is, strictly speaking, impossible to compare statistically two different periods in South African history with a view to ascertaining whether the National Party was more or less corrupt than its successor. What can be done, though, is to investigate corruption as a process, by studying how specific practices became established and how they developed. Only in this way do broad comparisons become feasible. Here, the evidence may suggest a certain continuity in the methods by which South Africa is governed inasmuch as specific techniques of corruption were common to both National Party and ANC governments. The study of corruption provides a platform for studying the continuing formation of the South African state.

Finally, I have been aware that the ANC itself has been strongly influenced by what one writer calls 'the basic rule of Stalinist hermeneutics: since the official media do not openly report trouble, the most reliable way to detect it is to look out for compensatory excesses in state propaganda: the more "harmony" is celebrated, the more chaos and antagonism there is in reality'.[4] Influenced by the theory and practice of Marxism-Leninism, the ANC has over many years developed a practice of managing information to which this observation has some relevance.

I hasten to say that it is quite normal for a political party and its leading members to emphasise whatever they consider their most commendable achievements and to gloss over less glorious aspects of the past. But in the case of the ANC and the SACP in exile, something more is afoot. One of the SACP's most distinctive characteristics in the last century was a dogmatic and highly ideological reading of history that it used to justify its current position. When the SACP changed political course, it changed the history correspondingly. It could not tolerate any other interpretation of the past. The ANC learned this way of representing history from the SACP, and retained it even after the Party had lost the effective hegemony over the ANC that had developed in exile. The ANC learned to live by certain historical myths.

By calling a certain version of history a 'myth', I do not mean that it is a fabrication. 'A myth, in its simplest definition, is a story with a meaning attached to it other than it seems to have at first,' the great Victorian critic John Ruskin tells us.[5] Political myths are stories about the past that are taken out of their actual historical context and presented as timeless truths.[6]

Any coherent society has certain myths, stories with deep meaning that people tell each other about the past and that help them to find their way forward. The job of historians is not necessarily to destroy national myths, since nations need them. But myths need to be reread, reinterpreted in the light of new facts and new thoughts, and updated where necessary.

This is a serious business because political myths are linked to an infrastructure of action and policy. The longer politicians try to maintain myths that run counter to the currents actually at work in society, the greater the certainty that some sort of correction will occur. 'Officially invented history always prepares its own destruction,' as Van Zyl Slabbert put it.[7] 'The burden of the great lie becomes too heavy to bear.'

The essence of the ANC's version of its own immediate past, propagated by means of official documents, speeches, monuments and commemorations,[8] is that the ANC initiated an armed struggle that, after much sacrifice, was the main factor forcing the apartheid government to negotiate in circumstances that handed effective victory to the representatives of the majority of the population. This view has been perpetrated in a genre of struggle history, with its subsets of exile, popular protest and the armed struggle itself, which, it has been rightly observed, 'suffers from a severe case of Whiggishness'.[9] The past is interpreted only in light of the present, considered to be a higher and better phase of history.

I have tried to indicate in this book how and why the myths most dearly held by the ANC today differ from history, and why these myths have ceased to be useful to South Africa. Although history is an assembly of stories about the past, it is not the same as myth.

It is not the first time that I have told roughly the same story. The present book has its origins in an earlier one called *Comrades Against Apartheid: The ANC and the South African Communist Party in Exile*, published in 1992. It was co-written by myself and a member of the SACP and the ANC, who used the pen name Tsepo Sechaba. After the unbanning of the ANC in 1990, Tsepo Sechaba and I reasoned that if South Africans were now at last able to become legal members of the ANC and the SACP, and were shortly to be able to vote for them or any other party, then they should be as fully informed as possible. The two of us believed that the South African public should be aware of a history that government censorship had previously prevented it from knowing. For more than a generation, it had been very difficult for South Africans to acquire any information on the ANC and the SACP other than the little their government told them, which was sometimes false and always slanted.

Leading members of the SACP, especially, did not like *Comrades*

Against Apartheid. In a published review, Jeremy Cronin (today the Party's deputy general secretary) did not dispute our description of the less glorious aspects of the ANC-SACP alliance but complained that we did 'not take nearly enough care to uncover [the] sociology of political exile'. He accused *Comrades Against Apartheid* of advancing 'a grand conspiratorial explanation for realities that often have more banal causes'.[10] In other words, he thought it wrong to attribute to the Party things that were really just accidents of history. The late Chris Hani, at that time the SACP's general secretary, also discussed the book. In regard to its allegation that the ANC's security service had developed a culture of intolerance and repression in exile that emanated largely from the Party itself, Hani said that this was 'sheer, ridiculous anti-communism'. He agreed that there had been a culture of intolerance in exile, but claimed that those most critical of it were Communist Party members, including himself.[11] Another leading Party member, Garth Strachan, the son-in-law of Ronnie Kasrils, wrote a review accusing the book of scandal-mongering and, again, of fostering a conspiracy theory. He also threw a handful of insults at my co-author Tsepo Sechaba.[12]

It was clear that the SACP was uncomfortable with revelations about its role in exile. It reacted by trying to discredit anyone who wrote on the subject without official permission.

Here we return to questions of method. Since history is not a pure science, why should one version of the past be regarded as better than another? A simple answer is because a satisfactory version of a given historical period has to take account of the known facts. When *Comrades Against Apartheid* was published, there were rather few of these precious items to be found, since the ANC and SACP had been remarkably successful in preventing information about their own past from being publicly known, other than the sanitised versions that they released for public consumption. Even that small store of information was little known to the South African public after decades of censorship. There were good reasons for being cautious about information on the ANC and SACP released by the South African government, their sworn enemy. In view of the paucity of information on the inner workings of the ANC when *Comrades Against Apartheid* was published, it is hardly surprising that the book contained errors, gaps and oversights.

In the present book, I have as far as possible tried to correct some of the errors in my earlier attempt at telling this story. Its basic line of analysis I believe to have stood the test of time.

        ★ ★ ★

I conclude with a note on some of the terms used in this book and other editorial matters.

Regarding terms for racial groups, I have used the system that is conventional in South Africa of referring to blacks, coloureds, Indians and whites. Although people are no longer assigned by law to racial categories as they were in apartheid days, categorisation is still used by the government and is socially recognised.

In regard to the quotations in the text, I have generally corrected spelling and obvious typographical errors except where it appears useful to quote errors verbatim.

Concerning personal names, there is a problem with many of the ANC members mentioned in this book because they used several names, sometimes with variant spellings. Where possible, I have adopted the form used by people themselves in documents they have signed. The sometime ANC treasurer-general Mendi Msimang, for example, often signed his name as Maindy. Many people who joined the ANC in exile after 1960 adopted noms de guerre, and in time the ANC came to insist on the use of these. Some people eventually began to use aspects of their birth name and their nom de guerre simultaneously, like Chris Hani (Chris was an assumed name, Hani an original one). I have tried to use whichever name is likely to be most familiar to readers. Joe Modise, for example, was also known

as Thabo More and Joseph More, but I have generally called him by
his original name.

Acknowledgements

History books may be signed by one person, but they always represent a team effort involving dozens of librarians, archivists, colleagues, referees and others. In this case, that has been over a period of 25 years.

It is impossible to name everyone who has contributed to this particular book, but I must mention John Daniel, who invited me to work as a researcher for the Truth and Reconciliation Commission; Loammi Wolf, who helped me get access to the Stasi archive in Berlin; and David Welsh, who read a draft of the text. Alfred LeMaitre was an expert editor. I am also most grateful to Maxi Schoeman and her colleagues in the Department of Political Sciences at the University of Pretoria for their hospitality in 2010 and their grant of a visiting fellowship that gave me an opportunity to do archival research in Gauteng. Archbishop Desmond Tutu has been gracious in giving his name to a chair that I hold at the Vrije Universiteit Amsterdam. I thank the authorities both there and at the African Studies Centre in Leiden, my main employer, for allowing me the time and facilities to work on this book. I am particular indebted to Paul Trewhela, for his constant help and for his close comments on a draft of this book. Among other scholars, librarians and archivists whom I must single out are those who helped me in the search for pictures, especially Catherine Kennedy and her colleagues at the South African History Archive, Michele Pickover, James Sanders and, above all, Kier Schuringa.

Some of the South Africans who provided me with photos requested anonymity, and there are also many other South Africans to whom I am indebted but who have asked me not to mention their names or who would probably not be happy if I did so. Thank you to all of them too.

Some passages in Chapter One follow closely an article published in the *Journal of Southern African Studies*.

As always, my greatest debt is to the woman I love, Gerrie.

Stephen Ellis
Amsterdam, June 2012

Notes

1 Chapter One: Call to Arms

1 South African National Defence Force (SANDF) Documentation Centre, Pretoria, AMI/MI archive group 14, MI/204/2/2/9, document 130: 'Notes of a Meeting at Mfuwe Game Lodge, 13 September, 1985', 30pp, by AH Bloom, 17 September 1985.

2 For more detail, see Stephen Ellis, 'The Genesis of the ANC's Armed Struggle in South Africa, 1948–1961', *Journal of Southern African Studies*, 37, 4 (2011), pp 657–76.

3 For an explanation of the terms used in regard to ethnic groups, see the Appendix.

4 Hermann Giliomee, *The Afrikaners: Biography of a People* (Tafelberg, Cape Town, 2003), pp 479–82.

5 Cf Adrian Guelke, *Rethinking the Rise and Fall of Apartheid: South Africa and World Politics* (Palgrave Macmillan, Basingstoke and New York, 2005), p 83.

6 Archive for Contemporary Affairs, University of the Free State, Bloemfontein, PW Botha papers, PV 203, 1/K6/1: 'Their Red Diary. Smuts-Hofmeyer-Government and Communism', tract written by PW Botha, secretary to the HNP information committee, 1948.

7 Govan Mbeki, *The Struggle for Liberation in South Africa: A Short History* (Mayibuye Centre, Bellville, and David Philip, Cape Town, 1992), pp 50–1.

8 Recalled by John Pule Motshabi in an open letter to Joe Slovo contained in the University of Cape Town Archives, BC1081, Simons papers, file O.5: Motshabi to Slovo, 5 November 1985.

9 CJB Le Roux, 'Umkhonto we Sizwe: Its Role in the ANC's Onslaught against White Domination in South Africa, 1961–1988' (PhD thesis, University of Pretoria, 1992), p 1.

10 Raymond Mhlaba, *Personal Memoirs: Reminiscing from Rwanda and Uganda. Narrated to*

Thembeka Mufamadi (Human Sciences Research Council and Robben Island Museum, Pretoria, 2001), pp 31, 37.

11 *Ibid,* pp 58–59.

12 South African History Archive (SAHA), Cullen Library, University of the Witwatersrand, Johannesburg, AL2460, Julie Frederikse interviews: interview with Jacob Zuma, circa 1986.

13 Elinor Sisulu, *Walter and Albertina Sisulu: In Our Lifetime* (David Philip, Cape Town, 2002), p 146; Nelson Mandela, *Long Walk to Freedom: The Autobiography of Nelson Mandela* (1994; Abacus edition, London, 1995), p 320.

14 Historical Papers, Cullen Library, University of the Witwatersrand, Johannesburg, Bernstein papers, AL3051, R4.1–4.4: notes for an autobiography.

15 Ben Turok, *Nothing But the Truth: Behind the ANC's Struggle Politics* (Jonathan Ball, Johannesburg, 2003), p 44.

16 Rowley Arenstein, interview with RW Johnson in *London Review of Books*, 13, 4 (21 February 1991), pp 22–23.

17 Sisulu, *Walter and Albertina Sisulu*, p 112.

18 Bernard Magubane et al, 'The Turn to Armed Struggle', in South African Democracy Education Trust (SADET), *The Road to Democracy in South Africa, Volume 1, 1960–1970* (Zebra Press, Cape Town, 2004), p 54.

19 ANC minutes of Inkatha/ANC consultative meeting, London, 29–30 October 1979, p 11. Copy in Archive for Contemporary Affairs, Bloemfontein, HJ Coetsee papers PV357, 1/A1/5.

20 Magubane et al, 'The Turn to Armed Struggle', p 54.

21 Clive Glaser, '"When Are they Going to Fight?" Tsotsis, Youth Politics and the PAC', in Philip Bonner, Peter Delius and Deborah Posel (eds), *Apartheid's Genesis, 1935–1962* (Ravan Press and Witwatersrand University Press, Johannesburg, 1993), pp 296–315.

22 Historical Papers, Cullen Library, Karis-Gerhart papers, A2675, pt I, folder 18: interview with Makiwane by Tom Karis and Gwendolen Carter, 1964.

23 Stephen Clingman, *Bram Fischer: Afrikaner Revolutionary* (David Philip, Cape Town, 1998), pp 202–05.

24 See the autobiography at http://www.sahistory.org.za/people/vella-pillay-0 [accessed 17 October 2011].

25 Rusty Bernstein, 'Comments on Francis Meli's Manuscript? History of the ANC', Bernstein papers AL 3051, R4.1-4.4.

26 Le Roux, 'Umkhonto we Sizwe', pp 49–51.

27 Bernstein, 'Comments on Francis Meli's Manuscript? History of the ANC'.

28 Govan Mbeki, *South Africa: The Peasants' Revolt* (Penguin, Harmondsworth, 1964) was written by a member of the SACP Central Committee.

29 *Nkrumah's Subversion in Africa* (Ministry of Information, Accra, no date [1966]) includes photos and other details.

30 Brian Bunting, *Moses Kotane, South African Revolutionary* (Inkululeko Publications, London, 1975), pp 199–205.

31 Mhlaba, *Personal Memoirs*, p 107.

32 Fanele Mbali, *In Transit: Autobiography of a South African Freedom Fighter* (Xlibris Corporation, online publisher, 2011), p 55.

33 Andrew Masondo, 'Sawing Electric Pylons', *Dawn* (souvenir issue, 1986), pp 21–23.

34 *Ibid.*

35 Edward Feit, *Urban Revolt in South Africa 1960–1964: A Case Study* (Northwestern

University Press, Evanston, IL, 1971), pp 96, 125–29.

36 Jeqe Buthelezi, 'The Struggle for Liberation Still Continues', ms, no date [1971], in University of Fort Hare (UFH), ANC archives, Lusaka mission, pt 2, box 53, folder 7. This ms gives significant information on the origins of MK, based partly on Buthelezi's recollection of his discussions in Cairo and Dar es Salaam with Raymond Mhlaba before the latter's arrest at Rivonia. Jeqe Buthelezi is a pseudonym – not to be confused with Chief Mangosuthu Buthelezi.

37 Historical Papers, Cullen Library, University of the Witwatersrand, ANC papers, AD2186/E15.

38 Rica Hodgson, in an undated interview with Julie Frederikse: SAHA, Frederikse collection, AL2460.

39 Magubane et al, 'The Turn to Armed Struggle', p 71.

40 Vladimir Shubin, *ANC: A View from Moscow* (1999; 2nd revised edn, Jacana, Auckland Park, 2008), p 5.

41 *Ibid*, pp 25–26.

42 Magubane et al, 'The Turn to Armed Struggle', p 81.

43 Irina Filatova, 'The Lasting Legacy: the Soviet theory of the National-Liberation Movement and South Africa', paper presented to the Liberation Struggles in Southern Africa workshop, University of Cape Town, 4–6 September 2008, p 16, suggests that the whole group travelled to China. Shubin, *ANC,* p 26, suggests that Dadoo went alone, but a photo of Pillay and Dadoo with Chairman Mao taken on 3 November 1960 shows this to be mistaken.

44 Magubane et al, 'The Turn to Armed Struggle', p 81, where Deng's name is written as Dang Tsia-Ping.

45 Photograph available at http://www.idcpc.org.cn/ziliao/tupian/ziliao/tupianji/cornerstone/1-5-5.htm [accessed 24 November 2011]. I am grateful to Professor Yang Lihua for providing this link.

46 *Ibid.* The meeting is depicted in the photo on the front cover of this book.

47 Information contained in an unpublished manuscript by Essop Pahad quoted in Shubin, *ANC,* pp 26–27.

48 I have been unsuccessful in attempts to find an account of the meeting in Chinese state archives.

49 Magubane et al, 'The Turn to Armed Struggle', p 81.

50 Filatova, 'The Lasting Legacy', p 16.

51 Shubin, *ANC,* p 29.

52 Filatova, 'The Lasting Legacy', p 7.

53 *Ibid.*

54 Shubin, *ANC,* p 24.

55 Filatova, 'The Lasting Legacy', p 2.

56 *Ibid*, p 4.

57 Document 82, p 188, in *South African Communists Speak: Documents from the History of the South African Communist Party 1915–1980* (Inkululeko Publications, London, 1981).

58 Simons Papers, O.1: J Simons to Kotzé, 20 April 1991.

59 Filatova, 'The Lasting Legacy', p 17. A substantial extract from the report is published as document 91 in *South African Communists Speak,* pp 200–211.

60 Simons papers, O.4: letter from Jack Simons to the editor of the *Cape Times,* 23 July 1993; Filatova, 'The Lasting Legacy', p 17, notes that Marquard's 1957 presidential address to the SAIRR was devoted to this subject.

61 Email from Iain Edwards, 5 October 2011.
62 Document 115 in *South African Communists Speak*, pp 284–320.
63 Filatova, 'The Lasting Legacy', p 15.
64 According to Vladimir Shubin, *cited in* ibid, p 18.
65 Simons papers, O.4: Jack Simons to the editor, *Cape Times*, 23 July 1993.
66 Ellis, 'The Genesis of the ANC's Armed Struggle', pp 661–64.
67 'The SACP Conference, December 1960. Extract from Notes Made by Bob Hepple in May/June 1964', document provided by Sir Bob Hepple.
68 Bernstein's own account is in his *Memory Against Forgetting: Memoirs from a Life in South African Politics, 1938–1964* (Viking, London, 1999), p 225.
69 Turok, *Nothing But the Truth*, pp 122–23.
70 Magubane et al, 'The Turn to Armed Struggle', p 82.
71 Bernstein, *Memory Against Forgetting*, p 224.
72 'Kampanje vir die vrylating van Nelson Mandela', 'uiters geheim' memorandum, circa 1981, Coetsee papers PV 357, 1/M1/48.
73 Buthelezi, 'The Struggle for Liberation still Continues'.
74 Joe Modise, 'The Happiest Moment in My Life', *Dawn* (souvenir issue, 1986), p 10.
75 Baruch Hirson, *Revolutions in My Life* (Witwatersrand University Press, Johannesburg, 2001), p 301.
76 Chris Vermaak, *The Red Trap: Communism and Violence in South Africa* (APB Publishers, Johannesburg, 1966), pp 55–56.
77 Magnus Gunther, 'The National Committee of Liberation/African Resistance Movement (ARM)', in SADET, *The Road to Democracy in South Africa*, Volume 1, pp 193–233.
78 Masondo, 'Sawing Electric Pylons', p 21.
79 Shubin, *ANC*, p 7.
80 *Ibid*.
81 See the remarks by John Pule Motshabi in the minutes of SACP Africa group meeting, 13 May 1982: Simons papers, O.7-2.
82 In an interview with Irina Filatova on 4 November 2004, quoted in Apollon Davidson and Irina Filatova, *Rossia I Yuzhnaia Africa: navedeniie mostov* (Russia and South Africa: Building Bridges) (Publishing House of the Higher School of Economics, Moscow, 2012), pp 220–21.
83 Magubane et al, 'The Turn to Armed Struggle', p 55.
84 Anthony Sampson, *Mandela: The Authorized Biography* (Alfred A Knopf, New York, 1999), p 189.
85 *Ibid*.
86 Police file on Nelson Mandela, confidential source. See also Shubin, *ANC*, p 44.
87 Sheridan Johns and R. Hunt Davis, Jr (eds), *Mandela, Tambo and the African National Congress: The Struggle against Apartheid, 1948–1990: A Documentary Survey* (Oxford University Press, New York, 1991), p 71.
88 Sampson, *Mandela*, p 136.
89 Letter from Mandela to the liquidator, Department of Justice, 23 October 1967: archives of the Nelson Mandela Foundation, unclassified.
90 Gerard Ludi, *Operation Q-018* (Nasionale Boekhandel, Cape Town, 1969), pp 31, 217.
91 Simons papers, O.7-2: Minutes of SACP Africa group meeting, 13 May 1982.
92 Hilda Bernstein interview with Padraig O'Malley, 25 August 2004, 'O'Malley: The Heart of Hope', available at http://www.nelsonmandela.org/omalley/index.php/

site/q/03lv00017/04lv00344/05lv01461/06lv01476.htm [accessed 23 October 2010].

93 Padraig O'Malley, *Shades of Difference: Mac Maharaj and the Struggle for South Africa* (New York, Viking Penguin, 2007), p 63, noting that other relevant sources are embargoed until 2030.

94 Email from Paul Trewhela to the author, 1 November 2011.

95 Shubin, *ANC*, p 7.

96 Turok, *Nothing But the Truth*, p 49. Joe Slovo, on page 130 of his autobiography *Slovo: The Unfinished Autobiography of ANC Leader Joe Slovo* (1995; Ocean Press edn, Melbourne and New York, 1997), describes the ultra-secretive method of election to the Central Committee.

97 Le Roux, 'Umkhonto we Sizwe', pp 94–95.

98 Slovo, *Slovo*, p 176.

99 Mandela, *Long Walk to Freedom*, p 320.

100 Quoted in Magubane et al, 'The Turn to Armed Struggle', p 73.

101 *Ibid*, p 88.

102 Mandela, *Long Walk to Freedom*, p 321.

103 South African History Online, www.sahistory.org.za [accessed 10 January 2011]. See also Mandela, *Long Walk to Freedom*, pp 321–22.

104 Mandela, *Long Walk to Freedom*, p 322.

105 Feit, *Urban Revolt*, p 178.

106 Mandela, *Long Walk to Freedom*, pp 323–24.

107 'Zuma Praises Albert Luthuli', 25 November 2010, News24, available at http://www.news24.com/SouthAfrica/Politics/Zuma-praises-Albert-Luthuli-20101124 [accessed 15 March 2011].

108 Scott Everett Couper, '"An Embarrassment to the Congresses?": The Silencing of Chief Albert Luthuli and the Production of ANC History', *Journal of Southern African Studies*, 35, 2 (2009), pp 331–48. Slovo, on p 172 of his autobiography, confirms that Luthuli 'was not a party to the decision [on violence], nor was he ever to endorse it'.

109 Ronnie Kasrils, *Armed and Dangerous: My Undercover Struggle against Apartheid* (Heinemann Educational, Oxford, 1993), pp 49–50.

110 Couper, '"An Embarrassment to the Congresses?"'.

111 Attributed to Rowley Arenstein by Professor Colin Bundy: panel discussion of the history of the SACP, 18 January 1991, University of the Western Cape, Simons papers, O.1. On Arenstein, see Feit, *Urban Revolt*, pp 267–8.

112 Interview with RW Johnson in *London Review of Books*, 13, 4 (21 February 1991), pp 22–23.

113 'Memorandum Presented to the Government of the Republic of Ghana by the African National Congress of South Africa', 10 May 1962, unclassified, Padmore Library, Accra. I am grateful to Jan-Bart Gewald for supplying a copy of this document.

114 Sifiso Mxolisi Ndlovu, 'The ANC in Exile, 1960–1970', in SADET, *The Road to Democracy*, Volume 1, p 435.

115 Joe Slovo, 'The Sabotage Campaign', *Dawn* (souvenir issue, 1986), p 24.

116 Mbeki, *The Struggle for Liberation in South Africa*, p 90.

117 Slovo, *Slovo*, p 177.

118 *Ibid*, p 170.

119 South African Study Group, northwest London, 'On the Communist Party', 1959, 12pp typescript, Simons papers, O.1.

120 Luli Callinicos, *Oliver Tambo: Beyond the Engeli Mountains* (David Philip, Cape Town, 2004), p 284.

121 Mac Maharaj, interviewed by Hilda Bernstein in 1991: http://www.nelsonmandela. org/omalley/index.php/site/q/03lv03445/04lv03996/05lv04011.htm [accessed 28 December 2010].

122 Mhlaba, *Personal Memoirs*, pp 111–12; Slovo, *Slovo*, p 173, gives the date as September 1961.

123 Ndlovu, 'The ANC in Exile', p 454.

124 Mhlaba, *Personal Memoirs,* p 115.

125 Paul Trewhela, 'Wilton Mkwayi: ANC Leader Imprisoned with Nelson Mandela', *The Independent*, [London] 29 July 2004, available at http://www.independent.co.uk/ news/obituaries/raymond-mhlaba-484366.html [accessed 27 July 2011].

126 Paul Trewhela, 'Raymond Mhlaba: ANC Leader Imprisoned with Mandela', *The Independent*, 23 February 2005, available at http://www.independent.co.uk/news/ obituaries/raymond-mhlaba-484366.html [accessed 20 May 2011].

127 Mhlaba, *Personal Memoirs*, p 117.

128 Interview with Wilton Mkwayi in SADET, *The Road to Democracy: South Africans Telling their Stories, Volume 1, 1950–1970* (Tsehai Publishers, Hollywood, CA, 2008), p 269.

129 Modise, 'The Happiest Moment in my Life'.

130 Shubin, *ANC*, p 20.

131 Fish Keitsing (compiled by Jeff Ramsay and Barry Morton), *Comrade Fish: Memories of a Motswana in the ANC Underground* (Pula Press, Gaborone, 1999), p 51.

132 Mkwayi interview in SADET, *The Road to Democracy: South Africans Telling their Stories, Volume 1*, p 274; interview with Justice 'Gizenga' Mpanza, ibid, pp 341–42.

133 Thomas Karis and Gail Gerhart, *From Protest to Challenge: A Documentary History of African Politics in South Africa, Volume 5* (Unisa Press, Pretoria, 1997), p 22.

134 Vermaak, *The Red Trap*, p 57.

135 The October 1961 attack is described in 'Memorandum Presented to the Government of the Republic of Ghana by the African National Congress of South Africa' by Oliver Tambo, Nelson Mandela and Robert Resha, 10 May 1962, Padmore Library, Accra.

136 Bernstein, *Memory Against Forgetting*, p 234.

137 HD Stadler, *The Other Side of the Story: A True Perspective* (Contact Publishers, Pretoria, 1997), p 23.

138 Reg Shay and Chris Vermaak, *The Silent War: The Fight for Southern Africa* (Galaxie Press, Rhodesia, 1971), p 144.

139 Paul Landau, 'The ANC, MK, and "The Turn to Violence" (1960–62)', *South African Historical Journal,* forthcoming.

140 Letter from Mandela to the liquidator, Department of Justice, 23 October 1967: archives of the Nelson Mandela Foundation, unclassified.

141 Quoted in Landau, 'The ANC, MK, and "The Turn to Violence" (1960–62)'.

142 Buthelezi, 'The Struggle for Liberation Still Continues'.

143 Cornelius Thomas, *Tangling the Lion's Tail: Donald Card, from Apartheid Era Cop to Crusader for Justice* (private publication, East London, 2007), pp 153–55.

144 Magubane et al, 'The Turn to Armed Struggle', p 128.

145 Thomas, *Tangling the Lion's Tail*, pp 88–89.

146 Vermaak, *Red Trap*, p 43.

147 Wilton Mkwayi interview published by SADET at http://www.freewebs.com/red-
locationmuseumhistory/wiltonmkwayi.htm [accessed 18 March 2011].

148 *Ibid.*

149 Mbali, *In Transit*, p 79.

150 Mandela, *Long Walk to Freedom*, p 369.

151 Tom Lodge, *Mandela: A Critical Life* (Oxford University Press, Oxford, 2006), p 98.

152 *Ibid*, p 99.

153 Interview with RW Johnson in *London Review of Books*, 13, 4 (21 February 1991),
pp 22–23.

154 Gerard Ludi, *The Communistisation of the ANC* (Galago Publishing, Alberton, 2011),
p 132.

155 Denis Goldberg, *The Mission: A Life for Freedom in South Africa* (STE, Johannesburg,
2010), p 111.

156 Joseph Albright and Marcia Kunstel, 'CIA Tip Led to '62 Arrest of Mandela', *The
Atlanta Constitution*, 10 June 1990, p A14; Peter J Schraeder, *United States Foreign
Policy Towards Africa: Incrementalism, Crisis and Change* (Cambridge University Press,
Cambridge, 1994), p 202.

157 Letter to the author by a former US diplomat, 14 March 1997.

158 James Sanders, *Apartheid's Friends: The Rise and Fall of South Africa's Secret Service* (John
Murray, London, 2006), pp 17–20.

159 Tom Mangold, *Cold Warrior: James Jesus Angleton: The CIA's Master Spy Hunter* (Simon
& Schuster, London and New York, 1991), pp 195–201.

160 'Kampanje vir die vrylating van Nelson Mandela', Coetsee papers PV 357, 1/M1/48. The
information contained in this memorandum was based on research by PC Swanepoel.
See following note.

161 PC Swanepoel, *Really Inside BOSS: A Tale of South Africa's Late Intelligence Service (and
Something about the CIA)* (private publication, Pretoria, 2008), pp 138–87.

162 *Ibid*, p 257.

163 Francis Meli, *South Africa Belongs to Us: A History of the ANC* (1988; James Currey,
London, 1989), pp 150–54.

164 Lauritz Strydom, *ANC: Masker af* (Oranjewerkers Promosies, Morgenzon, 1990),
pp 15–16. Gerard Ludi, *The Communistisation of the ANC*, p 127, claims that the informant was a contractor who had done work at Liliesleaf Farm.

165 Glenn Frankel, *Rivonia's Children: Three Families and the Price of Freedom in South Africa*
(Weidenfeld and Nicholson, London, 1999), p 25.

166 Shay and Vermaak, *Silent War*, pp 138–41.

167 Letter from David Kitson, in *London Review of Books*, 18, 10 (23 May 1996).

168 Natoo Babenia, *Memoirs of a Saboteur, as Told to Iain Edwards* (Mayibuye History and
Literature Series no 58, Mayibuye Books, Bellville, 1995), p 61.

169 *Ibid.*

170 Simons papers, O.7.2: 'Some Problems Before Us – A Discussion Document', no date
[1961].

171 Simons papers, O.7.1: 'The New Year – Some Tasks and Perspectives' [December
1961?].

172 Slovo, 'The Sabotage Campaign'.

173 Archiv der Zentralstellen, Berlin, MFS, Sekr. D. Min., 576, p 19: minute of talks on 30
November-1 December 1964.

174 Email from Paul Trewhela, 14 October 2010. Kotane's warning is also recorded as

'when you throw a stone at people they are going to come back and break your windows', quoted in Magubane et al, 'The Turn to Armed Struggle', p 73.

175 Karl Popper, *The Poverty of Historicism* (Routledge and Kegan Paul, London, 1957).

Chapter Two: The External Mission

1 Andy McSmith, 'Oliver Tambo: the Exile', *The Independent*, 15 October 2007.

2 Roger Fieldhouse, *Anti-Apartheid: A History of the Movement in Britain* (Merlin Press, London, 2005), p 27.

3 Venitha Soobrayan, *Yusuf Dadoo* (Maskew Miller Longman, Cape Town, 1993), pp 53–4.

4 Scott Thomas, *The Diplomacy of Liberation: The Foreign Relations of the ANC Since 1960* (International Library of African Studies, IB Tauris, London and New York, 1996), pp 35–41.

5 Shay and Vermaak, *Silent War*, p. 144.

6 Buthelezi, 'The Struggle for Liberation still Continues'.

7 University of Fort Hare (UFH), ANC Lusaka mission, pt 2, 35/2: Nancy to Ndima, 28 April 1964.

8 Joe Slovo, 'The Sabotage Campaign', *Dawn* (souvenir issue, 1986), pp 24–5.

9 UFH, ANC Lusaka mission, pt 2, 53/6: summary of reports dated 29 January 1965.

10 UFH, ANC Lusaka mission, pt 2, 35/2: undated memorandum. See also SADET, *The Road to Democracy in South Africa, Volume 1*, especially Gregory Houston, 'The post-Rivonia ANC/SACP Underground'.

11 UFH, ANC Lusaka mission, pt 2, 53/6: summary of reports dated 29 January 1965.

12 Eddy Maloka, *The South African Communist Party in Exile 1963–1990* (Africa Institute of South Africa, Research Paper no 65, Pretoria, 2002), p 15.

13 *Ibid*, p 11.

14 *Ibid*, p 12.

15 *Ibid*, p 13.

16 UFH, ANC Lusaka mission, pt 2, 35/12: report by Arthur Goldreich, 24 August 1964.

17 Slovo, 'The Sabotage Campaign', pp 24–25.

18 *Truth and Reconciliation Commission of South Africa Report* (5 vols, TRC/Department of Justice, Pretoria, 1998), 2, p 195.

19 Thomas, *Tangling the Lion's Tail*, pp 174–76.

20 Vladimir Shubin, 'Unsung Heroes: the Soviet Military and the Liberation of Southern Africa', in Sue Onslow (ed), *Cold War in Southern Africa: White Power, Black Liberation* (Routledge, London, 2009), p 157. Shubin uses variant spellings of the place name (while berating others for doing the same).

21 *Ibid*, p 158.

22 Irina Filatova, 'The ANC and the Soviets', 10 August 2011: http://www.politicsweb.co.za/politicsweb/view/politicsweb/en/page71619?oid=250154&sn=Detail&pid=71619 [accessed 19 August 2011].

23 Shubin, *ANC*, p 47.

24 Mayibuye Centre, University of the Western Cape, Bellville, ANC archives, London mission, box 1, folder 1: SACP London secretariat to Kotane, 12 April 1965.

25 UFH, ANC Lusaka mission, pt 2, 53/6: 'Draft Memorandum on our Financial

Situation and Problems', by Moses Kotane, 1 July 1965.

26 SADET, *South Africans Telling their Stories, Volume 1*, p 270.

27 *Ibid*, p 273.

28 Arianna Lissoni, 'Transformations in the ANC External Mission and Umkhonto we Sizwe, c.1960–1969', *Journal of Southern African Studies*, 35, 2 (2009), p 295.

29 UFH, ANC London mission (ex-Mayibuye), 10/1: minutes of SACP Central Committee meeting, 12 January 1967.

30 Quoted in Ndlovu, 'The ANC in Exile', p 445.

31 Obituary of Robert Resha by Alfred Kgokong Mqota, in Simons papers, P.1.

32 'Reply to the Central Committee of the South African Communist Party Statement Entitled "The Enemy Hidden Under the Same Colour"', February 1976, p 33, copy in SAHA AL2457, H.1.

33 ANC archives, Mayibuye Centre, London mission, box 2: 'Notes on the Discussions between a Delegation from the C.C. of the S.A.C.P. and the N.E.C. of the A.N.C.', no date, 12 pp.

34 Shubin, *ANC*, pp 31–32.

35 UFH, ANC Lusaka mission, pt 2, 53/6: 'Problems of the Congress Movement', no date [1966]. Italics in the original. See also Nhlanhla Ndebele and Noor Nieftagodien, 'The Morogoro Conference: A Moment of Self-Reflection', in SADET, *The Road to Democracy, Volume 1*, p 581.

36 Turok, *Nothing But the Truth*, p 228.

37 UFH, ANC Lusaka mission, pt 2, 53/5: 'Report of sub-Committee on Problems of the Congress Movement'. The subcommittee, which met on 24 August 1966, consisted of MK [Kotane], JB [Marks] and DN [Nokwe].

38 ANC archives, Mayibuye Centre, London mission, box 1: 'Directive on the Nature of the Forthcoming Conference', by OR Tambo, March 1969.

39 Lissoni, 'Transformations in the ANC External Mission and Umkhonto we Sizwe', p 296.

40 UFH, ANC Lusaka mission, pt 2, 53/6: political report of the National Executive Committee to the consultative conference of the ANC, April 1969.

41 Quoted in the obituary of Robert Resha by Alfred Kgokong Mqota, in Simons papers, P.1.

42 Thula Bopela and Daluxolo Luthuli, *Umkhonto we Sizwe: Fighting for a Divided People* (Galago, Alberton, 2005), p 45. Sibeko's own autobiography (with Joyce Leeson) is *Freedom in Our Lifetime* (Indicator Press, Durban, 1996).

43 Sibeko, *Freedom in Our Lifetime*, p 81.

44 Karis-Gerhart papers, pt I, folder 32: note of dinner conversation with Robert Resha by Tom Karis, 13 June 1964.

45 Magubane et al, 'The Turn to Armed Struggle', pp 55–56.

46 Karis-Gerhart papers, pt III, folder 16: memo by Amin Cajee, no date [1969].

47 Simons papers, P.29.4: anon. report, 2 pp typescript.

48 UFH, ANC Lusaka mission, pt.2, 65/2: ms. notes of National Executive Committee meetings, 24 and 30 September 1964.

49 Bopela and Luthuli, *Umkhonto we Sizwe*, p 40.

50 Kasrils, *Armed and Dangerous*, p 94.

51 Sibeko, *Freedom in Our Lifetime*, p 83.

52 Karis-Gerhart papers, A2675, pt III, folder 16: memo by Maurice Mthombeni, 1969.

53 Simons Papers, O.11.1: minutes of Unit 7 meeting, Lusaka, 1 September 1983.

54 Karis-Gerhart papers, pt III, folder 16: memo by Maurice Mthombeni, 1969.

55 Quoted in Ndlovu, 'The ANC in Exile', p 451, note 137.

56 Quoted in *ibid*, p 467.

57 Simons papers, P.29.4: anonymous report, 2 pp typescript.

58 Simons papers, P.1.1: 'Brief Autobiography', by John Pule Motshabi, document received on 7 June 1988.

59 SANDF, AMI/HDI, group 15, file 124; police memorandum on terrorism, 22 November 1968.

60 Karis-Gerhart papers, pt III, folder 16: memo by Maurice Mthombeni, 1969, which misspells Molaoa.

61 Bopela and Luthuli, *Umkhonto we Sizwe*, p 49.

62 Sisulu, *Walter and Albertina Sisulu*, pp 220–21.

63 Bopela and Luthuli, *Umkhonto we Sizwe*, p 49.

64 Simons papers, P.1.1: 'Brief Autobiography', by John Pule Motshabi, document received on 7 June 1988.

65 *Ibid*.

66 ANC, Second Submission to the TRC, 'Operations Report: The Department of Intelligence and Security', at http://www.justice.gov.za/trc/hrvtrans/submit/anc2.htm#Operations [accessed 10 August 2011].

67 Karis-Gerhart papers, pt III, folder 24: 'Issues Influencing my Thinking at Present', by JJ Hadebe, 1 March 1967.

68 Simons papers, P.1: Eric Mandzi, 'A short biography'. Manzi's name is spelt in various ways.

69 Simons papers, P.1.1: 'Brief Autobiography', pt 1, by John Pule Motshabi, document received on 7 June 1988.

70 Rendani Moses Ralinala et al, 'The Wankie and Sipolilo Campaigns', in SADET, *The Road to Democracy in South Africa, Volume 1*, p 500.

71 Simons papers, P.1.1: 'Brief Autobiography', pt 2, by John Pule Motshabi, document received on 7 June 1988.

72 Feit, *Urban Revolt*, p 253.

73 Sisulu, *Walter and Albertina Sisulu*, p 221.

74 Hugh Macmillan, 'The "Hani Memorandum" – Introduced and Annotated', *Transformation*, 69 (2009), pp 118 and 127, note 57.

75 See, eg, the draft budget in the papers at UFH, ANC London mission (ex-Mayibuye Centre files), 5/2.

76 UFH, ANC London mission (ex-Mayibuye Centre files), 10/2.

77 *Ibid*.

78 Mayibuye Centre, ANC London mission, box 13: 'Report on Maoists', no date [1967]. A marginal note in Dadoo's handwriting suggests that this document was submitted to him.

79 Vladimir Shubin, 'Yusuf Dadoo. Some Facts of his Life', para 5. http://www.sahistory.org.za/pages/people/special%20projects/dadoo-yusuf/pdfs/yusuf_dadoo_some_facts.pdf [accessed 11 April 2011].

80 Tom Lodge, *Sharpeville: An Apartheid Massacre and its Consequences* (Oxford University Press, Oxford, 2011), pp 234–79.

81 Also called Mendi Msimang. See the Appendix for an explanation.

82 Mayibuye Centre, ANC London mission, box 13: 'Report on Factionalism', 30 April 1972.

83 *Ibid.*

84 'NAT Workshop on Policy', no date [post-1990]. Confidential source.

85 Cf Hugh Lewin, *Stones Against the Mirror: Friendship in the Time of the South African Struggle* (Umuzi, Cape Town, 2011), p 59.

86 Simons papers, P.26.1: circular letter on the history of NAT by Sizakele Sigxashe, 8 July 1993.

87 *Ibid.*

88 Macmillan, 'The "Hani Memorandum"', p 118.

89 ANC, Second Submission to the TRC, 'Operations Report: The Department of Intelligence and Security' at http://www.justice.gov.za/trc/hrvtrans/submit/anc2.htm#Operations [accessed 10 August 2011].

90 Ndlovu, 'The ANC in Exile', p 426.

91 Note of dinner conversation with Thomas Karis, 13 June 1964: Karis-Gerhart papers, pt I, 32.

92 Kevin O'Brien, *The South African Intelligence Services: From Apartheid to Democracy, 1948–2005* (Routledge, London, 2011), p 37.

93 Thomas, *Tangling the Lion's Tail*, p 177.

94 Sanders, *Apartheid's Friends*, pp 9–17.

95 Houston, 'The post-Rivonia ANC/SACP Underground'.

96 SANDF, AMI/HDI group 15, file 124: memorandum by Captain Coetzee, 16 February 1968.

97 SANDF, AMI/HDI group 15, file 124: statement by Zolile Willie Nqose, 18 April 1968.

98 UFH, ANC Lusaka mission, pt 2, 29/4.

99 Ralinala et al, 'The Wankie and Sipolilo Campaigns', p 487.

100 SANDF, AMI/HDI group 15, file 124: statement by Zolile Willie Nqose, 18 April 1968.

101 Simons papers, P.5.1: Tambo to Comrade Ringo, 5 April 1969.

102 Thomas Nkobi, in *Dawn* (souvenir issue, 1986), p 39.

103 UFH, ANC Morogoro mission, 27/12: intervention by Alfred Kgokong in notes of the NEC meeting on 16 April 1967.

104 SANDF, AMI/HDI group 15, file 124: statement by Zolile Willie Nqose, 18 April 1968.

105 Bernard Magubane, *My Life and Times* (University of KwaZulu-Natal Press, Scottsville, 2010), p 146.

106 Bopela and Luthuli, *Umkhonto we Sizwe*, p 55. An account by one of the campaign organisers is Sibeko, *Freedom in Our Lifetime*, pp 87–90.

107 Simons papers, P.5.1: Tambo to Comrade Ringo, 5 April 1969.

108 *Ibid.*

109 UFH, ANC Lusaka mission, Department of International Affairs, 16/18: 'Speech Delivered by the NEC Representatives at the ANC Youth and Students Seminar', East Germany, 1–14 August 1971.

110 Ken Flower, *Serving Secretly: An Intelligence Chief on Record: Rhodesia into Zimbabwe, 1964 to 1981* (John Murray, London, 1987), p 108.

111 Ralinala et al, 'The Wankie and Sipolilo Campaigns', p 529.

112 Chris Hani, 'The Wankie Campaign', *Dawn*, souvenir issue, 1986, p 37.

113 Stadler, *The Other Side of the Story*, p 81.

114 Official ANC website, http://www.anc.org.za/100?t=Umkhonto%20we%20Sizwe

[accessed 20 March 2011].

115 Turok, *Nothing But the Truth*, p 230.

116 Nathan Shamuyarira, *Liberation Movements in Southern Africa* (8th annual Hans Wolff memorial lecture, Indiana University, Bloomington, IN, 1978), p 9.

117 Hani, 'The Wankie Campaign', p 37. Alternative accounts may be found in the biography of Basil February attached to the South African History Online newsletter, no 224, 6 January 2012.

118 Bopela and Luthuli, *Umkhonto we Sizwe*, p 55.

119 Simons papers, BC1081, P.29.6: list dated 14 December 1979.

120 UFH, ANC Lusaka mission, pt 2, 7/41: Keith [Mokoape?] to Nzo, no date [received 28 February 1980].

121 Ralinala et al, 'The Wankie and Sipolilo Campaigns', p 532.

122 *ANC Speaks: Documents and Statements of the African National Congress 1955–1976* (no place or date), p 116.

123 Shay and Vermaak, *Silent War*, pp 147–48.

124 Ralinala et al, 'The Wankie and Sipolilo Campaigns', pp 537–38.

125 Simons papers, P.1.1: 'Brief Autobiography', by John Pule Motshabi, document received on 7 June 1988.

126 Quoted in Ndlovu, 'The ANC in Exile', p 451. *Nkwenkwe* is a Xhosa word for a boy. During a search of the ANC's Morogoro mission papers in 2010, I was unable to locate key documents on this issue referred to by Ndlovu.

127 SANDF, AMI/HDI group 15, file 124: memorandum by Captain Coetzee, 16 February 1968.

128 Flower, *Serving Secretly*, p 108. The ZIPRA intelligence chief, Dumiso Dabengwa, has claimed that 'there were already units of the South African Army operating together with the Rhodesian army', but this appears to be inaccurate. 'ZIPRA in the Zimbabwe War of National Liberation', in Ngwabi Bhebe and Terence Ranger (eds), *Soldiers in Zimbabwe's Liberation War* (James Currey, London, 1995), p 27.

129 Flower, *Serving Secretly*, p 108.

130 Daan Prinsloo, *Stem uit die Wilderness: 'n Biografie oor Oud-Pres. P.W. Botha* (Vaandel Uitgewers, Mosselbaai, 1997), p 50.

131 Paul Matthysen, Matthew Kalkwarf and Michael Huxtable, *'Recce': A Collector's Guide to the History of the South African Special Forces* (30° South Publishers, Johannesburg, 2010), pp 22–23.

132 O'Brien, *The South African Intelligence Services*, pp 22–23.

133 Bodleian Library of Commonwealth and African Studies at Rhodes House, University of Oxford, TR Wade papers, box 1: memorandum on Rhodesia by FA Wearing, no date.

134 Matthysen et al, 'Recce', p 17.

135 cf David Welsh, *The Rise and Fall of Apartheid* (Jonathan Ball, Johannesburg and Cape Town, 2009), pp 198–203.

136 Botswana National Archives and Records Services, Gaborone: Office of the President series, OP 27/3/96: note by Commissioner of Police, 23 October 1968.

137 Macmillan, 'The "Hani Memorandum"', p 107. The following is based on Macmillan's introduction.

138 Janet Smith and Beauregard Tromp, *Hani: A Life Too Short* (Jonathan Ball, Johannesburg and Cape Town, 2009), pp 113–16.

139 Macmillan, 'The "Hani Memorandum"', pp 114–21, reproduces the memorandum itself.

140 Thabo More [Modise] to Malome [Moses Kotane], Morogoro, 16 July 1968. Confidential source.

141 Tseko Nell, 'Political Leadership in South Africa', *Sowetan*, 30 March 2012.

142 Macmillan, 'The "Hani Memorandum"', p 112.

143 *Ibid.*

144 Mayibuye Centre, Bunting papers, 136/12.8: 'Who's Who in the Expelled Group of Eight', 5 pp, no date [1975].

145 *Ibid.*

146 Macmillan, 'The "Hani Memorandum"', p 112.

147 UFH, ANC Lusaka mission, pt 2, 49/17: Pule to Nzo, 18 December 1981.

148 Mayibuye Centre, London papers, box 1: 'Directive on the Nature of the Forthcoming Conference', by OR Tambo, March 1969.

149 Maloka, *The South African Communist Party in Exile*, pp 15–17.

150 *Ibid*, p 17.

Chapter Three: The Party Triumphant

1 Magubane, *My Life and Times*, p 160.

2 *Ibid.*

3 *Ibid*, p 157.

4 Ndebele and Nieftagodien, 'The Morogoro Conference', p 597.

5 Turok, *Nothing But the Truth*, p 228.

6 Mayibuye Centre, Bunting papers, 136/12.8: 'Who's Who in the Expelled Group of Eight', 5pp, no date [1975].

7 Magubane, *My Life and Times*, p 160.

8 Simons papers, P.1.1: 'Brief Autobiography', by John Pule Motshabi, document received on 7 June 1988.

9 Maloka, *The South African Communist Party in Exile*, p 21.

10 Archiv der Zentralstellen, MFS, HAII, 28715: undated memorandum on the ANC.

11 'First National Consultative Conference: Report on the Strategy and Tactics of the African National Congress', 26 April 1969, http://www.anc.org.za/show.php?id=149 [accessed 14 April 2011].

12 Sol Dubula, 'Ten Years of Umkhonto we Sizwe', 1971, p 392, document 128 in *South African Communists Speak*.

13 'First National Consultative Conference: Report on the Strategy and Tactics of the African National Congress', 26 April 1969, http://www.anc.org.za/show.php?id=149 [accessed 14 April 2011].

14 Dale T McKinley, *The ANC and the Liberation Struggle: A Critical Political Biography* (Pluto Press, London, 1997), p 38.

15 Simons papers, P.8: 'Statement on the Expulsion from the A.N.C. (S.A.) …', 27 December 1975, issued by the eight expelled members.

16 Simons papers, P.1.1: 'Brief Autobiography', by John Pule Motshabi, document received on 7 June 1988.

17 Shubin, *ANC*, p 72.

18 Mabhida's autobiography is available from http://www.disa.ukzn.ac.za/webpages/

DC/bio00000000.026.021.000/bio00000000.026.021.000.pdf [accessed 21 March 2011].

19 'Further Submissions and Responses by the African National Congress to Questions Raised by the Commission for Truth and Reconciliation', 12 May 1997. http://www.anc.org.za/show.php?include=docs/misc/1997/trc2a.html [accessed 21 March 2011]. There also exists a printed version of this report dated 6 April 1997.

20 Stated by O'Brien, *The South African Intelligence Services*, p 77. No other source seems to confirm this, suggesting that the establishment of NAT may not have been a formal conference decision.

21 Hans-Georg Schleicher, 'GDR Solidarity: the German Democratic Republic and the South African Liberation Struggle', SADET, *The Road to Democracy in South Africa, Volume 3* (Unisa Press, Pretoria, 2008), p 1131.

22 Simons Papers, P.26.1: circular letter on the history of NAT by Sizakele Sigxashe, 8 July 1993.

23 Mayibuye Centre, ANC London mission, box 6.

24 *Ibid.*

25 *Ibid.* Some of the papers in this box appear to have been sent to Tambo under a covering letter dated 19 April 1969, but the archive's arrangement does not permit accurate dating.

26 UFH, ANC Morogoro mission, 27/3: memo by Morogoro office committee, 24 April 1974.

27 'Reply to the Central Committee of the South African Communist Party Statement Entitled "The Enemy Hidden Under the Same Colour"', SAHA, AL2457, H.1. Quotation at p 3.

28 *Ibid.*

29 *Ibid*, p 44.

30 Maloka, *The South African Communist Party in Exile*, p 25.

31 UFH, ANC Morogoro mission, 26/11: Shope to Ray [Simons], 1 August 1972.

32 Simons papers, P.8: 'Statement on the Expulsion from the A.N.C. (S.A.) ...', 27 December 1975, issued by the eight expelled members.

33 Mark Gevisser, *Thabo Mbeki: The Dream Deferred* (Jonathan Ball, Johannesburg and Cape Town, 2007), p 277.

34 Maloka, *The South African Communist Party in Exile*, p 33.

35 Gevisser, *Thabo Mbeki*, p 289.

36 UFH, ANC Lusaka mission, pt 2, 52/1: report of the secretariat, pt 2, no date [1970].

37 UFH, ANC Lusaka mission, pt 2, 49/19: Nkobi to Nzo, 13 October 1969. See also Hugh Macmillan, 'The African National Congress of South Africa in Zambia: The Culture of Exile and the Changing Relationship with Home, 1964–1990', *Journal of Southern African Studies*, 35, 2 (2009), pp 313–14.

38 Karis-Gerhart papers, pt III, folder 18: 'Memorandum by the ANC (SA) on the Implications and Consequences of Disciplinary Action ...', by Thomas Nkobi, 14 December 1970.

39 UFH, ANC Lusaka mission, pt 2, 53/6: 'A.N.C. Cadres at Kongwa', 6 pp, no date [1969].

40 Sifiso Mxolisi Ndlovu, 'The ANC's Diplomacy and International Relations', SADET, *The Road to Democracy in South Africa, Volume 2*, p 662; interview with ANC intelligence officer, 6 November 1989. The late Oscar Kambona, in an interview with the author, denied this allegation.

41 Karis and Gerhart, *From Protest to Challenge: Volume 5*, p 27.

42 Personal communication by Dr Jim Brennan.

43 Shubin, *ANC*, pp 78–79.

44 UFH, ANC Lusaka mission, pt 2, 49/20: 'Confidential Interim Report to RC Members', no date, apparently circulated by Tambo on 15 September 1970.

45 *Ibid.*

46 *Ibid.*

47 Shubin, *ANC*, p 80.

48 Mbali, *In Transit*, p 88.

49 The citation for an award of the Order of Luthuli in gold, published by the Presidency in 2005, is at http://www.thepresidency.gov.za/orders/042605/part3.pdf [accessed 7 March 2011].

50 Simons papers, P.5.2: J Simons to Moonsamy, 5 August [1969].

51 UFH, ANC Lusaka mission, pt 2, 5/34: letter from Maindy Msimang, 8 February 1972.

52 UFH, ANC Lusaka mission, Department of International Affairs, 13/39: September to Nzo, 24 April 1972.

53 Shubin, 'Unsung Heroes', p 158.

54 Obituary of Joe Slovo by Bill Keller, *The New York Times*, 7 January 1995.

55 Obituary of David Kitson by Harold Strachan, *Noseweek* 135 (January 2011).

56 Karis-Gerhart papers, pt I, folder 1: interview with Rowley Arenstein, 20 November 1990.

57 Shubin, *ANC*, pp 80–85.

58 Shay and Vermaak, *Silent War*, p 147.

59 Maloka, *The South African Communist Party in Exile*, pp 28–30.

60 Stadler, *The Other Side of the Story*, pp 29–30; Kasrils's own account is in *Armed and Dangerous*, pp 112–13.

61 Maloka, *The South African Communist Party in Exile*, p 36.

62 Thomas, *Tangling the Lion's Tail*, p 180.

63 PC Swanepoel, 'Secrets and Stories of Boers and Brits', unpublished ms.

64 *Ibid.*

65 Henry Pike, *A History of Communism in South Africa* (2nd edn, Christian Mission International of South Africa, Germiston, 1988), p 364.

66 Thomas, *Tangling the Lion's Tail*, p 180.

67 Patrick J Furlong, *Between Crown and Swastika: The Impact of the Radical Right on the Afrikaner Nationalist Movement in the Fascist Era* (Wesleyan University Press, Hanover, NH, 1991), pp 145–47.

68 Thomas, *The Diplomacy of Liberation*, p 61.

69 'Draft Proposal for a New Strategy of the African National Congress of South Africa', November 1970, anonymous, but given to Thomas Karis by Pascal Ngakane: Karis-Gerhart papers, pt III, folder 18.

70 Karis and Gerhart, *From Protest to Challenge, Volume 5*, pp 32–33.

71 Raymond Suttner, *The ANC Underground in South Africa: A Social and Historical Study* (Jacana, Auckland Park, 2008), pp 59–83.

72 UFH, ANC Lusaka mission, pt 2, 36/28: Thabo and Albert to National Executive Committee, 14 June 1975.

73 Kasrils, *Armed and Dangerous*, pp 116–21.

74 Gregory Houston and Bernard Magubane, 'The ANC Political Underground in the

1970s', in SADET, *The Road to Democracy in South Africa, Volume 2* (Unisa Press, Cape Town, 2007), p 402.

75 UFH, ANC Lusaka mission, pt 2, 36/28: Thabo and Albert to National Executive Committee, 14 June 1975.

76 Houston and Magubane, 'The ANC Political Underground in the 1970s', p 403.

77 *Ibid*, p 387.

78 Simons papers, P.1.1: 'Brief Autobiography', by John Pule Motshabi, document received on 7 June 1988.

79 *Ibid*.

80 'Reply to the Central Committee of the South African Communist Party Statement Entitled "The Enemy Hidden Under the Same Colour"', SAHA, AL2457, H.1, p 35.

81 UFH, ANC Lusaka mission, pt 2, 49/20: Nzo to A Makiwane, 22 January 1970.

82 *Ibid*: Nzo to A Makiwane, 10 August 1971.

83 'Further Submissions and Responses by the African National Congress to Questions Raised by the Commission for Truth and Reconciliation', 12 May 1997. http://www.anc.org.za/show.php?include=docs/misc/1997/trc2a.html [accessed 22 March 2011].

84 Magubane, *My Life and Times*, p 159.

85 Mayibuye Centre, ANC London mission, box 13: 'Report on Factionalism', 30 April 1972.

86 Magubane, *Life and Times*, p 155.

87 Mayibuye Centre, ANC London mission, box 13, undated report.

88 Mayibuye Centre, ANC London mission, box 13: 'Report on Factionalism', 30 April 1972.

89 *Ibid*.

90 *Ibid*.

91 *Ibid*.

92 Simons papers, P.8: 'Current Trends within the Organisation (ANC)', confidential memorandum, March 1972.

93 *Ibid*.

94 Simons papers, P.1.1: 'Brief Autobiography', pt 2, by John Pule Motshabi, document received on 7 June 1988.

95 UFH, ANC Lusaka mission, pt 2, 52/1: report of the secretariat, pt 2, no date [1970].

96 Turok, *Nothing But the Truth*, pp 224–5.

97 UFH, ANC Morogoro mission, 2/15: 'Report on Special Meetings of the A.N.C. (S.A.) African Members Resident in the U.K.', 7 pp.

98 UFH ANC Morogoro mission, 2/15: Liphoko to Tambo, 17 February 1975.

99 Interview with Wilton Mkwayi in SADET, *The Road to Democracy: South Africans Telling their Stories Volume 1*, p 272.

100 In October 2010, in a search at the National Archives and Records Service in Pretoria, I was unable to trace the correspondence between Kgokong/Mqota and Mkwayi.

101 Mayibuye Centre, ANC London mission, box 13: 'Guard the Unity of the Whole Movement', draft SACP document.

102 *Ibid*.

103 *Ibid*.

104 Imtiaz Cajee, *Timol: A Quest for Justice* (STE Publishers, Johannesburg, 2005).

105 'Reply to the Central Committee of the South African Communist Party Statement Entitled "The Enemy Hidden Under the Same Colour"', SAHA, AL2457, H.1, p 30.

106 Karis-Gerhart papers, pt III, folder 23: Liphoko to Nzo, 17 February 1975.
107 UFH, ANC Lusaka mission, pt 2, 49/20: Tambo to Nzo, 22 June 1970.
108 'Reply to the Central Committee of the South African Communist Party Statement Entitled "The Enemy Hidden Under the Same Colour"', p 20.
109 A copy of his speech is at UFH, Neame papers, 7/68.
110 Karis-Gerhart papers, pt III, folder 24: statement issued by Nzo, Lourenço Marques, 23 January 1976.
111 This name is also given as Milton Sethlopele.
112 Thomas, *The Diplomacy of Liberation*, p 163.
113 *Ibid.*
114 See Mayibuye Centre, Bunting papers, 136/12.8: 'Who's Who in the expelled Group of Eight', 5 pp, no date [1975] for some very hostile pen-pictures of the group.
115 'Reply to the Central Committee of the South African Communist Party Statement Entitled "The Enemy Hidden Under the Same Colour"'. Quotation at p 2.
116 Botswana National Archives and Records Services, Office of the President series, OP 27/46/176: 'Statement on the Expulsion from the A.N.C. (S.A.) ... Issued by the Expelled Eight Members', 27 December 1975.
117 Botswana National Archives and Records Services, Office of the President series, OP 27/46/128: Permanent Secretary to the President to head of Special Branch, 31 March 1976.
118 Turok, *Nothing But the Truth*, pp 224–25.
119 Magubane, *My Life and Times*, p 159.
120 SAHA, Frederikse collection, AL2460: interview with Rusty and Hilda Bernstein, 25 January 1987.
121 *Ibid.*
122 *Ibid.*
123 Magubane, *My Life and Times*, p 155.
124 Ndlovu 'The ANC in Exile', p 442.
125 SADET, *The Road to Democracy: South Africans Telling their Stories, Volume 1*, pp 19–20.
126 See Arenstein's interview with RW Johnson in *London Review of Books*, 13, 4 (21 February 1991), pp 22–23.
127 Simons papers, P.29.8: 'Proposals to Improve the Efficiency of the Working of the ANC of South Africa by Roma Unit', no date [1975].
128 *Ibid.*
129 Turok, *Nothing But the Truth*, p 227.
130 Gevisser, *Thabo Mbeki*, pp 458–61, on the rivalry with Slovo.
131 *Ibid*, p 295.
132 Simons papers, O.7.1: 'Guidelines', February 1978.
133 Simons papers, O.12: 'Comments on the Party Programme', no date.
134 Bopela and Luthuli, *Umkhonto we Sizwe*, p 49.
135 Mayibuye Centre ANC London mission, box 1: Matthews to Dadoo, 5 August 1972.
136 UFH, ANC Lusaka mission, Department of International Affairs, 16/18: 'Speech Delivered by the NEC Representatives at the ANC Youth and Students seminar', East Germany, 1–14 August 1971.
137 SAHA, AL2457, H.3: 'From Guerrillas to Policemen', 6 pp, 8 or 9 December 1974, pamphlet by the Workers' Organisation for Socialist Action.
138 Karis-Gerhart papers, pt III, folder 22: 'Interviews in Depth: Alfred Nzo', pamphlet published by LSM Information Centre, Richmond, BC, Canada, no date [1974].

139 JHP Serfontein, 'Amazing Peace Move by Top ANC Man', *Sunday Times*, 18 April 1976.
140 'Summary Record of a Meeting Held with Representatives of the ANC (S.A.) on 22nd March, 1976': Botswana National Archives and Records Services, Office of the President series, OP 27/46/98.
141 Karis-Gerhart papers, pt I, folder 32: interview with Joe Matthews, 21 July 1976.
142 Christopher Andrew and Vasili Mitrohkin, *The Mitrohkin Archive II: The KGB and the World* (Allen Lane, London, 2005), ch 23, especially pp 480–81.
143 Gordon Winter, *Inside BOSS, South Africa's Secret Police* (Penguin, Harmondsworth, 1981).
144 *TRC Report*, 2, p 17.
145 SAHA, AL2457, 5.5.2: ANC pamphlet.
146 Archiv der Zentralstellen, MFS Sekr. D. Min., 576, p 19: minute of KGB/Stasi talks on 30 November-1 December 1964.
147 Sue Onslow, 'The Cold War in Southern Africa: White Power, Black Nationalism and External Intervention', in Sue Onslow (ed), *Cold War in Southern Africa: White Power, Black Liberation* (Routledge, London and New York, 2009), p 25.

Chapter Four: New Strategies

1 Houston and Magubane, 'The ANC Political Underground in the 1970s', p 481.
2 Callinicos, *Oliver Tambo*, p 542.
3 Simons papers P.5.1: Kasrils to J Simons, 24 March 1980.
4 Simons papers, P.29.1: anonymous memorandum on people's war.
5 Houston and Magubane, 'The ANC Political Underground in the 1970s', p 481.
6 Maren Sæbø, 'A State of Exile: The ANC and Umkhonto we Sizwe in Angola, 1976–1989' (MA thesis, University of Natal, 2002), p 107.
7 Simons papers, P.29.1: anonymous memorandum on people's war.
8 Frederikse papers: interview with Francis Meli, June 1986.
9 *Ibid*.
10 SAHA, AL2457, 5.5.2: 'The ANC and the Black Consciousness Movement'.
11 *Ibid*.
12 Craig Williamson, interviewed by Tor Sellström, 23 April 1996: http://www.liberation-africa.se/intervstories/interviews/williamson/ [accessed 19 August 2011].
13 Leo Raditsa, *Prisoners of a Dream: The South African Mirage* (Prince George Street Press, Annapolis, MD, 1989), p 426.
14 'Guidelines Supplement and New Tasks', no date [1977], confidential source.
15 'Report by Cde J Gqabi', 11 August 1978, confidential source.
16 O'Malley, *Shades of Difference*, p 204.
17 *Ibid*.
18 *Ibid*, pp 204–05.
19 *Ibid*, p 205.
20 Howard Barrell, 'Conscripts to their Age: African National Congress Operational Strategy, 1976–1986' (DPhil, University of Oxford, 1993), p 171, who gives a later date for the appointment.

21 O'Malley, *Shades of Difference*, p 218.

22 Callinicos, *Oliver Tambo*, p 529.

23 'The Development of the Underground – the Need for a Scientific Approach?', 23 June 1983, confidential source.

24 'Guidelines Supplement and New Tasks', no date [1977], confidential source.

25 UFH, ANC Lusaka mission, subject files 124/204: Nzo to Politico-Military Council, 23 December 1983.

26 *Ibid.*

27 Maloka, *The South African Communist Party in Exile*, p 41.

28 Chitja Twala, 'The African National Congress Youth League's (ANCYL's) Role as the "Kingmaker": a Movement of post-Polokwane Blues?', *Journal for Contemporary History/Joernaal vir Eietydse Geskiedenis*, 34, 3 (2009), p 154.

29 Sæbø, 'A State of Exile', chapter 4.

30 James Ngculu, *The Honour to Serve: Reflections of an Umkhonto Soldier* (David Philip, Cape Town, 2009), pp 61–62.

31 ANC, 'The Shishita Report', p 16. Confidential source. See also David Beresford, *Truth is a Strange Fruit: A Personal Journey through the Apartheid War* (Jacana, Auckland Park, 2010), pp 48–49.

32 'Further Submissions and Responses by the African National Congress to Questions Raised by the Commission for Truth and Reconciliation', 12 May 1997: Operations Report: The Department of Intelligence and Security: http://www.justice.gov.za/trc/hrvtrans/submit/anc2.htm#Operations [accessed 10 August 2011].

33 Stephen Davis, 'Cosmopolitans in Close Quarters: Everyday Life in the Ranks of Umkhonto we Sizwe (1961-present)' (PhD, University of Florida, 2010), p 176.

34 Houston and Magubane, 'The ANC Political Underground in the 1970s', pp 468-75.

35 Stadler, *The Other Side of the Story*, p 41.

36 Barrell, 'Conscripts to their Age', p 166.

37 *Ibid*, p 188.

38 *Ibid*, pp 187–90.

39 Quoted in *ibid*, p 189.

40 O'Malley, *Shades of Difference*, p 222.

41 Houston and Magubane, 'Armed Struggle in the 1970s', pp 508–9.

42 Barrell, 'Conscripts to their Age', p 191.

43 Archiv der Zentralstellen, MFS, HAII, 28715: undated memorandum, p 17.

44 Callinicos, *Oliver Tambo*, p 527.

45 Simons papers, O.7.2: 'Draft Document Introducing Discussion on Structure etc.', no date [1980].

46 A draft of this important speech missing one vital page is in the Karis-Gerhart papers, pt III, folder 30.

47 UFH, ANC Lusaka mission, subject files 120/156: 'Minutes of the East NEC meeting'.

48 *Ibid.*

49 Martin Legassick, 'Myth and Reality in the Struggle against Apartheid', *Journal of Southern African Studies*, 24, 2 (1998), pp 445–46.

50 Karis-Gerhart papers, pt III, folder 27: 'Report on Meeting of ANC and Inkatha', 9pp, no date [September 1977].

51 See Chapter One, p 31.

52 Brian Morrow, as told to Laurence Piper, *'To Serve and Protect': The Inkathagate Scandal*

(Unisa Press, Pretoria, 2010), p xv.

53 Mzala, *Gatsha Buthelezi: Chief with a Double Agenda* (Zed Books, London, 1988), pp 10–11.

54 Coetsee papers, 1/A1/5: ANC minutes of Inkatha/ANC consultative meeting, 29–30 October 1979, 31 pp.

55 UFH, ANC Lusaka mission, subject files, 120/152: minutes of working committee meetings.

56 Coetsee papers, 1/A1/5: ANC minutes of Inkatha/ANC consultative meeting, 29–30≈October 1979.

57 UFH, ANC Lusaka mission, pt 2, 27/5: Hani to Nhlanhla, 17 November [1979].

58 Coetsee papers, PV357, 1/A1/5.

59 Callinicos, *Oliver Tambo*, p 529.

60 O'Malley, *Shades of Difference*, p 206. See also Barrell, 'Conscripts to their Age'.

61 O'Malley, *Shades of Difference*, p 204.

62 Mervyn Rees and Chris Day, *Muldergate: The Story of the Info Scandal* (Macmillan South Africa, Johannesburg, 1980).

63 'South African Defence Force Involvement in the Internal Security Situation in the Republic of South Africa', p 4, by HD Stadler, South African National Defence Force submission to the Truth and Reconciliation Commission.

64 Author's notes on Niel Barnard's testimony to the TRC, Durban, 14 July 1997.

65 Interview with security police intelligence officer, 11 June 1997.

66 'Penalties of Fighting Terrorism', *Aida Parker Newsletter* 3 (January 1984).

67 'Boek 1: Beleid. Die RSA se Belange en die RSA-Regering se Doel, Doelstellings en Beleid'. Copy in the possession of the author.

68 SSC meeting, 28 January 1980. The minutes of this and other SSC meetings were seen by the author in the course of research for the TRC in Durban in 1997–98.

69 FA Wearing, undated memorandum, TR Wade papers, box 1, Bodleian Library.

70 Stadler, *The Other Side of the Story*, p 36.

71 Interview with Col Eugene de Kock, Pretoria Central Prison, 3 March 1996.

72 UFH, ANC Lusaka mission, pt 2, 6/36: notes for a letter from Nzo to Zambian government, no date [1980].

73 Mwezi Twala and Ed Benard, *Mbokodo: Inside MK – Mwezi Twala. A Soldier's Story* (Jonathan Ball, Johannesburg, 1994), pp 29–36.

74 Wonga Welile Bottoman, *The Making of an MK Cadre* (LiNc publishers, Pretoria, 2010), pp 70–71; Kasrils, *Armed and Dangerous*, p 192.

75 Houston and Magubane, 'The ANC's Armed Struggle in the 1970s', pp 506–07.

76 Coetsee papers, PV357, AMV 8/4/Vol 1: Malan to Coetsee, 27 March 1980; SANDF, group 9, HS Ops 309/4: Chief of Staff (Intelligence) to Chief of Army, 27 May 1980.

77 Minutes of SSC meeting, 28 January 1980.

78 De Wet Potgieter, *Totale Aanslag: Apartheid se Vuil Truuks Onthul* (Zebra Press, Cape Town, 2007), pp 5–6.

79 Minutes of SSC meeting, 28 January 1980.

80 An easily accessible account of this operation is at: http://www.sahistory.org.za/silverton-siege-1980 [accessed 12 August 2011].

81 Simons papers, O.11-1: minutes of SACP unit 7 meeting, Lusaka, 18 April 1980.

82 *Ibid*, 28 March 1980.

83 *Ibid*, 27 May 1980.

84 SANDF, AMI/MI archive group 10, MI/204/2/2/9: memo from GD Colletts,

31 October 1980.

85 Houston and Magubane, 'The ANC's Armed Struggle in the 1970s', pp 506–07.

86 SANDF, AMI/MI archive group 14, MI/204/2/2/9/1Ops: memo by Admiral AP
    Putter, attached to Chief of Staff (Intelligence) to Chief of Army, 30 July 1981.

87 SSC minutes 11/80, 9 June 1980.

88 Peter Stiff, *Cry Zimbabwe: Independence – Twenty Years On* (Galago, Alberton, 2000),
    pp 59–65.

89 'SADF Barnacle and CCB Operations in SA', TRC document, confidential source.

90 *Ibid.*

91 SSC minutes 12/83, 30 July 1983.

92 Noted by the author in the archives of the Truth and Reconciliation Commission in
    1997.

93 SSC minutes, 27 August 1979, agenda item 8.

94 SANDF, Archive group 9, HS Ops 309/4: Chief of Staff (Intelligence) to Chief of
    Army, 27 May 1980.

95 Coetsee Papers, PV357, AMV 8/4/vol 1: Malan to Coetsee, 27 March 1980.

96 Detailed notes, almost certainly provided by the national serviceman Roland Hunter,
    who was convicted for passing information to the ANC, may be found in the Tambo
    papers at Fort Hare, box 2.4.

97 Interview with former SADF general, 27 May 1996.

98 Protocol on military counselling and training, top secret, 1979. Confidential source.

99 Kader Asmal and Adrian Hadland, with Moira Levy, *Politics in My Blood: A Memoir*
    (Jacana, Auckland Park, 2011), pp 65–66.

100 *Ibid*, and author's conversation with former ANC intelligence officer, Johannesburg,
    23 October 2010.

101 Botha papers, PV 203, 1/W1/9: anonymous memo [May 1977].

102 Author's interview with ANC intelligence officer, 6 November 1989.

103 Peter Stiff, *The Silent War: South African Recce Operations, 1969–1994* (Galago, Alberton,
    1999), p 319 *et seq.*

104 SANDF, CoS Ops group 3, vol II, HS OPS/204/2/2/9: 'Attack on ANC Bases:
    Mozambique – 29th January 1981'.

105 SAPA, 'Matola Raid Remembered', 29 October 2010: http://www.timeslive.co.za/
    local/article734004.ece/Matola-raid-remembered [accessed 15 August 2011].

106 Shubin, *ANC*, p 177.

107 South African History Online, newsletter 222, 9 December 2011: www.sahistory.org.
    za [accessed 18 December 2011].

108 'Lesotho Incident … the Whole Truth', *Paratus*, 34, 1 (January 1983), pp 18–22.

109 Report by Mathabatha Peter Sexwale, no date, confidential source. The raid is de-
    scribed by Stiff, *Silent War*, pp 412–26.

110 Beresford, *Truth is a Strange Fruit*, pp 102–07.

111 *White Paper on Aggression of November 25th 1981 Against the Republic of Seychelles* (Dept
    of Information, Victoria, Seychelles, no date); Mike Hoare, *The Seychelles Affair* (1986;
    Corgi edn, London, 1987).

112 Shipping Research Bureau (eds R Hengeveld and J Rodenburg), *Embargo: Apartheid's
    Oil Secrets Revealed* (Amsterdam University Press, Amsterdam, 1995), p 9.

113 *Ibid*, p 22.

114 Anton David Lowenburg and William H Kaempfer, *The Origins and Demise of South
    African Apartheid: A Public Choice Analysis* (University of Michigan Press, Ann Arbor,

1998), p 225.

115 PC Swanepoel, *Die Salem en Ander Oliegeheime* (private publication, Pretoria, 2002).

116 Clive Scholtz, 'Drive Now and Pay Forever – the Apartheid Way', in Shipping Research Bureau, *Embargo*, pp 260–61, 264–65.

117 Daniel Ammann, *The King of Oil: the Secret Lives of Marc Rich* (St Martin's Press, New York, 2009), p 191.

118 *Ibid*, pp 192–93.

119 Sasha Polakow-Suransky, *The Unspoken Alliance: Israel's Secret Relationship with Apartheid South Africa* (Vintage. New York, 2011).

120 See the interview with Eschel Rhoodie in *Noseweek* 2 (31 July 1993), p 5.

121 Prinsloo, *Stem uit die Wilderness*, p 68.

122 Interview with Eschel Rhoodie in *Noseweek* 2 (31 July 1993), p 5. This 1987 interview was published only after Rhoodie's death.

123 Ronen Palan, Richard Murphy and Christian Chavagneux, *Tax Havens: How Globalization Really Works* (Cornell University Press, Ithaca, NY, 2010).

124 Peter Gowan, *The Global Gamble: Washington's Faustian Bid for World Dominance* (Verso, London and New York, 1999). South Africa's role is entertainingly described in RW Johnson, *How Long Will South Africa Survive?* (Oxford University Press, New York, 1977), pp 67–111.

125 Alfred W McCoy, *The Politics of Heroin in Southeast Asia* (Harper & Row, New York, 1972).

126 Bob Woodward, *Veil: The Secret Wars of the CIA, 1981–1987* (Simon & Schuster, New York, 1987).

127 Steven Emerson, *Secret Warriors: Inside the Covert Military Operations of the Reagan Era* (GP Putnam's Sons, New York, 1988), p 222.

128 *Commission of Inquiry into the Alleged Smuggling of and Illegal Trade in Ivory and Rhinoceros Horn in South Africa* [Kumleben Commission] (Government Printer, Pretoria, 1996).

129 Alan Hirsch, *Season of Hope: Economic Reform Under Mandela and Mbeki* (University of KwaZulu-Natal Press, Scottsville, and International Development Research Centre, Ottawa, 2005), p 24.

130 'Reserve Bank's Smelly, Not-so-little, Secret', *Noseweek* 131 (September 2010). A copy of the report, compiled in 1999, is in my possession.

131 Annette Seegers, *The Military in the Making of Modern South Africa* (IB Tauris, London, 1996), p 286, note 16; for a detailed case study, see Frank Walsh, *Dangerous Deceits: Julian Askin and the Tollgate Scandal* (HarperCollins, London, 1999).

132 *Kommissie van Ondersoek na Sekere Moontlike Onreëlmatighede. Hoofverslag* [Harms Commission] (Staatsdrukker, Pretoria, 1989). Vermaas, formerly a lawyer to Department of Information chief Eschel Rhoodie, was convicted by the Pretoria Supreme Court on 111 charges in December 1996.

133 Quoted in Institute for Security Studies (author: Hennie van Vuuren) *Apartheid Grand Corruption: Assessing the Scale of Crimes of Profit in South Africa from 1976 to 1994* (ISS, Pretoria, 2006), p 45.

Chapter Five: The Grinding Stone

1 'NAT Workshop on Policy', no date [post-1990]. Confidential source.

2 *Ibid.*

3 Shubin, *ANC*, p 156.

4 Testimony of Andrew Masondo to the TRC, available at http://cryptomequintessenz. at/mirror.za-masondo.txt [accessed 5 April 2011].

5 Ngculu, *The Honour to Serve*, p 39.

6 Schleicher, 'GDR Solidarity', p 1131.

7 Archiv der Zentralstellen, MFS, HAII, 28715: undated memorandum on the ANC.

8 A handbook produced for training ANC and SWAPO security officers is 'Lehrkonzeption für Grundlehrgänge auf dem Gebiet der politisch-operativen Sicherung von Befreiungsoranisationen des südlichen Afrika', 1 September 1982, Archiv der Zentralstellen, MFS-JHS Potsdam, Mikrofilmstelle. Specifically on counterintelligence, 'Das Geheimdienstsystem der RSA …', June 1984, manual located in MFS, JHS, 24023.

9 ANC document quoted by Beresford, *Truth Is a Strange Fruit*, pp 99–101.

10 Twala and Benard, *Mbokodo*, p 55.

11 Davis, 'Cosmopolitans in Close Quarters', ch 4.

12 *Ibid*, p 159.

13 *Ibid*, ch 4 and especially pp 175–78.

14 Sworn affidavit by Ben Lekalake, 2 February 1993: confidential source.

15 'Further Submissions and Responses by the African National Congress to Questions Raised by the Commission for Truth and Reconciliation', 12 May 1997: 'Operations Report: The Department of Intelligence and Security' at http://www.justice.gov.za/ trc/hrvtrans/submit/anc2.htm#Operations [accessed 10 August 2011].

16 Ngculu, *The Honour to Serve*, p 102.

17 Bandile Ketelo et al, 'A Miscarriage of Democracy: the ANC Security Department in the 1984 Mutiny in Umkhonto we Sizwe', *Searchlight South Africa*, 5 (1990), p 38.

18 'Further Submissions and Responses by the African National Congress to Questions Raised by the Commission for Truth and Reconciliation', 12 May 1997: 'Operations Report: The Department of Intelligence and Security' at http://www.justice.gov.za/ trc/hrvtrans/submit/anc2.htm#Operations [accessed 10 August 2011].

19 Ketelo et al, 'A Miscarriage of Democracy', p 38.

20 UFH, ANC Lusaka mission, pt 2, 49/18: statement of the National Executive Committee to all members, 28 March 1979. See also Davis, 'Cosmopolitans', ch 4.

21 Sæbø, 'A State of Exile', p 95.

22 *Ibid*, p 98.

23 UFH, ANC Lusaka mission, subject files 120/152: minutes of working committee meeting, 11 January 1980.

24 *Ibid.*

25 'Guidelines Supplement and New Tasks', no date, confidential source.

26 *Sechaba*, 12, 3 (1978), p 23.

27 Twala and Benard, *Mbokodo*, p 83.

28 *TRC Report*, 3, pp 171–72.

29 UFH, ANC Lusaka mission, pt.2, 1/4: Makopo to Comrade Joe [Nhlanhla?], 2 June 1978.

30 Botswana National Archives and Records Services, Office of the President series, OP 27/46/94: record of a meeting held on 11 March 1976.

31 UFH, ANC Lusaka Mission, subject files 120/152: minutes of working committee meetings, 27 October 1979.

32 SAHA, AL 2457, 5.5.2: 'Their Case is Closed ...', flyer, no date.

33 Author's confidential interview. Keitsing, *Comrade Fish*, p 116, gives a brief description of the murder.

34 *TRC Report*, 2, p 335.

35 Mayibuye Centre, London papers, box 14: 'Problems of Social Behaviour in our Movement'.

36 UFH, ANC Lusaka mission, subject files, 120/143: decisions of the National Executive Committee, Luanda, 2–5 December 1981.

37 UFH, ANC Lusaka mission, subject files, 120/156: 'Minutes of the East NEC meeting'. See above, ch 4, notes 47 and 48.

38 Martin Legassick, *Armed Struggle and Democracy: The Case of South Africa* (Discussion paper no 20, Nordiska Afrikainstitutet, Uppsala, 2002), p 10.

39 UFH, ANC Lusaka mission, subject files 120/154: minutes of working committee meeting, 26 July 1980.

40 UFH, ANC Lusaka mission, subject files 120/150: minutes of working committee meeting, 13 May 1980.

41 UFH, ANC Lusaka mission, subject files 120/154: minutes of working committee meeting, 25 August 1980.

42 Karis-Gerhart papers, pt III, folder 36: Nzo to secretary of the Revolutionary Council, 14 September 1980.

43 ANC, Second Submission to the TRC, 'Operations Report: The Department of Intelligence and Security' at http://www.justice.gov.za/trc/hrvtrans/submit/anc2.htm#Operations [accessed 10 August 2011]

44 *Ibid*. This document claims that Piliso's appointment was in 1981, but the letter quoted in note 41 above clearly shows it as 1980.

45 Ketelo et al, 'A Miscarriage of Democracy', p 38.

46 'Cadre Policy', undated document. Confidential source.

47 Simons papers, O.7.2: minutes of meeting of SACP unit 7, Lusaka, 13 December 1981.

48 *Ibid*, 23 October 1982.

49 *Ibid*, 13 November 1982.

50 UFH, ANC Lusaka mission, subject files, 120/156: 'Minutes of the East NEC meeting'.

51 Gevisser, *Thabo Mbeki*, pp 461–4.

52 *Ibid*, pp 401–02.

53 UFH, ANC Lusaka mission, pt 2, 28/21: chairman, Regional Political Committee Lusaka, to Nzo, 2 October 1978.

54 UFH, ANC Lusaka mission, subject files, 124/154: minutes of working committee meeting, 11 July 1980.

55 Gevisser, *Thabo Mbeki*, p 470.

56 Simons papers, O11.1: 'Minutes of the Meeting of the Unit Held on February 11, 1980 at 3pm', handwritten.

57 'Guidelines for the Development of our Political Machineries in TX', SACP document, Lusaka, 20 September 1980. Confidential source.

58 Simons papers, O.12: handwritten notes on Party units, Lusaka region, 16 February 1980.

59 Shubin, *ANC*, p 191.
60 'Report: Commission of Inquiry into Recent Developments in the People's Republic of Angola' [Stuart Commission], 14 March 1984, p.4. Available at http://content.yudu.com/Library/A1ksvn/TheStuartCommissionR/resources/index.htm?referrerUrl= [accessed 6 December 2011].
61 Historical Papers, Cullen Library: Neame papers, A2729, B.2: 'On the Question of the Calling of a "Morogoro-type" Conference'.
62 Gevisser, *Thabo Mbeki*, p 422.
63 Obituary of Alan Brooks by Paul Trewhela, 2 September 2008: https://portal.fsw.leidenuniv.nl/politicsweb/view/politicsweb/en/,DanaInfo=.awxyCttrp1rm38rpOs5RGu+page71619?oid=101901&sn=Detail [accessed 30 March 2012]
64 Author's interview, Johannesburg, 24 September 2011.
65 UFH, ANC Lusaka mission, pt 2, 75/8: 'Recommendations on Discipline' by Nzo, no date [1981]
66 UFH, ANC Lusaka mission, subject files 120/154: minutes of working committee meeting, 26 July 1980.
67 UFH, ANC Lusaka mission, subject files 120/143: decisions of the National Executive Committee, 2–5 December 1981.
68 UFH, ANC Lusaka mission, subject files 125/218: circular letter by Nzo, no date.
69 UFH, ANC Lusaka mission, pt 2, 78/32: minutes of a meeting convened by the office of the treasurer-general, 7 February 1981.
70 UFH, ANC Lusaka mission, pt 2, 75/8: 'Recommendations on Discipline', by Nzo, no date [1981].
71 Confidential source.
72 Confidential source.
73 Twala and Benard, *Mbokodo*, p 55.
74 *Ibid.*
75 *Ibid*, p 105.
76 'Cadre Policy', undated document. Confidential source.
77 Ted Leggett, *Rainbow Vice: The Drugs and Sex Industries and the New South Africa* (Zed Books, London, 2002), p 41.
78 Author's interview with former head of the South African Narcotics Bureau, Centurion, 31 May 2012.
79 De Wet Potgieter papers, SAHA AL3283, A.2.1.9.1 and A2.1.9.2: interviews with Detective Warrant Officer Drummond Hammond, 25 February 2010.
80 Chris Steyn-Barlow, *Publish and Be Damned: Two Decades of Scandals* (Galago Books, Alberton, 2006), p 268.
81 Don Sipho, *Understanding Organised Crime and Corruption in South Africa* (Vaandel Publishers, Heiderand, 2009), p 141.
82 Misha Glenny, *McMafia: Crime Without Borders* (Bodley Head, London, 2008), pp 148–51.
83 Emails to the author from Neil Harper and John Austin, former Zimbabwean customs officers, 18 June 2011. The following account is based on this plus an interview with both gentlemen.
84 *Ibid.*
85 ANC Lusaka mission, subject files, 120/150: minutes of working committee meeting, 26 September 1980.
86 *Ibid.*

87 Email from South African investigative journalist, 20 February 2002.

88 Author's interview, Gaborone, 27 September 2011.

89 RW Johnson, *South Africa's Brave New World: The Beloved Country since the End of Apartheid* (Overlook Press, New York, 2010), pp 27–28.

90 *Ibid*, p 29. On the gangs in 1950s Alexandra, Philip Bonner and Noor Nieftagodien, *Alexandra: A History* (Witwatersrand University Press, Johannesburg, 2008), especially pp 8–9, 121, 152–53.

91 'Cadre Policy', undated document. Confidential source.

92 *Ibid*.

93 *Ibid*.

94 Author's email communication with former MK cadre, 4 October 2011.

95 UFH, ANC Lusaka mission, subject files 120/152: minutes of working committee meeting, 18 January 1981.

96 Botswana National Archives and Records Services, Office of the President series, OP 27/49: O'Brien Quinn to the Permanent Secretary to the President, 26 April 1982. I am grateful to Elisabetta Spano for providing me with a copy of this document.

97 Author's interview, 6 November 1989.

98 Botswana National Archives and Records Services, Office of the President series, OP 27/49: O'Brien Quinn to the Permanent Secretary to the President, 26 April 1982. Extensive inquiries by the author in Botswana in September 2011 failed to shed any further light.

99 See, eg Sipo E Mzimela, *Marching to Slavery: South Africa's Descent into Communism* (Soundview Publications, Atlanta, GA, 1993), p 33.

100 SANDF, HS OPS 204/2/2/9/1(A): minutes of meeting at special forces HQ, 3 December 1984, which misspells Nkobi's name.

101 Policy document attached to a briefing to the State Security Council, September 1983: confidential source.

102 Author's conversations with ANC source.

103 Stephan Terreblanche, 'Umkhonto Boss Linked to Crime', *Sunday Times*, 28 September 1986.

104 Simons papers, O.7.2: minutes of meeting of SACP unit 7, Lusaka, 23 October 1982.

105 'Some Aspects of Enemy Counter Guerrilla Tactics Compiled from our own Experience', NAT document, May 1984, confidential source.

106 Bottoman, *MK Cadre*, p 52.

107 *Ibid*, p 56.

108 UFH, ANC Lusaka mission, subject files 120/154: minutes of working committee meeting, 26 July 1980.

109 Paul Trewhela, *Inside Quatro: Uncovering the Exile History of the ANC and SWAPO* (Jacana, Auckland Park, 2009), p 13.

110 UFH, ANC Lusaka mission, subject files 120/152: minutes of working committee meeting 12 January 1981.

111 *Ibid*.

112 See Chapter Four, p 139.

113 Twala and Benard, *Mbokodo*, p 48.

114 Ngculu, *The Honour to Serve*, p 103.

115 Twala and Benard, *Mbokodo*, p 49; Ketelo et al, 'A Miscarriage of Democracy', p 40.

116 UFH, ANC Lusaka mission, subject files 120/152: minutes of working committee meeting, 5 March 1981.

117 *Ibid*, 26 March 1981.
118 Twala and Benard, *Mbokodo*, p 49.
119 *Ibid*.
120 UFH, ANC Lusaka mission, pt 2, 49/17: Motshabi to Mabhida, 30 November 1982.
121 UFH, ANC Lusaka mission, subject files, 124/204: fragment of an undated letter from the international department [1981].
122 Ngculu, *The Honour to Serve*, p 103.
123 Twala and Benard, *Mbokodo*, p 52.
124 *Ibid*, pp 52–3.
125 ANC, Second Submission to the TRC, section 3.2 [accessed 10 August 2011].
126 *Ibid*.
127 UFH, ANC Lusaka, subject files 120/152: minutes of working committee meeting, 3 April 1981.
128 *Ibid*.
129 Simons papers, P.29.4: 'Report on Political Progress. Covering Remarks', by Mark Shope, no date, mentioning Comrade Piper.
130 Ngculu, *The Honour to Serve*, p 77.
131 Shubin, *ANC*, pp 175–76.
132 UFH, Lusaka, subject files 124/204: memo by TM [Thabo More/Joe Modise?], 22 June 1981.
133 Karis-Gerhart papers, pt I, folder 18: Howard Barrell interview with Mac Maharaj, 3 February 1991.
134 Testimony supplied to the author by International Society for Human Rights, Frankfurt, 8 July 1992.
135 Karis-Gerhart papers, pt I, folder 18: Howard Barrell interview with Mac Maharaj, 3 February 1991.
136 ANC, 'The Shishita Report', p 9.
137 Simons papers, O.11.1: Minutes of SACP Unit 7 meeting, Lusaka, 15 July 1983.
138 Karis-Gerhart papers, pt I, folder 18: Howard Barrell interview with Mac Maharaj, 3 February 1991.
139 Simons papers, O.12: 'Summary of Unit Discussions and Reports', 1 August 1982.
140 Simons papers, O.12: ms notes by Jack Simons, recording a discussion with Comrade Maru on 9 April 1981.
141 UFH, ANC Lusaka mission, subject files, 124/204: fragment of an undated letter from the international department, circa 1981.
142 Simons papers, O.2: Raymond Nkuku, 'Late Comrade Sam Nkwe's Auto-Biography [sic]', 21 June 1984.
143 Karis-Gerhart papers, pt III, folder 34: minutes of working committee meeting, 1 September 1979.
144 ANC, 'The Shishita Report', p 10.
145 *Ibid*.
146 On Mahamba, see Ngculu, *The Honour to Serve*, p 100.
147 'Further Submissions and Responses by the African National Congress to Questions Raised by the Commission for Truth and Reconciliation', 12 May 1997: 'Operations Report: The Department of Intelligence and Security' at http://www.justice.gov.za/trc/hrvtrans/submit/anc2.htm#Operations [accessed 10 August 2011]
148 Testimony of Andrew Masondo to the TRC, available at http://cryptomequintessenz.

at/mirror.za-masondo.txt [accessed 5 April 2011: I was unable to recover the site on 21 June 2012].

149 ANC, 'The Shishita Report', pp 16–22.

150 'Further Submissions and Responses by the African National Congress to Questions Raised by the Commission for Truth and Reconciliation', 12 May 1997: 'Operations Report: The Department of Intelligence and Security' at http://www.justice.gov.za/trc/hrvtrans/submit/anc2.htm#Operations [accessed 10 August 2011]

151 See above, chapter 4, pp 120–21.

152 'Further Submissions and Responses by the African National Congress to Questions Raised by the Commission for Truth and Reconciliation', 12 May 1997: 'Operations Report: The Department of Intelligence and Security' at http://www.justice.gov.za/trc/hrvtrans/submit/anc2.htm#Operations [accessed 10 August 2011]

153 Davis, 'Cosmopolitans in Close Quarters', p 168.

154 Ketelo et al, 'A Miscarriage of Democracy', p 40.

155 Cf the testimony of Andrew Masondo to the TRC, available at http://cryptomequintessenz.at/mirror.za-masondo.txt [accessed 5 April 2011].

156 Botswana National Archives and Records Services, Office of the President series, OP 27/47/113: memo from head of Special Branch, 2 February 1977, recording the names of both men.

157 UFH, ANC Lusaka mission, pt 2, 28/12: Gordon Moshoeu to chief rep, Lusaka, 5 February 1987. There is also relevant material in Mzimela, *Marching to Slavery*, pp 36–39.

158 ANC, 'The Shishita Report', p 17.

159 The date 1982 figures on ANC lists, while 1983 is in the testimony of Andrew Masondo to the TRC, available at http://cryptomequintessenz.at/mirror.za-masondo.txt [accessed 5 April 2011]. Gordon Moshoeu's own account is in Stefaans Brümmer, 'NIA Bosses Named as "Torturers"', *Mail & Guardian*, 14–20 June 1996.

160 'Further Submissions and Responses by the African National Congress to Questions Raised by the Commission for Truth and Reconciliation', 12 May 1997: 'Operations Report: The Department of Intelligence and Security' at http://www.justice.gov.za/trc/hrvtrans/submit/anc2.htm#Operations [accessed 10 August 2011].

161 'Some Aspects of Enemy Counter Guerrilla Tactics Compiled from our own Experience', NAT document, May 1984, confidential source.

162 Simons papers, O.11.1: minutes of SACP Unit 7 meeting, Lusaka, 30 September 1981.

163 Simons papers, O.12: 'Summary of Unit Discussions and Reports', 1 August 1982.

164 Simons papers, O.11.1: minutes of SACP Unit 7 meeting, Lusaka, 1 September 1983.

165 Twala and Benard, *Mbokodo*, pp 99–100.

166 Ketelo et al, 'A Miscarriage of Democracy', p 41.

167 UFH, ANC Morogoro mission, box 4, 'Chief Representative 1985': Kgotso Katane to Tambo, 31 October 1985.

168 Twala and Benard, *Mbokodo*, p 57.

169 *Ibid*.

170 Cf Ketelo et al, 'A Miscarriage of Democracy', p 42.

171 'Report: Commision of Inquiry into Recent Developments in the People's Republic of Angola' [Stuart Commission], p 11.

172 UFH, ANC Morogoro mission, 27/1: meeting of special directorate, 15 January 1983.

173 Twala and Benard, *Mbokodo*, p 57.

174 *Ibid*.

175 UFH, ANC Lusaka mission, subject files, 124/204: fragment of an undated letter from the international department, circa 1981.

176 'Some Aspects of Enemy Counter Guerrilla Tactics Compiled from our own Experience', NAT document, May 1984.

177 UFH, ANC Lusaka mission, subject files, 124/204: fragment of an undated letter from the international department, circa 1981. Emphasis in original.

178 NAT document, 'Report about Wilton Mgungunyeka', 13 August 1985'. Confidential source.

179 Boroko to Tambo, 9 September 1985, confidential source.

180 Karis-Gerhart papers, pt I, folder 18: Howard Barrell interview with Mac Maharaj, 30 November 1990.

181 Affidavit of Joseph Tshepo Mamasela presented to the Harms Commission, 18 April 1990. Copy in the archives of the Independent Board of Inquiry, Sandton. Some background information on Mamesela, and corroboration of his testimony, is also contained in notes of interviews with former police captain Dirk Coetzee in the same archive.

182 'Some Aspects of Enemy Counter Guerrilla Tactics Compiled from our own Experience', NAT document, May 1984, confidential source.

183 SAHA, AL2457, 5.5.2: 'Their Case is Closed ...', flyer, no date.

184 Interview with ANC official, October 1989.

185 O'Malley, *Shades of Difference*, p 220.

186 '*Comrades Against Apartheid* – a Response ... by Tsepo Sechaba to a Review by Jeremy Cronin', unpublished ms, 1992, in the author's possession.

187 Quoted in Paul Holden and Hennie van Vuuren, *The Devil in the Detail: How the Arms Deal Changed Everything* (Jonathan Ball, Johannesburg and Cape Town, 2011), p 52.

188 Chapter Three, note 31.

189 Quoted in Holden and Van Vuuren, *The Devil in the Detail*, p 53.

190 Cf J Arch Getty and Oleg V Naumov, *The Road to Terror: Stalin and the Self-Destruction of the Bolsheviks, 1932–1939* (Yale University Press, New Haven and London, 1999).

191 'Lehrkonzeption für Grundlehrgänge auf dem Gebiet der politisch-operativen Sicherung von Befreiungsorganisationen des südlichen Afrika', 1 September 1982, Archiv der Zentralstellen, MFS-JHS Potsdam, Mikrofilmstelle.

192 Karis-Gerhart papers, pt I, folder 18: Howard Barrell interview with Mac Maharaj, 3 February 1991.

193 Archiv der Zentralstellen, MFS-HAII, 28726: situation report 89/V, 12 May 1983.

194 Simons papers, O.11.1: notes of Unit 7 meeting, 8 May 1982.

195 Author's interview with former CIA official, Washington, DC, 8 November 1988; see also Jacinto Veloso, *Memórias em Voo Rasante* (Papa-Letras, Lisboa, 2007), pp 167–68.

196 Author's interviews; cf 'Report: Commission of Inquiry into Recent Developments in the People's Republic of Angola' [Stuart Commission], 14 March 1984, p 18.

197 This is probably the speech by Joe Slovo published in *African Communist*, 95 (1983), pp 80–90.

198 Ketelo et al, 'A Miscarriage of Democracy', p 36.

199 Twala and Benard, *Mbokodo*, p 58.

200 *Ibid.*

201 Ketelo et al, 'A Miscarriage of Democracy', p 47.

202 Report of the Skweyiya Commission, October 1992, p 62. Available at http://anc.org.za/show.php?id=95 [accessed 8 December 2011].

203 Twala and Benard, *Mbokodo*, pp 58–60.

204 Ketelo et al, 'A Miscarriage of Democracy', p 45.

205 'Report: Commision of Inquiry into Recent Developments in the People's Republic of Angola' [Stuart Commission], 14 March 1984, p 22.

206 Author's interview with participant, Johannesburg, 24 September 2011; see also the eyewitness account by Bottoman, *The Making of an MK Cadre*, pp 139–48.

207 Transcript of ANC radio communication from Modise, 8 February 1984: confidential source.

208 Ketelo et al, 'A Miscarriage of Democracy', p 46.

209 Transcript of ANC radio communication from Hani, 9 February 1984: confidential source.

210 Transcript of ANC radio communication from Hani, no date: confidential source.

211 Transcript of ANC radio communication from Julius [Timothy] Mokoena, 9 February 1984: confidential source.

212 Transcript of ANC radio communications: confidential source.

213 Undated, handwritten note by Chris Hani: confidential source.

214 'Report: Commision of Inquiry into Recent Developments in the People's Republic of Angola' [Stuart Commission], 14 March 1984, p 2. One of the detainees reports that there were only 32, as Mwezi Twala had been taken to hospital after being shot.

215 Twala and Benard, *Mbokodo*, pp 63–69.

216 Transcript of ANC radio communication from Mbeki to Tambo, 17 February 1984: confidential source.

217 Ketelo et al, 'A Miscarriage of Democracy', p 49.

218 Twala and Benard, *Mbokodo*, pp 73–74.

219 'Report on the Developments', anonymous, 27 May 1984: confidential source.

220 *Ibid*.

221 *Ibid*.

222 Kasrils, *Armed and Dangerous*, p 251.

223 Interview with Victor Khumalo, in Evelien Groenink, 'Gekweld door Pretoria en het ANC', *de Volkskrant*, 3 July 1993, p 4.

224 'The Military Tribunal: Preliminary Report', no date, confidential source.

225 *Ibid*.

226 Callinicos, *Oliver Tambo*, p 461, is mistaken in writing that the sentences were commuted by Oliver Tambo.

227 Interview with Victor Khumalo, in Evelien Groenink, 'Gekweld door Pretoria en het ANC', *de Volkskrant*, 3 July 1993, p 4.

228 'Report on the Developments', anonymous, 27 May 1984: confidential source.

229 Julian Ozanne, 'ANC Commanders "Tortured Mutineers with Melting Plastic"', *Sunday Correspondent*, 8 April 1990.

230 'Report on the Developments', anonymous, 27 May 1984: confidential source.

231 UFH, ANC Lusaka mission 108/71: 'Report on the Death of Zaba Maledza', 28 November 1984.

232 Confidential source.

233 UFH, ANC Lusaka mission, 111/83: Rebecca Matlou to Comrade Nkhokheli, 15 October 1984. Rebecca Matlou was Ephraim Nkondo's sister-in-law. She later served as a Cabinet minister in South Africa under the name Sankie Mahanyele.

234 UFH, ANC Lusaka mission 108/71: Gessler Moses Nkondo to Tambo, 8 January 1985.

235 *Ibid*: Simon Makana to Gessler Moses Nkondo, 11 February 1985.
236 UFH, ANC Lusaka mission, subject files, 124/204: Msimang to Nzo, 18 October 1984.
237 UFH, ANC Lusaka mission 108/71: Mkwena to Lagu, 7 December 1984.
238 *Ibid*: Seabelo to Lagu, 16 December 1984.
239 *Ibid*.
240 UFH, ANC Lusaka mission, additions, 82/12: statement by Tambo to the ANC, 1 July 1991.
241 Trewhela, *Inside Quatro*, p 25.
242 UFH, ANC Lusaka mission 108/71: Makana to Gessler Moses Nkondo, 11 February 1985.
243 'ANC's Super Summit to Launch "Final Phase" of Attack', *Aida Parker Newsletter*, 28 February 1985.
244 *Africa Confidential*, 29, 24 (2 December 1988), pp 3–4. I was editor of the newsletter at that date and can verify the sources.
245 UFH, ANC Lusaka mission (ex-Mayibuye), 10/7: Msimang to Nzo, 9 December 1988.
246 Julian Ozanne, 'ANC Commanders "Tortured Mutineers with Melting Plastic"', *Sunday Correspondent*, 8 April 1990. On the circumstances of this report, see Rian Malan, *Resident Alien* (Jonathan Ball, Johannesburg and Cape Town, 2009), pp 224–25.
247 Ketelo et al, 'A Miscarriage of Democracy'.
248 Confidential interview with senior National Intelligence Agency official, 5 March 1997.
249 SAHA, Potgieter collection, AL3283, B.1.2.3.1: KZ Edwards, 'Strategy and Tactics of the ANC/SACP', May 1980.
250 Maritz Spaarwater, interview with Padraig O'Malley, 19 January 2003, at www.nelsonmandela.org/omalley [accessed 11 October 2010].
251 ANC, 'The Shishita Report', p 7.
252 Maritz Spaarwater, interview with Padraig O'Malley, 19 January 2003, at www.nelsonmandela.org/omalley [accessed October 2010].
253 Joseph Lelyveld, *Move Your Shadow: South Africa, Black and White* (Penguin, Harmondsworth, 1986), p 331.
254 Shubin, *ANC*, p 176.
255 Sæbø, 'A State of Exile', p 95.
256 Lelyveld, *Move Your Shadow*, p 331.
257 See, eg, Kasrils, *Armed and Dangerous*, pp 154, 187.
258 Quoted by Gavin Evans, 'Secret Histories', *Leadership*, 13, 5 (1994), p 16.
259 Jacques Pauw, *In the Heart of the Whore: The Story of Apartheid's Death Squads* (Southern Book Publishers, Johannesburg, 1991).
260 SANDF, archive group 9, HS OPS/309/4: Top-secret cable to General Gleeson, 9 February 1984.
261 Jacques Pauw, *Dances with Devils: A Journalist's Search for Truth* (Zebra Press, Cape Town, 2006), p 49
262 SANDF, HS OPS 204/2/2/9: memorandum ('geheim'), 5 July 1984; author's interview with former MK officer, 10 May 1996.
263 Tennyson Makiwane, interviewed by Thomas Karis and Gwendolyn Carter, 1964: Karis-Gerhart papers, pt I, folder 18.
264 Kasrils, *Armed and Dangerous*, pp 141–42.

265 Stephen Ellis and Tsepo Sechaba, *Comrades Against Apartheid: The ANC and the South African Communist Party in Exile* (James Currey, London, 1992), p 86.

266 Gary Kynoch, 'From the Ninevites to the Hard Livings: Township Gangsters and Urban Violence in South Africa', *African Studies*, 58, 1 (1999), pp 55–85.

267 Email from Neil Harper to Catholic Commission for Justice and Peace, 7 July 1999. Copy in the possession of the author.

268 *The Times* [Johannesburg], 7 July 1999.

269 Ketelo et al, 'A Miscarriage of Democracy', p 38.

Chapter Six: War Among the People

1 Reminiscing on 1 November 2006: http://www.southafrica.to/history/Apartheid/PW_Botha/PW_Botha.htm [accessed 12 November 2011].

2 'Kampanje vir die vrylating van Nelson Mandela', 'uiters geheim' memorandum, circa 1981, Coetsee papers PV 357, 1/M1/48.

3 Callinicos, *Oliver Tambo*, p 536.

4 Archiv der Zentralstellen, MFS, ZAIG, 6745/17–18: report 22 February 1984.

5 SAHA, AL2460, Frederikse papers: interview with Indres Naidoo, Lusaka, March 1987.

6 *Ibid.*

7 Archiv der Zentralstellen, MFS, ZAIG, 6726/183–4: Hauptverwaltung A to Generalmajor Irmler, 20 July 1984; MFS, HAII, 28726/22: situation report 44/VII, 9 July 1984.

8 Minutes of SSC 4/84: 5 March 1984.

9 Thula Simpson, '"Umkhonto we Sizwe, We are Waiting for You": The ANC and the Township Uprising, September 1984-September 1985', *South African Historical Journal*, 61 1, (2009), pp 158–77.

10 Ineke van Kessel, *'Beyond Our Wildest Dreams': The United Democratic Front and the Transformation of South Africa* (University Press of Virginia, Charlottesville, 2000), ch 3.

11 Callinicos, *Oliver Tambo*, p 538.

12 Alan Paton, in his address to the sixth congress of the Liberal Party shortly after the Sharpeville events, referred to the need for 'a nonviolent third force'. Alan Paton (ed Edward Callan), *The Long View* (Frederick A Praeger, New York, 1968), p 145.

13 Callinicos, *Oliver Tambo*, p 548.

14 *Ibid*, p 541.

15 Stadler, *The Other Side of the Story*, p 47.

16 Rian Malan, *My Traitor's Heart* (The Bodley Head, London, 1990), pp 245–64.

17 UFH, ANC Lusaka mission, subject files, 120/155: memo from Political Committee to Politico-Military Committee, 11 December 1985.

18 UFH, ANC Lusaka mission, subject files, 124/204: 'President's Message to the Progressive Forces of South Africa', no date [December 1986?].

19 Callinicos, *Oliver Tambo*, pp 558–59.

20 'Konsepstudiestuk: "Bevryde" Gebiede en Alternatiewe Strukture vir Bespreking: 1 April 1986', police document, confidential source.

21 UFH, ANC Lusaka mission, Department of International Affairs, 13/36: 'Some Guidelines on an Approach to the Building of the Underground', no date.

22 McKinley, *ANC*, p 77.
23 Stadler, *The Other Side of the Story*, p 179. The attitude of the ANC and the UDF towards necklacing is studied in Riedwaan Moosage, 'The Impasse of Violence: Writing Necklacing into a History of Liberation Struggle in South Africa' (MA thesis, University of the Western Cape, 2010).
24 Mac Maharaj, interviewed by Hilda Bernstein, 1991, available at www.nelsonmandela.org/omalley [accessed 11 November 2010].
25 O'Malley, *Shades of Difference*, p 235.
26 Mayibuye Centre, London mission, box 14: Schoon to Comrade Barbara [Masekela?] and Comrade Henry [Makgothi?], 18 June 1986. A copy of this document was also sent to Aziz Pahad in the ANC's London office.
27 *Ibid.*
28 *Ibid.*
29 Ngculu, *The Honour to Serve*, p 59.
30 UFH, ANC Lusaka mission, subject files, 124/204: memo by TM, 22 June 1981.
31 *Ibid.*
32 Simons papers, O.4: letter from Ray Simons, 31 August 1980.
33 Simons papers, O.7.2: memorandum, 7 March 1980.
34 Simons papers, O.8.6: 'Report on Bheki' by May, 18 July 1985.
35 Thomas, *The Diplomacy of Liberation*, p 157.
36 Christopher Andrew and Oleg Gordievsky, *KGB: The Inside Story* (Hodder & Stoughton, London, 1990), p 467.
37 Simons papers, O.7.2: Ray Simons, 'On the Question of Calling a "Morogoro-type" Conference', 3 pp, no date.
38 Historical Papers, Cullen Library, Neame papers, A2729, B2: 'On the Question of Calling a "Morogoro-type" Conference'.
39 Twala and Benard, *Mbokodo*, p 104.
40 Letter from Mabizela to Sithunyam, 10 June 1985: confidential source.
41 Simons papers, P.5: Motshabi to Slovo (open letter), 5 November 1985.
42 Cf the letter by 'Mkatashingo' and editorial comment in *Searchlight South Africa*, 6 (January 1991), pp 91–94.
43 Karis-Gerhart papers, pt I, folder 20: interview with Dikgang Masemola, February 1988.
44 Simons papers, O.7.1: 'Immediate Prospects for the SACP', 2 March 1993.
45 US Department of State, 'Communist Influence in South Africa', [1987], unclassified document in the possession of the author.
46 Simons papers, O.8.5: quoted in a letter to *Time* magazine by Tom Karis, 28 February 1987.
47 SANDF, AMI/MI group 14, MI/204/2/2/9: 'Vorderingsverslag tov ANC strategie vir periode 1 Jul-30 Sep 85', 'geheim'.
48 Stephen Davis, *Apartheid's Rebels: Inside South Africa's Hidden War* (Yale University Press, New Haven and London, 1987), pp 50–51.
49 'How the ANC Became a Communist Front', *Aida Parker Newsletter*, 9 June 1983.
50 Maloka, *The SACP in Exile*, pp 56–7.
51 Simon Adams, *Comrade Minister: The South African Communist Party and the Transition from Apartheid to Democracy* (Nova Science Publishers, Huntington, NY, 2001), appendix 1.
52 Statement by Jeremy Cronin, in Audrey Brown, 'Comrade Gorbachev Went Too Far,

Says SACP', *Vrye Weekblad*, 6–12 September 1991.

53 Unpublished ms in the possession of the author.

54 'Press Conference in Lusaka: Oliver Tambo', 25 June 1985: http://www.anc.org.za/show.php?id=4467 [accessed 11 November 2011].

55 ANC, *75 Years of Struggle* (London, 1987), copy in SAHA, AL2457, H.5.5.1.

56 James Myburgh, 'The ANC and the Boers', 20 September 2011: http://www.politicsweb.co.za/politicsweb/view/politicsweb/en/page71619?oid=256988&sn=Detail [accessed 27 June 2012].

57 *Financial Times* correspondent Patti Waldmeier, quoted in David Welsh and JE Spence, *Ending Apartheid* (Longman, Harlow, 2011), p 99.

58 Documents from the trial of Magnus Malan and others, Durban: memo by Admiral AP Putter, 27 November 1985. In the possession of the author.

59 Quoted in Stephen Ellis, 'The Historical Significance of South Africa's Third Force', *Journal of Southern African Studies*, 24, 2 (1998), p 274.

60 SSC 7/86: 12 May 1986.

61 Field Marshal Bernard Montgomery, quoted by Gwyn Prins and Robbie Stamp, *Top Guns and Toxic Whales: The Environment and Global Security* (Earthscan, London, 1991), p 32.

62 Notes of interview with Chris Hani and Steve Tshwete, 3 June 1988. Several international newspapers published similar interviews with Hani and Tshwete at this date.

63 Gail M Gerhart and Clive L Glaser, *From Protest to Challenge, Volume 6: Challenge and Victory, 1980–1990* (Indiana University Press, Bloomington, 2010), p 186.

64 Lisa Distelheim, 'ANC Approves Necklacing to Execute "Spies"', *Sunday Times* [London], 14 September 1986.

65 Letter from MK Brazo, 16 December 1985, confidential source.

66 'ANC Supports the Wimpy Bar Bombers', *The Citizen*, 29 January 1998.

67 Stadler, *The Other Side of the Story*, p 175.

68 Simons papers, P.29.4: '1987 Military Report and 1988 Annual Military Programme'.

69 'Combat Units', police document, 'uiters geheim' [14 March 1986]. Confidential source. A detailed account of one such combat unit is Peter Harris, *In a Different Time: The Inside Story of the Delmas Four* (Umuzi, Cape Town, 2008).

70 UFH, ANC archives, Lusaka mission, pt 2, 13/36: 'Some Guidelines on: an Approach to the Building of the Underground', no date [circa 1988].

71 UFH, ANC archives, Lusaka mission, pt 2, secretary-general's office, 54/11: Internal Political Committee, annual report 1988.

72 *Ibid.* A list of units inside South Africa is in UFH, ANC archives, Lusaka mission, pt 2, 35/1: 'Breakdown of Units Inside Ocean', 10pp [1988].

73 UFH, ANC archives, Lusaka mission, pt 2, secretary-general's office, 54/11: Internal Political Committee, annual report 1988.

74 Pippa Green, *Choice, Not Fate: The Life and Times of Trevor Manuel* (Penguin, Johannesburg, 2008), p 137.

75 Evans, 'Secret Histories', p 10.

76 Gavin Evans, 'Mbeki and Zuma: Between the Devil and the Deep Blue Sea', 30 December 2007. This blog appeared on Evans's website, www.gavinevans.net, but has subsequently disappeared from the web. I am grateful to Gavin Evans for supplying me with a copy.

77 Evans, 'Secret Histories', p 14.

78 Evans, 'Mbeki and Zuma: Between the Devil and the Deep Blue Sea'.

79 UFH, ANC archives, Morogoro mission, 5/39: Mabizela to Modise, 2 April 1985.

80 UFH, ANC archives, Lusaka mission pt 1, 114/119: Department of Legal and Constitutional Affairs, report of week ending 12 April 1986, by P Maduna.

81 Archiv der Zentralstellen, MFS, HAII, 28726, 52: memo by Gonschorek, East German ambassador in Lusaka, 13 June 1986.

82 'Report of Commission to Investigate Circumstances of Death of Three Comrades at Camp 32, Living Conditions of Inmates and Regulations of the Centre', 6 pp [1987]; 'Transference of Camp 32', 14 November 1987; 'Brief Report to NAT Directorate on a Short Visit to Camp 32', 9 December 1987. All three reports are from confidential sources.

83 Quoted on 1 November 2006: http://www.southafrica.to/history/Apartheid/PW_Botha/PW_Botha.htm [accessed 12 November 2011].

84 Archiv der Zentralstellen, MFS, HAII, 28726/22: situation report 108/VIII, 24 August 1984.

85 Allister Sparks, *Tomorrow is Another Country: The Inside Story of South Africa's Negotiated Revolution* (Struik Publishers, Sandton, 1994), pp 72–73. Shubin, *ANC*, pp 208–15, lists other contacts.

86 UFH, ANC Lusaka mission, 114/119: memorandum by Jack Simons to the constitutional committee, 12 February 1986.

87 *Ibid.*

88 Security police document, 'Skakelstukke ANC', veiligheidsverslag 90043765, 28 August 1990, confidential source.

89 Evans, 'Mbeki and Zuma: Between the Devil and the Deep Blue Sea'.

90 Piero Gleijeses, 'Cuito Cuanavale Revisited', *Mail & Guardian* Online, 11 July 2007: http://mg.co.za/article/2007-07-11-cuito-cuanavale-revisited [accessed 12 November 2011]. Gleijeses's analysis is based on declassified US and Cuban archives.

91 Jannie Geldenhuys, *At the Front: A General's Account of South Africa's Border War* (Jonathan Ball, Johannesburg and Cape Town, 2009), pp 1–3.

92 Hilton Hamann, *Days of the Generals: The Untold Story of South Africa's Apartheid-era Military Generals* (Zebra, Cape Town, 2001), pp 84–85, 94–95. See also Shubin, *ANC*, pp 227–78.

93 Chester A Crocker, *High Noon in Southern Africa: Making Peace in a Rough Neighbourhood* (1992; Jonathan Ball, Johannesburg, 1993), p 392.

94 Archiv der Zentralstellen, MFS, Hauptverwaltung Aufklärung, 52/000016, memo, 18 June 1988.

95 Prinsloo, *Stem uit die Wilderness*, p 317, and author's own interview with South African diplomat and military intelligence official, May 1996. Strauss's visit is mentioned in the minutes of the State Security Council meeting of 1 February 1988, SSC 2/88.

96 Dan O'Meara, *Forty Lost Years: The Apartheid State and the Politics of the National Party, 1948–1994* (Ravan Press, Randburg, and Ohio University Press, Athens, OH, 1996), p 354.

97 SSC 12/88: 20 June 1988.

98 UFH, ANC Lusaka mission, chief representative's office, 10/49: press release by Novosti, 22 March 1989.

99 Julia Preston, 'The Trial that Shook Cuba', *New York Review of Books*, 36, 19, (7 December 1989), pp 24–31.

100 SAHA, AL2457, 5.5.2: 'Mass Action for People's Power: Statement of the National Executive Committee on the 77th anniversary of the ANC', 8 January 1989.

101 *Ibid.*

102 UFH, ANC Lusaka mission pt 2, secretary-general's office, Internal Political Committee annual report 1988.

103 *Umsebenzi,* 5, 2 (1989), p 3.

104 Mac Maharaj, in a 1991 interview with Hilda Bernstein: http://www.nelsonmandela.org/omalley/index.php/site/q/03lv03445/04lv03996/05lv04011.htm [accessed 14 March 2012]. Other sources give 1985.

105 *Ibid*

106 O'Malley, *Shades of Difference*, p 244.

107 Stadler, *The Other Side of the Story*, p 91.

108 There is still a paucity of material on Vula, but see Conny Braam, *Operatie Vula: Nederlanders in het Ondergrondse Verzet tegen de Apartheid* (Meulenhoff, Amsterdam, 1992) and O'Malley, *Shades of Difference*, pp 239–389.

109 UFH (ex-Mayibuye), Lusaka mission, 45/2: notes of ANC/SIDA meeting, Lusaka, 8–11 December 1987. In financial year 1987–88, half of Swedish bilateral assistance, some US$420 million, went to southern Africa, and of this, half was for SWAPO and the ANC.

110 On the declaration, see Welsh and Spence, *Ending Apartheid*, p 113.

111 Gevisser, *Thabo Mbeki*, pp 528–29.

112 *The Path to Power*, available at http://www.sacp.org.za/main.php?ID=2638 [accessed 3 September 2011].

113 Archiv der Zentralstellen, MFS, HAII, 28715, pp 53–54: note of discussion, 28 March 1989.

114 Evans, 'Secret Histories', p 14.

115 *Ibid*, p 16.

116 *Ibid.*

117 Beresford, *Truth is a Strange Fruit*, pp 185–87.

118 Ellis and Sechaba, *Comrades Against Apartheid,* p 170.

119 Confidential source.

120 Karis-Gerhart papers, pt I, folder 32: Howard Barrell interview with Sue Rabkin, July-August 1989.

121 Interview with former ANC intelligence officer, Johannesburg, 17 October 2010. The accusations of tribalism are noted in a government secret intelligence report: 'Skakelstukke ANC', 15 August 1990, confidential source.

122 'Discussions with "Belinda"', London, 21 September 1985. Confidential source.

123 Marlene Burger, 'Gone with the Winds of Change', *Sunday Times*, 13 July 1997.

124 'Extracts from the Confessions of an Enemy Agent Ralph Mgcina Alias Fear …', confidential source.

125 Shubin, *ANC*, p 192.

126 Beresford, *Truth is a Strange Fruit*, pp 185–87, 234–36.

127 UFH, ANC Lusaka mission, pt 2, 35/4: memorandum by Sindiso [Mfenyana], 16 November 1988.

128 Philemon Ngwenya to Human Rights Lawyers, 23 May 1990. Confidential source.

129 Chikane to Tambo, 6 April 1989, confidential source.

130 'TZ's Story as He Presented It', confidential source.

131 Philemon Ngwenya to Human Rights Lawyers, 23 May 1990.

132 Stefaans Brümmer, 'Thami Zulu: In Search of Answers to an Old Query', *Mail & Guardian*, 31 May-6 June 1996.

133 Report of the Commission of Inquiry into the Death of Mzwakhe Ngwenya, 16 March 1990, confidential source.

134 Trewhela, *Inside Quatro*, pp 103–106.

135 Beresford, *Truth is a Strange Fruit*, pp 185–87, 234–36.

136 Evans, 'Mbeki and Zuma – Between the Devil and the Deep Blue Sea'.

137 *Ibid.*

138 'Never Again, Says Hani', *Vrye Weekblad*, 29 May 1992.

139 UFH, ANC Lusaka mission, pt 2, 35/2: statement by the Department of Information and Publicity, 31 May 1990.

140 TRC testimony by Philemon Ngwenya, 26 July 1996: http://www.justice.gov.za/trc/hrvtrans/soweto/ngwenya.htm [accessed 11 November 2011].

141 UFH, Nelson Mandela papers, 263/2: Jordan to Nhlanhla, 3 June 1991. Written in the margin is 'show Tata', indicating that the letter was to be shown to Mandela.

142 UFH, Nelson Mandela papers, box 263/12: document enclosed with DG Grewar to MJ Nhlanhla, 31 March 1994.

143 Author's interview with Comrade R, Lusaka, 20 March 1990. This is also referred to by Amnesty International, *South Africa: Torture, Ill-Treatment and Executions in African National Congress Camps* (AFR 53/27/92, London, 1992), p 10.

144 *Ibid*, pp 11–12.

145 Letter from M [name withheld] to Pastor Ndabazindle Musa, 27 October 1989, confidential source.

146 Author's phone interview with ANC intelligence officer, 9 September 1989.

147 UFH Tambo papers, 37/B8.1.1: McCann to Nzo, no date.

148 Trewhela, *Inside Quatro*, p 89.

149 *Ibid.*

150 Evans, 'Mbeki and Zuma – Between the Devil and the Deep Blue Sea'.

151 *Ibid.*

152 Mayibuye Centre, Lusaka mission, 69/1: Regional Political Committee report, Zambia, 3 October 1986.

153 UFH, ANC Lusaka mission, pt 2, secretary-general's office, 54/11: report by Kasrils to the NEC.

154 Twala and Benard, *Mbokodo*, pp 104–05.

155 UFH, ANC Lusaka mission, pt 2, 6/37: Manala E Manzini to Nzo, 10 November 1989. Political conditions at the camp were commented on by the Stasi, indicating how close was East German involvement in ANC affairs: telegram from Schunke to Ministerium für Staatssicherheit, 2 May 1989, MFS, HA II, 28716, 000105.

156 UFH, ANC Lusaka mission, pt 2, 6/37: Manala E Manzini to Nzo, 10 November 1989.

157 Twala and Benard, *Mbokodo*, p 109.

158 Meli to Lindiwe, 22 May 1987, confidential source.

159 'Mountaineer Doesn't Answer Any More … CIA and DMI against ANC and Ghana', *Top Secret*, (Autumn-Winter 1992), p 18. Also, author's personal interviews with Boakye-Djan and others involved.

160 Author's interview with security police officer, 2 May 1996.

161 'Mountaineer Doesn't Answer Any More … CIA and DMI against ANC and Ghana', *Top Secret*, (Autumn-Winter 1992), p 19; Trewhela, *Inside Quatro*, pp 115–16.

162 Evans, 'Secret Histories', p 16.

Chapter Seven: Homecoming

1 I am grateful to Paul Trewhela for the point outlined in the following paragraphs.

2 'Wilton Mkwayi', in SADET, *The Road to Democracy: South Africans Telling their Stories, Volume 1*, p 274: http://www.sadet.co.za/docs/RTD/stories/Stories%20-%20 Wilton%20Mkwayi.pdf [accessed 27 June 2012]

3 Coetsee papers, PV357, 1/A1/5: ANC minutes of Inkatha/ANC consultative meeting, 29–30 October 1979, p 30.

4 Appendix 1 to SSC minutes 1/85, 21 January 1985.

5 Minutes of SSC 5/85: 18 March 1985.

6 Minutes of SSC 6/85: 15 April 1985.

7 Interview with security police intelligence officer, 11 June 1997.

8 'Strategie vir die Bekamping van die Revolusionêre Klimaat', appendix to minutes of SSC 13/85, 26 August 1985.

9 Memorandum to State Security Council, 19 September 1985, appendix 1 to minutes of SSC 15/85, 23 September 1985. On the political effects of the banks' withdrawal and the 'Rubicon' speech, see Hermann Giliomee, 'The Rubicon Revisited', 20 August 2008: http://www.politicsweb.co.za/politicsweb/view/politicsweb/en/ page71619?oid=100899&sn=Detail [accessed 27 February 2012].

10 SSC, file 22/1/1/3/3.

11 *Ibid*, volume 1, especially the report by Brigadier BA Ferreira, 28 February 1986.

12 TRC amnesty application by Major General AJM Joubert, May 1997.

13 CA Fraser, *Revolusionêre Oorlogvoering: Grondbeginsels van Teeninsurgensie* (restricted circulation, 10 September 1986).

14 My vocabulary here is influenced by Rupert Smith, *The Utility of Force: The Art of War in the Modern World* (Penguin, London, 2006).

15 Nicholas Haysom, *Mabangalala: The Rise of Right-wing Vigilantes in South Africa* (Occasional paper no 10, Centre for Applied Legal Studies, University of the Witwatersrand, Johannesburg, 1986). A book-length official report on the organisation of vigilantes is Major General FMA Steenkamp, 'Alternatiewe Strukture as Faktor in die Rewolusionêre Aanslag teen die RSA' (unpublished, South African Police HQ, Pretoria, February 1987).

16 Thami Mali, *Chris Hani, The Sun That Set Before Dawn* (SACHED, Johannesburg, 1993), pp 28–29.

17 Anthea Jeffery, *People's War: New Light on the Struggle for South Africa* (Jonathan Ball, Johannesburg and Cape Town, 2009), p 54.

18 Interview with police researcher, 8 May 1996.

19 Interview with senior police officer, Durban, 16 May 1996.

20 Historical Papers, Cullen Library, Neame papers, B2: 'People's War Document', 19 November 1984.

21 O'Malley, *Shades of Difference*, p 269.

22 Jeremy Gordin, 'The Vuma Alumni', 12 June 2009: http://www.politicsweb.co.za/ politicsweb/view/politicsweb/en/page71619?oid=133047&sn=Detail [accessed 4 July 2012].

23 Steyn-Barlow, *Publish and Be Damned*, p 342.

24 Ray Joseph, 'The Rottweiler from Kuilsrivier', *City Press*, 27 March 2011.

25 Interview with Peter Gastrow, Cape Town, 25 May 1996.

26 Don Sipho, *Understanding Organised Crime and Corruption in South Africa* (Vaandel Publishers, Heiderand, 2009), p 172. Don Sipho is the pseudonym used by a former security police intelligence officer.

27 *Ibid*, pp 148–50.

28 TRC document.

29 Potgieter, *Totale Aanslag*, p 6.

30 Interview with Colonel Jan Breytenbach, in Ros Reeve and Stephen Ellis, 'An Insider's Account of the South African Security Forces' Role in the Ivory Trade', *Journal of Contemporary African Studies*, 13, 2 (1995), p 233.

31 Stephen Ellis, 'Africa and International Corruption: the Strange Case of South Africa and Seychelles', *African Affairs*, 95, 379 (1996), pp 165–96.

32 *Ibid*.

33 Potgieter, *Totale Aanslag*, p 6.

34 *Noseweek* 31 (February 2001), p 17.

35 'Zim Crime is Funding SA Military: Claim', *The Citizen*, 4 March 1994.

36 Potgieter, *Totale Aanslag*, p 38.

37 Marlene Burger and Chandré Gould, *Secrets and Lies: Wouter Basson and South Africa's Chemical and Biological Warfare Programme* (Zebra Press, Cape Town, 2002), p 80.

38 Janine Lazarus, 'The Shadowy World of Staal and "Big Alex"', *Sunday Star*, 25 February 1990. This article gave rise to a hearing before the South African media council that produced further information on the crime and security nexus.

39 Mandela's foreword to O'Malley, *Shades of Difference*, p 2.

40 Mayibuye Centre, Lusaka mission, 69/1: Regional Political Committee report, Zambia, 3 October 1986.

41 *Commission of Inquiry into the Alleged Smuggling of and Illegal trade in Ivory and Rhinoceros Horn in South Africa* [Kumleben Commission].

42 Personal communication by Fred Bridgland.

43 Potgieter papers, A.2.1.9.1 and A2.1.9.2: interviews with Detective Warrant Officer Drummond Hammond, 25 February 2010.

44 On Kalmanovitch, see Robert I Friedman, *Red Mafiya: How the Russian Mob has Invaded America* (Little, Brown, and Co, New York, 2000), pp 57–58.

45 Palazzolo's own version of his biography is at http://www.vrpalazzolo.com/ [accessed 29 March 2012]. On Palazzolo's debut in Ciskei, see 'A Cute Little Bankhaus in Bisho', *Noseweek* 9 (September 1994), usefully supplemented by a 2011 update available at http://www.noseweek.co.za/article/486/A-CUTE-LITTLE-BANKHAUS-IN-BISHO [accessed 3 September 2011].

46 Mayibuye Centre, Lusaka mission, 69/1: Regional Political Committee report, Zambia, 3 October 1986.

47 *Ibid*.

48 Craig Williamson, 'ANC Clandestine Operations', in Al J Venter (ed), *Challenge: Southern Africa Within the African Revolutionary Context* (Ashanti Publishing, no place, 1989), p 291.

49 Ivor Powell, 'How Military Intelligence Works', *Vrye Weekblad*, 27 November 1992.

50 Notes of a confidential briefing by senior officer of the NIA, 5 March 1997.

51 *Ibid*. The briefer was a former NIS official.

52 SAHA, AL2457, H.5.2: ANC minutes of PWV regional consultative conference, Lenasia, 2 September 1990.

53 'Skakelstukke ANC', veiligheidsverslag 90043765, 28 August 1990, confidential source.

54 ANC press release: 'Violence in the PWV Region', 26 July 1990. Copy in the possession of the author.

55 Ellis, 'The Historical Significance of South Africa's Third Force', p 261.

56 Morrow, *'To Serve and Protect': The Inkathagate Scandal*.

57 Rapule Tabane, 'From Revolutionary to President: What Mandela Has Meant to Me', *Mail & Guardian* Online, 18 July 2008: http://mg.co.za/article/2008-07-18-from-revolutionary-to-president-what-mandela-has-meant-me [accessed 15 November 2011].

58 *Ibid.*

59 Discussed by Guelke, *Rethinking the Rise and Fall of Apartheid*, pp 157–87.

60 Stuart Kaufman, 'South Africa's Civil War, 1986–1995', unpublished manuscript, p 30. Stuart Kaufman, Professor of Political Science and International Relations at the University of Delaware, has done field research on this issue.

61 Sparks, *Tomorrow is Another Country*; Patti Waldmeir, *Anatomy of a Miracle: The End of Apartheid and the Birth of the New South Africa* (Viking, London, 1997).

62 Ellis, 'The Historical Significance of South Africa's Third Force', p 263.

63 Chris Hani, 'Just How Possible is Peace?', the *African Communist*, 130 (1992), p 8.

64 David Niddrie, 'The Duel over Dual Power', *Work in Progress* 67 (June 1990), p 14.

65 Mandela's foreword to O'Malley, *Shades of Difference*, p 14.

66 Stadler, *The Other Side of the Story*, pp 76, 83–86.

67 Potgieter collection, AL3283, B1.2.1.: police submission to commission of inquiry regarding the prevention of public violence and intimidation.

68 Confidential police document.

69 Ellis, 'The Historical Significance of South Africa's Third Force'.

70 Wonder Hlongwa, 'Double Agent with Four Aliases Gets R5m', *Mail & Guardian*, 24 April 1998, http://mg.co.za/article/1998-04-24-double-agent-with-four-aliases-gets-r5m [accessed 29 July 2011]; Stefaans Brümmer and Hazel Friedman, 'New Evidence in Hani Death Plot', *Mail & Guardian*, 31 January 1997: http://www.mail-archive.com/yclsa-eom-forum@googlegroups.com/msg05633.html [accessed 29 July 2011]. See also Jenni Irish and Kevin Qhobosheane, 'South Africa', in Peter Gastrow (ed), *Penetrating State and Business: Organised Crime in Southern Africa* (ISS Monograph 89, Institute of Security Studies, Pretoria, 2003), especially p 122.

71 Stefaans Brümmer, 'Hints of Truth about Hani's Death, *Mail & Guardian*, 4–10 April 1997.

72 Peta Thornycroft, 'Dolinchek in from the Cold', *Sunday Tribune*, 20 February 1994.

73 Notes of a briefing by senior NIA officer, March 1997.

74 Steyn-Barlow, *Publish and Be Damned*, p 259.

75 *Ibid*, p 324.

76 Patrick Laurence, *Focus*, 17 (March 2000): http://www.hsf.org.za/resource-centre/focus/issues-11–20/issue-17-first-quarter-2000/the-future-of-the-nia [accessed 27 June 2012].

77 'South Africa: The Angolan Connections', *The Geopolitical Drug Despatch*, 79 (1998), pp 1–3.

78 Steyn-Barlow, *Publish and Be Damned*, p 342.

79 Author's interview with security police officer, 2 May 1996.

80 Paul Holden, *The Arms Deal in Your Pocket* (Jonathan Ball, Johannesburg and Cape Town, 2008), pp 258–59.

81 Adriaan Basson, 'Crony Capitalists on JZ's Coat-tails', *Mail & Guardian*, 5 March 2010, http://mg.co.za/printformat/single/2010-03-05-crony-capitalists-on-jzs-coattails/

[accessed 23 January 2012].

82 'Mary Braid, 'ANC Traded Charges for Party Donations', *The Independent*, 5 August 1996.

83 Kathi Austin, 'Illicit Arms Brokers: Aiding and Abetting Atrocities', *The Brown Journal of World Affairs*, 9, 1 (2002), pp 209–12, provides further detail.

84 Melle Leenstra, *Beyond the Façade: Instrumentalisation of the Zambian Health Sector* (African Studies Centre, Leiden, 2012), p 239.

85 Terry Crawford-Browne, *Eye on the Diamonds* (Penguin, Johannesburg, 2012).

86 'Gujarat Drug Bust to Dawood Dope Trail', 10 June 2004, *Indian Express*: http://www.indianexpress.com/oldStory/48707/ [accessed 29 July 2011].

87 Lionel Faull and Sam Sole, 'The Well-connected Mr KLamp', *Mail & Guardian*, 27, 42, 21–27 October 2011.

88 Julian Rademeyer, 'Slain Crime Boss "Just a Friend" – Moe', 23 March 2011: http://www.witness.co.za/index.php?showcontent&global%5B_id%5D=57556 [accessed 13 November 2011].

89 Sam Sole, 'Thabo's Boys vs Vula's Boys – the Sequel', *Mail & Guardian*, 15 December 2011.

90 Newton Kanhema, 'Men of War are Torn between Fear and Peace', *The Star International Weekly*, 20–26 October 1994.

91 Jim Peron, *Die, the Beloved Country* (Amagi Books, Saxonwold, and Liburne Press, London, 1999), p 101.

92 David Beresford, 'Jailbreaker Partied with SA Minister', *The Guardian*, 27 January 1998.

93 Adrian Hadland, 'Forgotten by the Leaders, Former Soldiers Turn to a Life of Crime', *The Sunday Independent*, 2 November 1997.

94 André Jurgens and Laurice Taitz, 'Mufamadi Fingers Rogue Guerrillas, Soldiers', *Sunday Times*, 2 November 1997.

95 Peron, *Die, the Beloved Country*, p 102.

96 BBC News, 'Robert McBride: South Africa Jails ANC ex-Police Chief', 9 September 2011: http://www.bbc.co.uk/news/world-africa-14855679 [accessed 21 April 2012].

97 UFH, Mandela papers, 263/2: Jordan to Nhlanhla, 3 June 1991.

98 Fred Bridgland, *Katiza's Journey: Beneath the Surface of South Africa's Shame* (Macmillan, London, 1997), pp 195–210.

99 UFH, Mandela papers, 263/2: Jordan to Nhlanhla, 3 June 1991.

100 Trewhela, *Inside Quatro*, p 115.

101 Patrick Laurence, 'Strange Death of Thami Zulu', *The Star*, 21 January 1992.

102 Interview with Eugene de Kock, 17 April 1998.

103 'Skakelstukke ANC', veiligheidsverslag 90043765, 28 August 1990, confidential source.

104 Charles Molele, 'Where is Modise's Money Man?', *Mail & Guardian*, 23 September 2011, supplemented by material from MK veteran Comrade S sent to the author by email, 30 September 2011.

105 Trewhela, *Inside Quatro*, pp 46–62.

106 Stefaans Brümmer, 'NIA Bosses Named as "Torturers"', *Mail & Guardian*, 14–20 June 1996.

107 Email message to the author, 6 February 2012.

108 Quoted in an unpublished obituary of Joe Modise by Sam Sole.

Chapter Eight: Perspectives

1 Fraser, 'Lessons Learnt from Past Revolutionary Wars', p 5.
2 Simons papers, O.5: J Simons to Motshabi, 20 January 1986.
3 Feit, *Urban Revolt*, p 100.
4 Simons papers, O.5: J Simons to Motshabi, 20 January 1986.
5 Bernstein papers, AL3051, R4.1-4.4: notes for an autobiography.
6 Turok, *Nothing But the Truth*, p 118.
7 This paragraph is a paraphrase of the analysis sent to me by Paul Trewhela via email on 1 November 2011.
8 Letter from Rusty Bernstein to John Saul, 8 June 2001, in *Transformation*, 64 (2007), p 142.
9 Quotations from Garth Strachan and Jeremy Cronin respectively, in Filatova, 'The ANC and the Soviets'.
10 Turok, *Nothing But the Truth*, p 50.
11 Interview with Padraig O'Malley, 19 January 2003, at www.nelsonmandela.org/omalley [accessed October 2010].
12 O'Malley, *Shades of Difference*, p 208.
13 Sæbø, 'A State of Exile', p 198.
14 Stadler, *The Other Side of the Story*, p 30.
15 Evans, 'Mbeki and Zuma – Between the Devil and the Deep Blue Sea'.
16 Jeremy Cronin, quoted in Adams, *Comrade Minister*, p 131.
17 Mandela's foreword to O'Malley, *Shades of Difference*, p 11.
18 Neville Alexander, quoted in Legassick, *Armed Struggle and Democracy*, p 7, note 4.
19 Moeletsi Mbeki, 'Death of a Socialist', *Work in Progress*, 89 (June 1993), p 11.
20 UFH, ANC Lusaka mission, 111/87: interview with Chris Hani, 21 January 1990.
21 Reg September, quoted above p 86.
22 Barrell, 'Conscripts to their Age'.
23 Smith, *The Utility of Force*, p 195.
24 Telephone interview with ANC member, 9 September 1989.
25 Above, p 64.
26 Above, p 86.
27 On the SACP's side, see 'The Enemy Hidden Under the Same Colour', document 131 in *South African Communists Speak*, pp 400–17.
28 See above, p 196.
29 Stephen Laufer, 'Scarlet Vindication for SACP's Violet', *Weekly Mail*, 16–22 July 1993.
30 Furlong, *Between Crown and Swastika*, pp 87–96; Christoph Marx, *Oxwagon Sentinel: Radical Afrikaner Nationalism and the History of the Ossewabrandwag* (Lit Verlag, Berlin, 2011), especially pp 478–514.
31 A description by Heribert Adam, quoted in Guelke, *Rethinking the Rise and Fall of Apartheid*, p 106.
32 Van Kessel, *'Beyond Our Wildest Dreams'*.
33 Simons papers, K.2.6: Jack Simons, 'South Africa's Civil War: Revolution and Counter-Revolution', unfinished ms, February 1989.
34 Kaufman, 'South Africa's Civil War, 1986-1995', p 4.
35 *Ibid.*
36 *Ibid*, p 29.

37 Stathis Kalyvas, *The Logic of Violence in Civil War* (Cambridge University Press, Cambridge, 2006).

38 Bopela and Luthuli, *Umkhonto we Sizwe*, pp 262–66.

39 Cf Smith, *The Utility of Force*, pp 289–92.

40 Rupert Taylor, 'Justice Denied: Political Violence in KwaZulu-Natal after 1994', *African Affairs*, 101, 405 (2002), pp 473–508.

41 Cf RW Johnson, 'The Class Purpose of the Zuma Regime', 19 January 2012, http://www.politicsweb.co.za/politicsweb/view/politicsweb/en/page71619?oid=275919&sn=Detail&pid=71616 [accessed 19 February 2012].

42 Jay Naidoo, *Fighting for Justice: A Lifetime of Political and Social Activism* (Picador Africa, Johannesburg, 2010), p 240.

43 O'Malley, *Shades of Difference*, p 245.

44 Naidoo, *Fighting for Justice*, p 240.

45 Pallo Jordan, 'Crisis of Conscience in the SACP', *Transformation*, 11 (1990), p 88.

46 See, eg, Cabinet memorandum 9/97: copy in Simons papers, Z.7.1.1.

47 Sarah Coleman, 'Mbeki's Tropical Storm', *World Press Review*, 51, 3 (March 2004).

48 'Chequered Future', interview with Deborah Posel, *The Guardian*, 5 May 2009.

49 Quoted in Sibongile Nkosi, 'Burn after Wearing – Township Kids' Hottest Fashion Statement', *Mail & Guardian*, 27, 43 (28 October-3 November 2011).

50 Allister Sparks, 'The Criminal Neglect of Burgeoning Youth Unemployment', *Business Day*, 6 July 2011.

51 Davis, 'Cosmopolitans in Close Quarters', p 299.

52 *Ibid*, p 196, especially note 266.

53 Anthony Minnaar, 'Self Defence Units or "Comtsotsi"/'Criminal Gangs', unpublished paper. Minnaar wrote a series of excellent papers on popular violence in the mid-1990s while he was at the Human Sciences Research Council. Some have been published in abridged form, such as in *Indicator SA*, 11, 2 (1994), pp 2–5.

54 Jeffery, *People's War*.

55 Eg, John Kane-Berman, *Political Violence in South Africa* (South African Institute of Race Relations, Johannesburg, 1993).

56 Mac Maharaj, 'History 101, Anyone?', www.timeslive.co.za [accessed on 18 March 2010]. Another scathing review by an ANC minister was by Pallo Jordan in *Focus*, 55 (2009), pp 50–2.

57 Interview with Hilda Bernstein, 1991, at http://www.nelsonmandela.org/omalley/index.php/site/q/03lv03445/04lv03996/05lv04011.htm [accessed 3 September 2011].

58 Filatova, 'The ANC and the Soviets', 10 August 2011.

59 Cassette recording of radio interview with Obbey Mabena, Kaya FM, no date.

60 Glenny, *McMafia*, part 1.

61 Eva Joly, *Est-ce dans ce monde-là que nous voulons vivre?* (Editions Les Arènes, Paris, 2003), p 208 et seq.

62 *Ibid*, pp 206–56.

63 Maritz Spaarwater, interview with Padraig O'Malley, 19 January 2003, at www.nelsonmandela.org/omalley [accessed October 2010]; McKinley, *ANC*, ch 5.

64 Mamphela Ramphele, *Laying Ghosts to Rest: Dilemmas of the Transformation in South Africa* (Tafelberg, Cape Town, 2008), especially pp 44–45.

65 Frederik van Zyl Slabbert, *The Other Side of History: An Anecdotal Reflection on Political Transition in South Africa* (Jonathan Ball, Johannesburg and Cape Town, 2006), p 156.

66 Mamphela Ramphele, 'Take Back the Power', *The Star*, 25 October 2009.

67 Van Zyl Slabbert, *The Other Side of History,* p 157.
68 Guelke, *Rethinking the Rise and Fall of Apartheid*, pp 214–15.
69 Author's interview, 10 May 1996.
70 Christophe Marx, 'From Trusteeship to Self-Determination: L.J. du Plessis' Thinking on Apartheid and his Conflict with H.F. Verwoerd', *Historia*, 55, 2 (2010), pp 50–75.

Appendix: A Note on Method

1 Meli, *South Africa Belongs to Us,* Janet Cherry, *Umkhonto weSizwe* (Jacana, Auckland Park, 2011), and many others.
2 Ramphele, *Laying Ghosts to Rest*, p 19.
3 *Ibid*, p 16.
4 Slavoj Zizek, 'Can You Give My Son a Job?', *London Review of Books*, 32, 20 (21 October 2010), p 9.
5 John Ruskin, *Queen of the Air: Being a Study of the Greek Myths of Cloud and Storm* (John Wiley & Son, New York, 1869), p 2.
6 Marx, *Oxwagon Sentinel*, pp 177–78.
7 Van Zyl Slabbert, *The Other Side of History,* p 42.
8 Cf Sabine Marschall, *Landscape of Memory: Commemorative Monuments, Memorials and Public Statuary in post-Apartheid South Africa* (Brill, Leiden and Boston, 2010).
9 Davis, 'Cosmopolitans in Close Quarters', pp 200–01.
10 'What Happened in Exile?', *Work in Progress*, 81 (1992), p 36.
11 'Hani Opens Up', *Work in Progress*, 82 (1992), p 18.
12 Garth Strachan, 'Indecent Obsession', *African Communist*, 129 (1992), pp 47–9.

Bibliography

Archive sources

Botswana
Gaborone
Botswana National Archives and Records Services
  Office of the President series

Germany
Berlin
Archiv der Zentralstellen
  Archives of the Ministerium für Staatssicherheit (MFS, or Stasi)

Ghana
Accra
Padmore Library
  Memorandum Presented to the Government of the Republic of Ghana by the African
  National Congress of South Africa, 10 May 1962

South Africa
Alice
University of Fort Hare, Liberation Archive
  Archives of the African National Congress
  Personal papers: Nelson Mandela, Sylvia Neame, OR Tambo
Bellville
University of the Western Cape, Mayibuye Centre
  Archives of the African National Congress
  Personal papers: Brian Bunting

Bloemfontein
University of the Free State, Archive for Contemporary Affairs
  Personal papers: PW Botha, PV 203; HJ Coetsee, PV357
Cape Town
University of Cape Town, Archives
  Personal papers: Jack and Ray Simons, BC1081
Johannesburg
The Nelson Mandela Foundation
  Letter from Mandela to the liquidator, Department of Justice, 23 October 1967
University of the Witwatersrand, Cullen Library
  (a) South African History Archive
    • Julie Frederikse interviews, AL2460
    • original SAHA collection, AL2457
    • personal papers: De Wet Potgieter, AL3283
  (b) Historical Papers
    • records of the African National Congress, AD 2186
    • Karis-Gerhart collection, A2675
    • personal papers: Lionel 'Rusty' Bernstein, AL3051; Sylvia Neame, A2729
Pretoria
National Archives and Records Service
  Minutes and files of the State Security Council: I consulted these documents in Durban while working with the Truth and Reconciliation Commission. They are now believed to be at the main office of the National Archives and Records Service in Pretoria.
South African National Defence Force (SANDF) Documentation Centre
Sandton
Human Rights Archive (HURISA)
  I consulted papers from the Harms Commission (whose report is listed below under *Kommissie van Ondersoek na Sekere Moontlike Onreëlmatighede*) in this archive in 1995. It is not clear whether it still exists.

United Kingdom
Oxford
Bodleian Library of Commonwealth and African Studies at Rhodes House
  Personal papers: TR Wade

Unpublished manuscripts[1]

African National Congress, 'The Shishita Report', confidential source.
Barrell, Howard, 'Conscripts to their Age: African National Congress Operational Strategy, 1976–1986' (DPhil thesis, University of Oxford, 1993).
Davis, Stephen, 'Cosmopolitans in Close Quarters: Everyday Life in the Ranks of Umkhonto we Sizwe (1961-present)' (PhD thesis, University of Florida, 2010).
Filatova, Irina, 'The Lasting Legacy: the Soviet Theory of the National-Liberation Movement and South Africa', paper presented to the Liberation Struggles in Southern

[1] During the course of research I have viewed many documents shown or given to me in confidence. These are listed in the notes where they are cited.

Africa workshop, University of Cape Town, 4-6 September 2008.

Fraser, CA, *Revolusionêre Oorlogvoering: Grondbeginsels van Teeninsurgensie* (restricted circulation, 10 September 1986). The English original is entitled 'Lessons Learnt from Past Revolutionary Wars'.

Hepple, Sir Bob, 'The SACP Conference, December 1960. Extract from Notes Made by Bob Hepple in May/June 1964', document kindly provided by Sir Bob Hepple.

Kaufman, Stuart, 'South Africa's Civil War, 1986–1995', Department of Political Science and International Relations, University of Delaware.

Le Roux, CJB, 'Umkhonto we Sizwe: Its Role in the ANC's Onslaught against White Domination in South Africa, 1961-1988' (PhD thesis, University of Pretoria, 1992).

Minnaar, Anthony, 'Self Defence Units or "Comtsotsi" Criminal Gangs'.

Moosage, Riedwaan, 'The Impasse of Violence: Writing Necklacing into a History of Liberation Struggle in South Africa' (MA thesis, University of the Western Cape, 2010).

Sæbø, Maren, 'A State of Exile: The ANC and Umkhonto we Sizwe in Angola, 1976– 1989' (MA thesis, University of Natal, 2002).

Sechaba, Tsepo, 'Comrades *Against Apartheid* – a Response … by Tsepo Sechaba to a Review by Jeremy Cronin', 1992.

Sole, Sam, obituary of Joe Modise.

Steenkamp, FMA, 'Alternatiewe Strukture as Faktor in die Rewolusionêre Aanslag teen die RSA' (South African Police HQ, Pretoria, February 1987).

Swanepoel, PC, 'Secrets and Stories of Boers and Brits'.

Newspapers and magazines

Africa Confidential

African Communist

Aida Parker Newsletter

Albright, Joseph, and Marcia Kunstel, 'CIA Tip Led to '62 Arrest of Mandela', *The Atlanta Constitution*, 10 June 1990, p A14.

Business Day, Johannesburg

The Citizen, Johannesburg

City Press, Johannesburg

Dawn

Focus

The Guardian, London

The Independent, London

Indicator SA

Kitson, David, letter to the *London Review of Books*, 18, 10 (23 May 1996).

London Review of Books

Mail & Guardian, Johannesburg

The New York Times

Noseweek

Ozanne, Julian, 'ANC Commanders "Tortured Mutineers with Melting Plastic"', *Sunday Correspondent* [London], 8 April 1990.

Paratus

Sechaba

Serfontein, JHP, 'Amazing Peace Move by Top ANC Man', *Sunday Times*, 18 April 1976.

South African Press Agency (SAPA)

Sowetan, Johannesburg

The Star, Johannesburg

The Star International Weekly, Johannesburg

Strachan, Harold, obituary of David Kitson, *Noseweek* 135 (January 2011).

The Sunday Independent, Johannesburg

The Sunday Star, Johannesburg

Sunday Times, Johannesburg

Sunday Times, London

Sunday Tribune, Durban

The Times, Johannesburg

Trewhela, Paul, 'Wilton Mkwayi: ANC Leader Imprisoned with Nelson Mandela', *The Independent*, [London] 29 July 2004.

— 'Raymond Mhlaba: ANC Leader Imprisoned with Mandela', *The Independent* [London] 23 Feb. 2005.

Umsebenzi

De Volkskrant, Amsterdam

Vrye Weekblad, Johannesburg

The Weekly Mail, Johannesburg

The Witness, Pietermaritzburg

Work in Progress, Johannesburg

Online sources

African National Congress (ANC), official website: http://www.anc.org.za

Department of Justice and Constitutional Development, South Africa: http://www.justice.gov.za

Digital Innovation South Africa: http://www.disa.ukzn.ac.za/

Evans, Gavin, 'Mbeki and Zuma: Between the Devil and the Deep Blue Sea', 30 December 2007: http://www.gavinevans.net

Filatova, Irina, 'The ANC and the Soviets', 10 August 2011: http://www.politicsweb.co.za/politicsweb/view/politicsweb/en/page71619?oid=250154&sn=Detail&pid=71619

Giliomee, Hermann, 'The Rubicon Revisited', 20 August 2008: http://www.politicsweb.co.za/politicsweb/view/politicsweb/en/page71619?oid=100899&sn=Detail.

Gleijeses, Piero, 'Cuito Cuanavale Revisited', Mail & Guardian online, 11 July 2007: http://mg.co.za/article/2007-07-11-cuito-cuanavale-revisited

Gordin, Jeremy, 'The Vuma Alumni', 12 June 2009: http://www.politicsweb.co.za/politicsweb/view/politicsweb/en/page71619?oid=133047&sn=Detail.

The Heart of Hope: interviews by Padraig O'Malley: http://www.nelsonmandela.org/omalley

Helen Suzman Foundation: http://www.hsf.org.za

Indian Express: http://www.indianexpress.com

International Department, Central Committee of the Chinese Communist Party: http://www.idcpc.org.cn

Mail & Guardian Online: http://mg.co.za

News24: http://www.news24.com/SouthAfrica/Politics/
Zuma-praises-Albert-Luthuli-20101124
The Nordic Documentation on the Liberation Struggle in Southern Africa Project:
http://www.liberationafrica.se
Politicsweb: http://www.politicsweb.co.za
Quintessenz: http://cryptomequintessenz.at
Red Location Museum: http://www.freewebs.com/redlocationmuseumhistory/
wiltonmkwayi.htm
Republic of South Africa, presidency: http://www.thepresidency.gov.za
Sipho, Dan: http://www.donsipho.com
South Africa Travel Online: http://www.southafrica.to
South African Communist Party: http://www.sacp.org.za
South African Democracy Education Trust: http://www.sadet.co.za
South African History Online: http://www.sahistory.org.za
Sunday Times [Johannesburg]: http://www.timeslive.co.za
Vito Palazzolo: http://www.vrpalazzolo.com
Yudu Free: http://content.yudu.com

Published books, chapters and articles

Adams, Simon, *Comrade Minister: The South African Communist Party and the Transition from Apartheid to Democracy* (Nova Science Publishers, Huntington, NY, 2001).

Ammann, Daniel, *The King of Oil: The Secret Lives of Marc Rich* (St Martin's Press, New York, 2009).

Amnesty International, *South Africa: Torture, Ill-Treatment and Executions in African National Congress Camps* (AFR 53/27/92, London, 1992).

ANC Speaks: Documents and Statements of the African National Congress 1955-1976 (no place or date).

Andrew, Christopher and Oleg Gordievsky, *KGB: The Inside Story* (Hodder & Stoughton, London, 1990).

Andrew, Christopher and Vasili Mitrohkin, *The Mitrohkin Archive II: The KGB and the World* (Allen Lane, London, 2005).

Anonymous, 'Mountaineer Doesn't Answer Any More … CIA and DMI against ANC and Ghana', *Top Secret*, (Autumn-Winter 1992).

—, 'South Africa: The Angolan Connections', *The Geopolitical Drug Despatch*, 79 (1998), pp 1-3.

Arenstein, Rowley, interview with RW Johnson in *London Review of Books*, 13, 4 (21 February 1991).

Asmal, Kader and Adrian Hadland, with Moira Levy, *Politics in My Blood: A Memoir* (Jacana, Auckland Park, 2011).

Austin, Kathi, 'Illicit Arms Brokers: Aiding and Abetting Atrocities', *The Brown Journal of World Affairs*, 9, 1 (2002).

Babenia, Natoo, *Memoirs of a Saboteur, as Told to Iain Edwards* (Mayibuye History and Literature Series no 58, Mayibuye Books, Bellville, 1995).

Beresford, David, *Truth is a Strange Fruit: A Personal Journey through the Apartheid War* (Jacana, Auckland Park, 2010).

Bernstein, Lionel, *Memory Against Forgetting: Memoirs from a Life in South African Politics, 1938-1964* (Viking, London, 1999).

—, letter to John Saul, 8 June 2001, in *Transformation*, 64 (2007).

Bonner, Philip and Noor Nieftagodien, *Alexandra: A History* (Witwatersrand University Press, Johannesburg, 2008).

Bopela, Thula and Daluxolo Luthuli, *Umkhonto we Sizwe: Fighting for a Divided People* (Galago, Alberton, 2005).

Bottoman, Wonga Welile, *The Making of an MK Cadre* (LiNc publishers, Pretoria, 2010).

Braam, Conny, *Operatie Vula: Nederlanders in het Ondergrondse Verzet tegen de Apartheid* (Meulenhoff, Amsterdam, 1992).

Bridgland, Fred, *Katiza's Journey: Beneath the Surface of South Africa's Shame* (Macmillan, London, 1997).

Bunting, Brian, *Moses Kotane, South African Revolutionary* (Inkululeko Publications, London, 1975).

Burger, Marlene and Chandré Gould, *Secrets and Lies: Wouter Basson and South Africa's Chemical and Biological Warfare Programme* (Zebra Press, Cape Town, 2002).

Cajee, Imtiaz, *Timol: A Quest for Justice* (STE Publishers, Johannesburg, 2005).

Callinicos, Luli, *Oliver Tambo: Beyond the Engeli Mountains* (David Philip, Cape Town, 2004).

Cherry, Janet, *Umkhonto weSizwe* (Jacana, Auckland Park, 2011).

Clingman, Stephen, *Bram Fischer: Afrikaner Revolutionary* (David Philip, Cape Town, 1998).

Coleman, Sarah, 'Mbeki's Tropical Storm', *World Press Review*, 51, 3 (March 2004).

Commission of Inquiry into the Alleged Smuggling of and Illegal Trade in Ivory and Rhinoceros Horn in South Africa [Kumleben Commission] (Government Printer, Pretoria, 1996).

Couper, Scott Everett, '"An Embarrassment to the Congresses?": The Silencing of Chief Albert Luthuli and the Production of ANC History', *Journal of Southern African Studies*, 35, 2 (2009).

Crawford-Browne, Terry, *Eye on the Diamonds* (Penguin, Johannesburg, 2012).

Crocker, Chester A, *High Noon in Southern Africa: Making Peace in a Rough Neighbourhood* (1992; Jonathan Ball, Johannesburg, 1993).

Cronin, Jeremy, 'What Happened in Exile?', *Work in Progress*, 81 (1992).

Dabengwa, Dumiso, 'ZIPRA in the Zimbabwe War of National Liberation', in Ngwabi Bhebe and Terence Ranger (eds), *Soldiers in Zimbabwe's Liberation War* (James Currey, London, 1995).

Davidson, Apollon and Irina Filatova, *Rossia I Yuzhnaia Africa: navedeniie mostov* (Russia and South Africa: Building Bridges) (Publishing House of the Higher School of Economics, Moscow, 2012).

Davis, Stephen, *Apartheid's Rebels: Inside South Africa's Hidden War* (Yale University Press, New Haven and London, 1987).

Ellis, Stephen, 'Africa and International Corruption: the Strange Case of South Africa and Seychelles', *African Affairs*, 95, 379 (1996).

—, 'The Historical Significance of South Africa's Third Force', *Journal of Southern African Studies*, 24, 2 (1998).

—, 'The Genesis of the ANC's Armed Struggle in South Africa, 1948-1961', *Journal of Southern African Studies*, 37, 4 (2011).

Ellis, Stephen and Tsepo Sechaba, *Comrades against Apartheid: The ANC and the South African Communist Party in Exile* (James Currey, London, 1992).

Emerson, Steven, *Secret Warriors: Inside the Covert Military Operations of the Reagan Era* (GP Putnam's Sons, New York, 1988).

Evans, Gavin, 'Secret Histories', *Leadership*, 13, 5 (1994).

Feit, Edward, *Urban Revolt in South Africa 1960-1964: A Case Study* (Northwestern University Press, Evanston, IL, 1971).

Fieldhouse, Roger, *Anti-Apartheid: A History of the Movement in Britain* (Merlin Press, London, 2005).

Flower, Ken, *Serving Secretly: An Intelligence Chief on Record: Rhodesia into Zimbabwe, 1964 to 1981* (John Murray, London, 1987).

Frankel, Glenn, *Rivonia's Children: Three Families and the Price of Freedom in South Africa* (Weidenfeld and Nicholson, London, 1999).

Friedman, Robert I, *Red Mafiya: How the Russian Mob has Invaded America* (Little, Brown, and Co, New York, 2000).

Furlong, Patrick J, *Between Crown and Swastika: The Impact of the Radical Right on the Afrikaner Nationalist Movement in the Fascist Era* (Wesleyan University Press, Hanover, NH, 1991).

Geldenhuys, Jannie, *At the Front: A General's Account of South Africa's Border War* (Jonathan Ball, Johannesburg and Cape Town, 2009).

Gerhart, Gail M, and Clive L Glaser, *From Protest to Challenge, Volume 6: Challenge and Victory, 1980-1990* (Indiana University Press, Bloomington, IN, 2010).

Getty, J Arch and Oleg V Naumov, *The Road to Terror: Stalin and the Self-Destruction of the Bolsheviks, 1932-1939* (Yale University Press, New Haven and London, 1999).

Gevisser, Mark, *Thabo Mbeki: The Dream Deferred* (Jonathan Ball, Johannesburg and Cape Town, 2007).

Giliomee, Hermann, *The Afrikaners: Biography of a People* (Tafelberg, Cape Town, 2003).

Glaser, Clive, '"When Are they Going to Fight?" Tsotsis, Youth Politics and the PAC', in Philip Bonner, Peter Delius and Deborah Posel (eds), *Apartheid's Genesis, 1935–1962* (Ravan Press and Witwatersrand University Press, Johannesburg, 1993).

Glenny, Misha, *McMafia: Crime Without Borders* (Bodley Head, London, 2008).

Goldberg, Denis, *The Mission: A Life for Freedom in South Africa* (STE, Johannesburg, 2010).

Gowan, Peter, *The Global Gamble: Washington's Faustian Bid for World Dominance* (Verso, London and New York, 1999).

Green, Pippa, *Choice, Not Fate: The Life and Times of Trevor Manuel* (Penguin, Johannesburg, 2008).

Guelke, Adrian, *Rethinking the Rise and Fall of Apartheid: South Africa and World Politics* (Palgrave Macmillan, Basingstoke and New York, 2005).

Gunther, Magnus, 'The National Committee of Liberation/African Resistance Movement (ARM)', in SADET, *The Road to Democracy in South Africa, Volume 1, 1960-1970* (Zebra Press, Cape Town, 2004).

Hamann, Hilton, *Days of the Generals: The Untold Story of South Africa's Apartheid-era Military Generals* (Zebra, Cape Town, 2001).

Hani, Chris, 'The Wankie campaign', *Dawn* (souvenir issue, 1986).

—, 'Hani Opens Up', interview with Hein Marais in *Work in Progress*, 82 (1992).

Harris, Peter, *In a Different Time: The Inside Story of the Delmas Four* (Umuzi, Cape Town, 2008).

Haysom, Nicholas, *Mabangalala: The Rise of Right-wing Vigilantes in South Africa* (Occasional paper no 10, Centre for Applied Legal Studies, University of the Witwatersrand, Johannesburg, 1986).

Hirsch, Alan, *Season of Hope: Economic Reform Under Mandela and Mbeki* (University of KwaZulu-Natal Press, Scottsville, and International Development Research Centre, Ottawa, 2005).

Hirson, Baruch, *Revolutions in My Life* (Witwatersrand University Press, Johannesburg, 2001).

Hoare, Mike, *The Seychelles Affair* (1986; Corgi edn, London, 1987).

Holden, Paul, *The Arms Deal in Your Pocket* (Jonathan Ball, Johannesburg and Cape Town, 2008).

— and Hennie van Vuuren, *The Devil in the Detail: How the Arms Deal Changed Everything* (Jonathan Ball, Johannesburg and Cape Town, 2011).

Houston, Gregory, 'The post-Rivonia ANC/SACP Underground', in SADET, *The Road to Democracy in South Africa, Volume 1, 1960–1970* (Zebra Press, Cape Town, 2004).

— and Bernard Magubane, 'The ANC Political Underground in the 1970s', in SADET, *The Road to Democracy in South Africa, Volume 2, 1970–1980* (Unisa Press, Pretoria, 2007).

Institute for Security Studies (author: Hennie van Vuuren) *Apartheid Grand Corruption: Assessing the Scale of Crimes of Profit in South Africa from 1976 to 1994* (ISS, Pretoria, 2006).

Irish, Jenni and Kevin Qhobosheane, 'South Africa', in Peter Gastrow (ed), *Penetrating State and Business: Organised Crime in Southern Africa* (ISS Monograph 89, Institute for Security Studies, Pretoria, 2003).

Jeffery, Anthea, *People's War: New Light on the Struggle for South Africa* (Jonathan Ball, Johannesburg and Cape Town, 2009).

Johns, Sheridan and R Hunt Davis, Jr (eds), *Mandela, Tambo and the African National Congress: The Struggle against Apartheid, 1948–1990: A Documentary Survey* (Oxford University Press, New York, 1991).

Johnson, RW, *How Long Will South Africa Survive?* (Oxford University Press, New York, 1977).

—, *South Africa's Brave New World: The Beloved Country since the End of Apartheid* (Overlook Press, New York, 2010).

Joly, Eva, *Est-ce dans ce monde-là que nous voulons vivre?* (Editions Les Arènes, Paris, 2003).

Jordan, Pallo, 'Crisis of Conscience in the SACP', *Transformation*, 11 (1990).

Kalyvas, Stathis, *The Logic of Violence in Civil War* (Cambridge University Press, Cambridge, 2006).

Kane-Berman, John, *Political Violence in South Africa* (South African Institute of Race Relations, Johannesburg, 1993).

Karis, Thomas and Gail Gerhart, *From Protest to Challenge: A Documentary History of African Politics in South Africa, Volume 5* (Unisa Press, Pretoria, 1997).

Kasrils, Ronnie, *Armed and Dangerous: My Undercover Struggle against Apartheid* (Heinemann Educational, Oxford, 1993).

Keitsing, Fish (compiled by Jeff Ramsay and Barry Morton), *Comrade Fish: Memories of a Motswana in the ANC Underground* (Pula Press, Gaborone, 1999).

Ketelo, Bandile, Amos Maxongo, Zamxolo Tshona, Ronnie Massango and Luvo Mbengo, 'A Miscarriage of Democracy: the ANC Security Department in the 1984 Mutiny in Umkhonto we Sizwe', *Searchlight South Africa*, 5 (1990).

Kommissie van Ondersoek na Sekere Moontlike Onreëlmatighede. Hoofverslag [Harms Commission] (Staatsdrukker, Pretoria, 1989).

Kynoch, Gary, 'From the Ninevites to the Hard Livings: Township Gangsters and Urban Violence in South Africa', *African Studies*, 58, 1 (1999).

Landau, Paul, 'The ANC, MK, and "The Turn to Violence" (1960-2)', *South African Historical Journal*, forthcoming.

Leenstra, Melle, *Beyond the Façade: Instrumentalisation of the Zambian Health Sector* (African Studies Centre, Leiden, 2012).

Legassick, Martin, 'Myth and Reality in the Struggle against Apartheid', *Journal of Southern African Studies*, 24, 2 (1998).

—, *Armed Struggle and Democracy: The Case of South Africa* (Discussion paper no 20, Nordiska Afrikainstitutet, Uppsala, 2002).

Leggett, Ted, *Rainbow Vice: The Drugs and Sex Industries and the New South Africa* (Zed Books, London, 2002).

Lelyveld, Joseph, *Move Your Shadow: South Africa, Black and White* (Penguin edition, Harmondsworth, 1986).

Lewin, Hugh, *Stones Against the Mirror: Friendship in the Time of the South African Struggle* (Umuzi, Cape Town, 2011).

Lissoni, Arianna, 'Transformations in the ANC External Mission and Umkhonto we Sizwe, c.1960-1969', *Journal of Southern African Studies*, 35, 2 (2009).

Lodge, Tom, *Mandela: A Critical Life* (Oxford University Press, Oxford, 2006).

—, *Sharpeville: An Apartheid Massacre and its Consequences* (Oxford University Press, Oxford, 2011).

Lowenburg, Anton David and William H Kaempfer, *The Origins and Demise of South African Apartheid: A Public Choice Analysis* (University of Michigan Press, Ann Arbor, 1998).

Ludi, Gerard, *Operation Q-018* (Nasionale Boekhandel, Cape Town, 1969).

—, *The Communistisation of the ANC* (Galago Publishing, Alberton, 2011).

McCoy, Alfred W, *The Politics of Heroin in Southeast Asia* (Harper & Row, New York, 1972).

McKinley, Dale T, *The ANC and the Liberation Struggle: A Critical Political Biography* (Pluto Press, London, 1997).

Macmillan, Hugh, 'The "Hani Memorandum" – Introduced and Annotated', *Transformation*, 69 (2009).

—, 'The African National Congress of South Africa in Zambia: The Culture of Exile and the Changing Relationship with Home, 1964-1990', *Journal of Southern African Studies*, 35, 2 (2009).

Magubane, Bernard, *My Life and Times* (University of KwaZulu-Natal Press, Scottsville, 2010).

—, Philip Bonner, Jabulani Sithole, Peter Delius, Janet Cherry, Pat Gibbs and Thozama April, 'The Turn to Armed Struggle', in SADET, *The Road to Democracy in South Africa, Volume 1, 1960-1970* (Zebra Press, Cape Town, 2004).

Malan, Rian, *My Traitor's Heart* (The Bodley Head, London, 1990).

—, *Resident Alien* (Jonathan Ball, Johannesburg and Cape Town, 2009).

Mali, Thami, *Chris Hani, The Sun That Set Before Dawn* (SACHED, Johannesburg, 1993).

Maloka, Eddy, *The South African Communist Party in Exile 1963-1990* (Africa Institute of South Africa, Research Paper no 65, Pretoria, 2002).

Mandela, Nelson, *Long Walk to Freedom: The Autobiography of Nelson Mandela* (1994; Abacus edn, London, 1995).

Mangold, Tom, *Cold Warrior: James Jesus Angleton: The CIA's Master Spy Hunter* (Simon & Schuster, London and New York, 1991).

Marschall, Sabine, *Landscape of Memory: Commemorative Monuments, Memorials and Public Statuary in post-Apartheid South Africa* (Brill, Leiden and Boston, 2010).

Marx, Christoph, 'From Trusteeship to Self-Determination: L.J. du Plessis' Thinking on Apartheid and his Conflict with H.F. Verwoerd', *Historia*, 55, 2 (2010).

—, *Oxwagon Sentinel: Radical Afrikaner Nationalism and the History of the Ossewabrandwag* (Lit Verlag, Berlin, 2011).

Masondo, Andrew, 'Sawing Electric Pylons', *Dawn* (souvenir issue, 1986).

Matthysen, Paul, Matthew Kalkwarf and Michael Huxtable, *'Recce': A Collector's Guide to the History of the South African Special Forces* (30° South Publishers, Johannesburg, 2010).

Mbali, Fanele, *In Transit: Autobiography of a South African Freedom Fighter* (Xlibris Corporation, online publisher, 2011).

Mbeki, Govan, *South Africa: The Peasants' Revolt* (Penguin, Harmondsworth, 1964).

—, *The Struggle for Liberation in South Africa: A Short History* (Mayibuye Centre, Bellville, and David Philip, Cape Town, 1992).

Mbeki, Moeletsi, 'Death of a Socialist', *Work in Progress*, 89 (June 1993).

Meli, Francis, *South Africa Belongs to Us: A History of the ANC* (1988; James Currey, London, 1989).

Mhlaba, Raymond, *Personal Memoirs: Reminiscing from Rwanda and Uganda. Narrated to Thembeka Mufamadi* (Human Sciences Research Council and Robben Island Museum, Pretoria, 2001).

Ministry of Information, Ghana, *Nkrumah's Subversion in Africa* (Ministry of Information, Accra, no date [1966]).

Mkatashingo, 'The ANC Conference: From Kabwe to Johannesburg', *Searchlight South Africa*, 6 (January 1991), pp 91–4.

Modise, Joe, 'The Happiest Moment in My Life', *Dawn* (souvenir issue, 1986).

Morrow, Brian, as told to Laurence Piper, *'To Serve and Protect': The Inkathagate Scandal* (Unisa Press, Pretoria, 2010).

Mzala, *Gatsha Buthelezi: Chief with a Double Agenda* (Zed Books, London, 1988).

Mzimela, Sipo E, *Marching to Slavery: South Africa's Descent into Communism* (Soundview Publications, Atlanta, GA, 1993).

Naidoo, Jay, *Fighting for Justice: A Lifetime of Political and Social Activism* (Picador Africa, Johannesburg, 2010).

Ndebele, Nhlanhla and Noor Nieftagodien, 'The Morogoro Conference: A Moment of Self-Reflection', in SADET, *The Road to Democracy in South Africa, Volume 1, 1960-1970* (Zebra Press, Cape Town, 2004).

Ndlovu, Sifiso Mxolisi, 'The ANC in Exile, 1960-1970', in SADET, *The Road to Democracy in South Africa, Volume 1, 1960-1970* (Zebra Press, Cape Town, 2004).

—, 'The ANC's Diplomacy and International Relations', SADET, *The Road to Democracy in South Africa, Volume 2, 1970-1980* (Unisa Press, Pretoria, 2007).

Ngculu, James, *The Honour to Serve: Reflections of an Umkhonto Soldier* (David Philip, Cape Town, 2009).

Nkobi, Thomas, untitled article in *Dawn* (souvenir issue, 1986), p.39.

O'Brien, Kevin, *The South African Intelligence Services: From Apartheid to Democracy, 1948-2005* (Routledge, London, 2011).

O'Malley, Padraig, *Shades of Difference: Mac Maharaj and the Struggle for South Africa* (New York, Viking Penguin, 2007).

O'Meara, Dan, *Forty Lost Years: The Apartheid State and the Politics of the National Party, 1948-1994* (Ravan Press, Randburg, and Ohio University Press, Athens, OH, 1996).

Onslow, Sue, 'The Cold War in Southern Africa: White Power, Black Nationalism and External Intervention', in Sue Onslow (ed), *Cold War in Southern Africa: White Power, Black Liberation* (Routledge, London and New York, 2009).

Palan, Ronen, Richard Murphy and Christian Chavagneux, *Tax Havens: How Globalization Really Works* (Cornell University Press, Ithaca, NY, 2010).

Paton, Alan (ed Edward Callan), *The Long View* (Frederick A Praeger, New York, 1968).

Pauw, Jacques, *In the Heart of the Whore: The Story of Apartheid's Death Squads* (Southern Book Publishers, Johannesburg, 1991).

—, *Dances with Devils: A Journalist's Search for Truth* (Zebra Press, Cape Town, 2006).

Peron, Jim, *Die, the Beloved Country* (Amagi Books, Saxonwold, and Liburne Press, London, 1999).

Pike, Henry, *A History of Communism in South Africa* (2nd edition, Christian Mission International of South Africa, Germiston, 1988).

Polakow-Suransky, Sasha, *The Unspoken Alliance: Israel's Secret Relationship with Apartheid South Africa* (Vintage, New York, 2011).

Popper, Karl, *The Poverty of Historicism* (Routledge and Kegan Paul, London, 1957).

Potgieter, De Wet, *Totale Aanslag: Apartheid se Vuil Truuks Onthul* (Zebra Press, Cape Town, 2007).

Preston, Julia, 'The Trial that Shook Cuba', *New York Review of Books*, 36, 19, (7 December 1989).

Prins, Gwyn and Robbie Stamp, *Top Guns and Toxic Whales: The Environment and Global Security* (Earthscan, London, 1991).

Prinsloo, Daan, *Stem uit die Wilderness: 'n Biografie oor Oud-Pres. P.W. Botha* (Vaandel Uitgewers, Mosselbaai, 1997).

Raditsa, Leo, *Prisoners of a Dream: The South African Mirage* (Prince George Street Press, Annapolis, MD, 1989).

Ralinala, Rendani Moses, Jabulani Sithole, Gregory Houston and Bernard Magubane, 'The Wankie and Sipolilo Campaigns', in SADET, *The Road to Democracy in South Africa Volume 1, 1960-1970* (Zebra Press, Cape Town, 2004).

Ramphele, Mamphela, *Laying Ghosts to Rest: Dilemmas of the Transformation in South Africa* (Tafelberg, Cape Town, 2008).

Rees, Mervyn and Chris Day, *Muldergate: The Story of the Info Scandal* (Macmillan South Africa, Johannesburg, 1980).

Reeve, Ros and Stephen Ellis, 'An Insider's Account of the South African Security Forces' Role in the Ivory Trade', *Journal of Contemporary African Studies,* 13, 2 (1995).

'Reply to the Central Committee of the South African Communist Party Statement Entitled "The Enemy Hidden Under the Same Colour"', February 1976, copy at SAHA AL2457, H.1.

Republic of Seychelles, Department of Information, *White Paper on Aggression of November 25th 1981 Against the Republic of Seychelles* (Victoria, Seychelles, no date).

Ruskin, John, *Queen of the Air: Being a Study of the Greek Myths of Cloud and Storm* (John Wiley & Son, New York, 1869).

Sampson, Anthony, *Mandela: The Authorized Biography* (Alfred A Knopf, New York, 1999).

Sanders, James, *Apartheid's Friends: The Rise and Fall of South Africa's Secret Service* (John Murray, London, 2006).

Schleicher, Hans-Georg, 'GDR Solidarity: the German Democratic Republic and the South African Liberation Struggle', SADET, *The Road to Democracy in South Africa, Volume 3, International Solidarity* (Unisa Press, Pretoria, 2008).

Scholtz, Clive, 'Drive Now and Pay Forever – the Apartheid Way', in Shipping Research Bureau, *Embargo: Apartheid's Oil Secrets Revealed* (Amsterdam University Press, Amsterdam, 1995).

Schraeder, Peter J, *United States Foreign Policy Towards Africa: Incrementalism, Crisis and Change* (Cambridge University Press, Cambridge, 1994).

Seegers, Annette, *The Military in the Making of Modern South Africa* (IB Tauris, London, 1996).

Shamuyarira, Nathan, *Liberation Movements in Southern Africa* (8th annual Hans Wolff memorial lecture, Indiana University, Bloomington, IN, 1978).

Shay, Reg and Chris Vermaak, *The Silent War: The Fight for Southern Africa* (Galaxie Press, Rhodesia, 1971).

Shipping Research Bureau (eds R Hengeveld and J Rodenburg), *Embargo: Apartheid's Oil Secrets Revealed* (Amsterdam University Press, Amsterdam, 1995).

Shubin, Vladimir, *ANC: A View from Moscow* (1999; 2nd revised edition, Jacana, Auckland Park, 2008).

—, 'Unsung Heroes: the Soviet Military and the Liberation of Southern Africa', in Sue Onslow (ed), *Cold War in Southern Africa: White Power, Black Liberation* (Routledge, London, 2009).

Sibeko, Archie, with Joyce Leeson, *Freedom in Our Lifetime* (Indicator Press, Durban, 1996).

Simpson, Thula, '"Umkhonto we Sizwe, We are Waiting for You": The ANC and the Township Uprising, September 1984–September 1985', *South African Historical Journal*, 61 1, (2009).

Sipho, Don, *Understanding Organised Crime and Corruption in South Africa* (Vaandel Publishers, Heiderand, 2009).

Sisulu, Elinor, *Walter and Albertina Sisulu: In Our Lifetime* (David Philip, Cape Town, 2002).

Slovo, Joe, 'The Sabotage Campaign', *Dawn* (souvenir issue, 1986).

—, *Slovo: The Unfinished Autobiography of ANC Leader Joe Slovo* (1995; Ocean Press edition, Melbourne and New York, 1997).

Smith, Janet and Beauregard Tromp, *Hani: A Life Too Short* (Jonathan Ball, Johannesburg and Cape Town, 2009).

Smith, Rupert, *The Utility of Force: The Art of War in the Modern World* (Penguin, London, 2006).

Soobrayan, Venitha, *Yusuf Dadoo* (Maskew Miller Longman, Cape Town, 1993).

South African Communists Speak: Documents from the History of the South African Communist Party 1915-1980 (Inkululeko Publications, London, 1981).

South African Democracy Education Trust (SADET), *The Road to Democracy in South Africa, Volume 1, 1960-1970* (Zebra Press, Cape Town, 2004).

—, *The Road to Democracy in South Africa, Volume 2, 1970–1980* (Unisa Press, Pretoria, 2007).

—, *The Road to Democracy in South Africa, Volume 3, International Solidarity* (Unisa Press, Pretoria, 2008).

—, *The Road to Democracy: South Africans Telling their Stories, Volume 1, 1950-1970* (Tsehai Publishers, Hollywood, CA, 2008).

Sparks, Allister, *Tomorrow is Another Country: The Inside Story of South Africa's Negotiated Revolution* (Struik, Sandton, 1994).

Stadler, Herman, *The Other Side of the Story: A True Perspective* (Contact Publishers, Pretoria, 1997).

Steyn-Barlow, Chris, *Publish and Be Damned: Two Decades of Scandals* (Galago Books, Alberton, 2006).

Stiff, Peter, *The Silent War: South African Recce Operations, 1969–1994* (Galago, Alberton, 1999).

—, *Cry Zimbabwe: Independence – Twenty Years On* (Galago, Alberton, 2000).

Strachan, Garth, 'Indecent Obsession', *African Communist*, 129 (1992).

Strydom, Lauritz, *ANC: Masker af* (Oranjewerkers Promosies, Morgenzon, 1990).

Suttner, Raymond, *The ANC Underground in South Africa: A Social and Historical Study* (Jacana, Auckland Park, 2008).

Swanepoel, PC, *Die Salem en Ander Oliegeheime* (private publication, Pretoria, 2002).

—, *Really Inside BOSS: A Tale of South Africa's Late Intelligence Service (and Something about the CIA)* (private publication, Pretoria, 2008).

Taylor, Rupert, 'Justice Denied: Political Violence in KwaZulu-Natal after 1994', *African Affairs*, 101, 405 (2002).

Thomas, Cornelius, *Tangling the Lion's Tail: Donald Card, from Apartheid Era Cop to Crusader for Justice* (private publication, East London, 2007).

Thomas, Scott, *The Diplomacy of Liberation: The Foreign Relations of the ANC Since 1960* (International Library of African Studies, IB Tauris, London and New York, 1996).

Trewhela, Paul, *Inside Quatro: Uncovering the Exile History of the ANC and SWAPO* (Jacana, Auckland Park, 2009).

Truth and Reconciliation Commission of South Africa Report (5 volumes, TRC/Department of Justice, Pretoria, 1998).

Turok, Ben, *Nothing But the Truth: Behind the ANC's Struggle Politics* (Jonathan Ball, Johannesburg, 2003).

Twala, Chitja, 'The African National Congress Youth League's (ANCYL's) Role as the "Kingmaker": a Movement of post-Polokwane Blues?', *Journal for Contemporary History/Joernaal vir Eietydse Geskiedenis*, 34, 3 (2009).

Twala, Mwezi and Ed Benard, *Mbokodo: Inside MK – Mwezi Twala. A Soldier's Story* (Jonathan Ball, Johannesburg, 1994).

Van Kessel, Ineke, *'Beyond Our Wildest Dreams': The United Democratic Front and the Transformation of South Africa* (University Press of Virginia, Charlottesville, 2000).

Van Zyl Slabbert, Frederik, *The Other Side of History: An Anecdotal Reflection on Political Transition in South Africa* (Jonathan Ball, Johannesburg and Cape Town, 2006).

Veloso, Jacinto, *Memórias em Voo Rasante* (Papa-Letras, Lisboa, 2007).

Vermaak, Chris, *The Red Trap: Communism and Violence in South Africa* (APB Publishers, Johannesburg, 1966).

Waldmeir, Patti, *Anatomy of a Miracle: The End of Apartheid and the Birth of the New South Africa* (Viking, London, 1997).

Walsh, Frank, *Dangerous Deceits: Julian Askin and the Tollgate Scandal* (HarperCollins, London, 1999).

Welsh, David, *The Rise and Fall of Apartheid* (Jonathan Ball, Johannesburg and Cape Town, 2009).

— and JE Spence, *Ending Apartheid* (Longman, Harlow, 2011).

Williamson, Craig, 'ANC Clandestine Operations', in Al J Venter (ed), *Challenge: Southern Africa Within the African Revolutionary Context* (Ashanti Publishing, no place, 1989).

Winter, Gordon, *Inside BOSS, South Africa's Secret Police* (Penguin, Harmondsworth, 1981).

Woodward, Bob, *Veil: The Secret Wars of the CIA, 1981–1987* (Simon & Schuster, New York, 1987).

INDEX